Advancing
Human Rights
in Social Work
Education

Advancing Human Rights in Social Work Education

EDITED BY

**Kathryn R. Libal, S. Megan Berthold,
Rebecca L. Thomas, and Lynne M. Healy**

Alexandria, Virginia

Published in the United States by the Council on Social Work Education, Inc.
All rights reserved. No part of this book may be reproduced or transmitted in any
manner whatsoever without the prior written permission of the publisher.

Library of Congress Cataloging-in-Publication Data

Advancing human rights in social work education / [edited by] Kathryn R. Libal,
S. Megan Berthold, Rebecca L. Thomas, and Lynne M. Healy.
        pages cm
Includes bibliographical references and index.
ISBN 978-0-87293-173-2 (alk. paper)
    1.Social work education. 2.Human rights.I. Libal, Kathryn, 1968–

HV11.A336 2014
361.3071—dc23

2014027993

Printed in the United States of America on acid-free paper that meets the
American National Standards Institute Z39-48 standard.

Council on Social Work Education
1701 Duke Street, Suite 200
Alexandria, VA 22314-3457
www.cswe.org

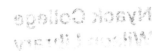

CONTENTS

SECTION II
Policy, Research, and Social Justice

ACKNOWLEDGMENTS

A project of this magnitude is based on the collaborative support of many. The co-editors would like to thank the CSWE Katherine A. Kendall Institute for International Social Work Education, the University of Connecticut Human Rights Institute, the University of Connecticut School of Social Work, and the University of Connecticut Center for International Social Work Studies for generous support of the working seminar "Advancing Human Rights in Social Work Education" held at the University of Connecticut School of Social Work, May 16-17, 2013. We are grateful for the support of the School of Social Work leadership, including particularly Dean Salome Raheim and Associate Dean for Academic Affairs Catherine Havens. Members of the staff, including Sandra Lane and Pamela Harrison, provided invaluable logistical support. MSW interns at the UConn Center for International Social Work Studies, Sasha Jay and Silvina Echegoyen, were key participants in organizing the seminar. Graduate students Kyle Barrett, Janelle Bryan, Michele Eggers, Brunilda Ferraj, Seiya Fukuda, and Judy Wyman Kelly took extensive notes on the seminar discussion. Daniel Melchor, alumnus, Sandra Lane, and Pamela Harrison also contributed to the success of the seminar. MSW student Nicole Seymour offered extensive editorial support during the book production process. Most of the chapters in this book are based on papers presented at the seminar. Due in large part to the rich exchanges at the 2.5 day seminar, compiling and editing the book has been rewarding. Thus, we also would like to acknowledge the high quality work of our participants, which made this book possible. Finally, we would like to thank Elizabeth Simon and her staff at CSWE Press for their expertise and unflagging assistance in seeing the project to its conclusion.

FOREWORD | *Vimla V. Nadkarni*

Social workers are professionals who work toward similar goals embedded in the human rights perspective: mobilizing social capital and supporting and enhancing people's potential to work for their development, as well as intervening with the social systems to better respond to the needs and assist in securing the rights of marginalized and disadvantaged groups in our society (Nadkarni, 2009). Today there is growing demand for social workers to adopt the human rights approach, particularly with increasing social and economic inequalities, poverty, religious and civil conflicts, disasters, and displacements of large populations, in rapidly changing societies. The violation of human rights has been aggravated with the negative outcomes of globalization, privatization, and liberalization that focus more on expansion of trade and markets than enhancement of human well-being, particularly in countries that have been forced to reduce state investment in social sectors such as health, education, and the social service. Adoption of the human rights perspective in social work education to address these issues cannot be contested.

The human rights perspective in social work education and practice is a natural corollary to the very foundation of social work, which aims to uphold the dignity and worth of every human being. The profession of social work has embraced this perspective in its work with people who are disadvantaged, marginalized, vulnerable, and discriminated against due to factors that range from the social, political, and economic to cultural and religious issues. However, the perspective has not been consciously integrated as work against the violation of human rights in social work education except in the last two decades of the profession, although there are many examples of social workers exemplified in this book who have been involved in civil and political rights, women's empowerment, labor rights, since the early part of the 1960s and 1970s.

This book is a welcome addition to the literature on reviewing and strengthening the human rights perspective within social work education. It includes attention to clinical and community practice, research, programming, and social policy development at all levels of interventions. It is unique because it provides very practical models for developing curricula around human rights and translating them into field education.

Clearly articulated in Chapter 1 are the benefits for the readers: "diverse authors discuss how the powerful idea of human rights can inform and transform social work education, and ultimately, professional practice." The volume is a primer on human rights in social work education because it explains in clear details how social work has positioned itself in the context of work on human rights in the United States and several other countries. There is some level of analysis of reasons why, despite the importance of social workers working within the human rights contexts, there has been resistance to adequate integration of concepts and translating the perspective into practice, research, and social policy in the U.S. environment.

Human Rights in South Asia

Among the South Asian countries, India is a signatory to the Universal Declaration of Human Rights (United Nations, 1948) and the other major human rights conventions and has shown some progress in implementing progressive laws such as the Right to Information and Right to Education Acts. Access to health care is also recognized as a right. Social workers in India have played leading roles in lobbying for land rights, forest rights for indigenous people, rights of people displaced by large dams, and many other issues. However, they have had to depend on a mass base of an empowered community, development practitioners, health and education activists, advocates, and other professionals to raise their voices against human rights violations and social injustices. Medha Patkar, a graduate of the Tata Institute of Social Sciences, became a social activist and social reformer and has recently joined a political party. She led the Narmada Bachao Andolan, a social movement of *adivasis*,[1] farmers, environmentalists, and human rights activists against large dams being built across the Narmada River. This movement caught international attention, and the World Bank was forced to withdraw its funds to build the dam unless the government fulfilled certain conditions, which included lowering the dam's height and ensuring adequate rehabilitation measures for the displaced people. Patkar has been fighting for the rights of the tribal people and the slum dwellers, the poorest of the poor, for more than a decade.

Although human rights are proclaimed to be universal and indivisible, in practice social workers experience and need to deal with conflicting rights in society. A glaring example is that of women and girls having less access to the right to education within some groups that remain highly patriarchal and religious. Sexual and reproductive rights are also denied to them. The issue of not advocating for the use of condoms as the means of preventing HIV/AIDS conflicts with the individual's right for protection against a terminal disease.

Policies made in one country can also work against the rights of human beings in other countries. The glaring example here is of the Mexico City Policy (Gag Rule) introduced by President George Bush in January 2001 (I had firsthand experience of this because I was the secretary-general of the Family Planning Association of India, which received funds from the International Planned Parenthood Federation [IPPF]). The Gag Rule prohibited organizations that received U.S. funds from providing abortion information, services, and care and from working on these issues even if their national governments requested them to do so. The IPPF rejected the Gag Rule and, as a result, lost significant amounts of funding. The IPPF and its member organizations such as the Family Planning Association of India had to seek alternative funding for continuing their work in the field of sexual and reproductive health and safeguarding the health and rights of women (IPPF, 2013).

Thus, working on human rights issues at both the micro and macro levels assumes that social workers will learn to assert themselves and fight against unfair and unjust systems when required. This is a great challenge in teaching human rights in social work education, and this could be one of the reasons social work schools may be reluctant to introduce the human rights perspective into the curricula because it often means working against the policies of the government. And university systems may not be ready to antagonize the state, especially if they depend on educational grants from the government or if they are public institutions.

India, like several other countries in the South Asian region, falls short of implementation of the human rights perspective, as is reported by the United Nations (UN) Office of the High Commissioner for Human Rights, Amnesty International, and other international and human rights organizations. The profession of social work also has not always been at the forefront on several such issues, although the scenario seems to be changing at least in India, where social work education is well-established and there is increasing awareness about viewing social work as a transformative discipline.

In India people's struggles for dignity and protection of their life and liberty continue. Sexual minorities came out in large numbers to demand their rights to be treated with dignity, to be accepted by the public health care system, and for change of laws such as the Indian Penal Code, which makes homosexuality an offence. Unfortunately, despite their efforts to appeal to the judiciary to decriminalize homosexuality in India, this was not accepted, and thus lesbian, gay, bisexual, and transgender (LGBT) communities continue to be discriminated against, incarcerated, and abused. The social work fraternity has played a major role in supporting the rights of LGBT communities.

Leading social workers have also been struggling for the rights of sex workers, including their rights to be treated as citizens, to practice their profession without fear and insecurity, and their right for shelter, sanitation, education for their children, and so on. On a more positive note, in the recent Supreme Court judgment in India, the *hijras* (transgender women in India) have been recognized as citizens (the so-called third gender) with rights to vote, health care, livelihood, and education. Disability and HIV/AIDS are other areas that have inspired social work educators and practitioners to fight for the rights of those affected to live with dignity and without discrimination. This has led to significant legislation such as the Persons With Disabilities (Equal Opportunities, Protection of Rights, and Full Participation) Act (1995), which also covers the rights of persons living with mental illness. Social work educators at the Tata Institute of Social Sciences, Mumbai, worked very closely with the Lawyers Collective (an organization started by advocates; http://www.law-yerscollective.org) to lobby for access to drugs and other rights for people living with HIV/AIDS.

Although social work education in India in the last decade seems to be appropriating the human rights perspective in its curricula, this is not uniform for all the social work educational institutions across the country. The Model Curriculum for Social Work Education developed on behalf of the University Grants Commission by the Tata Institute of Social Sciences and collaborating institutions in 2001 does not have any separate course on human rights (University Grants Commission, 2001). This concept is integrated into courses on ideologies of social work and social policy.

Social work education in South Asia is not a recognized discipline or profession like other social science disciplines and professions. Social work teachers and practitioners continue to struggle for recognition by society and the state. Historically, social work education has been influenced by western pedagogy, and at least in India most of the institutions continue with traditional courses borrowed from abroad. Since the University Grants Commission offered grants for teaching of human rights by colleges and universities, some institutions have taken advantage of this and training in human rights for social workers continues in an ad hoc manner. Very few institutions have integrated this perspective into their curricula.

One of the major factors for resistance to change has been the mushrooming of social work colleges without adequate infrastructure and quality education. There is also competition with management courses, and schools of social work are encouraged to offer human resource management courses as self-financed programs (because the state has been reducing funding for higher education and encouraging privatization and autonomy). This is focused more on industry and business than the social sectors. Thus, there is little motivation to assimilate the human rights perspective into social work education in these institutions.

There is also a lack of sustained national associations of social work in the country. Neither is there a national council to evaluate and accredit social work programs across the country. To correct this, the only strategy is to build a strong association for social work education, and this was launched on December 3, 2013, with funding support from the International Association of Schools of Social Work (IASSW). The association in India is in the process of formal registration. It is only through collective analysis and solidarity that it will be possible to transform social work education in India into an effective discipline with a human rights perspective. In South Asia this would need to be adapted to the specific contexts of the respective countries without compromising on human rights, equality, and social justice.

Linking with international organizations such as the IASSW also would facilitate recognition of the profession in South Asian countries. The IASSW's Committee on Human Rights has been very active, posting material on its website and holding seminars and training in human rights when opportunities arise. As a global social work education association, the IASSW has tremendous scope to make a difference by advocating for integration of the human rights perspective into social work education across the world. Lobbying with the UN Office of the High Commissioner for Human Rights and taking positions on various human rights violations as well as working in the field of social protection are areas where the IASSW along with the international partner organizations, namely the International Federation of Social Workers, International Council on Social Welfare, and regional associations of social work education, can make a difference in achieving their mission.

Key issues across South Asia include the denial of civil and political rights, armed conflict, the war on terror, violence against women, poverty, impunity, freedom of expression, human rights defenders at risk, and the death penalty (Amnesty International, 2013). Widespread poverty, food insecurity, and economic disparities continue to pose threats to the basic human rights and well-being of tens of millions of South Asians. Women, children, indigenous people, minority groups, lower castes, migrants, and displaced people face abuses and discrimination across the region (Amnesty International, 2013). Thus, the scope for social work education across Asia and globally to work on country-based and transnational issues through the human rights approach is tremendous.

I agree with Ife (2001) that we need passion and rage to take up human rights work—passion and commitment to uphold equality and justice, and anger against oppression and exploitation. Indigenous traditions in various parts of the world have respected holism, or comprehensiveness, in the relationship between humans and nature, but with so-called development we are moving away from it. Traditions within Buddhism and Confucianism, for instance, should be part of progressive social work. By working in oppressive structures, we too are prone to becoming part of that system if we do not constantly reflect, discuss, and act from a political and ideological stance. The orientation of social work education institutions to inculcate this human rights perspective in social work students is critical (Nadkarni, 2009).

This volume provides us with many excellent examples of human rights education and practice in social work education in the schools of social work in the United States and beyond, which will be most useful to social work educators, development practitioners, researchers, policy makers, and students. Some of the projects carried out in developing countries such as Jamaica, Costa Rica, Uganda, and Ghana in collaboration with U.S. universities provide a wider landscape of understanding about how social work education can address human rights issues through field education, research, social policy, program evaluation, doctoral programs, and interprofessional collaboration within low resource and poverty settings. The broad range of issues covered—from micro level health problems such as HIV/AIDS to the larger macro level issues of social justice, human trafficking, racism, water security, and problems of immigrant populations—contribute to the volume's significance.

References

Amnesty International. (2013). Asia and the Pacific human rights. Retrieved from
    http://www.amnestyusa.org/our-work/countries/asia-and-the-pacific

Ife, J. (2001). *Human rights and social work: Towards rights-based practice.*
    Cambridge, UK: Cambridge University Press.

International Planned Parenthood Federation (IPPF). (2013). Advocating against
    the Global Gag Rule. Retrieved from http://www.ippf.org/our-work
    /what-we-do/advocacy/global-gag-rule

Minority Rights Group International. (n.d.). Advasis. Retrieved from www.
minorityrights.org/5659/india/adivasis.html

Nadkarni, V. (2009). Human rights perspective in social work: Illustrations from
health social work. *Indian Journal of Social Work, 69*(2), 139–158.

Persons With Disabilities (Equal Opportunities, Protection of Rights, and Full
Participation) Act. (1995). Ministry of Social Justice and Empowerment,
Government of India. Retrieved from http://socialjustice.nic.in/pwdact1995.php

United Nations. (1948, December 10). Universal Declaration of Human Rights.
G.A. Res. 217 A (III). Retrieved from http://www.refworld.org/docid
/3ae6b3712c.html

University Grants Commission, Government of India. (2001). UGC model
curriculum on social work education. Retrieved from http://www.ugc.ac.in
/oldpdf/modelcurriculum/social_work_education.pdf

Endnote

1   *Adivasis* is a collective name used for the many indigenous people of India, also referred
to as the scheduled tribes (Minority Rights Group International, n.d.).

Diverse Human Rights Orientations to Curriculum Development

The first section of this volume includes chapters addressing varied approaches to integrating human rights within social work education. Lynne Healy, Rebecca Thomas, Megan Berthold, and Kathryn Libal provide a synopsis of the historical and current engagement of the social work profession in human rights. They address both the challenges and promise of incorporating broad and deep human rights content in social work curricula. Joseph Wronka presents human rights as the bedrock of the social work profession, showing how human rights is integral to generalist curriculum. His chapter also provides an introduction to core concepts to human rights-based practice in the profession, focusing especially on the relevance of the United Nations Universal Declaration of Human Rights (1948).

David Androff and Jane McPherson propose that a rights-based approach to social work practice provides an opportunity for social work education to bridge the micro–macro divide and to strengthen practice by promoting the rights of every human being, while recognizing the responsibility of states, communities, and organizations in protecting human rights. Megan Berthold indicates that core micro foundation and clinical practice courses in MSW programs are well-suited to the integration of teaching human rights and rights-based interventions. Through the use of case studies, vignettes, class exercises, and United

Nations documents, human rights-based interventions can be taught in micro foundation and clinical practice courses in addition to developing new courses.

The chapter by Elaine Congress provides an example of how Fordham University substantially revised its social work curriculum to focus on human rights and the related concept of human well-being. She underscores the necessity of faculty development and ongoing dialogue to increase faculty responsiveness to curricular changes. Susan Mapp provides insight into another way of integrating human rights content into the curriculum, showing how learning about human rights is central to international social work classes. She highlights potential strengths of comparing human rights issues and practices in other countries to those in the United States, asserting that human rights provide a bridge to connect the global and the domestic.

Kathryn Libal and Lynne Healy extend this theme, focusing on the importance of localizing human rights education to the domestic context through the lens of a specialized elective course at the MSW level. They bring the abstract nature of rights-based practice closer to home in the United States where many social work topics, such as food insecurity, systemic racism, and inadequate housing and homelessness can be framed as human rights as well as human needs. They highlight the potential of having students grapple with ethical dilemmas that occur within their field experience using a human rights lens.

Nivedita Prasad outlines a collaborative German master's program, Social Work as a Human Rights Profession. The program teaches the complaint mechanisms of the United Nations treaty bodies to enable students to bring attention to a particular problem and to actively use this mechanism to affect individual and social change and to identify social injustice with the human rights framework. Finally, Sandra Chadwick-Parkes identifies the challenge faced by Jamaican social work educators at the University of West Indies as one of creating a human rights culture among students so that principles taught in the classroom are connected to practice.

1 | Fulfilling the Rich Potential of Human Rights in Social Work Education: An Overview

Lynne M. Healy, Rebecca L. Thomas, S. Megan Berthold, and Kathryn R. Libal

As Jim Ife observed, "human rights represent one of the most powerful ideas in contemporary discourse" (2008, p. 1). In this volume, diverse authors discuss how the powerful idea of human rights can inform and transform social work education, and ultimately, professional practice. This introductory chapter begins by acknowledging the challenges educators face in introducing new perspectives and frameworks into the curriculum, identifying obstacles, and facilitating factors. We then move to a very brief definition of the field of human rights before addressing the question of why human rights is important to social work education. Next, we explore the compatibility of social work values and principles with human rights principles and review the history of the profession's involvement with human rights movements. Finally, we include a brief discussion of the rich potential of incorporating a deeper exploration of human rights frameworks and materials to enhance social work's contribution to human well-being.

Social work educators and practitioners in the United States have increasingly engaged human rights frameworks as they apply to everyday direct practice with clients, community organizing, and policy advocacy for broader social change. The growing interest in integrating human rights into social work education topically expands and conceptually deepens the work of earlier social work educators and practitioners (Healy, 2008). Authors in this volume advocate for further addition and expansion of human rights content. There are many challenges in recommending new areas of content for the social work curriculum, which many educators already consider overcrowded with diverse areas. Finding curriculum space is therefore one of the most serious challenges; others are faculty reluctance to embrace unfamiliar areas and, in some cases, lack of readily available teaching materials. Resistance can also be generated if instructors are not convinced of the relevance of human rights to pressing local social problems and core practice. Numerous chapters in the book discuss the importance of linking human rights to domestic issues and local practice.

Some scholars perceive clashes between human rights approaches and long-valued concepts, especially social justice and civil rights. Tensions between human rights and social justice, and the rationale for incorporating more than civil and political rights into the conception of rights, will be discussed further by contributing authors. It may be helpful at the outset to acknowledge the seminal contributions of the civil rights movement in the United States to the liberation of and movement for dignity and justice for oppressed groups, especially African Americans. The contributions of this movement to human rights are to be celebrated and built on as educators further embrace Martin Luther King Jr.'s call for advocacy for broad social and economic rights (Jackson, 2009).

There are also important facilitating factors for strengthening human rights in the social work curriculum, notably inclusion in official curriculum policy. This shift is reflected institutionally in the Council on Social Work Education's (CSWE) 2008 Educational Policy and Accreditation Standards (EPAS), which requires educators throughout the United States to incorporate human rights learning into generalist practice at the BSW level, as well as foundation and advanced practice curricula at the MSW level (McPherson & Abel, 2012).

Specifically, EPAS requires demonstrating competency in advocating for human rights (CSWE,2008).[1] As importantly, this document underscores that attending to human rights in the classroom and in practice is based in the very purpose of the social work profession, which is to "promote human and community well-being" (p. 1). The document states:

> Guided by a person and environment construct, a global perspective, respect for human diversity, and knowledge based on scientific inquiry, social work's purpose is actualized through its quest for social and economic jus-

tice, *the prevention of conditions that limit human rights*, the elimination of poverty, and the enhancement of the quality of life for all persons. (emphasis added; CSWE, 2008, p.1)

Reference to human rights is also made indirectly in Educational Policy 2.1.1, by citing the obligation of social workers to apply social work ethical principles to professional practice. The policy specifically cites the International Federation of Social Workers (IFSW) and International Association of Schools of Social Work (IASSW) *Ethics in Social Work, Statement of Principles* (2004a), which recognizes the binding nature of core human rights treaties linked to social work as a basis for establishing ethical social work practice. The Principles identify specific United Nations treaties as applicable to social work and compatible with its values.

Other facilitating factors are the compatibility of core social work and core human rights principles, and the considerable, but sometimes overlooked, history of social work involvement in human rights activism and scholarship. These will be addressed following a brief description of core human rights.

Defining Human Rights

Dominant understandings of the meaning of *human rights* in the United States commonly emphasize civil and political rights as the core human rights (Healy, 2008; Reichert, 2003). These include the right to life; to be free from torture and enslavement; to liberty and security of the person; recognition before the law; freedom of belief, thought, and expression; right to participate in politics and public life; freedom of association; right to marry; and the right to one's own language and community, particularly in countries with diverse ethnic, national, and religious groups. These rights are consonant with core values recognized by the U.S. Constitution and Bill of Rights and have been widely held as the human rights that matter most (Albisa, 2011). The legacy of successful civil rights mobilization in the 1950s to 1970s to address entrenched racism, sexism, ableism, as well as more recent gains for lesbian, gay, bisexual, transgender, and questioning (LGBTQ) populations has helped to reify the notion that civil rights are the human rights of greatest importance.

A second category of human rights known as social, economic, and cultural rights has yet to be recognized fully by the U.S. government and legal system but is crucial for the social work profession (Albisa, 2011; Lewis, 2009). Economic and social rights include the right to an adequate standard of living, adequate housing, food, health care, social protection/social security, and decent and fairly paid work and are elaborated in the International Covenant on Economic, Social and Cultural Rights (United Nations, 1966) and other human rights treaties.

Each of these rights has been elaborated by the UN Committee on Economic, Social and Cultural Rights in general comments that set specific governmental obligations, and the articulation of rights to adequate housing, health care, food, social protection, and an adequate standard of living entail enforcing rights as a matter of entitlement. Yet economic and social rights are not readily defended in the United States on constitutional grounds as legal entitlements (Albisa, 2011; Carmalt, Zaidi, & Yamin, 2011). Unlike many other countries that constitutionally define a right to housing or health care, for example, in the United States the Supreme Court has maintained that there is no constitutional protection for economic vulnerability or poverty. However, there is a small but growing awareness about international definitions, standards, and norms regarding economic and social rights (see, e.g., Center for Economic and Social Rights, 2010; CERD Working Group on Health and Environmental Health, 2008; Chilton & Rose, 2009; Gardiner, Irwin, & Peterson, 2009; Libal & Neubeck, 2013; McGill, 2012).

This stance is deeply exceptionalist within an international human rights law context; the effects of this resistance have extended beyond the halls of law to other domains, such as social work, as well. Thus, throughout human service professions, recognizing economic and social rights as human rights has lagged. Only in the past two decades has rights-based social work practice to realize the right to housing, food, health care, and an adequate standard of living emerged (Jewell, Collins, Gargotto, & Dishon, 2009; Reichert, 2003). Yet the potential of such engagement is also evident to social work educators. As Pyles (2006) notes,

As the discourse of civil rights propelled some of the changes that resulted in policies connected to the Great Society and the War on Poverty, it is certainly possible that human rights could propel a new anti-poverty agenda in the US. (p. 85)

A third category of rights, often called solidarity rights, must be realized in the collective and often require transnational cooperation and action to fulfill. These include such rights as the rights of indigenous peoples, the right to a clean environment, and the right to peace. Solidarity rights, the most controversial for (wealthy) nation states, are those implied by Article 28 of the Universal Declaration of Human Rights (UDHR; United Nations, 1948): "Everyone is entitled to a social and international order in which the rights and freedoms set forth in this Declaration can be fully realized." Solidarity rights are the most challenging to implement as they require considerable cooperation between countries, as chapters in this book related to immigrant and refugee rights, workers' rights, and the right to water illustrate.

Compatibility of Social Work and Human Rights

At the level of general values and underlying assumptions, social work and human rights share a common set of principles. Both are based on affirmation of the dignity and worth of human beings and assert that this worth is inherent and does not have to be earned. In a speech to the 1968 International Conference of Social Work, M. S. Gore summed up this link as follows:

the relevance of the Declaration [meaning the UDHR] for social work lies mainly in the fact that it unequivocally recognized the worth and dignity of the person ... Social work proceeds from the same basic assumption that every human individual is worthy in himself, independent of his material or social condition. (International Conference on Social Welfare, 1969, p. 57)

Although there has been historical interest in social work involvement in human rights in the United States (Healy, 2008), only recently have significant numbers of social work educators begun to link the ideals of advancing social justice with human rights. For many educators, invoking human rights in the classroom may entail citing the UDHR or noting the moral claim of achieving human rights without further elaborating what such a claim means. The relatively belated focus on human rights in the social work curricula has in part been shaped by reluctance to link social justice issues in the United States to human rights, which is part of a legacy of U.S. exceptionalism (Hertel & Libal, 2011; Reichert, 2003). Discussing human rights in the classroom or practice often meant focusing on the rights not being met for distant others— for individuals and groups in foreign countries.

Yet as several recent scholarly volumes have shown, human rights mobilization in the United States is no longer predominantly about waging campaigns for the realization of human rights in other countries (Armaline, Glasberg, & Purkayastha, 2011; Hertel & Libal, 2011; Pyles, 2006; Soohoo, Albisa, & Davis, 2009). Human rights mobilization has been localized or domesticated, and campaigns to bring human rights home to the U.S. context have resonated in professional fields such as public interest and family law, public health, medicine, family therapy, and social work (Chilton & Rose, 2009; MacNaughton, 2011; McDowell, Libal, & Brown, 2012)[2] Jewell, Collins, Gargotto, and Dishon (2009) argue that social workers often "gloss over" the value of social justice, "assuming that part of their daily work adheres to this ethical principle" (p. 311). Developing human rights-based approaches to community organizing, policy advocacy, and clinical social work with individuals, families, and groups helps to more clearly articulate how social justice may be realized. The authors assert that using a human rights framework pushes the profession to "incorporate new concepts and language that address the people's issues as rights instead of services that only assist in temporary relief" (p. 319).

Social work education has successfully taught about the dynamics of human oppression, including the roles of racism, sexism, heterosexism, ablism, and classism in undermining human potential and dignity. To some extent, civil rights is addressed in social work curricula through examining social policy formation and implementation, law and social work, or human oppression and social inequality. Other topics, such as children's rights, women's rights, and to a lesser extent workers' rights, have also been addressed. Yet the dominant approach to these topics has not linked such processes and conditions to the broader international movement to recognize human rights. And the relative lack of understanding of human rights theory and practice has often led critics to claim that the endeavor is mired in Western imperialism or the dangers of Enlightenment thought, which privilege the interests of the individual over community or broader collective interests. This image persists even in the face of growing scholarship and human rights practice, which stress the necessity of structural change and collective dimensions of rights claims, particularly with regard to health, food, housing, social security, and the effects of social inequality in its varied dimensions (see Chapter 14, this volume; Mishra, 2005; Pyles, 2006; Reichert, 2003).

Engagement of Social Work and Social Work Education in Human Rights

Although the limitations of its involvements as outlined here are real, the profession of social work has engaged with human rights in diverse ways. In 1988 the IFSW stated that "social work, since its conception, has been a human rights profession" (1988, p. 1). As noted earlier in this Introduction, the underlying values and premises of social work are fully congruent with those of human rights, quite probably more so than those of any other profession. Direct and substantive engagement in human rights as a profession has been considerable but also somewhat intermittent and not always well-recognized internally or externally.

Over the past 25 years social work has incorporated human rights language explicitly in its major global policy documents adopted by the IASSW and IFSW: the definition of social work (2000); *Ethics in Social Work: Statement of Principles* (2004a); the *Global Standards for the Education and Training of the Social Work Profession* (2004b) and the *Global Agenda for Social Work and Social Development* (2012). The IFSW issued a policy statement on human rights in 1988 and with the IASSW collaborated with the UN Centre for Human Rights (1994) to produce *Human Rights and Social Work: A Professional Training Manual*. Notably, this was the first in the UN professional training series in human rights. Later IFSW published a manual on children's rights (2002). Two decades prior to the 1988 statement, human rights was the theme of the 1968 International Conference of Social Work in celebration of the 20th anniversary of the signing of the UDHR. The papers published in the proceedings evidence serious social work attention to human rights (International Conference on Social Welfare, 1969).

Both international professional organizations maintain committees or task forces on human rights. Activities have included education and training seminars at regional and global conferences and advocacy for the rights of social workers who have been detained, charged, or otherwise harassed for defending human rights. Periodically, statements are issued on specific human rights violations. IASSW and IFSW are also involved in human rights issues through their representation as nongovernmental organizations (NGOs) with consultative status at the United Nations. Representatives of the IASSW, for example, participated in NGO consultations during the drafting of the Convention on the Rights of the Child in the 1980s, provided input to the Special Rapporteur on Extreme Poverty and Human Rights during the preparation of the Guiding Principles on Extreme Poverty and Human Rights in 2011–2012, and are participating with other NGOs in a working group on a possible Convention on the Rights of Older Persons.

In the United States individual social work leaders have spoken about and advocated for human rights, beginning with the founders of the profession. The work of Jane Addams is well-known, from her work to ensure equal access to basic city services in poor neighborhoods to her global efforts for peace. Edith Abbott encouraged social workers to engage with migration as a human rights issue (Abbott, 1927), and Julia Lathrop and Grace Abbott served on human rights committees of the League of Nations and the International Labour Organization (Healy, 2008). Bertha Reynolds was a passionate voice for human rights and for protection of civil rights during wartime (Reynolds, 1940). Whitney Young, executive director of the National Urban League, was a leader in the drive for racial equality, receiving the Medal of Freedom from President Johnson in 1969 in recognition of his civil rights work (Peebles-Wilkins, 2008). These are only a few among many social workers who have been active in many human rights issues. The list of social work human rights activists from other countries is also significant. Notably, the first document on children's rights was drafted by English social worker Eglantyne Jebb and adopted by the League of Nations in 1924.

It is more challenging to identify the human rights leaders of more recent decades. With the perspective of time, they will emerge. We can say that the profession of social work has participated in the major struggles to extend human rights to vulnerable groups, including racial minorities, women, persons with mental illness, immigrants, and LGBTQ persons. Human rights are also enhanced by social workers in many ways close to home. As Eleanor Roosevelt indicated, smaller actions close to home are the mainstay of human rights advancement (Roosevelt, 1958). In Connecticut, for example, new MSW graduates have launched rights-focused agencies, including True Colors, an agency to promote rights and dignity of LGBTQ youth; Families in Crisis, an organization to ensure rights of families of prisoners; and the Brazilian Alliance, founded to advocate for immigrant rights. Each of these exemplifies what may be the unique social work approach to human rights—providing services to fulfill rights while engaging in advocacy to further extend rights recognition.

Social work professional organizations have been significant players in human rights efforts. The American Association of Social Workers, a predecessor organization to the National Association of Social Workers (NASW), developed strong human rights-oriented platforms in the 1940s (Healy, 2008). NASW, although engaged in campaigns for rights of women, gays, and lesbians and the struggle for racial equality, among other human rights-oriented campaigns, took longer to issue an official policy statement on human rights. The International Policy on Human Rights was adopted as an official statement of the NASW at the 1999 Delegate Assembly and revised in 2008 (NASW, 2009). We note that examination of NASW's compilation of policy statements reveals an element of the American approach to human rights and one that has limited the profession's external reputation as a human rights profession. Many of the policy statements adopted over the years by Delegate Assemblies reflect issues of human rights, such as the association's positions on women's equality, corrections, the death penalty, gay issues, and many more. However, only the specific policy on international human rights fulsomely addresses human rights; most other policy statements lack any rights-based framing whatsoever. And when rights are invoked, it is often without reference to the legal bases for rights-claims, whether domestic or international.

The explicit involvement of U.S. social work education in human rights has increased recently. As already discussed, a major boost came in 2008 with the adoption of the revised Educational Policy and Accreditation Standards (CSWE, 2008). Previous statements have included the phrase "human rights," but the 2008 statement is the first to require preparation of students for human rights advocacy. The Katherine A. Kendall Institute of CSWE has identified human rights as one of its priority areas, and the CSWE Global Commission is also giving increased attention to the topic. In 2013 it announced formation of a special task force on human rights.

Globally, the IASSW has partnered with IFSW to draft and approve the documents noted previously. In the 1970s and 1980s member schools were required to sign a statement that they would uphold the principles of the UDHR in an effort to promote nondiscrimination and to address the situation of apartheid in South Africa. The 2004 Global Standards are the first official global document on guidelines for organization and content of social work education. The Standards contain several references to human rights (IFSW & IASSW, 2004b). Item 8.8 identifies the following curriculum purpose:

> Ensuring that social work students are schooled in a basic human rights approach, as reflected in international instruments, such as the Universal Declaration of Human Rights, the United Nations Convention on the Rights of the Child (1989) and the UN Vienna Declaration. (1993)

Beginning with publication of Ife's *Human Rights and Social Work* in 2001, many books and articles on social work and human rights have been published (e.g., Healy & Link, 2012; Hokenstad, Healy, & Segal, 2013; Ife, 2008; Mapp, 2014; Reichert, 2003; Reichert, 2007; Wronka, 2008). These are amply supplemented by the rich array of United Nations documents, reports, and papers from such organizations as Human Rights Watch and Amnesty International, all widely accessible on line. Availability of teaching materials has now changed from an obstacle to a facilitating factor for expansion of human rights education in social work.

Significance of the Volume: The Rich Potential of a Human Rights Approach

This book brings together the work of scholars who are actively engaged in research, teaching, and the development of educational models for furthering human rights in social work education. Joseph Wronka argues in this volume that human rights ought to serve as a "set of concrete and effective guiding principles for socially just intervention to substantively and legally mandate the fulfillment of human need and promotion of well-being." Other chapters expand on this idea with application to diverse curriculum areas and social issues. Although the curricular focus is on the United States, several chapters bring in perspectives on human rights and social work education from other parts of the world. Authors from Germany, Jamaica, and South Africa discuss challenges and innovative approaches in integrating human rights into social work education in their contexts. These examples stimulate creative thinking about additional curriculum advances.

Together the chapters in this volume provide exploration of educational models and innovations to introduce human rights into social work education in diverse ways. The examples span required courses in social work methods, policy, and research; specialized electives in international social work and human rights; travel study options; and exchange projects. Although this is not a curriculum manual, readers will glean ideas for course design and teaching strategies from the models discussed and find ample domestic and international reference material. Through the discussions and references, educators should discover ways to deepen their approaches to teaching human rights. The UDHR is truly an inspirational document, but social workers need to be introduced to a much broader and richer range of human rights materials and tools. These begin with the specialized treaties of specific relevance to social work and include country reports, shadow reports, United Nations treaty committee concluding comments, general comments explaining treaty provisions in depth, and complaint mechanisms, to name some. These will be referenced in the chapters that follow.

Conceptually the volume underscores several themes that merit ongoing scholarly discussion, including claims such as the ability of human rights to bridge macro/micro and global and local divides in U.S. social work. Moreover, many of the chapters enjoin social work educators to resist teaching human rights practice as solely about human rights violations covered widely as such in the media, such as human trafficking, torture, or other forms of state-sponsored violence against affected individuals and communities. Authors press readers to address more commonplace issues familiar to social work education and practice as human rights concerns, including child welfare, poverty, food insecurity, racism, and violence against women. Directly and indirectly, they encourage us as a profession to develop much clearer conceptualizations of what rights-based practice in mental health, child welfare, or the corrections systems should look like. Finally, the volume takes seriously the notion that social workers are crucial actors (either directly or indirectly) within any given society and thus have an obligation to have a fulsome understanding not only of what human rights are, but also how their practice potentially advances or hinders the human rights of those with whom they work.

References

Abbott, E. (1927). Human migration as a field of research. *Social Service Review*, 1(2), 258–269.

Albisa, C. (2011). Drawing lines in the sand: Building economic and social rights norms in the United States. In S. Hertel & K. Libal (Eds.), *Human rights in the United States: Beyond exceptionalism* (pp. 68–88). New York, NY: Cambridge University Press.

Anderson, C. (2003). *Eyes off the prize: The United Nations and the African American struggle for human rights (1944–1955)*. New York, NY: Cambridge University Press.

Armaline, B., Glasberg, D. S., & Purkayastha, B. (Eds.). (2011). *Human rights in our own backyard: Injustice and resistance in the United States*. Philadelphia, PA: University of Pennsylvania Press.

Carmalt, J. C., Zaidi, S., & Yamin, A. E. (2011). Entrenched inequity: Health care in the United States. In S. Hertel & K. Libal (Eds.), *Human rights in the United States: Beyond exceptionalism* (pp. 153–174). New York, NY: Cambridge University Press.

Center for Economic and Social Rights. (2010). *United States of America: Fact sheet no. 11.* New York, NY: Center for Economic and Social Rights.

CERD Working Group on Health and Environmental Health. (2008, January). *Unequal health outcomes in the United States: Racial and ethnic disparities in health care treatment and access, the role of social and environmental determinants of health, and the responsibility of the state. A report to the U.N. Committee on the Elimination of Racial Discrimination.* Retrieved from http://www.prrac.org/pdf /CERDhealthEnvironmentReport.pdf

Chilton, M., & Rose, D. (2009). A rights-based approach to food insecurity in the United States. *American Journal of Public Health, 99*, 1203–1211.

Council on Social Work Education (CSWE). (2008). *Educational policy and accreditation standards.* Retrieved from http://www.cswe.org/File.aspx?id= 13780

Gardiner, T. M., Irwin, A., & Peterson, C. W. (2009). No shelter from the storm: Reclaiming the right to housing and protecting the health of vulnerable communities in post-Katrina New Orleans. *Health and Human Rights Journal, 11*(2), 101–114.

Healy, L. M. (2008). Exploring the history of social work as a human rights profession. *International Social Work, 51*(6), 735–748.

Healy, L. M., & Link, R. J. (2012). *Handbook of international social work: Human rights, development, and the global profession.* New York, NY: Oxford University Press.

Hertel, S., & Libal, K. (Eds.) (2011). *Human rights in the United States: Beyond exceptionalism.* New York, NY: Cambridge University Press.

Hokenstad, M. C., Healy, L. M., & Segal, U. A. (2013). *Teaching human rights: Curriculum resources for social work educators.* Alexandria, VA: CSWE Press.

Ife, J. (2001) *Human rights and social work: Towards rights-based practice.* Cambridge, UK: Cambridge University Press.

Ife, J. (2008). *Human rights and social work: Towards rights-based practice* (Rev. ed.). Cambridge, UK: Cambridge University Press.

International Conference on Social Welfare (ICSW). (1969). *Social welfare and human rights: Proceedings of the Fourteenth International Conference on Social Welfare.* New York, NY: Columbia University Press.

International Federation of Social Workers (IFSW). (1988). Introduction to the policy papers. *International Policy Papers*, pp. 1–2. Geneva, Switzerland: Author.

International Federation of Social Workers (IFSW). (2002). *Social work and the rights of the child: A professional training manual on the UN Convention.* Retrieved from http://cdn.ifsw.org/assets/ifsw_124952-4.pdf

International Federation of Social Workers & International Association of Schools of Social Work. (2000). *Definition of social work.* Retrieved from http://ifsw.org /policies/definition-of-social-work/

International Federation of Social Workers (IFSW) & International Association of Schools of Social Work (IASSW). (2004a). *Ethics in social work: Statement of principles.* Retrieved from www.ifsw.org

International Federation of Social Workers (IFSW) & International Association of Schools of Social Work (IASSW). (2004b). *Global standards for the education and training of the social work profession.* Retrieved from http://cdn.ifsw.org /assets/ifsw_65044-3.pdf

International Federation of Social Workers (IFSW), International Association of Schools of Social (IASSW) Work, & International Council on Social Welfare (ICSW). (2012). *The global agenda for social work and social development.* Retrieved from www.iassw-aiets.org

Jackson, T. F. (2009). *From civil rights to human rights: Martin Luther King Jr. and the struggle for economic justice.* Philadelphia, PA: University of Pennsylvania Press.

Jewell, J. R., Collins, K. V., Gargotto, L., & Dishon, A. J. (2009). Building the unsettling force: Social workers and the struggle for human rights. *Journal of Community Practice, 17*(3), 309–322.

Lewis, H. (2009). "New" human rights? U.S. ambivalence toward the international economic and social rights framework. In C. Soohoo, C. Albisa, & M. F. Davis (Eds.), *Bringing Human Rights Home: A History of Human Rights in the United States* (Abridged ed., pp. 100–141). Philadelphia, PA: University of Pennsylvania Press.

Libal, K., & Neubeck, K. (2013). The rights of the child to an adequate standard of living: Applying international standards to the U.S. case. In L. Minkler (Ed.), *The state of economic and social rights: A global overview* (pp. 175–203). New York, NY: Cambridge University Press.

MacNaughton, G. (2011). Human rights frameworks, strategies, and tools for the poverty lawyer's toolbox. *Clearinghouse Review: Journal of Poverty Law and Policy*, January–February, 437–449.

Mapp, S. (2014). *Human rights and social justice in global perspective: An introduction to international social work* (2nd ed.). New York, NY: Oxford University Press.

McDowell, T., Libal, K., & Brown, A. (2012). Family therapy and human rights: Domestic violence as a case in point. *Journal of Feminist Family Therapy, 24*, 1–23.

McGill, M. (2012). Human rights from the grassroots up: Vermont's campaign for universal health care. *Health and Human Rights: An International Journal, 14*(1), 106–118.

McPherson, J., & Abell, N. (2012). Human rights engagement and exposure in social work: New scales to challenge social work education. *Research in Social Work Practice, 22*, 704–713.

Mishra, R. (2005). Social rights as human rights: Globalizing social protection. *International Social Work, 48*(1), 9–20.

National Association of Social Workers (NASW). (2009). International policy on human rights. In *Social work speaks: NASW policy statements, 2009–2012*. Washington, DC: NASW Press.

Peebles-Wilkins, W. (2008). Whitney Young. In T. Mizrahi and L. E. Davis (Eds.), *Encyclopedia of Social Work* (20th ed.). New York, NY: Oxford University Press.

Pyles, L. (2006). Toward a post-Katrina framework: Social work as human rights and capabilities. *Journal of Comparative Social Welfare, 22*(1), 79–88.

Reichert, E. (2003). *Social work and human rights: A foundation for policy and practice*. New York, NY: Columbia University Press.

Reichert, E. (Ed.). (2007). *Challenges in human rights: A social work perspective*. New York, NY: Columbia University Press.

Reynolds, B. C. (1940). Social workers and civil rights. *Social Work Today, 7*(9), 9–11.

Roosevelt, E. (1958, March 27). The great question: Remarks delivered at the United Nations in New York. Retrieved from: http://www.erooseveltudhr.org/

Soohoo, C., Albisa, C., & Davis, M. F. (2009). *Bringing human rights home: A history of human rights in the United States* (Abridged ed.). Philadelphla, PA: University of Pennsylvania Press.

United Nations Centre for Human Rights. (1994). *Human rights and social work: A manual for schools of social work and the social work profession* (Professional Training Series No. 1). Retrieved from http://www.ohchr.org/Documents /Publications/traininglen.pdf

United Nations. (1948, December 10). *Universal declaration of human rights.* G.A. Res. 217 A (III). Retrieved from http://www.refworld.org/docid /3ae6b3712c.html

United Nations. (1966, December 16). International covenant on economic, social, and cultural rights, G.A. Res. 2200A (XXI). Retrieved from http://www.ohchr.org/EN/ProfessionalInterest/Pages/CESCR.aspx

Wronka, J. (2008). *Human rights and social justice: Social action and service for the helping and health professions.* Thousand Oaks, CA: SAGE.

Endnotes

1   In the 2008 standards, EPAS 2.1.5 specifically addresses integrating human rights as a core competency. The document is currently under review but at this time the EPAS standards draft includes human rights as central to the values of social work.

2   Historian Carol Anderson (2003) has demonstrated that this localization has long been a part of U.S. history, but it has not been the dominant history on human rights in the United States. The early efforts of the National Association for the Advancement of Colored Persons (NAACP) included substantial mobilization to affect the new United Nations and secure commitment for challenging racial segregation in the United States as a human rights concern. By the mid-1950s, White supremacists had fused anticommunist and racist sentiments in a campaign to silence leaders of the NAACP and other groups through so-called red baiting. The organization chose to drop overt human rights language in their organizing efforts.

2 | Human Rights as the Bedrock of Social Justice:
Implications for Advanced Generalist Practice

Joseph Wronka

This chapter (1) presents select definitions of social justice, with particular attention to reasons that human rights principles ought to serve as its foundation; (2) discusses the meaning of human rights, with emphasis on the importance of the creation of a human rights culture and the human rights triptych; (3) examines implications for advanced generalist practice social work, roughly meta–macro (global), macro (whole population), mezzo (at-risk), micro (clinical), meta–micro (everyday life), and research interventions to fulfill human need, giving examples of integrating human rights within that framework; and (4) concludes with comments on social justice as struggle.

Select Definitions of Social Justice and Rationale for Human Rights as its Bedrock

Social justice, long a fundamental tenet of social work theory and praxis, is according to Barker (2003) "an ideal condition in which all members of a society have the same basic rights, protections, opportunities, obligations, and social benefits" (pp. 404–405). David Gil (2004), recent recipient of the Lifetime Achievement Award in Social Work, stated that

> a more generally accepted definition of social justice... [as] socially-established living conditions and ways of life that are conducive to the fulfillment of everyone's intrinsic needs and to the realization of everyone's innate potential, from the local to global levels. (p. 32; see also Gil, 2013)

An etymological definition of social justice, furthermore, is from the Latin *socius-i*, meaning "friends, allies, partners," and, in another context, "sharing, accompanying, acting together." *Sociare* means "to unite." The word *justice* comes from the Latin *iustus*, meaning "just, equitable, fair, mainly of persons," and in another context "what is fitting, what is right." Building on those etymological roots, *social justice* then "plainly concerns doing right among friends in ways that are equitable, fair and unite us" (Wronka, 2008, p. xx).

Although those definitions are worthwhile, they do not articulate the basic rights and obligations that all members of the human community have; what precisely are the ways of life conducive to the fulfillment of one's innate potential; and what actually is just, equitable, fair, fitting, and right among persons? The social construct of human rights, however, has been emphasized in major social work policy documents only since 2000. Furthermore, in 2008 the Council on Social Work Education (CSWE) asserted human rights as a core competency. This elaborates rather concretely and in educated layperson's terms the very important but rather ambiguous term of *social justice*, whose contours are often generally felt intuitively.

Thus, one may have an intuitive sense that homelessness or lack of health care is socially unjust. Certainly, it is unethical or, in the words of the Universal Declaration of Human Rights (UDHR; 1948), "shocks the conscience of humanity" to allow a homeless person to freeze in the cold. For that matter, equally shocking is to submit the healing of a sick child to market forces. These issues are specific violations of international legal mandates to fulfill human needs, as defined by the collective wisdom of the international community vis-à-vis the United Nations. People must change from having intuitive knowledge of this truth to actual awareness and move to overcome the injustice.

This powerful social construct of human rights arose out of the ashes of World War II. Officially coined by the United Nations in 1945, it reflected the failure of domestic sovereignty to stop the abuses of the Third Reich. The United States called the Conference of Evian (1938) to halt Hitler's transgressions, but not wishing to bring attention to other states' atrocities, such as public lynchings in the United States, policies of torture in Africa, and the Soviet's Gulag, the conference ended in failure (Buergenthal, Shelton, & Stewart, 2002). But after the deaths of an estimated 10 million innocents killed in the Holocaust and an estimated 92 million killed overall in the war with horrendous weapons such as nuclear bombs, the priority of domestic sovereignty was replaced by the idea of human rights, which now obliged all countries to adhere to them. Today no government would dare say that it is against human rights.

Given that ideas move people—as Eleanor Roosevelt, chair of the drafting committee for the United Nations Universal Declaration of Human Rights (1948), was fond of saying—this idea of human rights can unite us to overcome unfairness. In brief, to say that it is socially just to have health care and shelter does not have the specificity, power, and moral force as simply asserting that health care and adequate shelter are human rights. Stating the latter moves people not only individually, but also collectively and becomes a potent strategy for social change, thereby changing public sentiment. Indeed, Eleanor Roosevelt also wanted a series of human rights documents not in elitist language, but in language that could be readily understood by the educated layperson (Wronka, 1998).

A Bondei proverb asserts that sticks in a bundle are unbreakable. If united, human rights activists, or defenders, could overcome oppression to create a socially just world, to create, as Martin Luther King stated, the Beloved Community. Let us also not forget that Dr. King stated "It is necessary for us to realize that we have moved from the era of civil rights to the era of human rights... [as] clearly defined by the mandates of a humanitarian concern" (Human Rights Movement, 2013, p.2). Another luminary, Malcolm X, urged oppressed peoples of the world to see struggles as human rights rather than civil rights issues and to "use the United Nations' avenues, its Human Rights Commission... [as] more of a chance of getting meaningful results... and the moral support of the world" (Sterling Entertainment Group, 1992).

The words of Secretary General of the United Nations Ban Ki-Moon on World Social Justice Day, February 20, also reinforced the importance of human rights: "Equal opportunity, solidarity and *respect for human rights*, these are essential to unlocking the full productive potential of nations and peoples" (Ban, 2011; emphasis added). Navanethem Pillay (2011), UN High Commissioner for Human Rights, furthermore, stated:

> Social justice means life determined by human rights and equality. This is spelt out in the Universal Declaration of Human Rights for a life free from want and fear. And there are many U.N. conventions where states have undertaken obligations to ensure that all their policies and actions deliver on social justice and to respect the equality of all people. (p. 1)

Finally, let us not forget that the late Pope John Paul II said that the principles of the Universal Declaration ought to be lived in letter and in spirit (Catholics for the Common Good, 2013).

Human rights is the bedrock of social justice. Its role in social work theory and praxis is demonstrated by social work's recent pronouncements, compelling global historical antecedents, and statements by noted social justice and human rights leaders in the United States and United Nations. The Second Decade for World Human Rights Education (2004–2015) emphasizes integrating human rights into postsecondary, graduate, and professional education. Thus, it is a major challenge for the social work profession to effectively harness this idea to fulfill human need, promote well-being, and ultimately eradicate individual and social pathology.

Toward the Creation of a Human Rights Culture

This final analysis focuses on the creation of a human rights culture, which can be described as a "lived awareness of human rights in one's mind and heart, and dragged into our everyday lives" (Creating a Human Rights Culture, 2013, p. 2). To be sure, such a pithy statement is not that far removed from Eleanor Roosevelt's rather famous quote:

> Where after all do universal human rights begin?... in small places close to home... the neighborhood he [or she] lives in... the school or college he attends; the factory, farm, or office where he works. Such are the places

where every man, woman, and child seeks equal justice, equal opportunity, equal dignity without discrimination. Unless these rights have meaning there, they have little meaning anywhere. Without concerted citizen action to uphold them close to home, we shall look in vain for progress in the larger world. (Eleanor Roosevelt National Historic Site, 2014, p. 1)

Certainly, the profession of social work can play a substantive role in the formation of such a culture. The International Federation of Social Work (IFSW) stated that "from its inception social work has been a human rights profession" (United Nations Centre for Human Rights, 1994, p. 3). Although it is important to know one's rights, such cognitive awareness alone will not suffice. They must be known in a heartfelt way with passion and on an experiential, lived level, to borrow a phrase from phenomenology.

Perhaps the best way to comprehend the true meaning of human rights is to understand what René Cassin, often referred to as the father of human rights, called the Human Rights Triptych. The center panel is the Universal Declaration of Human Rights, the authoritative definition of human rights standards; the right panel is the documents following it, such as guiding principles, declarations, and conventions; and the left panel consists of implementation measures, generally institutional machinery, such as monitoring mechanisms, special rapporteurs, world conferences, and the Universal Periodic Review of the Human Rights Council.

The Center Panel of the Human Rights Triptych: The Universal Declaration of Human Rights

In brief, the General Assembly, although initially reluctant, endorsed the UDHR (United Nations, 1948) with no dissent on December 10, 1948. The UDHR is a compromise among various historical epochs and philosophical and spiritual systems. Increasingly referred to as *customary international law*, the UDHR consists of five crucial notions. The first is human dignity (Article 1); the second is nondiscrimination (Article 2); both notions reflect essential strands of some of the world's major religions such as the Judaic–Christian–Islamic tradition, Hinduism, and Buddhism. These religions also mirror social work's emphasis on spirituality and respect for cultural diversity. Thus, the only criterion to have one's dignity and rights is one's humanity, not one's gender, national or social origin, language, circumstances of birth, or other status. The third notion is civil and political rights (Articles 3–21), such as freedoms of speech, the press, peaceful assembly, and expression, largely mirroring the Age of Enlightenment and the U.S. Bill of Rights. They are also referred to as first generation or negative rights because they emphasize government's role not to intrude in people's lives. The fourth notion is that of economic, social, and cultural rights (Articles 22–27), such as rights to meaningful and gainful employment, rest and leisure, adequate shelter, medical care, security in old age, and education, mirroring for the most part the Age of Industrialization and the Soviet constitution of 1924. They are also referred to as second generation or positive rights because they emphasize government's role to do positive things to fulfill human need and promote well-being (Wronka, 2008).

Finally, there is the notion of solidarity rights (Articles 28–30), also referred to as third generation rights. Still in the process of conceptual elaboration, these rights are the product of postmodernism, reflecting largely the failure of domestic sovereignty. Emphasizing duties to the community and intergovernmental cooperation, they have come to mean rights to humanitarian disaster relief, international distributive justice, self-determination, development, protection of the cultural and common heritages of humanity (such as places of worship, the oceans, mountains, and space), and the right to environmental sustainability. It is important to emphasize that all of the above rights are indivisible and interdependent (What are human rights?, 2014). What, for example, is freedom of speech if a person is homeless and lives in a world at war?

The Right Panel: Guiding Principles, Declarations, and Conventions

The right panel consists of documents such as the Guiding Principles on Extreme Poverty and Human Rights (United Nations, 2012), the Declaration on the Rights of Indigenous Peoples (2007), and Principles for the Protection of Persons With Mental Illness and Improvement of Mental Health Care (United Nations, 1991). Documents with stronger judicial force are generally called conventions or covenants, which have the status of treaties. Some countries, such as the United States in its Supremacy Clause, have statements in their constitutions that assert that treaties when ratified shall "become the Supreme Law of the Land. ... And the judges bound thereby' (Article VI). Not many people know of that important clause, which former Attorney General Ramsey Clarke has called a "failure of our legal system" (personal communication, Human Rights Council, Geneva, 2012). This lack of awareness is also indicative of the failure and provincialism of the U.S. educational system, challenges that social workers in school and other settings can play a role in reversing. Certainly, the UN Guiding Principles on Extreme Poverty and Human Rights represent a breakthrough in eradicating extreme poverty (Redegeld, 2013), calling largely for a restructuring of global economic and social arrangements. Yet that document could be buttressed by an international convention (or treaty) to abolish extreme poverty, which since 2007 the IFSW and the International Association of Schools of Social Work (IASSW) have advocated in the fora of the Human Rights Council (Wronka, 2008, 2012, 2013; Wronka & Staub-Bernasconi, 2012).

In addition to the UN Charter—a treaty ratified by all member nations of the United Nations—there are nine major conventions: the International Covenant on Civil and Political Rights (United Nations, 1966a); the International Covenant on Economic, Social, and Cultural Rights (ICESCR; United Nations, 1966b); the Convention Against Torture (CAT; United Nations, 1984); the Convention on the Elimination of All Forms of Discrimination Against Women (CEDAW; United Nations, 1979); the Convention on the Elimination of All Forms of Racial Discrimination (United Nations, 1965); the Rights of the Child (CRC; United Nations, 1989); the Convention on the Protection of the Rights of All Migrant Workers and Members of Their Families (United Nations, 1990); the Convention on the Rights of Persons with Disabilities (United Nations, 2006); and the Convention for the Protection of All Persons from Enforced Disappearances (United Nations, 2010).

Generally, documents in the right panel of the triptych elaborate on rights the UDHR only touches on. Thus, the UDHR says simply, "Motherhood and childhood are entitled to special care and assistance" (Article 25); CEDAW and CRC establish what this special care and assistance means. For instance, CEDAW states that governments ought to "encourage the provision of necessary supporting social services to enable parents to combine family obligations with work responsibilities and participation in public life, in particular through promoting the establishment and development of a network of childcare facilities" (Article 11). They should also ensure "women appropriate services in connection with pregnancy, confinement and the post-natal period, granting free services where necessary, as well as adequate nutrition during pregnancy and lactation" (Article 12). Examples in CRC are the right of the child to be "registered immediately after birth … and the right from birth to a name, the right to acquire a nationality and, as far as possible, the right to know and be cared for by his or her parents" (Article 7); the right of the child "who is capable of forming his or her own views" to "express those views freely in all matters affecting the child, the views of the child being given due weight in accordance with the age and maturity of the child" (Article 12); and "the establishment of social programs to provide necessary support for the child and for those who have the care of the child" (Article 19).

Elaborating in part on the UDHR's notions of human dignity (Article 1) and the right to a standard of living for himself and his family (Article 25), the Guiding Principles on Extreme Poverty and Human Rights assert that we should no longer perceive those in extreme poverty as passive victims, poor helpless people to receive charity or to be rescued and unable to act for themselves. Rather, they are agents of change; rights holders to hold duty bearers, such as governments, private, and business entities accountable.

As a general rule, first there are guiding principles, then declarations, and finally conventions, which have more judicial force as discussed earlier. To emphasize, from 2007 to the present IFSW and IASSW have advocated for a convention to abolish extreme poverty before the Human Rights Council in Geneva, attempting to jump from guiding principles to an international convention in this instance. This urgent, if not emergency situation, is largely due to the growing gap between the poor and the rich in the 21st century (Carter Center, 2002), which also gave birth to many Occupy movements throughout the world (Zayas, 2012).

Elaborating on the right to participate in the cultural life of the community (UDHR, Article 27), the Declaration on the Rights of Indigenous Peoples (United Nations, 2007) asserts, for example, redress for deprivations of cultural values and ethnic identities; full guarantees against genocide; and the right to strengthen distinctive spiritual and material relations with lands, waters, and seas. Elaborating on the "right... to medical care" (UDHR, Article 25), the Principles on the Protection for Persons With Mental Illness asserts the need for appropriate disclosure of treatment in form and language understood by the patient and medication meeting the best health needs of the patient, not to be given for the convenience of others (Wronka, 2008).

The Left Panel: Implementation Measures

The left panel, undoubtedly the weakest part of the triptych with its emphasis on implementation, consists of UN charter and treaty-based approaches; the Universal Periodic Review; world conferences; and global commemorations of days, weeks, and decades deemed significant in the implementation of human rights principles. The former primarily consists of the appointment of special rapporteurs to examine and report on a particular theme and/or country that gained prominence in the global community. Such themes include racism and xenophobia (1993); violence against women (1994); extreme poverty (1998); the right to food (2000); the highest attainable standard of physical and mental health (2004); torture and other cruel, inhuman, or degrading treatment or punishment (2006); the right to freedom of expression and opinion (2010); the situation of indigenous peoples (2012); and the promotion of democracy and an equitable international order (2013). Treaty-based mechanisms also involve human rights monitoring committees that examine, with a spirit of creative dialogue, a country's progress vis-à-vis each article of the nine major conventions that a country ratified.

Implementation mechanisms can be extremely powerful tools for creating awareness of human rights principles. Ideally, this will result in a collective change of character for peoples and entire nations toward the creation of a human rights culture. One example is the plethora of laws and policies that have arisen in the last two decades to combat violence against women, not long after the special rapporteur's report on violence against women. Nongovernmental organizations (NGOs) also write their own shadow reports, which generally differ from government reports, such as statements on forced drugging, electro-shock, and mental health screening of children (Minkowitz, Galves, Brown, Kovary, & Remba, 2006) and indigenous peoples (Barnes, 2008).

The Human Rights Council set up the Universal Periodic Review Process when formed on March 15, 2006. Whereas only those countries that have ratified conventions go before the monitoring committees, all 192 members of the United Nations must submit a report every 4 years to the Human Rights Council concerning their efforts to adhere to human rights principles. Assisted by three troikas, member states are chosen by lots to review the country's report. (A country's reporting before the Human Rights Council can be viewed at http://www.unmultimedia.org/tv/webcast/c/un-human-rights-council.html.)

There are also world conferences. These are generally under the auspices of the United Nations, but in concert with numerous NGOs, which have become a powerful force governments must consider. An exception was the Conference on Peace in 1998 at The Hague, which was sponsored by NGOs rather than the governments of the United Nations. Some conference examples, with their attendant action plans, often revised every 5 years include population in Cairo (1994), women in Beijing (1995), food in Rome (1997), racism in Durban (2001), sustainability in Johannesburg (2002), the information society in Tunisia (2005), climate change in Copenhagen (2009), and sustainable development in Rio de Janeiro (2012).

Commemorating international days is another way to create awareness of human rights concerns and engage in questioning how to apply such values in socially just policies. Should we wish, as Gandhi said, to be the change we want to see in the world, such awareness might also result in major individual character transformation. Select international days are Holocaust Remembrance Day (January 27), World Social Justice Day (February 20), Women's Day (March 8), World Water Day (March 22), International Day for the Elimination of Racial Discrimination (March 21), International Day of the World's Indigenous Peoples (August 9), International Day of Peace

(September 21), International Day of Older Persons (October 1), World Day Against the Death Penalty and World Mental Health Day (both on October 10), International Day to Eradicate Extreme Poverty (October 17), International Day of Tolerance (November 16), Universal Children's Day (November 20), International Day of Persons with Disabilities (December 3), International Human Rights Day (December 10), and International Day of Solidarity (December 20). In general, a few days before and after an international day consist of a weeklong commemoration.

Examples of international years are Women's Year (1975), World's Indigenous Peoples (1993), Eradication of Extreme Poverty (1996), Oceans (1998), Sanitation (2008), Rapprochement of Cultures (2010), Forests (2011), and Cooperatives (2012). Examples of decades are Against Racism (1993–2003), Second Decade on Human Rights Education (2005–2015), Second International Decade for the Eradication Against Colonialism (2001–2010), Education for Sustainable Development (2005–2014), Action for Water for Life, (2006–2015), Second Decade for the Eradication of Extreme Poverty (2008–2017), and Fight Against Desertification (2010–2019).

Ultimately, the UN Charter, UDHR, guiding principles, declarations, conventions following it, and implementation mechanisms in general are only as powerful as public sentiment allows. The values of the Human Rights Triptych mirror the collective wisdom of almost the entire global community. They need discussion and debate in public fora, because research consistently demonstrates that only chosen values endure. Former Supreme Court Justice Brandeis's feeling that government is our omnipresent teacher has special relevance here.

For the sake of brevity, the above discussion mentioned only the triptych of the United Nations. The Organization of American States, the African Union, the European Union, and the Southeast Asian Human Rights Association, to mention a few, are regional organizations with their own documents and implementation mechanisms. Although their thrusts are similar to those from the United Nations, they appear to have different emphases, such as the European Charter emphasizing economic and social rights and the African Charter emphasizing rights to solidarity.

Implications for Advanced Generalist Social Work Education

These human rights principles, which represent societal values that have crystallized into rights, fulfill human needs and promote well-being. This creates a socially just world and has implications for advanced generalist social work education. This approach emphasizes multipronged levels of intervention to eradicate individual and social malaises. Although demarcation among levels is often blurred, such interventions can be classified roughly as global (meta–macro); whole-population (macro); at-risk (mezzo); clinical (micro); and everyday life (meta–micro) (Wronka, 2008, 2012; Wronka & Staub-Bernasconi, 2012).

Select examples that speak to the relevance of human rights principles on first the global level echo the words of Martin Luther King that "injustice anywhere is a threat to justice everywhere" (King, 1963). It emphasizes social work's concerns for every person, everywhere. This is often asserted by David Gil, and world citizenship is emphasized by Jane Addams, often referred to as the mother of social work. The Women's International League for Peace and Freedom—the organization for which Jane Addams was first co-president—exemplifies this approach through its concerns to eradicate the proliferation of nuclear arms, extreme poverty, and global social and economic inequities in general. The UN Charter has the status of treaty. It must be implemented in the United States (as least according to the federal constitution's Supremacy Clause discussed earlier) and commits all member states to promote full employment and the development of conditions favorable to economic and social progress. Implementation would help realize human rights for every person, everywhere, which is ultimately social work's mandate.

Additionally, implementation of the UN Charter and other facets of the human rights triptych, which are interrelated like guiding principles and reports of special rapporteurs, would alleviate violence against children. Research has demonstrated that violence against children can be a direct result of unemployment, underemployment, and lack of collective bargaining in the workplace (Gil, 1978). Full employment would also provide hope to the mentally ill, whose suffering is prefigured by despair. Such a global consciousness would also alleviate other malaises like AIDS. Policy makers and activists would seriously need to consider a socially just international order as enunciated throughout the triptych, thus ensuring that victims in developing countries have access to medications at reasonable prices.

During the dawn of the Third Phase of the World Program for Human Rights Education, human rights education has emphasized social media from the preschool to the professional levels. Using the media and other public venues for longstanding social change is a perfectly reasonable intervention on the whole population at the macro level, which generally encompasses interventions in only one country. The metaphor of putting out the burning ship to prevent victims from floating down the river is most amenable here; whereas, the meta–macro seeks interventions that will prevent all ships from burning in the oceans and seas, from which rivers flow. School social workers, for example, could then engage in creative discussions with administrators, teachers, and students for ways to include human rights principles in curricula. Or practitioners could ensure that professional agencies' policies are consistent with human rights documents on medical ethics and the protection of persons with mental illness. Social activists could also have public service announcements, develop human rights shows and even MTV skits that could help spread the word about human rights in an effort to expand people's consciousness. Indeed, teaching about the fundamental principles of human dignity, nondiscrimination, and rights to free expression, health care, and education that should promote tolerance and friendly relations among nations, as asserted in the UDHR, could easily create an attitude among people that no person shall be prejudiced against, or live in poverty or a global hostile environment. One poignant example is that human rights education has been found to be an effective antidote to bullying (Greene, 2006).

Working with vulnerable or at-risk populations is fundamental to social work theory and praxis (Staub-Bernasconi, 2012). Such vulnerable groups include children; undocumented immigrants; minorities; women; indigenous peoples; people with disabilities, including mental illness and substance abuse; workers vulnerable to employer whim; prisoners; and other groups as they evolve. As a human rights profession (Wronka, 2008; Staub-Bernasconi, 2012), social work must adhere to the following principle: Its professionals must view the aforementioned populations not as charity cases or research specimens, but rather as marginalized people whose voices need to be integrated into policy-making and who should be treated with human dignity. An extreme case was Nazi doctors indicted at Nuremberg for crimes against humanity. Other examples of mezzo- level interventions that derive from human rights documents are forming trade unions for the protection of workers' interests (ICESCR); maternity leave with pay and services for parents to balance family with outside work and public interests (CEDAW); maintenance of contact with both parents for the child in cases of separation and integration of an abused child into the community (CRC); and prohibiting torture by persons in an official capacity (CAT). The micro level is most associated with clinical social work, yet it almost entirely deals with the symptoms of an unjust social order, where other levels of intervention have failed.

Thus, social workers as a whole may strategize advocacy efforts for an amendment to the federal constitution for a right to adequate shelter as asserted in ICESCR. This would specify culturally appropriate housing at a reasonable cost, with adequate infrastructure and lighting, and nearness to employment by its monitoring committee. As an at-risk strategy social workers may organize workers to form a union for reasonable wages and job security. But if there is no right to shelter or collective bargaining, the person may become unemployed and homeless. Thus, the social worker might apply for a grant to construct a homeless shelter, and then not only administer it, but also counsel clients about searching for jobs. Ultimately, he or she would assist the client in overcoming learned helplessness, yet acknowledging somewhat paradoxically that they are victims of an unjust social order.

Also, other clients in hospital and outpatient settings ought to have treatment that is in accordance with such human rights documents as the Protections of Persons with Mental Illness. Thus, the clinician should be aware that diagnoses should not be given on the basis of membership in a minority group or class; no child should be given medication for the convenience of others; patients ought to know of alternatives to treatment, their length, and expense; treatment should be in the least restrictive environment.

At the meta–micro level, the level of the everyday life, social workers can encourage the use of peer groups as means of support. Alcoholics Anonymous, Narcotics Anonymous, Emotions Anonymous, Overeaters Anonymous, and Sex and Love Addicts Anonymous are examples of groups that every clinician knows can have a positive effect on clients and significant others. It is noteworthy here that CEDAW asserts the need for support groups for rural women. Furthermore, social workers can encourage the use of positive supports in a person's environment, an essential component of any psychosocial assessment.

Finally, both quantitative and qualitative research can constantly provide input into best practice models. The key here is that human rights ought to serve as the core modal point in the development, implementation, and evaluation of an intervention. A case in point is a comparison of the UDHR with the U.S. federal and state constitutions. A content analysis of those documents revealed that the U.S. Constitution, although exemplary in the areas of civil and political rights, is almost entirely lacking in economic, social, cultural, and solidarity rights. Former Supreme Court Justice Louis Brandeis urged that state constitutions ought to be laboratories of democracy. But they barely do any better; the only second generation right stated almost consistently is the right to education, which appeared in 41 constitutions (Wronka, 1998). Awareness of these gaps could easily move people to action in their own countries, such as the United States, where roughly 20% of children live in poverty, yet their government constantly touts itself as a leader of human rights.

Select Student Activities and Links to a Curriculum and Exemplary Group Project

If we define education in its etymological origin from the Latin *educare* meaning "to grow, nourish, strengthen," the idea of human rights as ultimately a way of life makes students extremely enthusiastic to apply it not only to their everyday lives, but also their social action projects. Whereas it is infused throughout the social work curriculum at Springfield College, here are select activities that students do in their social action group projects in a course titled Policy Implementation: Social Action in the Struggle for Human Dignity. They describe the relationship between human needs and the three sets of rights discussed earlier. Referring to Article 2 of the UDHR on nondiscrimination, they do a demographic of groups most affected as pertaining to race, gender, class, and/or other status. They trace a history of the problem through examining legislative, judicial, executive, and public discourse initiatives as they apply to the UDHR. Students also cite relevant major conventions and other guiding principles and declarations.

Students do not have to engage in all the social actions from the meta–macro to the meta–micro levels, but must engage in some substantive actions. These have included organizing readings of human rights documents, commemorating international days, passing bills to monitor states' compliance with international human rights standards, taking out Web pages and networking to sign and ratify certain conventions, urging pharmaceutical companies to abide by Article 28 of the UDHR asserting the "right to a just social and international order" as the basis for providing reasonably priced HIV medications to developing countries.

Students get "fired up" when the curriculum quotes James Grant (1994), former director of UNICEF, who cited social critic H. L. Mencken in speaking of the need for a "pathological belief in the occurrence of the impossible" (p. 9). For instance, students become aware of the UN Charter's assertion that full employment is a human right that must be implemented as the status of a treaty. They wonder why it is rarely in public discourse and alert others of its importance, along with human rights in general. Students also critique an article from *Social Work Speaks* from an advanced generalist perspective (see Wronka, 2008, and www.humanrightsculture.org for an essay on creating a human rights culture, links to human rights and social work resources, select videos, public service announcements, and opportunities to offer comments). An excellent student project on Violence Against Women illustrated an advanced generalist approach with a human rights/social justice orientation that followed the guidelines of the curriculum for the course Policy Implementation: Social Action in the Struggle for Human Dignity.

Social Justice as Struggle

In the final analysis, the challenge for social work education is how to integrate human rights into its theory and praxis to affect quality of life collectively and individually. This is a challenge more specifically for advanced generalist practice education. Challenges at the meta–macro level would necessitate massive global coalition building to have countries sign, ratify, and implement international treaties at considerable time and expense. On the macro level, countries inimical to human rights initiatives may attempt to stymie human rights education at the national level. Also, some school boards that might have links to elitist and profit-making companies might be threatened by some human rights documents that advocate collective bargaining. At the mezzo level, identifying at-risk groups might create a self-fulfilling prophecy in that, indeed, such groups might plummet further into society's malaises. These highlight the idea that social justice is a struggle.

The micro-level poses the possibility of working with only a few people and at considerable time and expense. The meta–micro may appear to negate professionalism. Another major challenge is that social work education must deal with the thorny problem of how to work both reactively and proactively. Thus, while counseling the homeless, the homeless keep on coming; while preventing the homeless from coming, the homeless may be dying in the streets.

Finally, we ought to keep in mind that the word *curriculum* is from the Latin *currere*, meaning to run and proceed, often within the context of good deeds and the learning of experience (Curriculum, 2013). Human rights is a powerful tool that ought to run through social work curricula. By keeping the concept of human rights in mind, good deeds and experiential learning can substantively address advanced generalist social work's multipronged levels of intervention and the challenges they pose.

References

Ban, K.-M. (2011). *Secretary generalia.org/wiki/Human_rights_movement right* Retrieved from http://www.facebook.com/note.php?note_id =200209326673008

Barker, R. L. (2003). *The social work dictionary* (5th ed.). Washington, DC: NASW Press.

Barnes, R. (2008). Report of the Indigenous Peoples and Nations Coalition: Racial injustice and crimes against humanity in Alaska: Article 15 of CERD urgent action. Retrieved from http://www2.ohchr.org/english/bodies/cerd /docs/ngos/usa/IPNCAlaskaReport.pdf

Buergenthal, T., Shelton, D., & Stewart, D. (2002). *International human rights in a nutshell*. St. Paul, MN: West.

Carter Center. (2002). President Jimmy Carter's acceptance speech for the Nobel Peace Prize. Retrieved from http://www.cartercenter.org/news/multimedia /GeneralTopics/NobelPeacePrize2002Speech.html

Catholics for the Common Good. (2013). Retrieved from http://ccgaction.org /node/879

Creating a Human Rights Culture. (2013). Retrieved from http://www .humanrightsculture.org

Curriculum. (2013). In *Wikipedia, the free encyclopedia*. Retrieved from http://en.wikipedia.org/wiki/Curriculum

Eleanor Roosevelt National Historic Site. (2014). Retrieved from http://www.nps .gov/elro/forteachers/classrooms/wheredohumanrightsbegin.htm

Gil, D. (1978). *Violence against children*. Cambridge, MA: Harvard University Press.

Gil, D. (2004). Perspectives on social justice. *Reflections, 10*(4), 32–39.

Gil, D. (2013). *Confronting injustice and oppression: Concepts and strategies for social workers* (2nd ed.). New York, NY: Columbia University Press.

Grant, J. P. (1994). Child health and human rights: Making the "impossible" possible. In National Research Council, *Child health and human rights*. Washington, DC: National Academies Press.

Greene, M. (2006). Bullying in schools: A plea for a measure of human rights. *Journal of Social Issues, 62*(1), 63–79.

Human rights movement. (2013). In *Wikipedia, the free encyclopedia*. Retrieved from http://en.wikipedia.org/wiki/Human_rights_movement

King, M. L., Jr. (1963, April 16). Letter from a Birmingham jail. Retrieved from http://www.africa.upenn.edu/Articles_Gen/Letter_Birmingham.html

Minkowitz, T., Galves, A., Brown, C., Kovary, M., & Remba, E. (2006). *Alternative report on forced drugging, forced electroshock, and mental health screening of children in violation of Article 7*. Retrieved from www.ushrnetwork .org/pubs/

Pillay, N. (2011). *Comments on social justice day*. Retrieved from http://www .youtube.com/watch?v=OlwLOIuSaxo

Redegeld, T. (2013). *UN guiding principles on extreme poverty and human rights: A breakthrough in tackling poverty*. Washington, DC: ATD Fourth World Movement.

Sterling Entertainment Group. (1992). *Malcolm X: Death of a prophet.* [Video] Available from Sterling Entertainment Group, Fort Mill, SC 29708.

Staub-Bernasconi, S. (2012). Human rights and their relevance for social work as theory and practice. In L. Healy & R. Link (Eds.), *Handbook of international social work: Human rights, development, and the global profession* (pp. 31–36). New York, NY: Oxford University Press.

United Nations. (1948). *Universal declaration of human rights.* G.A. Res. 217 A (III). Retrieved from http://www.refworld.org/docid/3ae6b3712c.html

United Nations. (1966a). *International covenant on civil and political rights.* G.A. Res. 2200A (XXI). Retrieved from http://www.ohchr.org/Documents /ProfessionalInterest/ccpr.pdf

United Nations. (1966b). *International covenant on economic, social, and cultural rights.* G.A. Res. 2200A (XXI). Retrieved from http://www.ohchr.org/EN /ProfessionalInterest/Pages/CESCR.aspx

United Nations. (1965). *International convention on the elimination of all forms of racial discrimination.* G. A. Res. 2106 (XX). Retrieved from http://www.ohchr .org/Documents/ProfessionalInterest/cerd.pdf

United Nations. (1979). *Convention on the elimination of all forms of discrimination against women.* G.A. Res. 34/180. Retrieved from http://www.ohchr.org /Documents/ProfessionalInterest/cedaw.pdf

United Nations. (1984). *Convention against torture and other cruel, inhuman or degrading treatment or punishment.* G.A. Res. 39/46. Retrieved from http://www.ohchr.org/Documents/ProfessionalInterest/cat.pdf

United Nations. (1989). *Convention on the rights of the child.* G.A. Res. 44/25. Retrieved from http://www.ohchr.org/Documents/ProfessionalInterest/crc.pdf

United Nations. (1990). *International convention on the protection of the rights of all migrant workers and members of their families.* G. A. Res. 45/158. Retrieved from http://www2.ohchr.org/english/bodies/cmw/cmw.htm

United Nations. (1991). *Principles for the protection of persons with mental illness and the improvement of mental health care.* Retrieved from http://www.ohchr. org/EN/ProfessionalInterest/Pages/PersonsWithMentalIllness.aspx

United Nations. (2006). *Convention on the rights of persons with disabilities.* G.A. Res. A/RES/61/106. Retrieved from http://www.ohchr.org/EN/HRBodies /CRPD/Pages/ConventionRightsPersonsWithDisabilities.aspx

United Nations. (2007). *Declaration on the rights of indigenous persons.* G.A. Res. 61/295. Retrieved from http://daccess-dds-ny.un.org/doc/UNDOC/GEN /N06/512/07/PDF/N0651207.pdf

United Nations. (2010). *Convention for the protection of all persons from enforced disappearance.* Retrieved from http://www.ohchr.org/Documents /ProfessionalInterest/disappearance-convention.pdf

United Nations. (2012). *Guiding principles on extreme poverty and human rights.* Retrieved from http://www.ohchr.org/Documents/Publications/OHCHR_ ExtremePovertyandHumanRights_EN.pdf

United Nations Centre for Human Rights. (1994). *Human rights and social work: A manual for schools of social work and the social work profession* (Professional Training Series No. 1). Retrieved from http://www.ohchr.org/Documents /Publications/traininglen.pdf

What are human rights? (2014). Retrieved from http://www.ohchr.org/en/issues /pages/whatarehumanrights.aspx

Wronka, J. (1998). *Human rights and social policy in the 21st century: A history of the idea of human rights and comparison of the United Nations Universal Declaration of Human Rights with United States federal and state constitutions* (Rev. ed.). Lanham, MD: University Press of America.

Wronka, J. (2008). *Human rights and social justice: Social action and service for the helping and health professions.* Los Angeles, CA: SAGE.

Wronka, J. (2012). Overview of human rights: The U.N. conventions and machinery. In L. Healy and R. Link (Eds.), *Handbook of international social work: Human rights, development, and the global profession* (pp. 439-446). New York, NY: Oxford University Press.

Wronka, J. (2013). An overview of human rights. In T. Hokenstad, L. Healy, & U. Segal (Eds.), *Teaching human rights: Curriculum resources for social work educators* (pp. 3–20). Alexandria, VA: CSWE Press.

Wronka, J., & Staub-Bernasconi, S. (2012). Human rights. In K. Lyons, T. Hokenstad, M. Pawar, N. Huegler & N. Hall (Eds.), *The SAGE handbook of international social work* (pp. 70–84). Los Angeles, CA: SAGE.

Zayas, A. (2012). *Report of the independent expert on the promotion of a democratic and equitable social order.* Retrieved from http://www.ohchr.org/Documents /HRBodies/HRCouncil/RegularSession/Session21/A-HRC-21-45_en.pdf

3 | Can Human Rights-Based Social Work Practice Bridge the Micro/Macro Divide?

David Androff and Jane McPherson

Social work is dedicated to helping oppressed members of society. Consensus on our professional values is encapsulated in the United States by the National Association of Social Workers Code of Ethics (2008), and informs myriad interventions, strategies, and roles for implementing these principles. The variability of practice techniques and methodologies within the field of social work practice has strengths and weaknesses. Abraham Flexner (1915) famously critiqued the lack of a singular practice method as one reason that social work failed to meet his standard of a profession. Despite his judgment, the multiplicity of ways that social workers can engage in resolving problems has also meant tremendous flexibility for practitioners.

However, many social workers do not avail themselves of the full range of practice options within the profession's toolbox. Social work education in the United States generally requires students to choose between micro and macro curricula, and most social workers specialize in either micro or macro practice. This divide limits the social work profession in practice, education, and research. Although specialization in advanced practice modalities is desirable and consistent with social work's ethical commitment to provide competent service, the split in perspectives is so large that it hampers practice and blunts the profession's impact.

This chapter investigates human rights-based practice's potential to bridge the micro/macro divide. A human rights approach to social work practice is an integrative approach linking the legal framework, language, and institutions of human rights with social work practice and demands intervention on the individual and societal levels. We begin with a review of the micro/macro divide, introduce human rights-based social work practice and its potential to bridge the divide, and present two case examples illustrating the potential of combining micro/macro practice perspectives. Narrative exposure therapy is an individually focused therapeutic intervention that contributes to social change, and truth and reconciliation commissions are macro-level interventions with implications for healing individuals.

The Micro/Macro Divide

Social work in the United States is typically divided between micro and macro emphases, between direct and indirect practice. The micro/macro divide dominates social work education, practice, and research in the United States but is less relevant around the world, particularly where micro-practice is less common (Healy, 2008a). This divide can be traced to divergent impulses in the profession's history, a tension between helping individuals versus working to improve social systems. We believe this division has restricted social work from fulfilling the profession's promise of social justice.

What Is the Divide?

The micro/macro divide is a separation of practice methods, curricula, and scholarship into two categories. The micro focuses on individuals and families and emphasizes interpersonal interactions between practitioners and clients (Johnson & Yanca, 2010). Micro practice is influenced by psychology, medicine, and education, and uses the practitioner's relationship with the client as a primary mode for intervention. Therefore, micro practice skills include relationship building, motivational interviewing, and therapeutic approaches. Micro social work curricula include assessment and treatment of mental disorders, treatment modalities (such as family therapy, cognitive-based therapy), and skills for interpersonal clinical practice with various populations. Scholarship in micro-level social work focuses on individual problems, direct practice approaches, clinical evaluations, and interpersonal theories.

The macro focuses on communities, organizations, and institutions (Meenaghan, Gibbons, & McNutt, 2005). Where micro approaches zero in on specific individuals, macro approaches take a bird's eye view to social problems. Macro practice emphasizes social planning, social policy, social action, and the administration and management of social service organizations. This form of practice draws from sociology, political science, economics, and business and seeks to intervene with the larger social structure in which social work clients are located. Practice skills include maximizing consumer participation, social planning for community change, social development, program development and evaluation, policy analysis, management and administration, budgeting, and grant writing. Macro social work curricula include program planning, managing human service organizations, community organizing, and agency or community-based research. Macro scholarship focuses on community and organizational assessment, program evaluation, social policy impact, and advocacy.

Where Does the Divide Come From?

The micro/macro divide is rooted in U.S. social work history. Social work was born an interdisciplinary project concerned with the application of knowledge in service of vulnerable populations, building on psychology, economics, medicine, and sociology. It may be expected that such diversity of disciplines would result in tension between practice approaches. Mary Richmond (1922) may have first coined the terms *micro* and *macro* social work practice. Social movements including the charity organization societies and the settlement house movement emphasized different levels of intervention. The micro/macro divide evolved from a split between individual casework and community and policy focused approaches. Micro practice retained a focus on helping individuals in need through direct engagement, whereas macro practice retained a focus on the transformation of the social structure.

Consequences of the Divide

The micro/macro divide reduces practitioners' ability to meet the needs of vulnerable populations, drains strength from the profession, and dilutes public awareness and recognition of social work (Austin, Coombs, & Barr, 2005). Practitioners exclusively focusing on individual or social concerns violate social work principles such as the person-in-environment perspective and ecological frameworks. In the United States most students specialize in micro practice, learn treatment-focused skills, and support for macro education is diminishing (Rothman & Mizrahi, 2014). Students are dissuaded from pursuing macro due to fears of fewer employment opportunities. This micro imbalance has been criticized for diverting social workers from their mission of social justice (Specht & Courtney, 1994). Macro practice has also been criticized as a historical remnant, marginal to contemporary social work, and for lacking specific practice skills (Rothman & Mizrahi, 2014). Most damaging are critiques that macro practitioners are disconnected from clients and not seen as significant players in policy, social activism, or social planning fields.

Specialization can lead to competent social work practice. However, expertise in one dimension of practice does not require blindness to others. The micro/macro divide in contemporary U.S. social work has reduced rather than enhanced social work practice. Rights-based practice should be examined in the context of other attempts to recombine micro/macro perspectives.

Previous Attempts to Bridge the Divide

Attempted resolutions have failed to sufficiently bridge micro/macro perspectives—and social work remains divided.

Generalist Practice

Generalist practice, based on the person-in-environment perspective and ecological theory, combines micro/macro through integrating interpersonal practice with policy and research (Kirst-Ashman & Hull, 2008; Miley, O'Melia, & DuBois, 2008). Generalist practice assumes practice skills, such as engagement, dialogue, assessment, and action, are transferrable regardless of level. Generalist practitioners assess individuals in their social environment and tailor interventions along a micro/macro spectrum. Generalist practice has been criticized for lacking a conceptual framework other than values, specific populations, or field of practice. Another criticism is that being overbroad prevents effective implementation. Generalist students have reported feeling unprepared for macro practice (Miller, Tice, & Harnek Hall, 2008). This is consistent with research indicating that students have less opportunity to learn macro skills (Koerin, Reeves, & Rosenblum, 2000).

Community-Centered Clinical Practice

Community-centered clinical practice focuses on strengthening neighborhoods and organizations while addressing interpersonal issues (Austin et al., 2005). Practice skills integrating clinical and community work include relationship building, assessment, helping processes and changing behaviors, effective use of self, empathy, and cultural sensitivity. This model requires a shared understanding of the micro/macro dimension of problems between practitioners and clients. Austin et al. (2005) provide an example of problematic student behavior that was dividing parents and teachers at an urban school. Practitioners implemented micro strategies of case management, crisis intervention, therapy, trust-building, and stress management. At a macro-level they formed parent/teacher groups, teacher support groups, research focus groups, a community advisory council, and collaborated with the teachers union.

Life-Course Perspective

The life-course perspective locates individual development within historical and cultural contexts (Hutchinson, 2005). Building from interdisciplinary collaboration the life-course perspective seeks to improve on existing life-cycle models of human development by acknowledging the role of historical and cultural forces on individual and family development. It combines a focus on an individual's sequence of life events and transitions with a historical focus of how cultural and social institutions shape individual lives. The result is a multidimensional understanding of intergenerational relationships, individual agency, and the influence of historical and social change on human behavior.

Public Health

The micro/macro divide is not unique to social work; micro/macro integration has been proposed in public health (Legge et al., 2007). Health, like social functioning, is affected by an interplay of micro/macro factors. Disease is manifested in individuals yet embedded in social structures; the social determinants of health include poverty and discrimination. The primary care model involves health care practitioners working within communities to alleviate health problems. It is hoped that practitioners, while focusing on immediate needs, will also inform policy. This approach has been criticized for overemphasizing clinical practice and ignoring social factors. The community development model focuses on structural dimensions through empowerment and access to resources. A public health micro/macro integration model combines meeting immediate health needs while addressing the social determinants of health. Building on concepts of "the personal is political" and "think globally, act locally," micro/macro integration combines assessment, goals, and interventions. Examples include older adults forming a peer support group, conducting outreach and education about their medical conditions, and advocating for policy change. Another involves a support group for women with disabilities who developed curricula to teach health care staff about their needs and lobbied organizations for wheelchair access and home visits for the homebound.

Human Rights and Social Work Practice

Through its focus on individual and collective rights within an international legal framework, a human rights-based approach to social work practice represents an opportunity to bridge the micro/macro gap. A human rights perspective is individually and universally focused and concerned with promoting the rights of every human being; also, it recognizes the responsibility of states and organizations in protecting rights. As such, human rights are difficult to categorize as either micro or macro in practice. Human rights, pertaining simultaneously to individual humans and universally to all humans, transcend the micro/macro divide.

Human rights can extend social work to new populations such as survivors of mass violence, torture, or human trafficking (Androff, 2011; Engstrom & Okamura, 2005), but a rights-based approach also provides a mechanism for defining many social work clients as survivors of rights abuses because poverty, hunger, homelessness, and domestic violence constitute human rights violations. Scholars argue the Universal Declaration of Human Rights (UDHR; United Nations, 1948) and the core international human rights treaties can bring rigor to social work practice, a quality that the "vague" (Mapp, 2008,

p. 24) and "outdated" (Reichert, 2011, p. 11) principle of social justice lacks (Pyles, 2006). A human rights approach reduces the emphasis on individual pathology by requiring that individual problems be seen in sociopolitical, structural context (Engstrom & Okamura, 2005; Lundy, 2011; Mapp, 2008). This empowers clients by redefining needs as entitlements or rights (Cemlyn, 2011; Lundy & van Wormer, 2007).

Human rights can help social workers educate clients about social structures (Barrett, 2011). Broadening assessment, human rights bridge "local and national issues with global concerns" (Healy, 2008b, p. 745) and allow social work to reorganize itself as a global profession in a world of international migration and neoliberal capitalism (Lundy, 2011; Midgley, 2007; Reichert, 2011). Some hope that human rights can repoliticize social work and support a critical theory of practice (Dominelli, 2007; Lundy, 2011).

What Is Human Rights Social Work Practice?

Although human rights-based social work practice is evolving, consensus exists that it requires knowledge of the UDHR and other relevant international agreements (Reichert, 2011). Key principles also include focus on strengths rather than pathology (Mapp, 2008); assessment that locates clients' individual problems in social and global contexts (Lundy, 2011); democratic, collaborative approaches to problem solving between worker and client (Ife, 2012); emphasis on the client's voice (Ife, 2012); advocacy (Healy, 2008a); and the importance of both micro and macro-level intervention (Wronka, 2008).

Human rights-based social work can be complicated by the contradictory role of social work in society. The profession advocates for social justice while operating within "a political and economic context that is based on, and supports, exploitation and inequality" (Lundy, 2011, p. 42). Still, human rights are tools that social workers can use to navigate these competing demands and come out fighting for social justice (Lundy, 2011; Reichert, 2011).

How Can Human Rights Combine Micro/Macro Perspectives?

Rights-based practice resolves the micro/macro divide by insisting on the necessity of both forms of action: individuals have the right to assistance, and unjust systems require change (Lundy, 2011; Lundy & van Wormer, 2007). Staub-Bernasconi (2012) proposes that micro practitioners include human rights violations on assessment protocols as a "diagnostic category" (p. 31), encouraging simultaneous micro/macro intervention. Lundy (2011) concurs that assessment should translate client needs into rights and lead to intervention on both levels.

Wronka (2008) provides an example of how a rights-based approach to homelessness entwines micro and macro approaches. Social workers advocate for the human right to shelter, strengthen prevention through protections for at-risk populations, directly provide shelter for the homeless, conduct research, and connect personally with homeless individuals through conversation. Reichert's (2011) example includes assessment of relevant human rights issues before the application of social work ethics. The skill of rights-oriented analysis allows social workers to navigate the inevitable conflicts that exist among human rights, established laws, agency policies, and cultural norms: Social workers must "develop techniques to analyze and critique potential conflict" (Reichert, 2006, p. xi). The final stage of practice is "taking action to realize human rights" in the context of ethical practice (Reichert, 2006, p. xi).

From the Micro to the Macro: Narrative Exposure Therapy (NET)

NET is a brief psychotherapeutic intervention designed to address posttraumatic stress disorder (PTSD) in survivors of mass violence and torture in settings such as refugee camps and postconflict zones (Schauer, Neuner, & Elbert, 2005). It is an individual-level intervention specifically designed for the context of massive human rights violations. NET has been used with children and adolescents (e.g., Rwandan genocide orphans, asylum seekers in Germany, Sri Lankan survivors of war and tsunami), adults (e.g., refugees from Sudan, Somalia, and Rwanda living in refugee camps; asylum seekers and refugees in Germany), and the elderly (Romanian survivors of political imprisonment) (McPherson, 2012). NET is a relatively new intervention (Schauer et al., 2005), but already there is good evidence to support its effectiveness in reducing PTSD symptoms (McPherson, 2012; Robjant & Fazel, 2010). NET combines micro and macro elements adapting strategies of two earlier trauma-treatment modalities, trauma-focused cognitive behavior therapy (TFCBT) and testimony therapy. TFCBT has been shown to be effective with a variety of PTSD sufferers (Bisson & Andrew, 2007; Foa & Meadows, 1997) and usually focuses on processing the survivor's worst memory. For individuals who have experienced torture and mass violence, there may be no single worst event that stands apart. NET therefore elicits autobiographies—including positive and negative memories—and contextualizes traumas as part of the survivors' lives as a whole (Schauer et al., 2005). Drawing on emotional processing theory, NET hypothesizes that repeated exposure to their own trauma narratives leads to healing through habituation to emotional and physiological responses (Bichescu, Neuner, Schauer, & Elbert, 2007). Psychotherapeutic approaches for survivors of human rights violations have often been criticized for "neglecting the context and for medicalizing the consequences of war," focusing on the micro to the neglect of the macro (Onyut et al., 2004, p. 94).

NET avoids this by incorporating testimony therapy, an intervention first used to treat survivors of Pinochet's political prisons in Chile, and which has been used effectively with Bosnian refugees in the United States (Cienfuegos & Monelli, 1983; Weine, Kulenovic, Pavkovic, & Gibbons, 1998). Testimony therapy aims to reorganize fragmented traumatic memories into a coherent narrative that emphasizes resilience and survival; the creation of a coherent testimony is believed to promote the cognitive and emotional processing of trauma (Neuner, Schauer, Roth, & Elbert, 2002). In NET, as in testimony therapy, the whole life of the individual is written down and then signed in a ritualized manner by witnesses. Beyond their personal value, the narratives produced in NET can be socially and politically meaningful in their documentation of human rights abuses (Bichescu et al., 2007). The testimonies can become evidence in the pursuit of justice, and the creation of testimony "helps the person to regain dignity and satisfies the survivor's need for justice" (Onyut et al., 2004, p. 94). On the micro-level the narrative contains the story that becomes the instrument of healing; on the macro-level it contains evidence of crimes. NET is designed for human rights practice, to serve survivors of severe human rights violations, and to create change at micro/macro-levels. Survivors require interventions capable of supporting "the psychological and social well-being of the individual, but extending to the repair of collective social structures"; such interventions help them "cope with the demands of a social world shattered by violence" (Mollica et al., 2004, p. 2062). NET therapists and researchers theorize that the low drop-out rates that characterize their studies are due to the utility of these written narratives for trauma-affected communities. For example, illiterate Sudanese refugees who received NET in a Ugandan refugee camp understood their narratives were a tool to make their voices heard. They encouraged their foreign therapists to publish the testimonies so that their situation would be remembered; they also wanted their children to know about their community's suffering during the war, and "hoped to pass on their biography to their children once they were living in peace and their children were educated" (Neuner, Schauer, Klaschik, Karunakara, & Elbert, 2004, p. 585). At clients' discretion, NET intervenes in the traumatic experience of individual lives for purposes such as tribunals, documenting a community's history, and promoting community healing. Clinical social workers practicing with refugee and migrant populations can employ this mental health intervention that seeks change on both micro and macro levels.

On the micro level, NET practitioners need diagnostic and therapeutic skills, experience working with trauma, and training in the NET procedure. They also should know the range of physical and psychological torture symptoms, behaviors that may trigger retraumatization in survivors, and their own needs for self-care (Engstrom & Okamura, 2005). On the macro level, social workers implementing NET need historical and political knowledge about the context of their clients' traumas and to expand their assessment to encompass human rights conditions in their clients' countries of origin (Fabri, 2001). In an implementation of NET with former Romanian political prisoners Bichescu et al. (2007) found it necessary to network with clients' larger systems. Though NET is an individual treatment, it was necessary to build trust with the community of survivors before being able to work effectively with individuals. To gain trust with individuals, the practitioners built trust with their political and social organizations (Bichescu et al., 2007). Proper deployment of NET requires knowledge of human rights, an ability to focus on a client's strengths and to contextualize his or her suffering, an emphasis on the client's voice and partnership within the therapeutic relationship, and assessment and intervention on the micro and macro levels.

From the Macro to the Micro: Truth and Reconciliation Commissions (TRCs)

TRCs represent how a macro human rights intervention can bridge the micro/ macro divide. Macro-level human rights interventions address systemic human rights violations and the failure of states and organizations responsible for protecting individual human rights. TRCs are macro interventions for responding to the aftermath of mass human rights violations (Hayner, 2001). TRCs entail consultations with victims, perpetrators, and community members and employ public forums to encourage dialogue between stakeholders. TRCs combine micro interventions by facilitating the healing of individuals with macro interventions for promoting social recovery (Androff, 2010a).

National or regional political bodies mandate TRCs to investigate human rights abuses. TRCs are typically created during political transitions, such as after a peace agreement ending armed conflict or the emergence of democracy after state repression. At their conclusion, TRCs produce a final report detailing their findings with recommendations for implementing reconciliation. Recommendations are commonly addressed to political bodies, public institutions, civil society organizations, and other macro-level actors, and sometimes to specific individuals. Recommendations have also been used to lobby for institutional and policy reforms. TRCs have been used in Africa, Latin America, Asia, and North America to promote social healing after conflict. Early TRCs were used in Latin America transitioning from military dictatorships. Following the popularity of the South African TRC, TRCs have been applied in diverse settings such as Timor-Leste, Sierra Leone, Peru, and Canada. More recently TRCs on a community level have been organized in North America, in settings as diverse as Greensboro, NC; Detroit, MI; and among tribal groups in Maine (Androff, 2012a).

TRCs bridge macro/micro practice dimensions in their twin functions of truth-seeking and reconciliation (Androff, 2010a). Truth-seeking is accomplished through detailed investigations into human rights violations (Androff,

2012b). These investigations consult official records as well as the testimony of victims, perpetrators, bystanders, and experts in relevant topics. In promoting reconciliation, TRCs employ restorative justice theory, which acknowledges that violence damages the social fabric, and attends to rebuilding relationships and reestablishing trust. Reconciliation activities vary by TRC but usually entail fostering mutual tolerance among formerly antagonistic groups (Androff, 2010b).

TRCs are considered human rights interventions because of their focus on human rights violations (Androff, 2012b). The human rights community has been involved in most TRCs. Often human rights lawyers conduct assessments of violations of international law. This requires detailed knowledge of international human rights law applied to specific local contexts. Sometimes evidence gathered in truth-seeking investigations has been used to prosecute perpetrators. This fosters accountability, a key element of rights-based practice. Whether TRCs contribute to justice or facilitate social healing, they can lay the foundation for prevention of further violence. TRCs have also contributed to building a human rights culture, setting new norms for conflict resolution, mutual respect, and peace.

TRCs are important for social work because they are a key strategy for repairing individuals and communities after violence (Androff, 2010a). If successful, TRCs can strengthen civil society, social functioning, and the provision and delivery of social services. TRCs promote pluralism and tolerance of diversity. In their use of local cultural strengths they evoke cultural competence. TRCs are about giving victims a voice to transform society. This promotes participation and self-determination, key aspects of rights-based practice. TRCs promote social justice through the protection of human rights in the wake of oppression and discrimination. TRCs encourage the participation of victims in the democratic process. TRCs use many macro social work practice skills (Androff, in press). Truth-seeking functions as a community needs assessment. TRCs identify community strengths throughout their investigations, and final reports contain assessments of community assets. Many TRCs result from political compromise between opposing groups; the resolution of violent conflict requires bargaining and negotiation skills. Implementing

TRCs, from selecting commissioners to planning public forums, requires community organizing skills. To ensure community engagement and attendance at events, macro practice skills such as outreach and recruitment are necessary. Community education and awareness campaigns can maximize a TRC's effect. Reconciling formerly antagonistic groups throughout the TRC process involves facilitating meaningful dialogue.

TRCs also involve micro practice skills (Androff, 2012c). To foster consensus, micro skills such as empathy, trust-building, and engagement are necessary to build relationships between divided people with histories of mistrust and abuse. To encourage victims, perpetrators, and community members to tell their stories, motivational interviewing and therapeutic support skills are valuable. This entails giving, respecting, and listening to the voice of victims. TRCs place individual voices in their cultural and political context. Many risk retraumatization during retellings of their stories; therefore, skills working with victims, preparing them for risks, and attending to traumatic symptoms are important. When participants require treatment, micro practitioners may provide services or make referrals. They may also assist with bereavement, grief, and helping people find closure. Micro practitioners can facilitate interpersonal reconciliation through restorative dialogue and, if possible, forgiveness processes. The micro practice skills of empathetic listening, validating, acceptance, nonjudgment, and the therapeutic use of self are invaluable to the success of TRCs.

Conclusion

This chapter argues that a human rights approach to social work practice can bridge the micro/macro divide. Rights-based approaches recontextualize individuals within their social environments and can refocus U.S. social work on its central social justice mission. We have highlighted two examples—NET and TRCs—as templates for human rights-based social work practice. Both examples exemplify critical elements of this approach: human rights knowledge, attention to voice, participatory approach, advocacy, and a dual micro/macro focus.

As new models of rights-based social work practice emerge, we must examine other social work modalities to adapt and recast them as human rights practices. Social work approaches such as trauma-informed and antioppressive practices could easily be expanded to include a rights-based assessment. In the United States, human rights-based practice would be particularly relevant with survivors of economic, social, and cultural rights violations who are frequent social work clientele in health care, child welfare, and income support settings.

Social work educators should incorporate human rights into teaching (McPherson & Abell, 2012; McPherson & Cheatham, in press). Students must be able to understand themselves and their clients as rights-holders (Reichert, 2006). The teaching of assessment should be broadened to include human rights violations (including violations of economic and social rights) (Staub-Bernasconi, 2012). Social work researchers must evaluate human rights approaches. Published evaluations of human rights practice in social work are few, and little can be asserted about the utility of rights-based practice. Research should investigate human rights protections, violations, practices, and institutions. In these ways, human rights-based social work practice can bridge the micro/macro divide and reassert our professional commitment to social justice.

References

Androff, D. (2010a). Truth and Reconciliation Commissions (TRCs): An international human rights intervention and its connection to social work. *British Journal of Social Work, 40*, 1960–1977.

Androff, D. (2010b). 'To not hate': Reconciliation among victims of violence and participants of the Greensboro Truth and Reconciliation Commission. *Contemporary Justice Review, 13*(3), 269–285.

Androff, D. (2011). The problem of contemporary slavery: An international human rights challenge for social work. *International Social Work, 54*(2), 209–222.

Androff, D. (2012a). Adaptations of Truth and Reconciliation Commissions in the North American context: Local examples of a global restorative justice intervention. *Advances in Social Work, 13*, 408–419.

Androff, D. (2012b). Can civil society reclaim the truth? Results from a community-based Truth and Reconciliation Commission. *International Journal of Transitional Justice, 6*(2), 296–317.

Androff, D. (2012c). Narrative healing among victims of violence: The impact of the Greensboro Truth and Reconciliation Commission. *Families in Society, 93*(1), 10–16.

Androff, D. (in press). A case study of a grassroots Truth and Reconciliation Commission from a community practice perspective. *Journal of Social Work.*

Austin, M, Coombs, M., & Barr, B. (2005). Community-centered clinical practice: Is the integration of micro and macro social work practice possible? *Journal of Community Practice, 13*(4), 9–30.

Barrett, J. (2011). Multicultural social justice and human rights: Strategic professional development for social work and counseling practitioners. *Journal for Social Action in Counseling and Psychology, 3*, 116–122.

Bichescu, D., Neuner, F., Schauer, M., & Elbert, T. (2007). Narrative exposure therapy for political imprisonment-related chronic post-traumatic stress disorder and depression. *Behaviour Research and Therapy, 45*, 2212–2220.

Bisson, J., & Andrew, M. (2007). Psychological treatment of post-traumatic stress disorder (PTSD). *Cochrane Database of Systematic Reviews, 18*, Art. No.: CD003388. doi: 10.1002/14651858. CD003388.pub3

Cemlyn, S. (2011). Human rights practice: Possibilities and pitfalls for developing emancipatory social work. *Ethics and Social Welfare, 2*, 222–242. doi:10.1080/17496530802481714

Cienfuegos, A., & Monelli, C. (1983). The testimony of political repression as therapeutic instrument. *American Journal of Orthopsychiatry, 53*, 43–51.

Dominelli, L. (2007). Human rights in social work practice: An invisible part of the social work curriculum? In E. Reichert (Ed.), *Challenges in human rights: A social work perspective* (pp. 16–43). New York, NY: Columbia University Press.

Engstrom, D., & Okamura, A. (2005). A plague of our time: Torture, human rights, and social work. *Families in Society, 85*, 291–300. doi: 10.1606/1044 -3894.1509

Fabri, M. (2001). Reconstructing safety: Adjustments to the therapeutic frame in the treatment of survivors of political torture. *Professional Psychology: Research and Practice, 32*, 452–457.

Flexner, A. (1915). Is social work a profession? *Proceedings of the National Conference of Charities and Correction, 42*, 576–590.

Foa, E., & Meadows, E. (1997). Psychosocial treatments for posttraumatic stress disorder. *Behaviour Research and Therapy, 38*, 319–345.

Hayner, P. (2001). *Unspeakable truths: Confronting state terror and atrocity.* New York, NY: Routledge.

Healy, L. (2008a). *International social work: Professional action in an interdependent world.* New York, NY: Oxford University Press.

Healy, L. (2008b). Exploring the history of social work as a human rights profession. *International Social Work, 51,* 735–748. doi:10.1177/0020872808095247

Hutchinson, E. (2005). The life course perspective: A promising approach for bridging the micro and macro worlds for social workers. *Families in Society, 86*(1), 143–152.

Ife, J. (2012). *Human rights and social work: Toward rights-based practice* (3rd ed.). New York, NY: Cambridge.

Johnson, L., & Yanca, S. (2010). *Social work practice: A generalist approach* (10th ed.). Upper Saddle River, NJ: Pearson.

Kirst-Ashman, K., & Hull, G. (2008). *Understanding generalist practice* (5th ed.). Chicago, IL: Nelson-Hall.

Koerin, B., Reeves, J., & Rosenblum, A. (2000). Macro-learning opportunities: What is really happening out there in the field? *Journal of Baccalaureate Social Work, 6,* 9–21.

Legge, D., Gleeson, D., Wilson G., Wright, M., McBride, T., Butler, P., & Stagoll, O. (2007). Micro macro integration: Reframing primary healthcare practice and community development in health. *Critical Public Health, 17*(2), 171–182.

Lundy, C. (2011). *Social work, social justice, and human rights: A structural approach to practice* (2nd ed.). Toronto, CA: University of Toronto Press.

Lundy, C., & van Wormer, K. (2007). Social and economic justice, human rights and peace: The challenge for social work in Canada and the US. *International Social Work, 50,* 727–739. doi:10.1177/0020872807081899

Mapp, S. (2008). *Human rights and social justice in a global perspective.* New York, NY: Oxford University Press.

McPherson, J. (2012). Does narrative exposure therapy reduce PTSD in survivors of mass violence? *Research in Social Work Practice, 22,* 29–42.

McPherson, J., & Abell, N. (2012). Human rights engagement and exposure in social work: New scales to challenge social work education. *Research in Social Work Practice, 22,* 704–713. doi:10.1177/1049731512454196

McPherson, J., & Cheatham, L. P. (in press). Measuring human rights impact in social work education: The One Million Bones example. *Journal of Social Work Education.*

Meenaghan, T., Gibbons, W., & McNutt, J. (2005). *Generalist practice in larger settings: Knowledge and skills concepts.* Chicago, IL: Lyceum Books.

Midgley, J. (2007). Development, social development, and human rights. In E. Reichert. (Ed.), *Challenges in human rights: A social work perspective.* New York, NY: Columbia University Press.

Miller, S., Tice, C., & Harnek Hall, D. (2008). The generalist model: Where do the micro and macro converge? *Advances in Social Work, 9*(2), 79–90.

Miley, K., O'Melia, M., & DuBois, B. (2008). *Generalist social work practice: An empowering approach* (6th ed). Boston, MA: Allyn & Bacon.

Mollica, R., Lopes Cardozo, B., Osofsky, H., Raphael, B., Ager, A., & Salama, P. (2004). Mental health in complex emergencies. *Lancet, 364,* 2058–2067. doi: http://dx.doi.org/10.1016/S0140-6736(04)17519-3

National Association of Social Workers. (2008). Code of ethics. Retrieved from https://www.socialworkers.org/pubs/code/code.asp

Neuner, F., Schauer, M., Klaschik, C., Karunakara, U., & Elbert, T. (2004). A comparison of narrative exposure therapy, supportive counseling, and psychoeducation for treating posttraumatic stress disorder in an African refugee settlement. *Journal of Consulting and Clinical Psychology, 72*(4), 579–587. doi:10.1037/0022-006X.72.4.579

Neuner, F., Schauer, M., Roth, W., & Elbert, T. (2002). A narrative exposure treatment as intervention in a refugee camp: A case report. *Behavioural and Cognitive Psychotherapy, 30,* 205–209.

Onyut, L. P., Neuner, F., Schauer, E., Ertl, V., Odenwald, M., Schauer, M., & Elbert, T. (2004). The Nakivale Camp mental health project: Building local competency for psychological assistance to traumatized refugees. *Intervention, 2,* 90–107.

Pyles, L. (2006). Toward a post-Katrina framework: Social work as human rights and capabilities. *Journal of Comparative Social Welfare, 22,* 79–88. doi: 10.1080/17486830500523086

Richmond, M. (1922). *What is social casework?* New York, NY: Russell Sage Foundation.

Reichert, E. (2006). *Understanding human rights: An exercise book.* Thousand Oaks, CA: SAGE.

Reichert, E. (2011). *Social work and human rights: A foundation for policy and practice* (2nd ed.). New York, NY: Columbia University.

Robjant, K., & Fazel, M. (2010). The emerging evidence for narrative exposure therapy: A review. *Clinical Psychology Review, 30,* 1030–1039. doi: 10.1016/j.cpr.2010.07.004

Rothman, J., & Mizrahi, T. (2014). Balancing micro and macro practice: A challenge for social work. *Social Work, 59*(1), 91–93.

Schauer, M., Neuner, F., & Elbert, T. (2005). *Narrative exposure therapy: A short-term intervention for traumatic stress disorders after war, terror and torture.* Gottingen, Germany: Hogrefe & Huber.

Specht, H., & Courtney, M. (1994). *Unfaithful angels: How social work abandoned its mission.* New York, NY: Free Press.

Staub-Bernasconi, S. (2012). Human rights and their relevance for social work as theory and practice. In L. Healy, & R. Link (Eds.), *Handbook of international social work: Human rights, development and the global profession* (pp. 30–36). New York, NY: Oxford University Press.

United Nations. (1948, December 10). Universal declaration of human rights. G.A. Res. 217 A (III). Retrieved from http://www.refworld.org/docid/3ae6b3712c.html

Weine, S., Kulenovic, A., Pavkovic, I., & Gibbons, R. (1998). Testimony psychotherapy in Bosnian refugees: A pilot study. *American Journal of Psychiatry, 155,* 1720–1726.

Wronka, J. (2008). *Human rights and social justice: Social action and service for the helping and health professions.* Thousand Oaks, CA: SAGE.

4 | Teaching Human Rights in Core Micro Foundation and Clinical Practice Classes:
Integration of Clinical Examples of Human Trafficking and Torture

S. Megan Berthold

Social work students who aspire to be caseworkers or clinical social workers should be prepared to identify and appropriately address human rights violations in their everyday practice. They may encounter violations experienced by their clients due to such harms as domestic violence, childhood sexual abuse, elder abuse, or community violence and/or more systemic violations perpetrated by their agency or the larger systems within which their clients interact (e.g., inappropriate use of chemical or physical restraints in a psychiatric hospital, solitary confinement of youth in adult prisons under the guise of protecting them). The harm may have both immediate and lasting effects that become a focus of attention for the survivor and social worker.

Social work programs are mandated by the Council on Social Work Education (CSWE) in its Educational Policy and Accreditation Standards (Educational Policy 2.1.5) to address human rights and economic justice as a core competency in its curriculum (Council on Social Work Education, 2008). The National Association of Social Workers (NASW) adopted a policy that promotes that social work theory and knowledge should be built on a foundation of human rights (NASW, 2008a). Core micro foundation and casework practice courses in MSW programs are well-suited to the integration of the teaching of human rights and rights-based interventions. These courses provide ample opportunity for drawing a link between the NASW Code of Ethics and various human rights principles and mechanisms and for the use of examples of human rights based interventions to illustrate and develop core practice competencies covered in these courses.

This chapter provides examples of how human rights-based interventions can be integrated into the teaching of required micro foundation and casework practice courses in the MSW curriculum. I draw case material from social work practice with survivors of two types of harms, human trafficking and state-sponsored torture, but the analysis and discussion has relevance for other domains of human rights violations. I also make connections between individual harm and human rights violations and mechanisms. Finally, I describe vignettes, classroom strategies, and methods that engage students in applying core casework/clinical and cross-cultural practice principles grounded in principles of rights-based intervention, exploring common challenges as well.

Definitions of Human Trafficking and Torture

The United States first passed legislation in 2000 to protect victims of human trafficking. This legislation was in keeping with international standards and has been reauthorized several times in the ensuing years. The Victims of Trafficking and Violence Protection Act of 2000 (P.L. 106-386) defines "severe forms of trafficking in persons" as

a) sex trafficking in which a commercial sex act is induced by force, fraud, or coercion, or in which the person induced to perform such an act has not attained 18 years of age; or

b) the recruitment, harboring, transportation, provision, or obtaining of a person for labor or services, through the use of force, fraud, or coercion for the purpose of subjection to involuntary servitude, peonage, debt bondage, or slavery (Sec. 103, 8).

A victim need not be physically transported from one location to another for the crime to fall within definitions of the United States Criminal Code, which defines *human trafficking* as "the act of compelling or coercing a person's labor, services, or commercial sex acts. The coercion can be subtle or overt, physical or psychological" (*United States Criminal Code*, Title 18, Chapter 77).

There has been great debate, on the other hand, about how to define torture. The most widely used definition of torture internationally is contained in Article

1 of the United Nations Convention Against Torture and other Cruel, Inhuman or Degrading Treatment or Punishment (UNCAT; United Nations, 1984):

> "torture" means any act by which severe pain or suffering, whether physical or mental, is intentionally inflicted on a person for such purposes as obtaining from him or a third person information or a confession, punishing him for an act he or a third person has committed or is suspected of having committed, or intimidating or coercing him or a third person, or for any reason based on discrimination of any kind, when such pain or suffering is inflicted by or at the instigation of or with the consent or acquiescence of a public official or other person acting in an official capacity. It does not include pain or suffering arising only from, inherent in or incidental to lawful sanctions (Article 1.1).

Although the United States is a signatory to the UNCAT, it adopted a narrower interpretation of what constitutes torture than most of the rest of the world (see Torture Victims Relief Act, 18 *USC* 2340(1) 1998). The Bush Administration, for example, infamously held that torture did not include waterboarding and was limited to acts that might implicate organ failure. The U.S. government has faced fierce criticism from within and outside the United States for this. Although the controversial legal memoranda related to torture were eventually overturned, some charge that the U.S. involvement in and definition of torture have harmed its credibility and standing in the world. A bipartisan task force on detainee treatment by the United States found that it was beyond dispute that the United States practiced widespread torture, and that the torture memos "remain a stain on the image of the United States, and the memos are a potential aid to repressive regimes elsewhere when they seek approval or justification for their own acts" (Constitution Project, 2013, p. 5).

One of the challenges in the classroom may be helping social work students grapple with the contradictions inherent in the U.S. stance on torture. "The United States may not declare a nation guilty of engaging in torture and then exempt itself from being so labeled for similar if not identical conduct" (Constitution Project, 2013, p. 3). Students should also be prepared to handle the distress experienced by some of their clients who fled torture seeking refuge and safety in the United States, when they discover that U.S. officials have also engaged (and may still be engaging) in acts of torture. Social work students need experience and skills to enable them to explore the complexities of the situation with their clients, attend to the distress, and identify and appropriately address possible transference reactions toward them as Americans, without becoming defensive. These same skills can be applied to other retraumatizing or challenging clinical situations students may encounter.

Understanding the context of clients' experience is vital. In the case of torture, for example, social work students are made aware of relevant contextual factors such as (a) the harm is intentional; (b) it involves severe pain and suffering that may be physical, psychological, and/or spiritual; (c) it evokes feelings of betrayal by governmental officials; and (d) it involves loss of power and control. There may be additional individual aspects of the experience, such as those related to the meaning of sexual torture in a society where the survivor risks being disowned, shunned, divorced, and/or becoming the victim of an honor killing if others learn of what happened.

Case Vignettes—Application to Course Material

Two case vignettes are provided here that illustrate some of the experiences of clients who have been subjected to human trafficking and torture. The names and other identifying information in all case material have been changed to protect confidentiality, and aspects of each case are a composite from more than one survivor. These cases have been presented in micro foundation and casework MSW courses by the author with additional layers (discussed later in this chapter) added sequentially throughout the course to build core knowledge, attitude, and skill competencies in a phased way over time. These vignettes are used at various points in the curriculum to develop practice competencies while also teaching about human rights.

"Song"—Standing Up to Her Traffickers

Song, a foreign student in the United States who came from Asia in her late teens, was eager to work. She was not able to support herself with the relatively modest funds her parents were able to provide and was lured into a seemingly legitimate office job. Over the course of a few weeks her hours became longer and longer until her employer's expectations exceeded what anyone could reasonably consider as normal. When Song complained that she was exhausted, the threats started. Song's employers made sure she knew they had close ties to organized crime in her homeland. Eventually, the hard labor turned into sexual slavery when Song was forced to sleep with up to 10 men a day. When Song resisted, she was injected with drugs or told that if she did not comply the traffickers would harm her parents.

Song began to cut her arms and upper thighs, almost daily, and drink heavily. In an effort to put an end to the extreme stress and shame that she felt, she overdosed on a combination of alcohol and sleeping pills, ending up in the hospital. Song spoke to a hospital social worker about her experiences. She was connected with a local nonprofit that worked with trafficking survivors and discharged to their shelter. The nonprofit referred her to a social worker who was a trauma therapist experienced in providing forensic and intensive clinical services to survivors of trafficking.

As part of qualifying for a T visa (granting her legal nonimmigrant status and a route toward permanent residency in the United States), Song cooperated with the authorities in their investigation and prosecution of her traffickers. This was a retraumatizing yet ultimately empowering process for Song. Her legal and treatment team provided strong support, psychological preparation, and treatment throughout. She was granted a T visa and filed a civil lawsuit against the traffickers. Her mother died before Song's T visa was granted. Her father later came to the United States to support Song during the trial. Song (and her therapist) testified in great detail about her experiences and the effects of those experiences in her civil case. Her traffickers were sitting facing Song, smirking and glaring at her during her testimony. The trial lasted several weeks. Song was hospitalized after revealing to her therapist a plan to kill herself.

Song ultimately won her civil case and was awarded substantial damages. More important to Song than the monetary compensation she received was the sense of justice and empowerment she felt for having stood up to her traffickers and seen them convicted. With continued therapy, Song stopped engaging in self-injurious behavior and has had no suicide attempts for the last several years. She returned to school and married.

"Myo"—Sustained by Commitment to His Cause

Myo, a student activist in an opposition democracy movement, was imprisoned and tortured on five occasions by the military in his country. His longest imprisonment lasted for several years. The military used many methods of torture against Myo, trying to get him to denounce his allegiance to his opposition group and disclose the identities and whereabouts of his associates. Myo was kept in shackles, including during long hours of hard manual labor in the hot sun. He was suspended from the ceiling by his arms, interrogated, beaten, and subjected to electric shocks.

Myo never cooperated with his torturers. Each time that he was released from prison he continued his work with the opposition party and spoke to the media. He knew that in doing so he risked being picked up, imprisoned, and tortured again. Eventually Myo decided that his life was in danger and that he could better serve his party in exile where he could freely speak and exercise his political opinion. Myo was granted asylum in the United States.

Although Myo struggled with some symptoms related to his torture (e.g., nightmares, traumatic memories, sleep disturbance) at the time that his social work clinician first met him soon after his escape, Myo did not present with any mental health condition contained in the American Psychiatric Association's *Diagnostic and Statistical Manual of Mental Disorders* (DSM-IV-TR; APA, 2000). For example, he did not meet the avoidance/numbing criteria to be diagnosed with posttraumatic stress disorder (PTSD), as epitomized by his talking openly to the media and public about his experiences. Myo quickly obtained a job and was able to function well in his daily life. Reflecting on the critical ingredients that contributed to his resilience, Myo identified the following: his hope for a better society, his Buddhist philosophy of life and long-term daily meditation practice, support he received from family and fellow activists, and his deep commitment to his cause.

Connections Between Individual Harm and Human Rights Violations

Human-perpetrated trauma such as torture and trafficking (but also domestic violence and child abuse) can affect individuals across multiple domains of their lives including cognitive (e.g., memory loss, confusion, difficulty concentrating), psychological (e.g., feeling loss of control, powerless, trapped, or helpless; numbness; grief; reliving the trauma; hopelessness; shame; dehumanization), behavioral (e.g., suicidal and self-injurious behavior; substance use or abuse), physical (e.g., difficulty sleeping, nausea, fatigue, pain), existential/spiritual (e.g., loss or questioning of faith, despair), and relational (e.g., breakdown in trust, withdrawing from or clinging to others, strained interpersonal relationships). Torture survivors have high rates of psychiatric disorders (14%–74%), chronic PTSD and depression being most prominent (Kinzie, Jaranson, & Kroupin, 2007). These conditions also are common in trafficking survivors (Oram, Stöckl, Busza, Howard, & Zimmerman, 2012). Other common psychological responses experienced by survivors of torture and trafficking are somatic and/or dissociative complaints, substance abuse, other anxiety conditions such as panic disorder, and enduring personality changes. Psychotic symptoms and conditions are less common but do occur. Students can be taught that they should be cautious not to misdiagnose symptoms of distress as psychosis, when they might be better understood as a posttraumatic response.

The case of Myo can be used to explore the many consequences of the traumatic experiences of their clients that go beyond anything found in the DSM. They are introduced to the concept that torture can profoundly alter one's capacity to trust others and form interpersonal bonds, retain a sense of identity, maintain faith in a system of justice, and sustain a sense of existential meaning and hope. They deepen their understanding of the differential effect of trauma as they become aware that individuals who were tortured due to mistaken identity may experience worse outcomes, in part due to the difficulty of making sense of the existential question, "Why me?"

Students explore how gross human rights violations such as torture and human trafficking also frequently have a profound effect on family and society. For example, they are taught that the goal of torture typically is to harm rather than to cause death (although death sometimes occurs) and to exert social control, silencing and oppressing the opposition. The perpetrators accomplish this by returning the tortured individual alive but greatly changed to society to serve as an example to others, spreading fear in those who might otherwise challenge the authorities. The bonds uniting families and communities sometimes are targeted and break down as a result of torture or human trafficking. In some societies a woman who is raped in the context of human trafficking or torture is disowned by family and shunned by community members. In extreme cases the woman may be stoned to death or become the victim of an honor killing. The torture survivor's loved ones are often at-risk of being threatened, tortured themselves, forced into hiding, "disappeared" (abducted by the authorities and often clandestinely killed), or openly murdered as authorities look for or try to put pressure on their primary target. Some victims of trafficking report that their traffickers have threatened to harm or kill their family members if the person does not cooperate with them. Social work students are encouraged to consider not only the effects of trafficking and torture on the individual and his or her family, but also to make connections between individual harm and human rights violations.

Social work faculty can make a direct link between the case material presented here and relevant human rights' violations and mechanisms in their courses. One of the key United Nations' protocols relevant to human trafficking is the Optional Protocol to the Convention on the Rights of the Child on the sale of children, child prostitution, and child pornography (United Nations, 2000b). In the Concluding Observations to the United States of this Optional Protocol, the United Nations Committee on the Rights of the Child (2013) recommended that the United States strengthen the systematic training of social workers and other professional groups on the Optional Protocol.

Social work students in foundation and casework courses have found it important to understand that although the United States ratified this Optional Protocol in 2001, it opposed joining the Convention on the Rights of the Child (CRC; United Nations, 1989) and is only one of three states that have not ratified the CRC as of 2014 (along with Somalia and South Sudan). This provides an opportunity for highlighting the role that social work caseworkers/clinicians can play in community organizing, advocacy, and policy practice to promote human rights. For example, students may be engaged in the Campaign for U.S. Ratification of the CRC. In doing so they might develop a campaign to educate others at their school or in the community on the issue and advocate for them to urge the Senate to ratify the CRC. Alternatively, or in addition, students may provide clinical and/or practical support to children and their families, enabling them to provide testimony in support of the CRC at public forums or events.

Additional human rights mechanisms that are relevant to the topics presented here include several that involve prohibitions against slavery, forced labor, servitude, and the slave trade: Article 4 of the Universal Declaration of Human Rights (United Nations, 1948); Article 8 of the International Covenant on Civil and Political Rights (United Nations, 1966a); and the 2000 United Nations Protocol to Prevent, Suppress, and Punish Trafficking in Persons, Especially Women and Children (United Nations, 2000c; Palermo Protocol, supplementing the United Nations Convention Against Transnational Organized Crime, 2000a). In addition, Article 7 of the International Covenant on Economic, Social and Cultural Rights (United Nations, 1966b) addresses the right to just and favorable work conditions (e.g., fair remuneration, safe and healthy work conditions).

Relevant human rights mechanisms and principles for working with torture survivors include the United Nations Convention Against Torture and Other Cruel, Inhuman or Degrading Treatment or Punishment (CAT; United Nations, 1984) that includes an absolute prohibition against torture and requires states not to return a person to a country in which there is a substantial likelihood that she or he may be tortured; the nonrefoulement principle contained in CAT and in the International Covenant on Civil and Political Rights (United Nations, 1966a); and the right of those subject to expedited removal from the United States to be provided a credible fear screening by a U.S. Customs and Immigration asylum officer on entry to the United States to determine whether they have a credible fear of being persecuted or tortured if returned to their homeland.[1] By facilitating the understanding of these human rights mechanisms that underlie their work, social work students are provided with a strong platform from which to advocate for humane, just, and responsive policies and treatment for all.

Teaching Core Micro Foundation and Casework Skills and Knowledge

Students are introduced to micro foundation and casework social work content through a case-based approach that uses problem-based learning principles to augment didactic training. Some of the methods used to teach this material and build progressive mastery of skills over the course of graduate training are critical analysis of case vignettes, live and video observation, simulation of mock cases, and supervised role plays. The author has integrated this approach in MSW Micro Foundation Practice, Clinical Conditions, and Casework With Vulnerable and Resilient Populations courses. Some of the core areas are identified here, including the application of relevant cross-cultural practice principles and approaches within a framework of cultural humility; the teaching of casework practice engagement, assessment, and intervention skills (including assessing and building on client strengths and resilience); making the link between human rights and core ethical principles/foundational values of social work; and developing strategies to resolve complex ethical dilemmas. The case vignettes related to torture and human trafficking presented here can also provide an opportunity for developing core trauma competencies and clinical reasoning in students for working with survivors of other forms of trauma. Integrating the development of these knowledge areas, skills, and attitudes into micro foundation and core casework courses will provide a solid foundation for social work students to later engage in advanced trauma-informed and evidenced-based practice training (CSWE, 2012; Layne, Fields, Moyse-Steinberg, Krishna, & Dinov, 2009; New Haven Trauma Competencies, 2013). Supervised internship experiences throughout the MSW program allow students to apply classroom-based knowledge to simple and later more complex cases in the field. Students integrate their case-based field learning into written assignments in core courses and apply knowledge from the theoretical, clinical, and empirical literature to client cases they have worked with.

The cases of Song and Myo illustrate a number of relevant cultural humility practice related issues. Song, for example, was not able to return to her country to be with her dying mother, as she would have forfeited her chance to continue to pursue her T visa application. Her attorney attempted to get an exemption to this policy so that Song could see her mother before she died but Song's mother passed away before this appeal could be processed. Song's grief process was complicated by the shame and stigma she experienced related to not being with her mother at the time of her death or at the funeral, a meaning shaped by her native culture. Her suicidal desires and attempts were in turn influenced by her belief that killing herself was the honorable choice in her situation given the meaning of rape and sexual activity outside marriage in her culture and her lack of filial duty. It was devastating for her to have to testify and have others testify about her experiences in front of her father. Song's only consolation was her knowledge that her father did not understand the words spoken in court due to a language barrier. Elaboration of the course of therapy with Song by adding additional layers of the vignette allows for discussion of cultural and individual variation in the expression of distress and in clients' view of mental health and social work services as well as strategizing about how best to engage and work across these differences.

Song's case also affords the opportunity to build students' knowledge and skills related to assessment and intervention. For example, in addition to assessing Song's vulnerabilities and conducting a psycho-social-cultural assessment of the impact of her trafficking experience on her mental state, students are guided to assess her strengths and resilience such as the factors that enabled her to open up to the hospital social worker and her courage to confront her traffickers in open court. Song's case also introduces students to various cross-cultural issues related to diagnosis, including the appropriateness of giving a diagnosis based on the DSM-5 (APA, 2013), developed in the West, to a non-Western individual. Students explore the possible relevance of one or more idioms of distress found in members of her culture in better explaining the effects of her experiences. Students are trained to understand the differences between self-injurious and suicidal behavior and engage in thorough ongoing risk assessment and safety planning. Students are encouraged to think about how they might frame Song's case and write it up in the context of her T-visa application and court case and about the various ways that they can help to prepare her psychologically for trial.

The case vignettes of Song and Myo may be used to help students develop foundational skills such as engagement, developing mutual working agreements, formulating goals, connecting with important resources, engaging in interdisciplinary collaboration, envisioning and working toward a positive future, and employing a culture- and trauma-informed approach to intervention. For example, drawing on principles from the self-trauma model for working with survivors of complex trauma, students can be taught the importance of and how to provide and ensure safety and stability; adopt a respectful approach that provides support and validation in the context of a therapeutic relationship; provide psychoeducation on trauma and trauma symptoms; provide stress reduction or affect regulation training; provide cognitive interventions to address harmful or debilitating trauma-related beliefs, assumptions, and perceptions; work with clients (as and when appropriate) to develop a coherent narrative about their trauma(s); process traumatic memories, usually involving guided self-exposure; process relational issues in the context of a positive therapeutic relationship; engage in exploration activities that increase self-awareness and self-acceptance; and teach mindfulness (Briere, 2002; Briere & Scott, 2012). These are important skills for social workers to develop and are valuable for working with a broad array of clients.

These cases can also be used to help students make connections between micro and macro social work practice. For example, Song's case provides the opportunity for casework students to learn about the need and avenues for more states to pass safe-harbor laws that can be one critical part of the solution[2] (ECPAT-USA, n.d.).

Contemporary or modern slavery (human trafficking) and torture violate universal human rights as well as social work ethics. Although the term *human rights* is not explicitly included in the NASW Code of Ethics, the code does promote policies that protect the rights, equity, and social justice of all people (NASW, 2008b). As Rodgers (2009) stresses, social workers should "embrace a human rights perspective in their practice because it promotes the core values of social work, including human dignity, self-worth, equality, and social justice for all" (para. 44). The mission of the social work profession is, in part, to protect the rights of vulnerable and oppressed populations. Those who are persecuted by trafficking or torture are certainly vulnerable and oppressed and have had their rights violated. Among the core values of the profession of social work are social justice, respecting the inherent dignity and worth of the person, and the right to self-determination (NASW, 2008b), all values that are not upheld when people are trafficked or tortured. Case-based learning using cases such as those of Song and Myo assist students in making the link between human rights violations and the social work code of ethics.

Resilience and Posttraumatic Growth

It is important for social work students to understand the resilience of survivors of human rights violations. Although those who are subjected to torture or human trafficking are vulnerable to developing a host of distressing symptoms and functional challenges, resilience is the most common outcome of potentially traumatic events (Bonanno, Westphal, & Mancini, 2011). Resilience is a dynamic process. Resilient individuals, families, or communities demonstrate the ability to positively adapt and cope effectively in the face of substantial trauma, threats, and stress as well as bounce back after extreme stress and return to stable functioning (Bonanno et al., 2011; Southwick, Litz, Charney, & Friedman, 2011). Students explore the various resilience factors that enabled Myo to endure his repeated and long-term torture and function effectively, and they examine contextual and individual differences relevant to the clients they are serving in their internships.

Posttraumatic growth is another important area to include in the curriculum and can be illustrated using clinical material with survivors of torture and human trafficking. Posttraumatic growth represents a positive change in trauma survivors such that their posttrauma level of adaptation exceeds their pretrauma level (Tedeschi & Calhoun, 2004). It may be manifested in a variety of domains such as a greater appreciation for life, a sense of new life possibilities, an enhanced sense of personal strength, enhanced ability to engage in intimate relationships, and spiritual development. Remaining or regaining connection with political or religious/spiritual identity or with a strong support system may promote resilience, healing, and posttraumatic growth (Basoglu, Mineka, et al., 1994; Basoglu, Paker, et al., 1997; Holtz, 1998; Moio, 2008).

Strategies for Addressing Challenges

A variety of challenges in teaching this material and integrating it into core micro foundation and casework practice courses may arise. For example, some students may initially find it difficult to see the relevance to their practice area as only a minority of MSW students may have had exposure to or aspire to work with survivors of trafficking or state-sponsored torture. The author has found it possible and effective to enhance students' awareness that various human rights violations occur in the United States and apply practice principles presented in articles about work with torture survivors to other cases they are working with. For example, Fabri's (2001) article elaborates the need and techniques for developing a therapeutic relationship and reconstructing safety with torture survivors, yet has relevance more generally for sound clinical principles of engagement with other clients. Ortiz's (2001) chapter describes what it feels like to be a survivor of trauma (in her case, torture) and to receive services from a clinician, emphasizing what is or what is not helpful. Students have found this enlightening for their work with diverse client populations.

Some social work students may find the case material related to torture and trafficking distressing and employ various defense mechanisms to tolerate their distress, such as distancing or avoidance. Instructors can use this as an opportunity to build knowledge and skills related to practitioner self-awareness and the ability to manage their own reactions to the trauma material of their clients to promote practitioner skills and self-care while minimizing the risk of retraumatizing the survivors they work with (Piwowarczyk, Moreno, & Grodin, 2000). Faculty can also introduce the topics of vicarious trauma and self-care (Saakvitne, Pearlman, & Staff of the Traumatic Stress Institute/ Center for Adult and Adolescent Psychotherapy, 1996; Stamm, 1999), as well as vicarious resilience (Engstrom, Hernandez, & Gangsei, 2008) to social work students, because a strong grounding in these areas is relevant to all methods and specialty areas of practice (even if the social worker is not engaged in casework/clinical practice).

Presenting these cases provides a chance to dispel some common myths and preconceived notions, modeling for students the importance of being aware of one's biases and assumptions and not letting them negatively affect one's practice. For example, students can be educated that trafficking happens within the United States (not just across international borders); it is not limited to sex trafficking (but also includes labor and services); and males, females, children and older adults can be targeted (U.S. Department of State, 2014).

Conclusion

MSW students may not have worked with refugee and immigrant populations, including survivors of trafficking and torture. However, developing competency to provide social work services to refugees and immigrants has become important as their numbers throughout the United States have increased. This paper illustrates how case-based and problem-based learning can be used to teach human rights-based practice principles and build competencies in social work students taking micro foundation and casework classes. This was accomplished through exploration of clinical examples of human trafficking and torture, but the principles are relevant to working effectively with a broad range of populations.

Social workers are very likely to encounter a broad range of clients whose rights to nondiscrimination, life, security of their body/person, and freedom from slavery (upheld in the International Covenant on Civil and Political Rights, UNCAT, and other human rights mechanisms) have been violated. Social work educators should assist their students to develop the capacity to think about and respond to situations such as domestic violence, child abuse, elder abuse, human trafficking, and torture as human rights violations. For example, these issues are about the abuse of power, domination, and control, which social workers certainly have a role to play in countering at multiple levels through the adoption of a human rights-based approach to casework/clinical practice. Adopting such an approach to practice can be inherently therapeutic.

References

American Psychiatric Association (APA). (2000). *Diagnostic and statistical manual of mental disorders* (4th ed.). Washington, DC: Author.

American Psychiatric Association (APA). (2013). *Diagnostic and statistical manual of mental disorders* (5th ed.). Arlington, VA: American Psychiatric Publishing.

Basoğlu, M., Mineka, S., Paker, M., Aker, T., Livanou, M., & Gok, S. (1997). Psychological preparedness for trauma as a protective factor in survivors of torture. *Psychological Medicine, 27*(6), 1421–1433.

Basoglu, M., Paker, M., Paker, O., Ozmen, E., Marks, I., Incesu, … & Sarimurat, N. (1994). Psychological effects of torture: A comparison of tortured with nontortured political activists in Turkey. *American Journal of Psychiatry, 151*(1), 76–81.

Bonanno, G. A., Westphal, M., & Mancini, A. D. (2011). Resilience to loss and potential trauma. *Annual Review of Clinical Psychology, 7,* 511–535.

Briere, J. (2002). Treating adult survivors of severe childhood abuse and neglect: Further development of an integrative model. In J. E. B. Myers, L. Berliner, J. Briere, C. T. Hendrix, T. Reid, & C. Jenny (Eds.), *The APSAC handbook on child maltreatment* (2nd ed.) (pp. 175–202). Newbury Park, CA: SAGE Publications.

Briere, J., & Scott, C. (2012). *Principles of trauma therapy: A guide to symptoms, evaluation, and treatment* (2nd ed.). Thousand Oaks, CA: SAGE Publications.

Constitution Project. (2013). *The report of The Constitution Project's Task Force on Detainee Treatment.* Washington, DC: Author.

Council on Social Work Education (CSWE). (2008). *Educational policy and accreditation standards.* Retrieved from http://www.cswe.org/File.aspx?id= 13780

Council on Social Work Education (CSWE). (2012). *Advanced social work practice in trauma.* Alexandria, VA: Author. Retrieved from http://www. cswe.org/Accreditation/EPASImplementation.aspx

ECPAT-USA (n.d.) *Advocate for protective laws and policies.* Retrieved from http://www.ecpatusa.org/advocate-for-protective-laws-and-policies

Engstrom, D., Hernandez, P., & Gangsei, D. (2008). Vicarious resilience: A qualitative investigation into its description. *Traumatology, 14*(3), 13–21.

Fabri, M. R. (2001). Reconstructing safety: Adjustments to the therapeutic frame in the treatment of survivors of political torture. *Professional Psychology: Research and Practice, 32,* 452–457.

Holtz, T. (1998). Refugee trauma versus torture trauma: A retrospective controlled cohort study of Tibetan refugees. *Journal of Nervous and Mental Disease, 186*(1), 24–34.

Immigration and Nationality Act of 1952. (1952). Pub. L. No. 82-414, 66 Stat. 163.

Kinzie, J. D., Jaranson, J. M., & Kroupin, G. V. (2007). Diagnosis and treatment of mental illness. In P. F. Walker & E. D. Barnett (Eds.), *Immigrant medicine* (pp. 639–651). Philadelphia, PA: Saunders Elsevier.

Layne, C. M., Fields, P. J., Moyse-Steinberg, D., Krishna, M., & Dinov, I. (2009, November).Making evidence-based practice user friendly: Integrating clinical-proficiency and data-proficiency training across the social work curriculum. In V. Strand (Chair), *Preparing graduate social work students for evidence-based trauma intervention.* Symposium conducted at the Annual Program Meeting of the Council on Social Work Education, San Antonio, TX.

Moio, J. A. (2008). *Resiliency and recovery: An exploration of meaning and personal agency for women survivors of state sponsored torture* (Doctoral dissertation). Available from Dissertations and Theses database (UMI No. 3346914) .

National Association of Social Workers. (2008a). International policy on human rights. In *Social work speaks: NASW policy statements 2009–2012* (8th ed.) (pp. 209–217). Washington, DC: NASW Press.

National Association of Social Workers (NASW). (2008b). Code of ethics of the National Association of Social Workers. Retrieved from http://www. socialworkers.org/pubs/code/code.asp

New Haven Trauma Competencies. (2013, April 25–28). *Advancing the science of education, training and practice in trauma: Developing the New Haven model.* Working conference funded by the U.S. Department of Health & Human Services, Agency for Healthcare Research and Quality. New Haven, CT.

Oram, S., Stöckl, H., Busza, J., Howard, L. M., & Zimmerman, C. (2012). Prevalence and risk of violence and the physical, mental, and sexual health problems associated with human trafficking: Systematic review. *PLoS Medicine, 9*(5), 1–13. doi:10.1371/journal.pmed.1001224

Ortiz, D. (2001). The survivors' perspective: Voices from the center. In E. Gerrity, T. M. Keane, & F. Tuma (Eds.), *The mental health consequences of torture* (pp. 13–64). New York, NY: Klewer Academic/Plenum Publishers.

Piwowarczyk, L., Moreno, A. S., & Grodin, M. (2000). Health care of torture survivors. *JAMA, 284*(5), 539–541. doi:10.1001/jama.284.5.539

Rodgers, J. A. (2009). Global social work practice, human rights, social work ethics and human responsibilities: The challenge [Editorial]. *Journal of Global Social Work Practice, 2*(2). Retrieved from www.globalsocialwork.org/vol2no2 /RodgersEditorial.html+&cd=2&hl=en&ct=clnk&gl=us&client=firefox-a

Saakvitne, K. W., Pearlman, L. A., & Staff of the Traumatic Stress Institute/ Center for Adult and Adolescent Psychotherapy. (1996). *Transforming the pain: A workbook on vicarious traumatization.* New York, NY: Norton.

Southwick, S. M., Litz, B. T., Charney, D., & Friedman, M. J. (Eds.). (2011). *Resilience and mental health: Challenges across the lifespan.* New York, NY: Cambridge University Press.

Stamm, B. H. (Ed.). (1999). *Secondary traumatic stress: Self-care issues for clinicians, researchers, & educators* (2nd ed.). Lutherville, MD: Sidran Press.

Tedeschi, R. G., & Calhoun, L. G. (2004). Posttraumatic growth: Conceptual foundations and empirical evidence. *Psychological Inquiry, 15*(1), 1–18.

Torture Victims Relief Act of 1998. (1998). 18 *USC* 2340 (1).

United Nations. (1948). *Universal declaration of human rights.* G.A. Res. 217 A (III). Retrieved from http://www.refworld.org/docid/3ae6b3712c.html

United Nations. (1966a). *International covenant on civil and political rights.* G.A. Res. 2200A (XXI). Retrieved from http://www.ohchr.org/Documents /ProfessionalInterest/ccpr.pdf

United Nations. (1966b). *International covenant on economic, social, and cultural rights.* G.A. Res. 2200A (XXI). Retrieved from http://www.ohchr.org /EN/ProfessionalInterest/Pages/CESCR.aspx

United Nations. (1984). *Convention against torture and other cruel, inhuman or degrading treatment or punishment.* G.A. Res. 39/46. Retrieved from http://www.ohchr.org/Documents/ProfessionalInterest/cat.pdf

United Nations. (1989). *Convention on the rights of the child.* G.A. Res. 44/25. Retrieved from: http://www.ohchr.org/Documents/ProfessionalInterest/crc.pdf

United Nations. (2000a). *Convention against transnational organized crime.* G.A. Res. 55/25. Retrieved from http://www.refworld.org/docid/3b00f55b0.html

United Nations. (2000b). *Optional protocol to the convention on the rights of the child on the sale of children, child prostitution and child pornography.* G.A. Res. 54/263. Retrieved from http://www.unhcr.org/refworld/docid/3ae6b38bc.html

United Nations. (2000c). Protocol to prevent, suppress and punish trafficking in persons, especially women and children, supplementing the United Nations convention against transnational organized crime. Retrieved from http://www .unhcr.org/refworld/docid/4720706c0.html

United Nations Committee on the Rights of the Child. (2013). *Concluding observations: CRC optional protocol (sale of children/prostitution/pornography)— United States of America.* Retrieved from http://www2.ohchr.org/English /bodies/crc/docs/co/CRC_C_OPSC_USA_CO_2.doc.

U.S. Department of State. (2014). *Human trafficking report 2014*. Retrieved from http://www.state.gov/j/tip/rls/tiprpt/2014/index.htm

Victims of Trafficking and Violence Protection Act of 2000. (2000, October 28). 114 Stat. 1464, Pub. L. 106–386.

Endnotes

1 Provided under the U.S. Immigration and Nationality Act of 1952 (1952) (as amended in § 208(b)(2)(A), 241(b)(3)(B), 8 CFR 208.16(d), and 8 CFR 208.17 (1996)).

2 Safeharbor laws: promote a client-centered approach; require training for first responders, including law enforcement, on how to identify and assist victims as well as exempt children from prosecution for prostitution; increase the penalties for traffickers and buyers; and encourage the development of a statewide system of care involving collaboration between interdisciplinary teams.

5 | Developing a Curriculum Based on Human Rights and Social Justice

Elaine Congress

Social work has long been viewed as a human rights profession (Healy, 2008). Almost 20 years ago the United Nations published a book about human rights for social work practitioners and educators (United Nations Centre for Human Rights, 1994), and 1995–2004 was declared the Decade for Human Rights Education (Steen & Mathiesen, 2005). Whereas the first phase (2005–2009) of the World Programme for Human Rights Education focused on elementary and secondary education, the emphasis of the current phase (2010–2014) is on higher education. Thus, a focus on human rights in social work education is most timely. Although human rights education has been included in higher education in many schools of social work, Fordham University was one of the first to develop a whole curriculum rooted in human rights and social justice. This chapter discusses the process.

Literature Review

Although a number of books by social work authors have addressed human rights issues (Healy & Link, 2011; Ife, 2008; Reichert, 2003; Wronka, 2008) over the last decade, the first book on curriculum resources that specifically addresses human rights in social work education was published last year (Hokenstad, Healy, & Segal, 2013). A decade ago teaching about human rights seems to have been absent from the social work curriculum. A review of titles and descriptions of social work courses indicated that schools of social work had limited content on human rights (Steen & Mathiesen, 2005). The study found that as indicated by course titles and descriptions, 91% of social work schools surveyed did not have any courses on human rights. This was in sharp contrast to law schools, where only 12% of schools reported that they did not have human rights courses.

Why has social work, a profession that seems firmly rooted in human rights values, been slow to embrace teaching about human rights? Reichert (2011) argues that until recently social work educators may have had limited understanding of human rights. Thus, teaching faculty about human rights seems to be a first step in developing a plan to integrate human rights content into the social work curriculum.

Teaching students about human rights seems deeply connected to the core concepts of social work. Since its inception social work has been value-based, and a core value of social work, as expressed by the International Federation of Social Workers (IFSW) and International Association of Schools of Social Work (IASSW) in their joint Statement of Ethical Principles, includes "a respect for the inherent worth and dignity of all people, and the rights that follow from this" (IFSW & IASSW, 2004, p. 1). Although the current National Association of Social Workers (NASW) Code of Ethics (2008) does not specifically mention human rights, the core value/principle of social work, namely the "respect for the inherent dignity and worth of each person" (p. 2), certainly relates to the recognition of each person as having human rights.

The growing interest in social work education in teaching human rights is reflected in the recent Council on Social Work Education (CSWE) Education Policy and Accreditation Standards (EPAS; 2008). In Educational Standard 2.5.1 social work educators are advised to teach students about human rights. To help social work educators achieve this goal, CSWE recently published a manual on teaching about human rights to provide resources on this topic (Hokenstad et al., 2013). Reichert (2008) has suggested exercises that can be used to help students, as well as professional social workers, integrate human rights into their practice.

Despite the growing interest in human rights, there have been few attempts to measure students' attitudes and behaviors in regard to human rights. One notable exception is McPherson and Abel's (2012) development of two scales, Human Rights Engagement in Social Work (HRESW) and Human Rights

Exposure in Social Work (HRXSW). An initial attempt to validate these scales involved a sample of 287 social workers, and the authors concluded that both these measures indicated adequate reliability and validity.

The measures can be used independently or together. The HRXSW measures how much a social work curriculum has exposed students to human rights principles, whereas the HRESW measures their engagement in human rights principles or "their passion for human rights and social work" (p. 711). A significant finding from McPherson and Abel's (2012) study was that both MSW and BSW students had higher rates of engagement in human rights principles than exposure. In fact, exposure to human rights predicted only 9% of human rights engagement. This requires further study because social work educators hope that increased exposure to human rights content will positively influence their engagement with human rights issues.

A Model for Integrating a Human Rights Curriculum Into a School of Social Work

Over the last 5 years Fordham has revised its entire curriculum to focus on human rights. Leading up to this curriculum revision, a number of faculty development sessions were organized to provide all faculty with a greater understanding of human rights. This addressed a concern that Reichert (2008) had raised that social work educators were reluctant to teach an area about which they had little knowledge.

Process

What led up to the decision to change? There were a number of reasons:

- When we started this odyssey, Fordham was scheduled for reaffirmation in 3 years and, thus, if we wanted to bring about curriculum change it was important to begin the process early to complete the assessment portion of the self-study.
- Fordham wanted an overarching theme on which to ground our curriculum. We needed a consistent theme and orientation throughout our program.

- Although we were a Jesuit school—the motto *cura personalis* (care for the entire person) and social justice were overarching themes—there was a need to make students more aware of these themes throughout the curriculum.
- An increasing number of faculty members were interested in international work and had become concerned about human rights issues around the world. Several faculty members had been involved with the United Nations and had become familiar with the Universal Declaration of Human Rights (UDHR; United Nations, 1948) and other human rights treaties.
- Given our interest in becoming more international, human rights seemed to be a better overall theme than social justice alone.

A few well-respected faculty members initiated the idea of having human rights as an overarching theme. As faculty members know, bringing about a major change in curriculum is never easy, and there were opponents and proponents of this new curriculum idea. The proponents expressed the belief that the change would distinguish Fordham as unique, reflect more closely our mission, and acknowledge how our students and our clients were much more international than ever before. There were a number of opponents to changing the curriculum. The complaints ranged from "if it's not broke, don't fix it," to "we don't have time for this before reaffirmation," "we have problems here that are more social justice focused," and finally that "human rights are too abstract to translate into actual practice."

Faculty members in support of the change initiated a number of important steps to foster the transformation. An early decision that was made was to include social justice in our human rights framework, so our curriculum was renamed Human Rights and Social Justice. Faculty members argued that human rights and social justice were two separate concepts. Faculty members who taught macro practice were more readily amendable to adopting a human rights perspective throughout the curriculum, whereas those who taught clinical practice courses were not as comfortable with how human rights could be integrated. The International/Global faculty committee, which had developed case vignettes that focused on different immigrant families, provided some assistance. Elements from these clinical case examples could be easily translated into human rights language, noting the obstacles families encountered in realizing these rights.

As field education is an important component in social work education, the fieldwork director was involved in discussions about revising the curriculum. It was necessary to include human rights in fieldwork evaluation forms and also educate the many field instructors about our new orientation. To accomplish this, the focus of field education training for new and experienced field instructors included orientation to the human rights framework.

Education for Faculty Members and Adjuncts

Although some faculty members felt very comfortable and had much knowledge about adopting a human rights framework, others believed that their knowledge was limited. To help bring all faculty members aboard in terms of their knowledge about human rights, Fordham sponsored several faculty development sessions on human rights. Joseph Wronka, one of the contributors to this book and a highly regarded expert on human rights, was one of the guest lecturers.

As in other schools of social work, Fordham has many adjuncts that serve as classroom teachers and as faculty advisors. Many of these people had much agency experience, and some had doctorates and had taught successfully at Fordham for many years. Yet they had varying degrees of understanding about human rights. Thus, special educational sessions were organized for adjuncts to provide instruction about human rights content and how it could be integrated into their courses. Adjunct faculty members also were invited to participate in area curriculum meetings where faculty members discussed how to integrate human rights into specific courses.

Curriculum Outline

The introductory course required for all students as they begin their MSW studies is Human Rights and Social Justice. The master syllabus for this course describes the content in the following way: "This is the signature course of our program. The course provides the foundation for all courses." The course is divided into four modules:

1) The Social Work Profession: The course begins with an overview of the evolution of the social work profession, its values, the Code of Ethics, and the overarching mission of the profession.

2) Social Justice: This component traces the evolution of the understanding and definitions of social justice. Students are exposed to various theories and perspectives of social justice and explore their effects on social work and social policy.

3) Human Rights: This component traces the origins and evolution of human rights and its effects on society. Students are exposed to the three generations or levels of human rights. They also learn about the various organizations guiding the promotion of human rights globally and how these factors have influenced social work and social policy.

4) Integration of Social Work, Social Justice, and Human Rights: Students begin to critically analyze the intersection of social work values, human rights, and social justice perspectives and how this integrated approach might influence social work practice. Students examine diverse social problems and issues through the lens of this integrated approach.

In this course students are introduced to the major human rights documents, beginning with the UDHR, and move into a consideration of other relevant human rights documents including the International Covenant on Civil and Political Rights (United Nations, 1966a) and the International Covenant on Economic, Social, and Cultural Rights (United Nations, 1966b). Students learn about the three generations of human rights: negative rights, positive rights; and collective rights. Students also are introduced to documents such as the UN Declaration of Rights of Indigenous Peoples (United Nations, 2007), the Convention on the Elimination of All Forms of Discrimination against Women (United Nations, 1979), and the Declaration of Rights of Persons with Disabilities (United Nations, 2008). Teaching students about United Nations human rights treaties that focus on vulnerable populations is especially important because of social work education's commitment to teaching students about discrimination directed toward special populations.

In this course students are introduced to two main documents on ethics, the IFSW and IASSW Statement of Ethical Principles (2004) and the NASW Code of Ethics (2008). The CSWE EPAS advises social work educators to teach students about using these documents in ethical decision-making. The Statement of Ethical Principles outlines ethical guidelines for social workers around the world. Social work is described as promoting "social change, problem solving in human relationships, and the empowerment and liberation of people to enhance well-being... Principles of human rights and social justice are fundamental to social work" (IFSW/ IASSW, 2004, p. 1) and presented as an overarching approach to the professional work that students will do. According to this ethics statement, social workers can promote human rights through respecting the right to self-determination, promoting the right to participation, treating each person as a whole, and identifying and developing strengths. The final section of this statement looks at professional conduct.

In contrast, the NASW Code of Ethics focuses first on six principles (values) for social workers and then includes 154 professional standards. Although the term *human rights* does not specifically appear in the NASW Code of Ethics, the last group of standards looks at social workers' responsibilities to the larger society, the duty to promote policies and practices that guarantee rights to all regardless of nationality, race, religion, ethnicity, disability, immigration status, age, or sexual orientation.

The course concludes with teaching students about integrating human rights and social justice. We not only want students to be able to identify the human rights of all people, but also to examine how they are violated and what social workers can do in fighting against policies and institutions that interfere with people securing their basic rights. One way this is done is through linking human rights to various well-beings. Well-beings that we have identified are economic well-being, political well-being, educational well-being, social well-being, mental well-being, physical well-being, and spiritual well-being. We take this approach because it helps students translate theoretical concepts into a practice model and also moves from more of a deficit perspective of lack of human rights to focus on strengths and social work goals.

Integrating Human Rights Into Different Courses

Each course in the curriculum has been revised to include content on human rights. The UDHR provides a common platform for citing human rights principles, although courses often use the UDHR as a starting point only.

Two required courses at Fordham, as well as many other schools of social work, focus on human behavior in the social environment. Steen (2012) proposes that the human rights perspective fits well with the person-in-environment paradigm that is paramount in these courses. Human rights can be applied to micro, mezzo, and macro perspectives of human behavior in the social environment. In terms of micro practice, social work students learn about promoting the human rights of their clients, many of whom may lack sufficient financial resources for adequate food and housing. From a mezzo perspective, students learn how communities and agencies promote or detract from the promotion of human rights. For example, a community with a high crime rate certainly is not conducive to the promotion of clients' rights for safety of person (UDHR, Article 3), or a community that contains no stores that offer fresh produce does not promote clients' right to a standard of living that promotes health (Article 25). Conversely, communities with libraries and recreational centers promote clients' rights to education, rest, and leisure (Articles 24 and 26). Finally, macro social and political institutions can affect the human rights of clients. For example, when certain populations such as young Black men are more commonly picked up by the police for questioning, this may challenge the human right of protection from arbitrary arrest and detention (Article 9) and equal protection before the law (Articles 6–7).

Although a human rights perspective seems very applicable to human behavior and social environment courses, it also can be integrated into other courses. For example, in research courses students learn about historical and current examples in which human rights were violated. For example, with the Tuskegee research African American men were not able to benefit from the latest medical treatments for syphilis and thus were denied their right to health

(UDHR, Article 25). More currently, students learn about the importance of Institutional Review Board (IRB) reviews to protect the rights of vulnerable populations. In conducting their own research, students learn about ethical practices that promote human rights (Rubin & Babbie, 2011).

Policy courses provide opportunities for students to examine which policies promote and detract from human rights. In required policy courses students learn how to analyze United States policies such as the Social Security Act (1935) and the Personal Responsibility and Work Opportunity Reconciliation Act (PRWORA, 1996). The way that policies are written to exclude or minimize advantages for certain populations are also addressed. Students are encouraged to think critically about who is included or excluded in these policies. For example, even the greatly lauded Social Security Act rewarded only those in regular documented employment with disability or retirement benefits. Many who worked minimally, whose work was not recorded, or who received very low wages were not eligible.

PRWORA, which was and still is more controversial, excluded many on welfare who were not able to find work or were not United States citizens. This and other policies can be examined through a human rights lens. Which policies prevented people from realizing their human right to sufficient income to maintain an adequate standard of living? Another important factor is how policies are translated into administrative procedures and practices. Even though a policy may seem to support opportunities to maintain an adequate standard of living, the way policies are administered in practice may deny certain groups equal opportunities.

Generalist practice courses are a place in the curriculum where students learn how to translate human rights into actual practice with their clients. Students are able to identify occasions when their clients were not accorded the right "to a standard of living adequate for the health and wellbeing of (their) family, including food, clothing, housing and medical care and necessary social services" (UDHR, Article 25). Students learn about interventions they can use to help their clients achieve this right.

A focus on human rights should not only be found in introductory, human behavior, policy, or research courses, but also should be included in clinical or administrative MSW curriculum. Students in a clinical concentration learn how denial of human rights such as fear of arbitrary arrest (UDHR, Article 9), fear of deportation (Articles 13 and 15), or denial of the right to an adequate standard of living (Article 25) can contribute to mental/behavioral health problems of their clients. Advocating for clients' rights as well as learning how to empower their clients to advocate for their rights can be incorporated into clinical practice classes. In macro practice administration classes students develop managerial and leadership skills to use as social work administrators. Students can learn how to develop administrative policies that provide equal access and opportunities for all. They study how to advance within an organization a human rights atmosphere that promotes mutual respect and provides equal opportunities for all employees.

Turning the Abstract Into Actual Practice

A continuing challenge in teaching about human rights, however, is that a discussion on human rights may seem very abstract to students and far removed from their daily work with clients. To help students operationalize human rights and relate it to their own practice, human rights standards were linked to different well-beings of clients. Although the term *well-being* has different meanings in social work education, it can most clearly be linked to a social work assessment of basic needs (Gamble, 2012). To help students think of human rights in terms of their own practice, global human rights principles can be applied to local problems and needs. Using the language of well-being, rather than a focus on lacks and needs, is certainly compatible with a social work focus on goals and strengths.

Physical and economic well-being are linked to the right to an adequate standard of living to maintain health (UDHR, Article 25). For example, a family in the South Bronx facing eviction and forced to eat only rice for the last three nights because of lack of income certainly lacks physical and economic well-being and has not been accorded the human right to an adequate standard of living.

To help students understand more clearly how human rights are linked to clients' well-being, Maschi and Congress (2010) developed a human rights well-being assessment tool and map to teach students about human rights. In preparation for completing the Human Rights Well-Being Assessment students learn about the three types of human rights: civil and political rights; social and cultural rights; and collective rights. As stated previously, a study of these rights can be abstract and quite remote, although students as adult learners need to apply abstract concepts to their daily experiences (Gitterman, 2004). Thus, students are immediately encouraged to apply abstract human rights to the daily well-being of their clients.

To understand how human rights link to well-being, the following well-beings were defined (Maschi & Congress, 2010):

- Economic well-being: sufficient resources to meet basic needs (economic and social rights) such as food, clothing, shelter, and health, as well as the means to participate in the civic life of the community
- Educational well-being: the right to free and compulsory elementary and secondary education and readily available resources for higher education
- Political and legal well-being: the right of all individuals to participate in the political process in a fair and just manner, as well as the right to due process under the law. Protection from discrimination based on gender, religion, race, and sexual orientation is guaranteed.
- Social and cultural well-being: each individual has the right to his or her own cultural beliefs.
- Physical well-being: freedom from the risk of preventable disease and untimely death and the right to receive needed health care
- Mental well-being: internal state whereby individuals are able to recognize their strengths and are able to cope with the normal stresses of life, work productively, and make a contributions to the community
- Spiritual well-being: belief in a meaning and purpose in life, as well as a place in universe

Connecting Human Rights With Well-Being

Students are first asked to complete the information shown in Figure 1, which provides them the opportunity to link all the articles in the UDHR to specific domains of well-being. The Human Rights Well-Being Assessment tool (Figure 2) provides students the opportunity to assess the well-beings of their clients, examining strengths as well as the obstacles clients face. Then students are asked to link well-beings to specific human rights concepts. Whereas Figure 1 promotes a deductive approach from the abstract human rights to the specific well-being, completion of Figure 2 enables students to move from the specific well-being identified in clients and families to the overarching abstract human rights principles.

As a final step, students are asked to complete a human rights map (Figure 3; see also Appendix, which gives a suggested exercise for students). A human rights map is a paper-and-pen visual assessment tool developed as an individual, family, or group assessment, planning, and intervention instrument. Although resembling an ecomap, this process uses a human rights framework. It helps make the relationship between human rights and well-being much more apparent to the student. An advantage of developing a human rights map is that it provides a visual representation of the person/family in relation to well-being and rights.

Although most countries have approved the UDHR because these rights "are (generally) accepted by the global community" (IASSW & IFSW, 2004, p. 1), there have been some objections to a human rights approach to social work practice. A goal of social work education is to develop a capacity for critical thinking (CSWE, 2008). We have found it important to teach students not only about the human rights perspective, but also critiques of this approach. Human rights doctrines with a focus on individuals have been seen as primarily a Western construct that places a higher value on individual freedom over collective perspectives. Ife (2008) suggests that some have criticized a human rights perspective as primarily an outgrowth of Enlightenment thinking, but presents the counter argument that a human rights moral philosophy has been around for many years, predating the Enlightenment. Although the term *human rights* may not have been used, human rights has been expressed in many different cultures and religious traditions.

Figure 1   **Human rights and well-being assessment (Source: Maschi & Congress, 2010)**

HUMAN RIGHTS AND WELL-BEING	ASSESSMENT
Person/Family/Population:	
Directions: The Human Rights and Well-Being Assessment can be used to classify and assess relevant well-being information for an individual, family, or vulnerable population in general. Gather bio-, psycho-, sociopolitical information about person or family.	
Domains of Well-Being	
1. **Physical Well-Being:** List essential strengths/obstacles for person, family, or population for person, family, or population	
2. **Mental Well-Being:** List essential strengths/obstacles for person, family, or population	
3. **Spiritual Well-Being:** List essential strengths/obstacles for person, family, or population	
4. **Cultural Well-Being:** List essential strengths/obstacles for person, family, or population	
5. **Legal Well-Being:** List essential strengths/obstacles for person, family, or population	
6. **Political Well-Being:** List essential strengths/obstacles for person, family, or population	
7. **Economic Well-Being:** List essential strengths/obstacles for person, family, or population	
8. **Educational Well-Being:** List essential strengths/obstacles for person, family, or population	
9. **Social Well-Being:** List essential strengths/obstacles for person, family, or population	

Source: Maschi & Congress, 2010

Figure 2 Universal Declaration of Human Rights: 30 articles by three generations of human rights (positive, negative, and collective) and well-being

Client Name or Population: _____   Date: _____

		PHY	MEN	SPIR	SOC	CULT	ECO	EDU	POL	LEG
	Article 1. All human beings are born free and equal in dignity and rights. They are endowed with reason and conscience and should act towards one another in a spirit of brotherhood.									
Gen	**First generation–negative rights (civil and political articles 2-21) - To ensure freedom from the "curtailment of individual liberty"**									
1	Article 2. Everyone is entitled to all the rights and freedoms set forth in this Declaration, without distinction of any kind, such as race, color, sex, language, religion, political or other opinion, national or social origin, property, birth or other status. Furthermore, no distinction shall be made on the basis of the political, jurisdictional or international status of the country or territory to which a person belongs whether it be independent, trust, non-self-governing or under any other limitation of sovereignty.									
1	Article 3. Everyone has the right to life, liberty and security of person.									
1	Article 4. No one shall be held in slavery or servitude; slavery and the slave trade shall be prohibited in all their forms.									
1	Article 5. No one shall be subjected to torture or to cruel, inhuman, degrading treatment or punishment.									
1	Article 6. Everyone has the right to recognition everywhere as a person before the law.									
1	Article 7. All are equal before the law and are entitled without any discrimination to equal protection of the law. All are entitled to equal protection against any discrimination in violation of this Declaration and against any incitement to such discrimination.									

(continued)

Figure 2 (continued)

1	Article 8. Everyone has the right to an effective remedy by the competent national tribunals for acts violating the fundamental rights granted him by the constitution or by law.			
1	Article 9. No one shall be subjected to arbitrary arrest, detention or exile.			
1	Article 10. Everyone is entitled in full equality to a fair and public hearing by an independent and impartial tribunal in the determination of his rights and obligations and of any criminal charge against him.			
1	Article 11. (1) Everyone charged with a penal offence has the right to be presumed innocent until proved guilty according to law in a public trial at which he has had all the guarantees necessary for his defense. (2) No one shall be held guilty of any penal offence on account of any act or omission which did not constitute a penal offence, under national or international law, at the time when it was committed. Nor shall a heavier penalty be imposed than the one that was applicable at the time the penal offence was committed.			
1	Article 12. No one shall be subjected to arbitrary interference with his privacy, family, home or correspondence, nor to attacks upon his honour and reputation. Everyone has the right to the protection of the law against such interference or attacks.			
1	Article 12. No one shall be subjected to arbitrary interference with his privacy, family, home or correspondence, nor to attacks upon his honour and reputation. Everyone has the right to the protection of the law against such interference or attacks.			
1	Article 13. (1) Everyone has the right to freedom of movement and residence within the borders of each state. (2) Everyone has the right to leave any country, including his own and to return to his country.			
1	Article 14. (1) Everyone has the right to seek and to enjoy in other countries asylum from persecution. (2) This right may not be invoked in the case of prosecutions genuinely arising from non-political crimes or from acts contrary to the purposes and principles of the United Nations.			

(continued)

Figure 2 (continued)

1	Article 15. (1) Everyone has the right to a nationality. (2) No one shall be arbitrarily deprived of his nationality nor denied the right to change his nationality.					
1	Article 16. (1) Men and women of full age, without any limitation due to race, nationality or religion, have the right to marry and to found a family. They are entitled to equal rights as to marriage, during marriage and at its dissolution. (2) Marriage shall be entered into only with the free and full consent of the intending spouses. (3) The family is the natural and fundamental group unit of society and is entitled to protection by society and the State.					
1	Article 17. (1) Everyone has the right to own property alone as well as in association with others. (2) No one shall be arbitrarily deprived of his property.					
1	Article 18. Everyone has the right to freedom of thought, conscience and religion; this right includes freedom to change his religion or belief, and freedom, either alone or in community with others and in public or private, to manifest his religion or belief in teaching, practice, worship and observance.					
1	Article 19. Everyone has the right to freedom of opinion and expression; this right includes freedom to hold opinions without interference and to seek, receive and impart information and ideas through any media and regardless of frontiers.					
1	Article 20. (1) Everyone has the right to freedom of peaceful assembly and association.					
1	Article 21. (1) Everyone has the right to take part in the government of his country, directly or through freely chosen representatives. (2) Everyone has the right of equal access to public service in his country. (3) The will of the people shall be the basis of the authority of government; this shall be expressed in periodic and genuine elections which shall be by universal and equal suffrage and shall be held by secret vote or by equivalent free voting procedures.					

(continued)

Figure 2 (continued)

Gen	Second generation-positive rights (economic, social, & cultural rights; articles 22- 27)				
2	Ensure social justice, freedom from want and participation in the social, economic and cultural aspects of life.				
2	Article 22. Everyone, as a member of society, has the right to social security and is entitled to realization, through national effort and international co-operation and in accordance with the organization and resources of each State, of the economic, social and cultural rights indispensable for his dignity and the free development of his personality.				
2	Article 23. (1) Everyone has the right to work, to free choice of employment, to just and favorable conditions of work and to protection against unemployment. (2) Everyone, without any discrimination, has the right to equal pay for equal work. (3) Everyone who works has the right to just and favorable remuneration ensuring for himself and his family an existence worthy of human dignity, and supplemented, if necessary, by other means of social protection.				
2	Article 24. Everyone has the right to rest and leisure, including reasonable limitation of working hours and periodic holidays with pay.				
2	Article 25. (1) Everyone has the right to a standard of living adequate for the health and well-being of himself and of his family, including food, clothing, housing and medical care and necessary social services, and the right to security in the event of unemployment, sickness, disability, widowhood, old age or other lack of livelihood in circumstances beyond his control. (2) Motherhood and childhood are entitled to special care and assistance. All children, whether born in or out of wedlock, shall enjoy the same social protection.				
2	Article 26. (1) Everyone has the right to education. Education shall be free, at least in the elementary and fundamental stages. Elementary education shall be compulsory. Technical and professional education shall be made generally available and higher education shall be equally accessible to all on the basis of merit. (2) Education shall be directed to the full development of the human personality and to the strengthening of respect for human rights and fundamental freedoms. It shall promote understanding, tolerance and friendship among all nations, racial, or religious groups, and shall further the activities of the United Nations for the maintenance of peace. (3) Parents have a prior right to choose the kind of education that shall be given to their children.				

(continued)

Figure 2 (continued)

2	Article 27. (1) Everyone has the right freely to participate in the cultural life of the community, to enjoy the arts and to share in scientific advancement and its benefits. (2) Everyone has the right to the protection of the moral and material interests resulting from any scientific, literary or artistic production of which he is the author.
Gen 3	Third generation-collective rights (rights of social & political involvement beyond personal to national-regional levels; article 28), Ensure collective vision of the right to social and economic development beyond personal to national and international
3	Article 28. Everyone is entitled to a social and international order in which the rights and freedoms set forth in this Declaration can be fully realized.
Other Articles	
	Article 29. (1) Everyone has duties to the community in which alone the free and full development of his personality is possible. (2) In the exercise of his rights and freedoms, everyone shall be subject only to such Obstacles as are determined by law solely for the purpose of securing due recognition and respect for the rights and freedoms of others and of meeting the just requirements of morality, public order and the general welfare in a democratic society. (3) These rights and freedoms may in no case be exercised contrary to the purposes and principles of the United Nations.
	Article 30. Nothing in this Declaration may be interpreted as implying for any State, group or person any right to engage in any activity or to perform any act aimed at the destruction of any of the rights and freedoms set forth herein.

Note: PHY=physical well-being; MEN=mental well-being; SPIR=spiritual well-being; SOC=social well-being; CUL=cultural well-being; ECO=economic well-being; EDU=educational well-being; POL=political well-being; LEG=legal well-being;

Source: Maschi & Congress, 2010; adapted from United Nations, 1948

Figure 3 **Human rights map template**

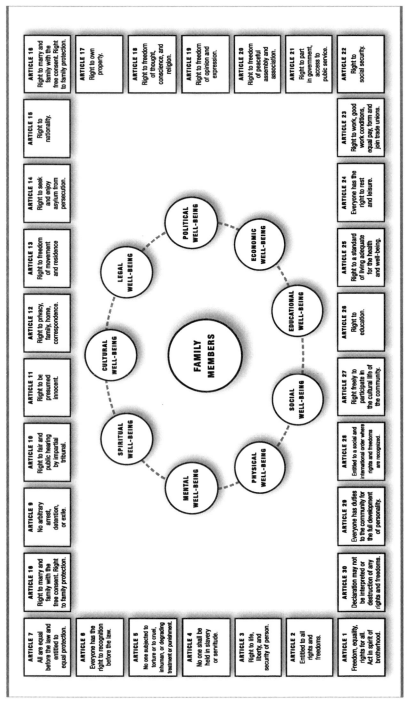

ARTICLE 16
Right to marry and family with the free consent. Right to family protection.

ARTICLE 17
Right to own property.

ARTICLE 18
Right to freedom of thought, conscience, and religion.

ARTICLE 19
Right to freedom of opinion and expression.

ARTICLE 20
Right to freedom of peaceful assembly and association.

ARTICLE 21
Right to part in government, access to public service.

ARTICLE 22
Right to social security.

ARTICLE 15
Right to nationality.

ARTICLE 14
Right to seek and enjoy asylum from persecution.

ARTICLE 13
Right to freedom of movement and residence

ARTICLE 12
Right to privacy, family, home, correspondence.

ARTICLE 11
Right to be presumed innocent.

ARTICLE 10
Right to fair and public hearing by impartial tribunal.

ARTICLE 9
No arbitrary arrest, detention, or exile.

ARTICLE 16
Right to marry and family with the free consent. Right to family protection.

ARTICLE 7
All are equal before the law and entitled to equal protection.

ARTICLE 6
Everyone has the right to recognition before the law.

ARTICLE 5
No one subjected to torture or to cruel, inhuman, or degrading treatment or punishment.

ARTICLE 4
No one shall be held in slavery or servitude.

ARTICLE 3
Right to life, liberty, and security of person.

ARTICLE 2
Entitled to all rights and freedoms.

ARTICLE 1
Freedom, equality, rights for all. Act in spirit of brotherhood.

ARTICLE 30
Declaration may not be interpreted or destruction of any rights and freedoms.

ARTICLE 29
Everyone has duties to the community for the full development of personality.

ARTICLE 28
Entitled to a social and international order where rights and freedoms are recognized.

ARTICLE 27
Right freely to participate in the cultural life of the community.

ARTICLE 26
Right to education.

ARTICLE 25
Right to a standard of living adequate for the health and well-being.

ARTICLE 24
Everyone has the right to rest and leisure.

ARTICLE 23
Right to work, good work conditions, equal pay, form and join trade unions.

POLITICAL WELL-BEING

ECONOMIC WELL-BEING

LEGAL WELL-BEING

EDUCATIONAL WELL-BEING

CULTURAL WELL-BEING

FAMILY MEMBERS

SOCIAL WELL-BEING

SPIRITUAL WELL-BEING

PHYSICAL WELL-BEING

MENTAL WELL-BEING

Source: Maschi & Congress, 2010

Does a focus on human rights as the primary and universal perspective on ethical practice for social workers promote a Western developed world perspective that may not be appropriate for social workers from less developed countries? In his book, *Professional Imperialism: Social Work in the Third World*, Midgley (1981) argued that the human rights orientation of our ethical codes may be promoting a "professional imperialism" because the codes were developed primarily by social workers in developed countries. More recently, Yip (2004) addressed how the social work profession regards cultural diversity. He contends that Western social workers give lip service only to "mild diversity" (p. 603) in that there is some respect for diverse cultural beliefs and practices, but beliefs about the universality of human rights prevails. Although Western countries and social workers support a human rights perspective, Chinese cultures promote a perspective that is based on responsibilities. Flynn (2005) also argues that human rights is primarily an individualistic model and ignores the collective. He advocates that to teach effectively about human rights, a focus on responsibilities is also needed. Furthermore, African perspectives have been critical of the Western human rights perspective based on individualism and personal freedom. A focus on connection to the community is seen as the prevailing value for social work practice in Africa (Graham, 2002; Osei-Hwedie, Ntseane, & Jacques, 2006).

Are universal human rights and cultural relativism compatible? Yip (2004) takes the most radical approach, proposing a cultural relativist approach rather than the Western universalist human rights perspective, whereas Healy (2008) proposes a "stance in the middle of the universalist relativism continuum" (p. 24). A strict cultural relativist perspective might be detrimental to women, especially in terms of intimate partner violence (Healy, 2008). Hugman (2008) points out that there is not a strict dichotomy between all those in Western countries being against domestic violence, whereas those in non-Western countries condone domestic violence. There are those in the West who do not oppose violence against women, and there are many, especially social workers, in non-Western countries who do not support legal and cultural policies that promote the oppression of women. Gray and Fook (2004) and Noble (2004) have proposed that an inductive approach is better, that is, beginning with what is considered normative in specific countries and moving up to a consideration of what is universal among social workers everywhere, rather than beginning with a universalist approach.

The UDHR promotes the rights of individual people rather than communities or collectives of people, although other human rights treaties and mechanisms recognize the importance of collective enjoyment of rights. The focus on the rights of individuals in many Western countries has been translated into a concern for individual privacy and confidentiality. This is most apparent in the United States, where the NASW Code of Ethics has 18 provisions on confidentiality—more than any other topic in the Code of Ethics (Congress, 2013). Although not as strong a theme, confidentiality and privacy are also included in the IFSW and IASSW Social Work: Statement of Ethical Principles. Yet both locally and globally, many share a more collective approach to confidentiality and privacy.

Human rights doctrines propose that each person is entitled to the same or equal human rights, whereas social work education has stressed the importance of culturally competent practice in addressing cultural, racial, and ethnic diversity. Even among those who accept a human rights perspective, there are concerns. Webb (2009) argues that a focus on diversity and difference may take social work education away from concepts of sameness and equality, which he views as fundamental to realizing human rights for all.

An important part of educating students about human rights is to introduce them to the different beliefs and controversies surrounding human rights, ranging from those who oppose the approach completely to those who promote the rights as absolute dictums. Students need the opportunity to discuss and debate in the classroom about human rights doctrines and critiques.

Conclusion

Teaching social work students about human rights seems most appropriate because of social work's firmly rooted values of respect for all people, self-determination, focus on strengths, and promotion of well-being. Using a human rights map to help students link abstract human rights to different well-beings of their clients is a useful way to help students learn to operationalize human rights. Because teaching students about human rights and, more specifically, this model is so new, there has been little research on its effectiveness as a teaching model. This would be an important next step.

Finally, because an important purpose of social work education is to increase students' capacity for critical thinking, it is not sufficient to teach social work students only about human rights principles stemming from the UDHR and other human rights instruments. Students need to be exposed to controversies around human rights, especially to critiques that interpret a human rights orientation as primarily based on a Western orientation that supports individual freedom and rights over a collective or community approach. As social work education becomes more international, students need to learn how to integrate education about human rights with other perspectives to be more respectful and inclusive of the different values and beliefs of their clients and other colleagues around the world.

References

Congress, E. (2013). Global ethical principles and dilemmas. In L. Healy & R. Link (Eds.), *Handbook of international social work* (pp. 297–302). New York, NY: Oxford University Press.

Council on Social Work Education (CSWE). (2008). *Educational policy and accreditation standards.* Retrieved from http://www.cswe.org/File.aspx?id=13780

Flynn, D., 2005. What's wrong with rights? Rethinking human rights and responsibilities. *Australian Social Work 58*(3), 244–256.

Gamble, D. (2012). Well-being in a globalised world: Does social work know how to make it happen? *Journal of Social Work Education 48*(4), 669–689.

Gitterman, A. (2004). Interactive androgagy. *Journal of Teaching in Social Work 24*(3/4), 95–112.

Graham, M. (2002). *Social work and African-centred worldviews.* Birmingham, UK: Venture Press.

Gray, M., & Fook, J. (2004). The quest for a universal social work: Some issues and implications. *Social Work Education 23*(5), 625–644.

Healy, L. (2008). *International social work: Professional action in an interdependent world.* New York, NY: Oxford University Press.

Healy, L., & Link, R. (2011). *Handbook of international social work: Human rights, development and the global profession.* New York, NY: Oxford Publishing Company.

Hokenstad, T., Healy, L., & Segal, U. A. (Eds.). (2013). *Teaching human rights: Curriculum resources for social work educators.* Alexandria, VA: CSWE Press.

Hugman, R. (2008). Ethics in a world of difference. *Ethics and Social Welfare 2*(2), 118–132.

Ife, J. (2008). *Human rights and social work: Toward rights based practice.* Melbourne, AU: Cambridge Publishing Company.

International Federation of Social Workers & International Association of Schools of Social Work (IFSW & IASSW). (2004). *Ethics in social work: Statement of principles.* Retrieved from www.ifsw.org

Maschi, T., & Congress, E. (2010, March 20). Visualizing human rights and wellbeing: A human rights map. Presentation at the Association of Baccalaureate Social Work Program Directors conference, Atlanta, GA.

McPherson, J., & Abell, N. (2012). Human rights engagement and exposure: New scales to challenge social work education. *Research on Social Work Practice 22*(6), 704–713.

Midgley, J. (1981). *Professional imperialism: Social work in the third world.* London, UK: Heinemann.

National Association of Social Workers. (NASW). (2008). *Code of ethics.* Washington, DC: NASW.

Noble, C. (2004). Social work education, training and standards in the Asia-Pacific region. *Social Work Education, 23*, 527–536.

Osei-Hwedie, K., Ntseane, D., & Jacques, G. (2006). Searching for appropriateness in social work education in Botswana: The process of developing a master in social work (MSW) programme in a "developing" country. *Social Work Education, 25*, 569–590.

Reichert, E. (2003). *Social work and human rights: A foundation for policy and practice.* Thousand Oaks, CA: SAGE.

Reichert, E. (2006). *Understanding human rights: An exercise book.* Thousand Oaks, CA: SAGE.

Reichert, E. (2011). Human rights in social work: An essential basis. *Journal of Comparative Social Welfare 27*(3), 207–220.

Rubin, A., & Babbie, E. (2011). *Research methods for social work* (7th ed.) Belmont, CA: Thomson/Brooks-Cole.

Steen, J. A. (2012). The human rights philosophy as a values framework for the human behavior course: Integration of human rights concepts in the person-in environment perspective. *Journal of Human Behavior in the Social Environment* *22*(7), 853–862.

Steen, J. A., & Mathiesen, S. (2005). Human rights education: Is social work behind the curve? *Journal of Teaching in Social Work, 25*(3/4), 143–156.

Webb, S. 2009. Against difference and diversity in social work: The case of human rights. *International Journal of Social Welfare, 18*(3), 307–316.

United Nations. (1948). *Universal declaration of human rights.* G.A. Res. 217 A (III). Retrieved from http://www.refworld.org/docid/3ae6b3712c.html

United Nations. (1966a). *International covenant on civil and political rights.* G.A. Res. 2200A (XXI). Retrieved from http://www.ohchr.org/Documents/ProfessionalInterest/ccpr.pdf

United Nations. (1966b). *International covenant on economic, social, and cultural rights.* G.A. Res. 2200A (XXI). Retrieved from http://www.ohchr.org/EN/ProfessionalInterest/Pages/CESCR.aspx

United Nations. (1979). *Convention on the elimination of all forms of discrimination against women.* G.A. Res. 34/180. Retrieved from http://www.ohchr.org/Documents/ProfessionalInterest/cedaw.pdf

United Nations. (2007. *Declaration on the rights of indigenous persons.* G.A. Res. 61/295. Retrieved from http://daccess-dds-ny.un.org/doc/UNDOC/GEN/N06/512/07/PDF/N0651207.pdf?OpenElement

United Nations. (2008). *Convention on the rights of persons with disabilities.* G.A. Res. A/RES/61/106. Retrieved from http://www.ohchr.org/EN/HRBodies/CRPD/Pages/ConventionRightsPersonsWithDisabilities.aspx

United Nations Centre for Human Rights. (1994). *Human rights and social work: A manual for schools of social work and the social work profession* (Professional Training Series No. 1). Retrieved from http://www.ohchr.org/Documents/Publications/traininglen.pdf

Wronka, J. (2008). *Human rights and social justice: Social action and service for the helping and health professions.* Thousand Oaks, CA: SAGE.

Yip, K. S. (2004). A Chinese cultural critique of the global qualifying standards for social work education. *Social Work Education 23* (5), 597–612.

Appendix: Suggested Exercise for Students

This case example has been adopted from a presentation given by Maschi and Congress (2009).

Ellen is an 18-year-old Hispanic female. In September 2009 she enrolled for her first year at a school for students with a diagnosis of emotional disturbance. Ellen currently resides with her mother and a 16-year-old sister who attends the same school. Ellen's mother is an immigrant from Peru, and Spanish is the only language spoken in the home. Ellen reports that her family prides itself on its culture and places an emphasis on maintaining Peruvian traditions. Ellen and her family members are also very involved in their Pentecostal church. When Ellen was 2 years old her mother and father separated, and Ellen and her sister see their father once a year on Christmas day. Ellen does not have an interest in pursuing a relationship with her father or his new wife. Ellen's mother has recently started a new factory job. She has reported that her family experiences financial difficulties and that the stress of paying the bills affects the family emotionally. Ellen started working at Rite Aid in September 2009 after school and on weekends to earn extra money to help her mother with the bills. Her Individualized Educational Plan reports that Ellen has a history of sexual abuse and has been diagnosed with bipolar disorder. She has an extensive psychiatric history including three hospitalizations and outpatient treatment. Ellen has been suspended five times and expelled twice from school due to ongoing negative behavioral problems. Currently, Ellen reported to a school counselor that she is experiencing increased anxiety and depression because of her past sexual abuse history, an ongoing stressful relationship with her sister, and adjusting to a new school and a new job. She shows symptoms of an eating disorder, including restricting her food intake, purging, and obsessing about food. She has a history of cutting and states that she often feels the urge to cut as a release from all the stress in her life. Ellen reports that she currently is having strong impulses to cut again and is having suicidal thoughts. She has been able to verbalize the immense stress, anxiety, and sadness she experiences daily, and she is very open about her struggle with her current coping mechanisms including her eating disorder and self-injurious behavior. Ellen also expressed that she had

fallen behind at school, is concerned about maintaining her school enrollment, and really wants to graduate.

(Case written by a second year MSW student.)

Steps:

1) Complete Figure 1, which connects human rights with various well-beings.
2) On Figure 2 look at the bio-psycho-social well-beings of the client and
   the family. List the strengths and obstacles for each family member in
   terms of the well-beings. Link each family member's well-beings with
   the specific human rights article.
3) Complete the map in Figure 3, which describes graphically how
   the well-beings are linked with different provisions of the Universal
   Declaration of Human Rights.

6 | Human Rights as a Framework for Teaching International Social Work

Susan Mapp

Although the Universal Declaration of Human Rights (UDHR) was adopted by the United Nations in 1948, it has only been since the inclusion of the phrase "human rights" in the 2008 Educational Policy and Accreditation Standards that large numbers of social work faculty members have begun to be aware of the international human rights documents and include them in courses (Council on Social Work Education, 2008; United Nations, 1948). Although some faculty members have been working in this area for a long time, for others it is new territory, and they are seeking to learn how human rights can be integrated into an already overburdened curriculum. Both the profession of social work and the covenants, conventions, and other human rights documents are primarily focused on populations at high risk for violations of their rights; thus, there is a natural fit between social work values and human rights.

Human rights provides an ideal framework for teaching issues in international social work—whether in separate courses or integrated within other courses. Although not perfect, these documents provide an agreed-on standard for the minimally acceptable base for human dignity and can be used to examine practice at all system levels, from the individual to the global.[1] Practicing from a rights-based approach helps focus the issues by framing what should be occurring, as defined by the appropriate international human rights documents, as contrasted with what is occurring. This helps social workers move from a needs-based approach, in which we provide only what we think we can afford, to working to make sure all peoples have what they need to reach their potential.

Although it cannot be ignored that violations of human rights are frequent in the Global North (see Chapters 7, 11, and 21), for certain issues they can be even more evident in the Global South. Due in large part to growing global awareness, an increasing number of social work students are interested in social problems in other nations and in learning how they can effect change there. As discussed previously, the covenants and conventions of the United Nations and other documents provide a natural framework for examining and affecting these issues. Examining what is occurring in other nations can also help to contrast that with our own to help students examine where the United States is doing well and where it needs improvement. Thus, this chapter explores different topics that are often explored under the term *international social work* and discusses the different human rights documents that are applicable to those topics. Although the discussed topics do not represent the totality of the issues that could be examined, they are among the most common.

Human Trafficking

Awareness of human trafficking has been increasing exponentially. Currently, 21 million people are in situations of human trafficking around the world. Although the majority of them are trafficked within their own nations, approximately 30% are trafficked across international borders (International Labour Organization, 2012). Thus, U.S. social workers may work within this nation with U.S. citizens who have been trafficked or foreign nationals who have been trafficked here. They may also work in other nations with citizens of that nation who have been trafficked or foreign nationals who have been trafficked there. For example, in India, Indian citizens are vulnerable to trafficking, as are citizens of neighboring countries such as Nepal. It is extremely rare for U.S. citizens to be trafficked to other nations, although it does occur (U. S. Department of State, 2012).

Although the term *human trafficking* has been in use for some time, it was not formally defined in international law until 2000, when the United Nations Convention against Transnational Organized Crime was opened for signature and entered into force. A standard definition was needed to help states coordinate their antitrafficking efforts and provide services to those who had been trafficked (United Nations Office on Drugs and Crime, 2013). Three protocols supplemented this convention—the Protocol to Prevent, Suppress, and Punish Trafficking in Persons, especially Women and Children being the relevant one. It is sometimes referred to the Palermo Protocol, even though there are actually three protocols. This protocol entered into force in 2003 and defines trafficking as follows (United Nations Office on Drugs and Crime, 2004):

> "Trafficking in persons" shall mean the recruitment, transportation, transfer, harbouring or receipt of persons, by means of the threat or use of force or other forms of coercion, of abduction, of fraud, of deception, of the abuse of power or of a position of vulnerability or of the giving or receiving of payments or benefits to achieve the consent of a person having control over another person, for the purpose of exploitation. Exploitation shall include, at a minimum, the exploitation of the prostitution of others or other forms of sexual exploitation, forced labour or services, slavery or practices similar to slavery, servitude or the removal of organs. (p. 42)

Within general human rights documents, there are articles related to the prohibition of trafficking. Article Four of the UDHR (United Nations, 1948) relating to the prohibition of slavery is the most applicable within that document to the issue of human trafficking, and Article 6 of the Convention on the Elimination of all Forms of Discrimination Against Women (CEDAW; United Nations, 1979) prohibits trafficking and the exploitation of prostitution. Article 34 of the Convention on the Rights of the Child (CRC; United Nations, 1989) requires ratifying states to protect children from sexual exploitation, whereas Article 35 more specifically requires states to take measures to prevent child trafficking.

In 2000 two optional protocols to the CRC were opened for signature: the Sale of Children, Child Prostitution, and Child Pornography (United Nations, 2000a) and Involvement of Children in Armed Conflicts (United Nations, 2000b). Although the United States has not ratified the convention itself, it has ratified these optional protocols. Because the use of child soldiers is considered to be a form of labor trafficking (U.S. State Department, 2011), both protocols address trafficking. The International Labour Organization's Convention Number 182 (1999), which defines the worst forms of child labor, also notes the use of children in armed conflicts as a type of trafficking. Interestingly, the sexual exploitation of children is broken out into a separate item within Article 3:

a) all forms of slavery or practices similar to slavery, such as the sale and trafficking of children, debt bondage and serfdom and forced or compulsory labour, including forced or compulsory recruitment of children for use in armed conflict;

b) the use, procuring or offering of a child for prostitution, for the production of pornography or for pornographic performances

The U.S. Trafficking Victims Protection Act (TVPA) and its subsequent reauthorizations are quite similar in definition to the Palermo Protocol related to trafficking, although the TVPA does not include organ trafficking—only labor and sexual exploitation. In both, the means defined (force, fraud and coercion) are not required if the person is a child. Nor is movement required in either; people can be, and are, trafficked where they live.

Human trafficking has gained increased media attention in recent years, and many students have now heard of this issue, in contrast to even a few years ago. However, many are unaware of the actual definition of trafficking and rely on media images and depictions for information, resulting in a focus on sex trafficking over labor trafficking and foreign victims over domestic ones, although this latter focus is changing in the media. However, there is still a media focus on cases related to force, over fraud and coercion, or examining how children can be lured into these situations.

Although trafficking is easy to condemn, it can be more difficult for students to understand how these situations are created; how do people become trafficked? A variety of tools on the Internet can help students understand these complex issues. An excellent multimedia tool for students to use outside the classroom is MTV's Backstory (http://thebackstory.mtv.com), which walks students through the story of how different individuals became ensnared in human trafficking in an interactive manner. Another tool to help them understand the role they play in furthering these conditions is Slavery Footprint, in which participants take a survey about what they own and then calculate how many slaves likely participated in the making of those goods (http://slavery-footprint.org/survey).

The Palermo Protocols and the TVPA were developed from a legal standpoint and serve to define human trafficking for prosecution in a court of law. The Palermo Protocol (United Nations Office on Drugs and Crime, 2004) states only that, "each State Party shall *consider* implementing measures to provide for the physical, psychological and social recovery of victims of trafficking in persons" (emphasis added, p. 44). The TVPA hinges adult access to services on cooperation with prosecution efforts unless the survivor can demonstrate severe trauma. In addition, antitrafficking campaigns often fail to recognize those who have been trafficked as empowered actors. This can be seen in the name of U.S. governmental campaigns such Rescue and Restore and Innocence Lost.

Therefore, another exercise for students is to have them develop documents from a rights-based framework, which assumes that there are certain things to which people are entitled to assure they can reach their full potential. What would a law based on human rights include? To which services would survivors be entitled? How would it change the current model to operate from the point of view of the survivor as opposed to that of law enforcement?

Issues Women Face

Women face a broad variety of threats to their human rights as a result of their gender. In recognition of their more vulnerable status, the United Nations developed CEDAW (United Nations, 1979). This convention defines discrimination to include both intentional discrimination and acts that have a discriminatory effect and looks at women's actual lives, as opposed to the laws that exist within a nation, to determine whether the rights set forth in CEDAW are being met (United Nations, 2009a). This focus helps examine issues on a broader societal level and includes institutional discrimination.

Thus, ratifying nations must work to eradicate harmful practices that result in poor outcomes for females such as violence and unequal access to schools.

However, a weakness of CEDAW and all human rights documents is that ratifying nations may post reservations to specific articles as an opt-out mechanism. CEDAW has more reservations than any other human rights treaty (United Nations, 2009b). The most common article to which reservations are noted is Article 16, which states that men and women are to be considered equal in marriage; the second most common is Article 2, which requires ratifying states to recognize the equality of men and women in law (Freeman, 2009). These articles are considered to be core principles of CEDAW; the UN considers these "impermissible reservations" (United Nations, 2009c). The use of Sharia law within a nation is often the basis for a posted reservation. However, after review many countries have withdrawn their reservations (Freeman, 2009).

An excellent area for debate within the classroom is the relative merit of these three positions. Is it better, morally and ethically speaking, to not ratify the document as the United States has done, than to ratify it but post reservations to core elements, or to ratify it and fail to achieve its desired outcomes (the situation of all ratifying nations)? Although some students may feel that it is better not to ratify if the nation posts reservations or fails to achieve them, other students may say that it weakens our international position to scold others for human rights violations if we have not even ratified the documents. Other students may add that it is better to have something to aim for than to declare it cannot be done.

The articles of CEDAW can be used to support the human rights base of specific issues. Girls have unequal access to education. The majority of children out of school are girls, leading to the fact that almost two-thirds of illiterate adults in the world are female (UNESCO, 2011), a situation addressed in Article 10. Article 16 includes the issue of child marriage; more than 67 million women aged 20 to 24 worldwide were married before the age of 18 (UNICEF, 2011). Females have unequal access to health care (Article 12) throughout their lives, resulting in higher rates of mortality in girls than boys as well as maternal mortality (Hvistendahl, 2011; United Nations Population

Fund, n.d.). Access to equitable employment is an issue that clearly bridges the Global North and Global South and is addressed in Article 11.

Other issues are not specifically named, but can be inferred. For example, the issue of female genital cutting, while not specifically named in CEDAW, is considered to be addressed by Articles 10 and 12 on education and health care, respectively (Committee on the Elimination of Discrimination Against Women, 1990). Numerous articles are considered to establish the right of women to be free from gender-based violence, both within the family and without: Articles 2, 5, 11, 12, and 16 (Committee on the Elimination of Discrimination Against Women, 1989).

Refugees and Asylum-Seekers

The Geneva Conventions of 1949 (International Committee of the Red Cross, 1949) are the central documents for the humane treatment of people involved in conflict, whether they are combatants or civilians, and all nations of the world are party to these conventions. Although people sometimes erroneously refer to the Geneva Convention, in fact there is a set of four conventions and three additional protocols reflecting the evolving state of war since the first convention in 1864.

The Universal Declaration of Human Rights supports the principles found in the Geneva Conventions. Article 5 states that "No one shall be subjected to torture or to cruel, inhuman or degrading treatment or punishment," and Article 14 provides the right to asylum. The primary document in establishing who is a refugee, together with their rights and responsibilities, is the 1951 convention relating to the Status of Refugees (United Nations, 1951), together with its 1967 protocol (United Nations, 1967).

The American Red Cross (2011) states that

the Geneva Conventions apply in all cases of declared war, or in any other armed conflict between nations. They also apply in cases where a nation is partially or totally occupied by soldiers of another nation, even when there is no armed resistance to that occupation. (p. 2)

This statement provides an area for debate in the classroom. According to the administration of George W. Bush, the Geneva Conventions did not apply in the War on Terror because it was not a declared war. However, the United States did occupy Iraq and Afghanistan and captured people there who were then held at Guantanamo Bay. Did the U.S. government have the legal authority to do so? A report by an independent think tank, the Open Society Justice Initiative, has concluded that it is "indisputable" that the United States tortured prisoners captured during the War on Terror (Cobain, 2013), in violation of the Convention Against Torture (United Nations, 1984) and the Geneva Conventions. Is this defensible in light of the information that was sought to prevent future attacks? The authors of the report state that this program was "counterproductive" (Cobain, 2013), and therefore not effective. The United States also held Omar Khadr for 10 years, who was 15 years old at the time of capture and therefore should have been protected under the optional protocol relating to child soldiers. Was this ethical because he was captured after killing a U.S. soldier?

Another ethical situation for debate is the Israeli occupation of the West Bank. The United Nations Human Rights Council ruled that Israeli settlements in the West Bank are a violation of the Geneva Conventions, specifically the fourth one regarding transfer of civilians into occupied territory (Cumming-Bruce & Kershner, 2013). Israel states that this is based on a misinterpretation of this convention. The Israeli government states that it is not an occupying power because it has held these territories for decades, and furthermore that this convention is aimed at preventing the forced transfer of civilians whereas Israel's settlements are populated by those who move there voluntarily (Levinson & Zarchin, 2012).

One of the ways in which social workers may work in international social work without leaving their own borders is through working with refugees and asylum seekers. As noted, the UDHR and the 1951 Refugee Convention provide these rights; however, how nations have worked with those claiming this right has been very controversial. Australia and the United States have been condemned by human rights groups for their treatment of asylum-seekers. Australia has also been condemned by the United Nations ("UN condemns,"

2013). In these nations, as well as others, it is the first reaction to detain those seeking asylum, to assure they do not pose a security threat to that nation and that their claim is valid. Thus, this creates an area ripe for debate: How does a government balance the rights of asylum-seekers with the duty to protect its borders, as well as be fiscally responsible? This issue may become even more controversial since two young men who planted bombs in Boston in 2013 had been granted asylum to be in the United States. The following paragraph details some of the major issues that have arisen in these nations as a result.

In the United States, treatment of asylum-seekers has been found to vary greatly depending on who is assessing the claim. Treatment varies significantly at different airports, for example. At some airports asylum-seekers are strip-searched, shackled, and put in detention facilities or fail to have their statements of persecution recorded (United States Commission on International Religious Freedom, 2005). At others, this is not the case. Immigration judicial decisions have also been found to vary significantly by judge and by region of the country (Wasem, 2011).

In 2012 Australia reopened its detention facilities for asylum-seekers on the islands of Manus and Nauru. These facilities have drawn condemnation from the United Nations High Commissioner for Refugees and Amnesty International due to the inadequate housing facilities, lack of access to legal representation to process their claims, and negative effects on physical and mental health ("Activists rap," 2013; Amnesty International, 2012a). In 2013 the government of Australia stated that no one arriving by boat without a visa would be considered for asylum in Australia even if determined to be a genuine refugee ("Australia to send," 2013). The use of for-profit prison facilities for asylum-seekers has exploded in the United States, Australia, and the United Kingdom, increasing concerns about adequate treatment. In the United States for-profit facilities do not have to follow the same standards as government facilities, nor must they report on their activities as government facilities do ("Private prisons," 2012). Despite findings of abuse and lethal neglect across these nations, these for-profit companies do not lose their contracts, worth billions of dollars (Bernstein, 2011).

Issues Children Face

The document that focuses on human rights for children is the CRC (as noted previously, the CRC has two optional protocols related to issues of child trafficking). For years this 1989 update of the Declaration of the Rights of the Child had been ratified by every country except two: the United States and Somalia. Now that South Sudan has become a nation, it joins this small group. Somalia has been unable to ratify due to lack of a functioning government until 2012. The main barrier in the United States has been the parental rights movement. This group fears that ratification of the CRC would remove their rights as parents, including their rights to homeschool their children and to use corporal punishment. The defeat of the convention on the Rights of Persons with Disabilities (United Nations, 2006) in 2012 was led by those who feared it would give the United Nations the right to determine U.S. law, especially as it pertained to raising children (Helderman, 2012).

However, in 1957 the U.S. Supreme Court ruled in *Reid v. Covert* that no international treaty has the ability to override the U.S. Constitution. Additionally, the United States has previously designated United Nations conventions as "non-self-executing," in which they do not automatically become law but are carefully reviewed to determine their compatibility with U.S. law. Thus, a classroom use of this issue can be to urge students to take action on this issue by advocating for ratification. Advocating for social justice is a core value of social work, and this can be a mechanism for doing so (see materials at www.childrightscampaign.org for ideas of advocacy techniques).

The most vivid violations of children's rights tend to be around areas of child labor and child maltreatment. Article 32 states that children must be protected from economic exploitation, defined as "any work that is likely to be hazardous or to interfere with the child's education, or to be harmful to the child's health or physical, mental, spiritual, moral or social development." ILO Convention 182, which came into force in 2000, defines the worst forms of child labor as slavery (including trafficking, debt bondage, forced labor, and child soldiers); sexual exploitation (including prostitution, pornography, and stripping); using a child for illicit activity (especially in the area of drugs); and work that is considered hazardous due to its nature or how it is done (International Labour

Organization, 1999). Approximately 215 million children worldwide were engaged in some form of child labor in 2010, about 115 million of whom were engaged in hazardous work. Sixty percent of child laborers work in the area of agriculture (International Labour Organization, 2010). Therefore, this is an enormous issue that affects people in the United States because goods we purchase may have been produced with child labor (see previously mentioned tool on our Slavery Footprint). Additionally, children also labor in agriculture here in the United States. Children working in this industry lack the protections afforded to other working children, including minimum working age limits, limits on the number of hours worked, and standards regarding exposure to toxins and handling dangerous equipment. A bill to extend these protections to agricultural businesses has been languishing in Congress since 2003 (Children's Act for Responsible Employment/CARE Act).

Child maltreatment occurs in all nations. An estimated 86% of children between the ages of 2 and 14 experience physical or psychological aggression from their families; two thirds experience physical aggression (UNICEF, 2009). Article 19 of the CRC provides that the state will ensure that all children are protected from child maltreatment. However, even within a culture there are different definitions of what is maltreatment. For example, in the United States there is no single clear-cut definition of child physical abuse; some would include corporal punishment, whereas others would not. Therefore, having students develop a definition of child maltreatment can be a classroom exercise. Which resources they draw on can be informative. Do students rely solely on their own opinions, or do they seek out research on the effects of various practices on children and base their definitions on the outcome for children? How do they balance cultural differences?

International adoption and surrogacy are other ethical areas for debate. Are these practices that social workers should support because they create families, or are international adoption and surrogacy inherently oppressive and do they take advantage of the globally weaker nature of the sending countries to the benefit of the receiving countries? The Convention on the Protection of Children and Co-Operation in Respect of Intercountry Adoption (commonly called the Hague Convention on Intercountry Adoption) was developed in

1993 to attempt to maintain ethical practices for international adoption (Hague Conference on Private International Law, 1993). It was ratified by the United States in 2007. It sets minimum standards for international adoptions to protect all parties—birthparents, adoptive parents, and the children being adopted. The first priority must be to attempt to have children remain with their birth parents and ensure that international adoption is an option only after attempts at familial reunification or domestic placement have failed. However, is it ethical to remove a few select children and leave the conditions unchanged? Additionally, the matter of international surrogacy is largely unregulated, with situations that resemble that of trafficking. Women are often given legal contracts in languages they cannot read and kept housed until the birth (Rotabi & Bromfield, 2012).

Tying it all Together

Regardless of nation, those most at risk for human rights violations are those who are impoverished, targets of discrimination, and who lack access to education. These are issues that often intertwine (Mapp, 2014). For truly effective action to occur on these issues, the core issues that create them must be addressed. Therefore, the United Nations created the Millennium Development Goals (MDGs). With a 2015 achievement goal, these eight goals were designed to address core human rights violations that inhibited full human development. Despite their almost complete lack of attention in the United States, the MDGs have been a driving force for development since adoption. Substantial progress has been made on many issues, including extreme poverty, education of girls, child and maternal mortality, and reduced deaths from AIDS (United Nations, 2013).

However, with the global recession, the aid given by nations in the Global North, especially to the Least Developed Countries, has been affected. Although the goal is for the wealthy nations to give 0.7% of their gross national income (GNI), they are currently giving only 0.3% according to the Organisation for Economic Co-operation and Development (OECD; 2012). This aid has also been shifting to the middle income countries such as China, India, and Indonesia rather than the Least Developed Countries. Whereas aid overall fell 4% from 2011 to 2012, it fell by 8% in Sub-Saharan Africa (Tran, 2013). The United States contributes the largest absolute amount, but due to the size of the nation it only equates to 0.2% of GNI (OECD, 2012).

Students can learn about and become engaged with community organizing and activism around these goals. The websites of organizations such as the Millennium Campaign (http://www.endpoverty2015.org) and One.org (www.one.org) inform people about the goals, steps that are being taken to achieve them, and opportunities for activism. It could be as simple as signing a petition or writing a letter, but students can also learn about the hands-on work that is being done to attain these goals. As of this writing, the post-2015 goals are being developed, a process students can follow (Open Working Group for Sustainable Development Goals, 2014).

Conclusion

As has been shown, there is a broad variety of pedagogical tools for teaching human rights using the vehicle of issues relating to international social work. Students can learn about the human rights documents, how the existing situation violates them, and opportunities for intervention and advocacy. This chapter offers only a starting point, and many more issues could be included. These issues can also be examined specifically within the United States, rather than focusing on other nations, to help students comprehend the human rights violations that occur within this nation. Regardless of approach, however, it is essential to have students learn these core rights to which all humans are entitled.

References

Activists rap Australia's offshore processing of migrants. (2013, January 14). *IRIN News*. Retrieved from http://www.irinnews.org/printreport.aspx?reportid=97243

American Red Cross. (2011). *Summary of the Geneva Conventions of 1949 and their additional protocols*. Retrieved from http://www.redcross.org/images/MEDIA _CustomProductCatalog/m3640104_IHL_SummaryGenevaConv.pdf

Amnesty International. (2012). *Nauru camp: A catastrophe with no end in sight*. Retrieved from http://www.amnesty.org/en/library/info/ASA42/002/2012/en

Australia to send all boatpeople to poverty-hit Papua New Guinea. (2013, July 23). *South China Morning Post.* Retrieved from http://www.scmp.com

Bernstein, N. (2011, September 28). Companies use immigration crackdown to turn a profit. *New York Times.* Retrieved from http://www.nytimes.com

Cobain, I. (2013, April 16). U.S. torture of prisoners is "indisputable", independent report finds. *The Guardian.* Retrieved from http://www.guardian .co.uk

Committee on the Elimination of Discrimination Against Women. (1989). *General recommendation no. 12.* Retrieved from http://www.un.org /womenwatch/daw/cedaw/recommendations/recomm.htm

Committee on the Elimination of Discrimination Against Women. (1990). *General recommendation no. 14.* Retrieved from http://www.un.org /womenwatch/daw/cedaw/recommendations/recomm.htm

Council on Social Work Education (CSWE). (2008). *Educational policy and accreditation standards.* Retrieved from http://www.cswe.org/File.aspx?id= 13780

Cumming-Bruce, N., & Kershner, I. (2013, January 31). UN panel Says Israeli settlement policy violates law. *New York Times.* Retrieved from http://www .nytimes.com

Freeman, M. A. (2009). *Reservations to CEDAW: An analysis for UNICEF.* Retrieved from http://www.unicef.org/gender/files/Reservations_to_CEDAW -an_Analysis_for_UNICEF.pdf

Hague Conference on Private International Law. (1993). *Convention on the protection of children and co-operation in respect of intercountry adoption.* Retrieved from http://www.hcch.net/upload/conventions/txt33en.pdf

Healy, L. M. (2008). Exploring the history of social work as a human rights profession. *International Social Work, 51,* 735–748.

Helderman, R. S. (2012, December 4). Senate rejects treaty to protect disabled around the world. *Washington Post.* Retrieved from http://articles .washingtonpost.com/2012-12-04/politics/35624605_1_treaty-disabled -children-americans-with-disabilities-act

Hvistendahl, M. (2011). *Unnatural selection: Choosing boys over girls, and the consequences of a world full of men.* Jackson, TN: Public Affairs.

International Committee of the Red Cross (ICRC). (1949, 12 August). *Geneva convention relative to the protection of civilian persons in time of war (fourth Geneva convention),* 75 UNTS 287, Retrieved from http://www.refworld.org /docid/3ae6b36d2.html

International Labour Organization. (1999). *Convention 182 – Convention concerning the prohibition and immediate action for the elimination of the worst forms of child labour.* Retrieved from http://www.ilo.org/public/english /standards/relm/ilc/ilc87/com-chic.htm

International Labour Organization. (2010). *Facts on child labour 2010.* Retrieved from http://www.ilo.org/wcmsp5/groups/public/@dgreports/@dcomm /documents/publication/wcms_126685.pdf

International Labour Organization. (2012). *ILO global estimate of forced labour 2012: Results and methodology.* Retrieved from http://www.ilo.org/sapfl /Informationresources/ILOPublications/WCMS_182004/lang--en/index.htm

Levinson, C., & Zarchin, T. (2012, July 9). Netanyahu-appointed panel: Israel isn't an occupying force in West Bank. *Haaretz.* Retrieved from http://www .haaretz.com/news/diplomacy-defense/netanyahu-appointed-panel-israel-isn-t -an-occupying-force-in-west-bank-1.449895

Mapp, S. (2014). *Human rights and social justice in a global perspective: An introduction to international social work* (2nd ed). New York, NY: Oxford University.

Open Working Group on Sustainable Development Goals. (2014). *Introduction and proposed goals and targets on sustainable development for the Post 2015 Development Agenda.* Retrieved from http://sustainabledevelopment.un.org /content/documents/4523zerodraft.pdf

Organisation for Economic Co-operation and Development (OECD). (2012). *United States.* Retrieved from http://www.oecd.org/dac/stats/USA.gif

Pollack, D., & Rosman, E. (2012). An introduction to treaties for international social workers. *International Social Work, 55(3), 417–427*

Private prisons profit from illegal immigrants. (2012, August 2). *CBS News.* Retrieved from http://www.cbsnews.com/8301-201_162-57485392/ap -private-prisons-profit-from-illegal-immigrants

Reid v. Covert, 351 U.S. 487 (1957).

Rotabi, K. S., & Bromfield, N. F. (2012). The decline in intercountry adoptions and new practices of global surrogacy: Global exploitation and human rights concerns. *Affilia, 27*, 129–141. doi: 10.1177/0886100912444102

Tran, M. (2013, April 3). Aid from rich countries falls for second year in a row, says OECD. *The Guardian.* Retrieved from http://www.guardian.co.uk/global -development/2013/apr/03/aid-rich-countries-falls-oecd

UN condemns Australia's indefinite detention of refugees as "inhumane." (2013, August 22). *The Guardian.* Retrieved from http://www.theguardian.com

U. N. panel says Israeli settlement policy violates law. *New York Times*. Retrieved
   from http://www.nytimes.com/2013/02/01/world/middleeast/un-panel-says
   -israeli-settlement-policy-violates-law.html?_r=0

UNESCO. (2011). *Adult and youth literacy.* Retrieved from http://www.uis.
   unesco.org/FactSheets/Documents/FS16-2011-Literacy-EN.pdf

UNICEF. (2009). *Progress for children.* Retrieved from http://www.unicef.org/
   protection/files/Progress_for_Children-No.8_EN_081309(1).pdf

UNICEF. (2011). *Child protection from violence, exploitation, and abuse:
   A statistical snapshot.* Retrieved from http://www.childinfo.org/files/
   ChildProtection__from_violence_exploitation_abuse.pdf

United Nations. (1948). *Universal declaration of human rights.* G. A. Res. 217 A
   (III). Retrieved from http://www.refworld.org/docid/3ae6b3712c.html

United Nations. (1951). *Convention relating to the status of refugees.* G. A. Res. 429
   (V) of 14 December 1950. Retrieved from http://www.ohchr.org/EN
   /ProfessionalInterest/Pages/StatusOfRefugees.aspx

United Nations. (1967). *Protocol relating to the status of refugees.* G. A. Res. 2198
   (XXI) of December 1966. Retrieved from http://www.ohchr.org/EN
   /ProfessionalInterest/Pages/ProtocolStatusOfRefugees.aspx

United Nations. (1979). *Convention on the elimination of all forms of discrimination
   against women,* G.A. Res. 34/180. Retrieved from http://www.ohchr.org
   /Documents/ProfessionalInterest/cedaw.pdf

United Nations. (1984). *Convention against torture and other cruel, inhuman or
   degrading treatment or punishment,* G.A. Res. 39/46. Retrieved from
   http://www.ohchr.org/Documents/ProfessionalInterest/cat.pdf

United Nations. (1989). *Convention on the rights of the child.* G.A. Res. 44/25.
   Retrieved from http://www.ohchr.org/Documents/ProfessionalInterest/crc.pdf

United Nations. (2000a). *Optional protocol to the convention on the rights of the
   child on the sale of children, child prostitution and child pornography,* G. A. Res.
   54/263. Retrieved from http://www.ohchr.org/Documents
   /ProfessionalInterest/crc-sale.pdf

United Nations. (2000b). *Optional protocol to the convention on the rights of
   the child on the involvement of children in armed conflict,* G. A. Res. 54/263.
   Retrieved from http://www.ohchr.org/Documents/ProfessionalInterest/crc
   -conflict.pdf

United Nations. (2006). *Convention on the rights of persons with disabilities.* G. A.
   Res. A/RES/61/106. Retrieved from http://www.ohchr.org/EN/HRBodies
   /CRPD/Pages/ConventionRightsPersonsWithDisabilities.aspx

United Nations. (2009a). *About the convention*. Retrieved from http://www.unifem
.org/cedaw30/about_cedaw/index.html

United Nations. (2009b) *CEDAW success stories*. Retrieved from http://www
.unifem.org/cedaw30/success_stories/

United Nations. (2009c). *Reservations to CEDAW*. Retrieved from http://www
.un.org/womenwatch/daw/cedaw/reservations.htm

United Nations. (2013). *#MDGMomentum*. Retrieved from http://www.un.org
/millenniumgoals

United Nations Office on Drugs and Crime. (2004). *United Nations convention
against transnational organized crime and the protocols thereto.* Retrieved from
http://www.unodc.org/documents/treaties/UNTOC/Publications/TOC
%20Convention/TOCebook-e.pdf

United Nations Office on Drugs and Crime. (2013). *United Nations convention
against transnational organized crime and the protocols thereto.* Retrieved from
http://www.unodc.org/documents/treaties/UNTOC/Publications/TOC
%20Convention/TOCebook-e.pdf

United Nations Population Fund (UNFPA). (n.d.). *Technical resources*. Retrieved
from http://www.endfistula.org/public/pid/7433

United States Commission on International Religious Freedom. (2005). *Report on
asylum seekers in expedited removal*. Retrieved from http://www.uscirf.gov/index.
php?option=com_content&task=view&id=1892

U. S. Department of State. (2011). *Trafficking in persons report 2011*. Retrieved
from http://www.state.gov/j/tip/rls/tiprpt/2011/index.htm

U. S. Department of State. (2012). *Trafficking in persons report 2012*. Retrieved
from http://www.state.gov/j/tip/rls/tiprpt/2012/

Wasem, R. E. (2011). Asylum and "credible fear" issues in U.S. immigration
policy. *Congressional Research Service*. Retrieved from *www.fas.org/sgp/crs
/homesec/R41753.pdf*

Endnotes

1   See Healy (2008) and Pollack and Rosman (2012) for introductions to such human
rights documents. The Office of the High Commissioner for Human Rights maintains
an updated collection of treaties, country reports (concluding observations on country progress toward human rights realization), and documents of the Human Rights
Council that set human rights standards (see www.ohchr.org).

7 Bringing Human Rights Home in Social Work Education

Kathryn R. Libal and Lynne M. Healy

Where, after all, do universal rights begin? In small places, close to home—so close and so small that they cannot be seen on any maps of the world. Yet they are the world of the individual person; the neighborhood he lives in; the school or college he attends; the factory, farm or office where he works. Such are the places where every man, woman, and child seeks equal justice, equal opportunity, equal dignity without discrimination. Unless these rights have meaning there, they have little meaning anywhere. Without concerned citizen action to uphold them close to home, we shall look in vain for progress in the larger world.

—Eleanor Roosevelt, "In Our Hands," remarks delivered at the United Nations in New York on March 27, 1958 (United Nations, n.d.)

More than 50 years ago Eleanor Roosevelt recognized what social work educators and practitioners in the United States have begun to understand in recent years: Human rights education and practice are often inherently local efforts, carried out in places "close to home" rather than primarily in terms of advocacy related to issues in other countries. Over the past 15 years the number of social work programs in the United States introducing human rights content has increased (Dewees & Roche, 2001; McPherson & Abel, 2012; Steen & Mathieson, 2005). Responding to growing interest in the field, the Council on Social Work Education (CSWE) included human rights in the 2008 Educational Policy and Accreditation Standards (EPAS), in effect mandating that all BSW and MSW programs achieve an outcome related to human rights (CSWE, 2008). Although the profession of social work has a long history in human rights (Healy, 2008), explicit use of human rights language and curriculum to prepare social workers to join mainstream human rights advocacy is new to many educators, and programs are still searching for best practices in human rights education (Ife, 2008).

In this chapter we argue that human rights education must be linked to students' practice (whether in micro, mezzo, or macro contexts), if it is to play a meaningful role in professional education. In the United States, students should be helped to apply internationally relevant concepts and the principles expressed in globally agreed treaties to national and local social issues and social work practice. We provide a rationale and suggested design for a model course that "brings human rights home." Courses on human rights routinely introduce students to the major international human rights treaties, United Nations (UN) treaty bodies and mechanisms, and sometimes to other aspects of the official human rights machinery such as the work of special rapporteurs on various human rights concerns, the Human Rights Council, and rights-based work in the International Labour Organisation. Courses often highlight specific human rights abuses or problem areas such as human trafficking, child soldiers, female genital mutilation, child marriage or rape as a weapon of war; often, the focus is on atrocities in other countries. In taking this approach, educators may unintentionally reinforce students' tendency to see human rights as other countries' concerns. Such understandings are inadvertently steeped in a legacy of U.S. exceptionalism, which is a widely held view that human rights matters are largely concerns external to the United States and the norms and processes to realize human rights bear little relation to domestic politics, policy making, and social work practice (Libal & Hertel, 2011).

Knowledge of specific human rights principles and processes elaborated in treaties and complaint procedures is essential underpinning for additional learning but, alone or combined with study of human rights atrocities in other countries, does not provide social workers with a solid background for human rights practice.

Rationale for Localizing Human Rights Education in Social Work

Social work is a practice profession and emphasizes the application of knowledge to real life problems. Its members work directly with individuals, groups, communities, and institutions to address social and personal problems and to advocate for more just social structures and conditions. Social work is, therefore, primarily a locally based profession, because most of its members will practice close to home. As Lundy (2006) observed, "social workers are in position to witness social injustice and human rights violations on a daily basis" (p. 121). Expressing surprise that professionals do not regularly use human rights approaches in practice, she states: "Social justice and human rights need to be foundational principles for social work policy and practice in working with individuals, families or communities and a starting point for the profession rather than the end result" (p. 121).

Educators can help students identify human rights as relevant and applicable to their professional roles as social work practitioners and advocates (McPherson & Abel, 2012; Steen, 2012). Otherwise, there is a danger that human rights education will address only the knowledge dimension of the important trilogy of knowledge, values, and skills for practice. This recommendation resonates with those from the United Nations Educational, Scientific and Cultural Organization (UNESCO). In its plan of action for human rights education in higher education, UNESCO encourages identification of "human rights skills and competences" with attention to values and attitudes as well as knowledge and skills. The plan recommends that educators "employ experiential learning methodologies that enable learners to understand and apply human rights concepts to their lives and experiences, including community research and/or service" (UNESCO, 2012, p. 24). Social work authors have recognized this, recommending extensive use of case examples and opportunities for engaging in social action (Berthold, 2015; Gamble & Weil, 2010; Reichert, 2003; United Nations Centre for Human Rights, 1994).

It is important to note that we are not suggesting abandonment of the global elements of human rights education. As other chapters in this volume emphasize, human rights provides a natural link connecting the local and the global, and global advocacy is important to the profession and the advancement of its role in the human rights movement. The model course we describe here includes attention to the global human rights machinery, international as well as domestic cases, key policy statements from the international social work organizations, and attention to issues of refugees and migration that clearly demonstrate the local–global connections.

EPAS as a Partial Guide

The inclusion of human rights in the Preamble and statement of social work values in EPAS is important in advancing human rights education. Of particular note is that human rights is included in one of the 10 competency standards that all professional programs must achieve. Educational Policy Standard 2.1.5 requires all students to be prepared to advocate for enhanced human rights and social justice (CSWE, 2008). It states the following (italics added for emphasis):

> Each person, regardless of position in society, has basic *human rights*, such as freedom, safety, privacy, an adequate standard of living, health care, and education. Social workers recognize the global interconnections of oppression and are knowledgeable about *theories of justice and strategies to promote human and civil rights*. Social work incorporates social justice practices in organizations, institutions, and society to ensure that these *basic human rights* are distributed equitably and without prejudice. Social workers:
> - understand the forms and mechanisms of oppression and discrimination;
> - advocate for human rights and social and economic justice; and
> - engage in practices that advance social and economic justice (CSWE, 2008, p. 5).

Inclusion of this standard is an important step forward. However, as written it illuminates several challenges in teaching human rights in the United States. The standard uses the term "basic human rights" without defining which human rights are "basic." It also refers to "human and civil rights," separating rights into categories rather than reflecting the principle of indivisibility. We applaud the emphasis on advocacy, but hope that future guidelines will also emphasize the applicability of rights-based approaches to all forms of social work practice. These concerns are further addressed in the presentation of a model for a human rights and social work course that follows.

Insights From a Model Course

Building on our experiences in developing and teaching a course titled Human Rights and Social Work, we offer a model for curriculum building and teaching in U.S. social work programs. The example described here is an elective course in an MSW program (Libal & Healy, 2013). It was developed as part of a transdisciplinary movement to bring human rights home, in terms of integrating human rights learning into universities and communities (Anderson, 2003; Armaline, Glasberg, & Purkayastha, 2011; Soohoo, Albisa, & Davis, 2009). We expect infusion of human rights principles to help social workers recognize and address harms and omissions in social policies and to help practitioners enhance the realization of rights for those accessing social services. These efforts have a long history at the host university, and both the school of social work and the university have provided institutional support for developing coursework and creating faculty and student learning environments to gain fluency in the international human rights system.

A core aim of the course is to help students understand that human rights practice takes place at various levels and that as social workers they can be involved in the shaping of rights-based practice regardless of their workplace or community. In the elective, human rights is presented as

- a system of international laws and accountability mechanisms;
- a set of globally agreed standards;
- a perspective to guide social work practice, both micro and macro;
- a conceptual frame to guide development of social and economic policy; and
- a framework for ethical decision-making in concert with professional ethics.

The last three themes are the subject of this chapter. In presenting human rights as a framework and a perspective to guide practice, policy development, and ethical decision-making, human rights is brought "home." It is further localized to the U.S. context by using human rights examples from the United States (in our case) and in requiring students to adapt and apply human rights treaties to local practice and policy issues.

Balancing Local and Global in Course Design

One past survey of curricula in the United States revealed that specialized courses on human rights are not commonly offered (Steen & Mathieson, 2005) but are growing in number as social work educators become more familiar with human rights. In the case described in this chapter, a number of supportive factors led to the development and approval of a specialized course on human rights. These included a longstanding commitment to an international perspective and content; faculty interest and expertise; and an active human rights focus at the university level. Over almost two decades the University of Connecticut has been building human rights programs based on conferences, research groups, undergraduate and graduate courses, certificates, an undergraduate major, and hosting visiting scholars. The School of Social Work has participated in many of these efforts and has sponsored several conferences and seminars on human rights dating back to at least 2002. Thus, the environment for introducing a new course was a supportive one.

The course provides theoretical, conceptual, and practical foundation for social workers to engage in human rights-based social work practice. Students gain an understanding of the international human rights system, social work's contribution to achieving human rights within the United States and in an international social work context, and how international human rights principles can be applied to practice. We have found that the course offers both a bridge between global and local realms as well as between micro and macro conceptualizations of practice. In course evaluations students have briefly encapsulated the relevance of the course in terms of their own practice:

- "Human rights is the umbrella for all that I do as a community organizer."
- "As a case worker it is very easy to get tunnel vision. I want to see the bigger picture."
- "It is our obligation—people in poverty don't know their rights."
- "I work in disabilities; human rights are talked about but not adhered to."

Although these statements may seem obvious, ongoing dialogue, reflection, and engagement in local human rights concerns demonstrate that students can readily make connections between human rights ideas and ideals and social work practice.

Course objectives state that students will develop a good familiarity with human rights bodies, mechanisms, and treaty content. This means fostering critical engagement with how human rights treaties operate in international law and the strengths and weaknesses of the treaty-monitoring process for inculcating human rights at local, national, and international levels. We aim for students to gain an understanding of key concepts in human rights, such as civil, political, social, economic, and cultural rights; the indivisibility and interdependence of rights; cultural relativism versus universalism; rights and/versus responsibilities, the public/private divide in human rights debates; and the idea of U.S. exceptionalism. By the end of the course students should be familiar with the major United Nations human rights treaties and the work of the Office of the High Commissioner for Human Rights, as well as other human rights processes that are carried out through the Human Rights Council, particularly through special rapporteurs on particular human rights issues. We also seek to foster student understanding of how civil society (including social work organizations) plays a critical role in the realization of human rights through grassroots education, advocacy, and shadow reporting processes at the United Nations.

More directly linked to social work in the United States, the course helps students develop a basic awareness of human rights and how such rights relate to social work policies and practices, including an understanding of social work as a human rights profession. The course enhances students' ability to discern ways social work can contribute to the achievement of human rights domestically and internationally; to examine how international human rights principles can be applied to social work practice and ethical dilemmas that may arise from such efforts; and to be active social work professionals advocating for the realization of human rights domestically and internationally.

Course outcomes are conveyed in competency-oriented language, although as an elective it meets the EPAS standards on human rights and social and economic justice only for self-selected students. We note that development of the elective has had a spread effect in encouraging infusion of human rights content in other parts of the curriculum, especially our required course Human Oppression and Social Policy Analysis. Course outcomes are linked to specific assignments and reflect the overarching goal to familiarize students with rights-based practice. These outcomes are as follows:

- Be able to define and discuss core human rights concepts
- Demonstrate through class discussions and a course paper a beginning understanding of core human rights treaties and the UN human rights system and practices as they apply domestically and internationally
- Demonstrate in the course assignments the ability to locate and use key human rights resources
- Demonstrate the use of a human rights framework to analyze a key social problem or vulnerability that women, children, immigrants and refugees, and other severely disadvantaged groups face
- Apply a human rights based approach to social work practice through discussions and a final paper on their social work practice
- Be able to identify for social work action human rights issues domestically and internationally

The course has been taught in a workshop format, which is commonly employed at our school. The course meets 1 day a month for an 8-hour session throughout the semester. Students prepare readings and assignments in advance of each session and in class engage course content through a variety of learning processes, including lectures related to formal human rights concepts and treaty mechanisms, discussions of readings focusing on application of ideas to social work settings, viewing film clips, analyzing case exercises, and learning from guest lecturers who are often practitioners in either local or international contexts. The format has been helpful in facilitating in-depth discussion, but could certainly be modified to a more traditional weekly model or even to modules for other courses.

Curriculum Design and Teaching Methodologies

As previously noted, the course interweaves attention to global and domestic human rights movements and issues, with a particular focus on consideration and application of international norms and practices within the United States generally and in our state in particular. Curricular materials are now quite rich within social work (Hokenstad, Healy, & Segal, 2013; Ife, 2008; Mapp, 2014; Reichert, 2003, 2006; Wronka, 2008), and relevant human rights documentation is readily available through the UN Office of the High Commissioner for Human Rights and numerous human rights organizations, governmental websites, and educational institutions and professional associations. For the course we draw on a range of sources, including primary human rights documentation from the United Nations (treaties, general recommendations or comments, findings from individual complaints mechanisms, etc.), human rights organizations (see especially the rich corpus of reports on human rights issues in the United States that is produced by Human Rights Watch), and treaty monitoring reporting by governments and civil society organizations who are engaged in shadow reporting. We also draw extensively on social work scholarship, which is increasing yearly, balancing attention to the United States and other countries' human rights and social work concerns.

The first session provides an overview on human rights, including the formation of the United Nations system that includes treaty and charter mechanisms and an overview of social, economic, cultural, civil, and political rights through the Universal Declaration of Human Rights (United Nations, 1948), International Covenant on Civil and Political Rights (United Nations, 1966a), and International Covenant on Economic, Social and Cultural Rights (United

Nations, 1966b). Students are introduced to social work involvement in the formation and application of human rights practices through readings, lecture, and discussion. During the first session we also introduce students to the idea of U.S. exceptionalism—or the limited participation of the U.S. government in the international system and the reasons for lack of familiarity on the part of the vast majority of U.S. citizens (and social workers) with formal human rights processes (Hertel & Libal, 2011).

In the remaining sessions we attempt to balance discussion of international and domestic cases that illustrate human rights mobilization and practice; key controversies or dilemmas in domestic and international use of human rights; and above all, encourage students to seek information to inform rights-based policy making, organizing, or direct practice. We familiarize students with a range of human rights documentation that elaborates the content and meaning of human rights treaties, including general comments, documents of the special rapporteurs of the Human Rights Council, and country reports and concluding observations of treaty body committees, and shadow or alternative reports of civil society organizations.

Topics include human rights, values, and social work ethics; universalism and cultural relativism as it relates to social work ethics; adapting social and economic rights mobilization tactics from other countries to local and state initiatives in the United States; women's and children's human rights; rights-based frameworks for challenging structural racism and social inequality; and rights of immigrants, asylum-seekers and refugees. Throughout there is a focus on what rights-based practice may mean regardless of type of agency or job that a social worker may fill.

A key theme throughout the course is the meaning of social and economic rights, particularly because addressing poverty and social inequality have been dominant questions in the U.S. profession throughout its history. This has been identified in previous social work scholarship as a key arena for social work engagement, particularly in terms of building an understanding of and capacity to promote social and economic justice (Reichert, 2006; Staub-Bernasconi, 2007). Thus, throughout the course we challenge students to consider value-based questions of social policy. For example, why does the

United States formally recognize a right to education, particularly at the state level, but not a right to health care, adequate housing, or food? Students critique related policy statements from *Social Work Speaks* (National Association of Social Workers, 2012a) regarding health care, housing, food, poverty, as well as women's issues, child welfare, and teen pregnancy using a human rights lens. Students compare and contrast framing in *Social Work Speaks* policy statements with rights-based analyses assigned as class readings. For children's rights, for example, they consider Libal, Mapp, Ihrig, and Ron (2011), Lewis (2011), and Link (2007). They also examine the International Policy on Human Rights (National Association of Social Workers, 2012b) and debate the extent to which that statement engages domestic human rights concerns.

Racism is another key topic for bringing human rights into the domestic context. How does racism at structural and interpersonal levels contribute to the violation of the rights of persons of color within the United States, in particular disproportionate experiences of poverty (New York City CERD Working Group, 2007; UN United Nations Committee on the Elimination of Racial Discrimination, 2008)? We underscore the importance of covering the Convention on the Elimination of All Forms of Racial Discrimination (CERD), one of the few core treaties ratified by the United States, in achieving our objective of bringing human rights home. Wronka (2008) cites the importance of using the U.S. self-report on CERD as a teaching tool. In its 2013 report the government acknowledges that "the path toward racial equality has been uneven, racial and ethnic discrimination still persists, and much work remains to meet our goal of ensuring equality for all" (United States Department of State, 2013, para. 2). Students are often surprised to see the government acknowledge failures to overcome structural racism, to see the range of issues addressed in the government report, and discuss the relevance of tackling racism through a human rights lens.

Another important way in which we bring home human rights in our social work classroom is to highlight the ongoing social mobilization in communities and states that draws on human rights-based approaches. These include efforts such as the Philadelphia-based organization Witnesses to Hunger, which uses an explicit right to food framework (Chilton, Rabinowich, Council, &

Breaux, 2009; Chilton & Rose, 2009), and the work of New York University's International Human Rights Clinic (2013), which published the first comprehensive human rights report on the right to food in the United States. Using this approach, paired with the documentary *A Place at the Table*, students participate in a class exercise to develop a rights-based advocacy campaign to secure the right to adequate food for the nearly 15% of U.S. residents who are food insecure. Related to health, students consider the Vermont Worker's Center's Healthcare Is a Human Right Campaign. Launched in early 2008, the campaign resulted in the adoption of an act that leads to a single-payer universal insurance plan based on human rights principles (McGill, 2012; Rudiger, 2011). A major shadow report facilitated by the Urban Justice Center in New York provides an opportunity to consider how legal advocates and social justice activists (including community-based social workers) have partnered to draw attention to a variety of forms of structural racism as a human rights concern in New York City (New York City CERD Working Group, 2007). Drawing student attention to shadow reporting processes by nongovernmental organizations provides insights into how they could participate in such efforts at varying levels (e.g., Libal & Harding, 2015).

Bringing Human Rights Home in Student Practice

After being introduced to major human rights principles, processes, and examples of rights-based mobilization, students are ready to apply their knowledge. The final project requires students to apply what they have learned about global human rights mechanisms and ideas to a policy issue in Connecticut or to develop a rights-based analysis of a practice case in their own work or field placement. Practice assignments are strongly encouraged. Topics have ranged widely and have addressed matters deeply familiar to the profession. A sampling of such topics includes the following:

- Criminalization of mental illness
- DREAM Act at state and federal levels
- Access to health care for transgendered persons
- Reproductive rights of girls in state care

- The right to marry regardless of sexual orientation
- Developing supports for adolescents aging out of foster care
- Overrepresentation of minorities in child protection services
- Access to health care for patients on Medicare
- Felon disenfranchisement
- Supplemental Nutrition Assistance Program and adequacy of benefits through a human rights lens
- Food insecurity and children's rights in Connecticut
- Educational disparities and the achievement gap for children in foster care
- Challenging indiscriminate use of psychotropic drugs within inpatient settings
- Homelessness as a human rights concern in Hartford, CT
- Building a rights-based movement to end gender-based violence
- The right of the child to participate in child protection processes

Overwhelmingly, students have chosen topics that address the interdependence of rights, with a majority of projects substantially focusing on economic and social rights issues.

One of the challenges of teaching this course has been to illustrate the relevance and applicability of rights-based work regardless of method or concentration. In our program students gain advanced practice skills in one of five methods: casework, group work, administration, policy practice, and community organization. Although approximately two thirds of students in our MSW program are case work or group work students, they have comprised about half of those enrolled in the elective. To ensure broad relevance to social work, we incorporate direct service discussion cases in class and ensure attention to both micro and macro practice throughout the course. The final assignment, dealing with how human rights ideas relate to practice, regardless of agency setting or type of social work one does, has been a crucial part of the success of the course.

Some of the richest analyses have come from our casework and group work students, who analyzed particular incidents or practices in their work settings through a rights-based lens. One student came to recognize that the entrenched processes of removing children from their families for physical neglect and racial disproportionality in these processes must be understood through a human rights lens. Another student grappled with the realization that although inpatient treatment centers for mental illness may espouse a patient's bill of rights, actual treatment sometimes followed a business model over a patient-centered model. Students identified ways they could seek allies within their organizations to begin reexamining whether chemical restraints are used in patients' best interest. Finally, one student placed in a school field setting examined the ordinary practice of sending children to so-called screaming rooms to address behavioral concerns in the classroom. Applying principles from the Convention on the Rights of the Child (United Nations, 1989), the student highlighted how such practices violated the child's right to education, safety, and security, and the obligation of school officials to find other means to address disruption in the classrooms that adhered to norms of social inclusion and nonhumiliating treatment.

Policy practice and community organizing students have applied rights-based lenses to issues across the human rights spectrum, including, for example, examining models of rights-based advocacy to end punitive policies that result in the expulsion or criminalization of children for truancy or other minor infractions in schools (see the Dignity in Schools Campaign, 2011, which uses an explicit human rights frame); opposing felon disenfranchisement (following with American Civil Liberties Union and Human Rights Watch campaigns that use a human rights lens); and reframing access to supportive housing services as a human rights concern.

Although students have very astutely made links with relevant human rights standards and practices, one area of concern for some has been how to bridge the gap between their knowledge and understanding of human rights and social justice and that of social work practitioners, community leaders, and politicians with whom they may interact on a given campaign. As the instructors for the course, we have begun to incorporate dialogue on how to move understandings to action much earlier in future courses. The model outlined by Barbera (see Chapter 14), which includes action projects spanning two semesters, may offer a stronger opportunity for such rich engagement, reflection, and support of rights-based social work practice.

Educational Challenges

Dewees and Roche (2001) identified three challenges for U.S. educators in teaching human rights: the principle of indivisibility and lack of recognition of economic and social rights (or, as we have discussed it, U.S. exceptionalism); the tension between universalism in human rights and social work focus on multiculturalism; and "the political action implications of human rights analyses" (p. 141). We identify a number of additional challenges: student frustration and disillusionment with the official human rights system; addressing controversial and sensitive issues; ensuring respect for human rights within the classroom; and the need to help students identify a way to move forward with their concerns.

After introduction to the treaties and examination of human rights abuses across the world, some students express frustration with the international human rights regime. They question whether the treaties and perhaps even the concept of rights are useful when mechanisms for enforcement are limited and egregious violations so common. These reactions may be reinforced by presumptions of U.S. superiority and resistance to participation in the international human rights regime. Several teaching strategies can be helpful: using positive examples of how some countries are using the moral force of the documents and processes to improve their own policies, practices, and institutions (such as advancements made in child welfare systems in many countries in response to the Convention on the Rights of the Child [United Nations, 1989]); presenting the treaties as remarkable achievements in negotiating globally approved language on so many principles important to social work; and emphasizing the positive aspects of participation in the global system to effect change. As others have described it, human rights "offers a powerful, unsettling, and hopeful message to students" (Dewees & Roche, p. 152). Wronka (2008), acknowledging the difficult nature of human rights content, stresses the importance of optimism and hope. He encourages educators to instill in students that "despite setbacks, it is of absolute importance to keep a pathological belief in the impossible and the vision of hope that human rights/social justice work entails" (p. 265).

Teaching human rights to groups of students who come from diverse cultures and hold different religious and family values can cause discomfort and even conflict in the classroom. Some students will express personal feelings of guilt—perhaps about everyday behaviors such as purchasing shoes made by child labor—or discomfort in wrestling with tensions between cultural relativism and universal rights. Veterans and other students may have negative reactions to examination of U.S. violations of human rights, such as a discussion of treatment of prisoners at Guantanamo. We used the book *Asylum Denied* (Kenney & Schrag, 2008) to illustrate the interconnections of global and domestic issues, in this case with the asylum-seeking process endured by a Kenyan man trying to get asylum in the United States. The book details a torturous process of bureaucratic delays, administrative arrogance, and injustice by State Department and court officials. It was difficult for many students to face the human rights violations committed by their own government described in the book. There is no way to teach human rights without addressing difficult and controversial topics. What is essential is building a culture of mutual respect in the classroom to ensure that students can engage with the content and express their ideas and concerns without fear of being labeled or ostracized—in other words, to create a human rights culture in the classroom (Wronka, 2008).

Finally, as students identify human rights concerns in their field placement or employment agencies and their own social work practice, they may need support and guidance in moving forward. Human rights advocacy is not easy, and it is often not popular (Morgaine, 2009). For example, which steps can students who work in large bureaucratic systems take to carry out rights-based practice? How can one proceed when rights-based approaches challenge long-accepted norms in agencies of any size (Lewis, 2011)? Which risks are inherent in human rights work in various contexts (United Nations Centre for Human Rights, 1994)? Educators can use discussion case vignettes to involve students in working groups to identify opportunities and risks in various courses of action and generate ideas for feasible interventions. It is important to ground the discussion in real-world practice and help students consider "the variety of responses that they would expect to receive, or have already received, in response to their promotion of human rights" and identify supports they may need to continue these efforts in their future professional roles (Dewees & Roche, 2001, p. 151).

Conclusion

Our experience in teaching a course dedicated to human rights is that students are able to appreciate the potential contribution of a rights-based approach to social work and to begin to apply this to practice situations. Over the semester, most students move from excitement over discovering the world of human rights treaties and machinery, to discouragement over the inherent failures of compliance, to renewed enthusiasm for the possibilities of a human rights orientation. The tendency of some students to become disillusioned or overly cynical can be tempered by stressing throughout the semester that human rights are a work in progress that requires ongoing engagement at many levels. This progression is also aided by devoting significant attention to domestic human rights issues and to connections to social work practice and advocacy roles. Through these efforts human rights are brought home to social work in the United States.

We recognize that the model of a specialized course, especially an elective, may have limited effects on shaping social work practice because it can reach only a modest number of students. Infusion of human rights content across the curriculum may be preferable, but this approach presents a new set of challenges for curriculum design and teaching. Comprehensive infusion requires faculty buy-in, and faculty, too, are products of U.S. exceptionalism. Merry and Shimmin (2011) note that Americans, even progressives, are skeptical about "the power of human rights language to move domestic audiences" and question whether there is value added by adoption of human rights approaches (p. 128). Infusion models are likely to require faculty development efforts to familiarize instructors with the human rights literature and essential concepts relevant to their courses. These would follow careful curriculum planning to locate appropriate elements of human rights education in selected foundation courses and develop assessment tools to evaluate student learning across the curriculum.

It will be helpful if the next draft of EPAS provides guidelines to strengthen curriculum for human rights in social work practice. Inclusion of human rights in the 2008 version was an important step forward. However, in this edition of EPAS human rights is tied to advocacy, suggesting a narrow role for human rights learning and perhaps a single curriculum location for human rights content. Optimally, as presented earlier, human rights is accepted as a relevant practice orientation for micro and macro practice, a conceptual frame for the development and analysis of social policy, and a guide for ethical decision-making in concert with codes of professional ethics. Further, it locates U.S. social work within the global profession and social work within the global interdisciplinary movement for human rights.

A final recommendation is for follow-up research to assess whether the model course has had the hoped-for effects on practice. Judging by performance on course assignments, we are confident that students were able to apply global concepts to their own practice and domestic policy issues. To determine whether the in-class learning is applied after graduation, and if so, whether a rights-based orientation makes a difference, will require further study.

References

Anderson, C. (2003). *Eyes off the prize: The United Nations and the African American struggle for human rights (1944–1955).* New York, NY: Cambridge University Press.

Armaline, W. T., Glasberg, D. S., & Purkayastha, B. (Eds.) (2011). *Human rights in our own backyard: Injustice and resistance in the United States.* Philadelphia, PA: University of Pennsylvania Press.

Berthold, S. M. (2015). *Human rights-based approaches to clinical social work.* New York, NY: Springer.

Chilton, M., Rabinowich, J., Council, C., & Breaux, J. (2009). Witnesses to Hunger: Participation through Photovoice to ensure the right to food." *Health and Human Rights, 11*(1), 73–85.

Chilton, M., & Rose, D. (2009). A rights-based approach to food insecurity in the United States. *American Journal of Public Health, 99*(7), 1203–1211.

Council on Social Work Education. (2008), *Educational policy and accreditation standards.* Alexandria, VA: Author.

Dewees, M., & Roche, S. E. (2001). Teaching about human rights in social work. *Journal of Teaching in Social Work, 21*(1/2), 137–155.

Dignity in Schools Campaign. (2011). National Week of Action on School Pushout, October 4–11, 2014. Retrieved from http://www.dignityinschools.org/

Gamble, D. N., & Weil, M. (2010). *Community practice skills: Local to global perspectives.* New York, NY: Columbia University Press.

Healy, L. (2008). Exploring the history of social work as a human rights profession. *International Social Work, 51*(6), 735–748.

Hertel, S., & Libal, K. (2011). *Human rights in the United States: Beyond exceptionalism.* New York, NY: Cambridge University Press.

Hokenstad, T., Healy, L., & Segal, U. A. (Eds.) (2013). *Teaching human rights: Curriculum resources for social work educators.* Alexandria, VA: CSWE Press.

Ife, J. (2008). *Human rights and social work: Towards rights-based practice* [Revised ed.]. Cambridge, UK: Cambridge University Press.

International Human Rights Clinic. (2013). *Nourishing change: Fulfilling the right to food in the United States.* New York, NY: New York University School of Law.

Kenney, D. N., & Schrag, P. G. (2008). *Asylum denied: A refugee's struggle for safety in America.* Berkeley, CA: University of California Press.

Lewis, M. (2011). The human rights of children in conflict with the law: Lessons for the US human rights movement. In S. Hertel & K. Libal (Eds.), *Human rights in the United States: Beyond exceptionalism* (pp. 255–273). New York, NY: Cambridge University Press.

Libal, K. R., & Harding, S. (2015). *Human rights-based approaches to community practice in the United States.* New York, NY: Springer Publications.

Libal, K., & Healy, L. M. (2013). Human rights and social work. In M. C. Hokenstad, L. M. Healy, & U. A. Segal (Eds.), *Teaching human rights: Curriculum resources for social work educators.* Alexandria, VA: CSWE Press.

Libal, K., & Hertel, S. (2011). Paradoxes and possibilities: Domestic human rights policy in context. In S. Hertel & K. Libal (Eds.), *Human rights in the United States: Beyond exceptionalism* (pp. 1–22). New York, NY: Cambridge University Press.

Libal, K., Mapp, S.A., Ihrig, E., & Ron, A.V. (2011). The Convention on the Rights of the Child: Children can wait no longer for their rights. [Commentary] *Social Work, 56*(4), 367–370.

Link, R. (2007). Children's rights as a template for social work practice. In E. Reichert (Ed.), *Challenges in human rights: A social work perspective* (pp. 215–238). New York, NY: Columbia University Press.

Lundy, C. (2006) Social work's commitment to social and economic justice: A challenge to the profession. In N. Hall (Ed.), *Social work: Making a world of difference* (pp. 115–128). Berne, Switzerland: IFSW and Fafo.

Mapp, S. C. (2014). *Human rights and social justice in a global perspective: An introduction to international social work* (2nd ed.). New York, NY: Oxford University Press.

McGill, M. (2012). Human rights from the grassroots up: Vermont's campaign for universal healthcare. *Health and Human Rights: An International Journal, 14*(1), 106–117.

McPherson, J., & Abel, N. (2012). Human rights engagement and exposure: New scales to challenge social work education. *Research on Social Work Practice, 22*(6), 704–713. doi: 10.1177/1049731512454196.

Merry, S. E., & Shimmin, J. (2011). Domestic violence and human rights in the United States. In S. Hertel & K. Libal (Eds.), *Human rights in the United States: Beyond exceptionalism* (pp.113–131). New York, NY: Cambridge University Press.

Morgaine, K. (2009). "'How would that help our work?' The intersection of domestic violence and human rights in the United States." *Violence Against Women, 17*(1), 6–27.

National Association of Social Workers. (2012a). *Social work speaks* (9th ed.). Washington, DC: NASW Press.

National Association of Social Workers. (2012b). International policy on human rights. In *Social work speaks* (9th ed.). Washington, DC: NASW Press.

New York City CERD Working Group. (2007). *Race realities in New York City: A NYC CERD shadow report.* New York, NY: Urban Justice Center.

Reichert, E. (2003). *Social work and human rights: A foundation for policy and practice.* New York, NY: Columbia University Press.

Reichert, E. (2006). *Understanding human rights: An exercise book.* Thousand Oaks, CA: SAGE Publications.

Rudiger, A. (2011, November 6). Reviving progressive activism: How a human rights movement won the country's first universal health care law. *New Politics.*

Retrieved from http://newpol.org/content/reviving-progressive-activism-how-human-rights-movement-won-country%E2%80%99s-first-universal-health

Soohoo, C., Albisa, C., & Davis, M. F. (Eds.). (2009). *Bringing human rights home: A history of human rights in the United States* (Abridged ed.). Philadelphia, PA: University of Pennsylvania Press.

Staub-Bernasconi, S. (2007). Economic and social rights: The neglected human rights. InE. Reichert (Ed.), *Challenges in human rights: A social work perspective* (pp. 138–161). New York, NY: Columbia University Press.

Steen, J. A. (2012). The human rights philosophy as a values framework for the human behavior course: Integration of human rights concepts in the person-in environment perspective. *Journal of Human Behavior in the Social Environment, 22*(7), 853–862.

Steen, J. A., & Mathiesen, S. (2005). Human rights education: Is social work behind the curve? *Journal of Teaching in Social Work, 25*(3/4), 143–156.

United Nations. (n.d.). *Human rights for all.* Retrieved from http://www.un.org/en/globalissues/briefingpapers/humanrights/quotes.shtml

United Nations. (1989, November 20). Convention on the rights of the child. G.A. Res. 44/25. Retrieved from http://www.ohchr.org/Documents/ProfessionalInterest/crc.pdf

United Nations Centre for Human Rights. (1994). *Human rights and social work: A manual for schools of social work and the social work profession.* Geneva, Switzerland: United Nations Centre for Human Rights with IASSW and IFSW.

United Nations. (1948, December 10). Universal declaration of human rights. G.A. Res. 217 A (III). Retrieved from http://www.refworld.org/docid/3ae6b3712c.html

United Nations. (1966a, December 16). International covenant on civil and political rights, G.A. Res. 2200A (XXI). Retrieved from http://www.ohchr.org/Documents/ProfessionalInterest/ccpr.pdf

United Nations. (1966b, December 16). International covenant on economic, social, and cultural rights, G.A. Res. 2200A (XXI). Retrieved from http://www.ohchr.org/EN/ProfessionalInterest/Pages/CESCR.aspx

United Nations Committee on the Elimination of Racial Discrimination (UN CERD). (2008, May 8). Consideration of reports submitted by states parties under Article 9 of the Convention, Concluding observations of the Committee on the Elimination of Racial Discrimination: United States of America. CERD/C/USA/CO/6. Retrieved from http://www.refworld.org/docid/4885cfa70.html

UNESCO. (2012). *World programme for human rights education: Second phase plan of action.* Retrieved from www.unesco.org

United States Department of State. (2013, June 12). *Periodic report of the United States of America to the United Nations Committee on the Elimination of Racial Discrimination concerning the International Convention on the Elimination of All Forms of Racial Discrimination.* Retrieved from http://www.ushrnetwork.org /sites/ushrnetwork.org/files/periodic_icerd_report_of_the_usg_2013.pdf

Wronka, J. (2008). *Human rights and social justice: Social action and service for the helping and health professions.* Thousand Oaks, CA: SAGE Publications.

8 Teaching the Use of Complaint Mechanisms of UN Treaty Bodies as a Tool in International Social Work Practice

Nivedita Prasad

Historically speaking, there has been some debate about whether social work is a human rights profession, even though social work pioneers such as Jane Addams, Alice Salomon, and Eglantine Jebb left no doubt that their understanding of social work was very clearly linked to social justice and human rights (Healy, 2008). But in the last two decades there has been a mutual understanding within the profession on the international level that social work is certainly one of the human rights professions. This understanding is growing outside the profession as well. For example, *Régis Brillat,* head of the Department of the European Social Charter, asserted that "social workers are human rights workers" during the 2013 European Network for Social Action (ENSACT) conference.

On the national level, in Germany the topic of social workers as human rights workers is still debated. Silvia Staub-Bernasconi, a Swiss professor, initiated the German master's program, Social Work as a Human Rights Profession, in 2002. In the meantime an internationalization of the program in cooperation with the following universities is in preparation:

- Alice Salomon University of Applied Sciences, Berlin
- Centrum for Post Gradual Studies of Social Work, Berlin
- Coburg University of Applied Sciences and Arts
- Ilia State University, Georgia
- Malmö University, Department of Social Work
- University of Gothenburg, Department of Social Work

- University of Ljubljana, Department for Social Justice and Inclusion
- University of Strathclyde, School of Applied Social Sciences

The German master's program translates "the often very abstract and appellative discourse on human rights into the theory and practice of social work" (Alice Salomon University of Applied Sciences [ASH], 2013, p. 4):

> *The main aim* is the development of a general *professional self-conception* based on the *"triple mandate of social work,"* meaning that the universally known "double mandate of social work" on behalf of the addressees and the society/providers is complemented by a third mandate on behalf of the profession: this consists of science-based theories of action, intervention as well as the principles of the professions code of ethics. (emphases added, p. 6)

The Importance of Documents of the International Association of Schools of Social Work (IASSW) and the International Federation of Social Workers (IFSW)

Unfortunately, the German Association of Social Workers has not yet been able to formulate a national code of ethics, leaving students and social workers in a profession without a national code of reference. For an understanding of social work as an ethically reflected human rights profession, the following documents are therefore of major importance for social work students and social workers (in Germany):

1) The United Nations Centre for Human Rights (1994): *Human Rights and Social Work*
2) IFSW and IASSW (2000): *Definition of Social Work*
3) IFSW and IASSW (2004a): *Ethics in Social Work*
4) IFSW and IASSW (2004b): *Global Standards for the Education and Training of the Social Work Profession*
5) IFSW European Region (2010): *Standards in Social Work Practice Meeting Human Rights*

6) IFSW, IASSW, and the International Council on Social Welfare
[ICSW] (2012): *Global Agenda*

All of these documents leave no doubt that human rights is a core issue of
the social work profession; they

> introduce human rights as a central regulatory concept for training and
> practice ... however, the demands which resulted from these documents are
> still far from being common knowledge in the 'scientific and professional
> community' let alone implemented. Wherever they have actually been
> adopted and integrated into education and training, this is being done in
> very diverse ways. (ASH et al., 2013, p. 4f)

The German master's program encourages students to use these documents in everyday social work practice as a source of ethical reference, when
employers and/or state institutions ask them to provide services that are not in
the mandate of social work (for example, the surveillance of the departure of
migrants, the ethically problematic practice of collecting data on the ethnicity
of drug consumers, or requests for information from immigration authorities
to make it easier to deport service users).

To support our graduates in their social work practice, since 2011 they have
received certificates with their diplomas stating that "the graduate has voluntarily committed her/himself to work according to the International Code
of Ethics of the IASSW/IFSW" (IFSW & IASSW, 2004a). We will evaluate
in the future whether this supplement is helpful in practice. There was some
anxiety that employers might even avoid hiring people who remind them that
they might refuse services for ethical reasons. The Swiss Association of Social
Workers (Avenir Social) goes a step farther. Since 2013 they have sent their
members certificates containing a reference to the national code of ethics. It
asks them to commit themselves to perform services in reference to the code of
ethics and to consider displaying the certificate in their workplaces.

In addition to the above mentioned documents, a core body of social work
literature (Healy, 2008; Healy & Link, 2011; Ife, 2001; Reichert, 2003, 2007;

Staub-Bernasconi, 2009, 2010; Wronka, 2008) provides the basis of a professional understanding of social work as a human rights profession and helps create a professional identity. It is important to move beyond these general principles and statements, however, to teach social work students how to use various human rights mechanisms in their practice. In the remainder of this chapter I focus on the use of complaint mechanisms of United Nations (UN) treaty bodies (or committees) as a means to help students to implement their theoretical and ethical knowledge in everyday practice.

The "Right to Have Rights"

Hannah Arendt's (1951/2009) quote the "right to have rights" (p. 614) is more than 60 years old, but unfortunately still applies to a considerable number of people, some of whom are users of social work services. In countries such as Germany the following groups are systematically excluded from access to justice/state protection or have a very limited access to justice:

- Undocumented migrants
- Unidentified trafficked people
- Unaccompanied minors
- Domestic workers of diplomats
- People on so-called terror lists
- Migrants who have committed serious crimes
- Small children
- People in prisons
- People in psychiatric facilities
- People with severe mental disabilities

In some other countries (e.g., Uganda, Jamaica, Belize, Iran) the same applies to homosexuals, sex workers (e.g., the United States, China, Azerbaijan), and people who are HIV positive (e.g., Ukraine, Namibia).

These groups are not just vulnerable, they are virtually powerless and have few resources enabling them to change their situation on their own. Therefore, they need to rely on services such as those provided by social workers. But if social workers use only the principles and practices of their national legal system, they may have very little to offer. In some cases compliance with the law forbids even serving these groups. In Germany, for example, assisting undocumented migrants in social work practice can end in the criminalization of a social worker, leading some social workers to the conclusion that they cannot assist undocumented migrants. Keeping in mind that social work is a profession with a normative frame of reference, social workers are obliged to assist groups and individuals who "do not have the right to have rights" (Arendt, 1951/2009, p. 614). In such contexts the international human rights framework is crucial to combat the effects of social injustice.

Why Do We Need to Teach How to File Complaints?

If you ask students of social work whose human rights are most violated in Germany, they respond similarly: asylum seekers, undocumented migrants, people with disabilities, and women who have experienced violence. These groups are vulnerable because they historically (individually and structurally) have been discriminated against, their vulnerability is not temporary, and they have very few resources to combat this vulnerability on their own.

An analysis of cases against Germany that have been taken to the United Nations[1] shows that most often it is not people who belong to vulnerable groups who file complaints. Only one individual complaint has been brought against Germany before the Committee of the Convention on the Elimination of All Forms of Discrimination Against Women (CEDAW; UN, 1979) or the Committee of the Convention Against Torture and Other Cruel, Inhuman or Degrading Treatment or Punishment (CAT; UN, 1984). Two complaints have been taken to the committee of the Convention on the Elimination of All Forms of Racial Discrimination (CERD; UN, 1965) and, as of April 2013, 19 complaints were raised to the Human Rights Committee, which is the treaty body of the International Covenant on Civil and Political Rights (ICCPR; UN, 1966). Only three of all these 23 complaints actually deal with issues of vulnerable groups. One deals with racially motivated violence by the police (*Mohamed Musa Gbondo Sama v. Germany*, 2009), one was brought by a migrant woman whose husband had been deported (*Aduhene, Claudia, and*

Agyeman, Daniel v. Germany, 2008), and another was a recent decision from the CERD Committee on the issue of freedom of speech versus impugned speech (*Turkish Union in Berlin/Brandenburg v. Germany*, 2013). All the other cases against Germany filed with UN treaty bodies have been brought by more powerful groups, such as fathers with custody problems, scientologists, or guards of the former East German border.

To file an individual complaint to the UN, the person needs to have significant resources, including knowledge, money, legal representation, and considerable courage. Taking a case to the UN means that one is suing the state. Even though in theory the UN has designed its complaint mechanisms in a way that should enable people whose rights have (allegedly) been abused to complain on their own, in practice, this happens very rarely.[2] Social workers could help fill this representation gap. But to do so, they must possess certain theoretical and practical knowledge to bring these issues to the attention of UN treaty bodies, either with or on behalf of their service users, to achieve not only individual but also structural change.

What Do We Need to Teach?

An overview of existing human rights conventions[3] and their complaint mechanisms is the starting point to get an understanding of the UN human rights protection system. Besides providing insight into the mechanisms, the overview enables students to learn to differentiate between codified human rights and human rights that have been universally expressed but are not yet codified into conventions with complaint mechanisms. Knowledge about a convention includes an overview of opinions of the treaty body about their convention. Committees publish their opinions in general comments or recommendations, in Concluding Observations, and in their jurisprudence.

General Comments/Recommendations

Many conventions were adopted in the 1970s or even earlier; the general comments written by members of the treaty committee ensure that the conventions remain relevant and that the specific content of the human rights norms is interpreted or elaborated. For example, the CEDAW, adopted in 1979, includes no provision against violence against women but many provisions on discrimination against women. The CEDAW committee therefore published two general recommendations, Number 12 and Number 19 (UN Committee on the Elimination of Discrimination Against Women, 1989, 1992), declaring violence against women to be a form of discrimination against women. The Committee stated:

> [T]he Convention in article 1 defines discrimination against women. The definition of discrimination includes gender-based violence, that is, violence that is directed against a woman because she is a woman or that affects women disproportionately. It includes acts that inflict physical, mental or sexual harm or suffering, threats of such acts, coercion and other deprivations of liberty. Gender-based violence may breach specific provisions of the Convention, regardless of whether those provisions expressly mention violence" (UN Committee on the Elimination of Discrimination Against Women, 1992, para. 6).

Thus, the Committee left no doubt that violence against women obviously falls under the scope of the CEDAW, even though it is not mentioned in the initial convention.

Another example is General Comment No. 20, "Non-Discrimination and Social, Economic and Cultural Rights," of the UN Committee for Economic, Social, and Cultural Rights (2009). The International Covenant on Economic, Social and Cultural Rights (ICESCR; UN, 1966b) states in Article 2.2. that state parties to the convention should guarantee that they will not discriminate on the basis of race, color, sex, language, religion, political or other opinion, national or social origin, property, birth, or other status. In General Comment No. 20 the committee declared that sexual orientation is subsumed under "other status," taking a very clear stand that discrimination based on sexual orientation is covered by the ICESCR.

The development of general comments is a transparent process in which treaty bodies regularly ask for contributions from civil society members. Practicing social workers and students of social work are well-suited to contribute to the development of general comments. The German nongovernmental organization (NGO) Ban Ying, for example, has regularly contributed to the development of general comments. It was successful in advocating the UN Committee on the Protection of the Rights of all Migrant Workers and Members of Their Families (hereafter, Committee on Migrant Workers) to address the issue of domestic workers in diplomatic households in its first general comment on migrant domestic workers (UN Committee on Migrant Workers, 2011). This was possible even though Germany has not ratified the migrant workers' rights convention. Such contributions are neither very time-consuming nor do they require any financial resources or a long-term work plan. They require only expertise on the issue on debate. In many cases committees initiate so-called thematic debates on the respective issue; these debates are public events in Geneva, which can be visited by students.

EXERCISE: *Compilation of a Document on Minimum Human Rights Standards*

Students are asked to choose one issue, such as violence against women, poverty, or undocumented migrants, and scan the conventions mentioned above to find out which convention and general comments protect the vulnerable group. This provides students with a human rights frame of reference for one vulnerable group and gives them an idea about how universal human rights have been codified. They also get an idea of which human rights have not (yet) been codified. In a second step students can be encouraged to work out a lobbying plan for the codification of a not-yet codified human right.

Complaint Mechanisms

To understand the different means of accessing the UN protections system, the five complaint mechanisms (shadow reporting, individual complaints to relevant human rights committees, initiating an inquiry procedure, petitioning a UN special rapporteur, and the Universal Periodic Review) are introduced in detail in the master's program. The challenges and benefits of the different mechanisms are discussed, enabling students to decide which complaint mechanism is the most appropriate for a case in a specific country. Shadow reporting and the individual complaint mechanism, the most frequently used methods, are described in more detail in following paragraphs.

Shadow Reporting

Committees regularly survey the implementation of their convention in countries that have ratified it. For this purpose, states must report regularly to the committee, and civil society members have the possibility to write critical reports—so called shadow reports—on deficits in the implementation of the convention. Preparing a shadow report (also called alternative reports) is a very good opportunity to evaluate daily social work practice from a human rights perspective. These reports are also a very good source of grassroots information in other countries, giving an insight into human rights violations.

Concluding Observations

Each UN committee must take equal notice of both country and civil society shadow reports. After having a so-called constructive dialogue with states, the committee publishes concluding observations regarding how the convention has been implemented and recommendations that should contribute to an improvement of the human rights situation. These concluding observation documents give an understanding of the interpretations of the convention. For example, intersexed people advocating for their human rights in Germany were not certain whether the abuses they experienced would be recognized by UN treaty bodies as of form of torture or other cruel, inhuman, or degrading treatment. Intersexuelle Menschen e.V. (Association of Intersex People, 2011) wrote a shadow report to the CAT in 2011. The Committee Against Torture took the information very seriously, which led to four recommendations to the German state regarding the situation of intersex people (UN CAT, 2011). That the committee addressed the concerns in the review of Germany's compliance with the Convention Against Torture shows that coerced "gender corrections" ("surgical and medical alterations") experienced by some intersexed people are a form of torture, inhuman, or degrading treatment (UN Committee Against Torture, 2011, para. 20).

EXERCISE: Monitoring Compliance of Treaty Obligations

Students are asked to work on one country and one UN convention. They are encouraged to collect information from a country different from the one they live in or a country of origin. For the assignment they are asked to investigate whether this country has

1) ratified the convention;
2) submitted a report to the treaty body (if yes, they are asked to review the last state report and discuss three main issues raised there);
3) NGOs who submitted shadow reports (if yes, students examine the last shadow report and mention three main issues of concern); and/or
4) a follow-up program addressing concluding observations of the UN committee.

Preparing contributions to shadow reports can be done during a study program. Research conducted by students can easily be designed to collect information for a shadow report. Academic institutions are entitled to submit information, so students can actually submit a complaint to the UN with information they gathered in the course of their studies. A group of students of the German master's program course Social Work as a Human Rights Profession contributed to a shadow report to the UN Committee on Economic, Social, and Cultural Rights (WSK-Allianz, 2011). They claimed that the German state violated the rights of poor people by not providing them with sufficient minimum social benefits. Their shadow report was based on research done during their studies to find out how people living on state benefits survive. The Committee on Economic, Social, and Cultural Rights took a clear stand on poverty in Germany on behalf of those who drew on state benefits (UN Committee on Economic, Social, and Cultural Rights, 2011, para. 24).

Students who live in a country that has not ratified the respective convention can prepare contributions to shadow reports on other countries, for example, in a class on international social work. Reporting on other countries can help protect civil society members in countries such as Belarus. But such action also runs the risk of neocolonial continuity. Discussing this dilemma in class and finding an ethically sound way of handling it can be very informative for students.

Individual Complaints

Individuals who believe that their rights guaranteed by a UN convention have been or will be violated by a state have the opportunity to complain to the respective UN treaty body. To file a complaint, many requirements must be fulfilled (Bayesfky, 2002; Office of the UN High Commissioner for Human Rights, 2008). A social work study program that teaches students only how to take a complaint to the UN might not be very effective, because it is very unlikely that all future social workers will take complaints to the UN. It is the so-called passive use of jurisprudence, which can be a very powerful resource in social work practice and a very valuable source of knowledge in social work theory. In many cases, a real complaint is not necessary because threatening a state with a complaint to the UN is enough to motivate them to react. This demonstrates that the knowledge of these mechanisms alone can be a very powerful tool in (social work) practice.

Passive use of jurisprudence also means giving students knowledge of cases that are relevant for their everyday work. For many social workers the UN is very far away, with very little practical implication for their daily work. Decisions of UN treaty bodies show the practicability of human rights. Decisions against other states can be used for their own cases, because usually they are typical of international social work. Therefore, they can be used to pressure states and national courts, strengthen argumentation in a similar case, and in the best case even prevent further human rights violations.

Individual complaints filed with UN committees by people belonging to vulnerable groups are cases that deal with issues of relevance in many countries; that is, cases of international social work. For example, in the case *Hudoyberganova v. Uzbekistan*, the UN Human Rights Committee (2004) recognized that denying a woman who wears a headscarf access to university is a clear violation of civil rights under the ICCPR. Banning clothing understood to be Muslim plays a very important role in many European countries and is therefore an issue of relevance for social work with migrants.

Another relevant case for working with migrants is *Mr. Z.B.A.H v. Denmark* (CERD Committee, 1999). Mr. Z.B.A.H, a Tunisian national living and working in Denmark with a permanent visa married to a Danish woman, was denied a loan by a bank because of his nationality. The bank argued that it did not want to risk losing money, because Mr. Z.B.A.H could return to Tunisia without fulfilling the terms of the loan. Mr. Z.B.A.H tried to file a complaint in Denmark but was not successful. The Danish courts held that it is legitimate to differentiate between citizens and noncitizens. For this reason, Mr. Z.B.A.H. took the case to the UN committee monitoring the CERD. The CERD Committee argued that nationality is no guarantee for a loan to be paid back; other criteria, such as having a job, is more likely to ensure that somebody will pay back a loan. The committee further commented that Danes can also leave the country without completing loan repayment. Therefore, the committee came to the conclusion that CERD was violated by Denmark because Denmark was not able to provide Mr. Z.B.A.H with an effective remedy against racism. Even though this decision applied to only one person in one country, it has important implications for addressing racism as a matter of human rights today. This case underscores that although CERD allows states to differentiate between citizens and noncitizens, the decision leaves no doubt that nationality is not an acceptable criterion of differentiation if it is being used only to mask racism.

For social workers who work in shelters for abused women, the cases *Sahde Goekce v. Austria* (UN Committee on the Elimination of Discrimination Against Women, 2007a) and *Fatima Yildirim v. Austria* (UN Committee on the Elimination of Discrimination Against Women, 2007b) can be of great help. The women in these cases experienced extreme domestic violence for years. After leaving their husbands, both women applied for protection orders, which were ignored by the perpetrators. Both women turned to the police asking for their husbands to be detained when they continued to be threatened. The police refused to detain the men, arguing this would be a disproportionate intervention. As a result, the women were killed by their respective husbands. Austrian NGOs decided to take these cases to the CEDAW committee, arguing that the convention had been violated by Austria because not all appropriate measures were taken to protect the right to personal security and life of the two women. The CEDAW committee came to the conclusion that Austria had indeed violated CEDAW, taking a very clear position by stating "the perpetrator's rights cannot supersede women's human rights to life and to physical and mental integrity" (UN Committee on the Elimination of Discrimination Against Women, 2007a, para. 12.1.5). Even though this case was against Austria, all shelters that work with abused women unfortunately had to learn that protection orders can only protect if the perpetrators are willing to obey them. Using this decision in everyday practice would mean pushing police and prosecutors to take all appropriate measures to protect women, which could also mean detaining violent men to save women's lives.

Besides providing remedies for individuals, these decisions can be very help-ful in obtaining structural change, because all decisions also contain a list of recommendations that the committee would like to see implemented to ensure that the human rights abuse will not be repeated in future. In the cases against Austria, the government changed laws and regulations as a result of the com-plaint—a change for which lobby groups had unsuccessfully being lobbying for years. The decision of the CEDAW Committee accelerated these overdue regulations. This case also shows that taking a case to the UN can be more effective than struggling for structural change on the national level.

An overview of the jurisprudence of a committee gives the deepest under-standing of how the convention actually remains alive. The ICCPR, the oldest convention with a complaint mechanism, has dealt with more than 1,500 complaints. Therefore, maintaining an overview of the jurisprudence of the ICCPR committee is not very realistic, but websites such as Bayefsky.com make it easier to look for cases by content. Other conventions such as CEDAW and CERD[4] have rather new complaint mechanisms, making it less difficult to monitor the jurisprudence showing how committees interpret their conven-tions. (For a comprehensive overview of cases of violence against women, see Edwards [2011]. For selected cases from the CAT Committee see UN (2008), and for selected cases from the CERD Committee see UN [2012].)

Strategic Litigation

Strategic litigation (i.e., taking a case to a UN treaty body to obtain structural change for a whole group) is a method that is seldom taught in social work classes. Many international NGOs such as the Open Society Justice Initiative or AIRE International have specialized in strategic litigation, but these organizations are not easily accessible for people whose human rights have been violated. The gap between those whose human rights have been abused and those who want to take these issues to international courts is very wide. Social work could play a key role in the identification of human rights abuses because social workers are regularly in touch with people who are at risk of having their human rights violated. Social workers can also take over the role of translating complicated judicial structures to service users, enabling them to make informed decisions in their cases. Strategic litigation is very time-consuming and people who have the courage to tell their stories for strategic litigation often need support for years; this can be provided by social workers.

Cooperation in cases of strategic litigation can be very challenging, because it requires cooperation between lawyers or large international NGOs, the person whose human rights have been violated, and social workers. These interests often conflict with each other; for example, a lawyer might want to be sure she or he wins the case, whereas the social worker might be interested only in the structural change, and the person affected wants a public apology and/or compensation. Also, it is very difficult to judge at the end whether the litigation was successful, because each party might have a different understanding of success. For example, the German NGO Ban Ying (2003) tried to convince the CEDAW Committee to open an inquiry procedure against Germany, because of that state's treatment of the domestic workers of diplomats. The committee decided not to investigate Germany, so legally speaking this case was lost. Practically speaking, this complaint was very successful because the German government, pushed by the threat of a UN committee investigation, fulfilled most of the demands of the NGO before CEDAW even published its decision, improving the working situation of all (legal) domestic workers of diplomats.

Success in other cases might mean giving a service user a realistic opportunity to send her or his experiences to the UN in the form of a complaint. A social worker can even file a complaint knowing that the case will be lost but still decide to do so to bring an issue to the attention of the human rights community or for the personal satisfaction of a service user. Preparing students for strategic litigation from a social work perspective is a challenge in social work education that needs to be elaborated further.

Decisions Clarify Misconceptions

Besides providing individual remedies and suggestions for structural change, UN jurisprudence is also very helpful in clarifying misconceptions and giving practical explanations of what basic principles of human rights actually mean. A state that argues that human rights can only be violated by a state authority will have to take notice of the fact that treaty bodies such as the CEDAW Committee have held states responsible for acts committed by individuals because the state did not protect people in their premises or did not provide effective remedies (e.g., in the previously mentioned cases against Austria and Denmark).

The most recent case against Germany concerns balancing freedom of speech versus dissemination of racist ideology (UN Committee on the Elimination of Racism, 2013). This case was taken up by the Turkish Union in Berlin-Brandenburg (TBB), which is the largest NGO representing Turkish migrants in Germany. The TBB complained to the CERD Committee that a very prominent German politician was spreading racist ideas about Turks and other minorities. People who tried to prosecute the speaker for hate speech were not successful, because the German judiciary declared these statements to be covered by freedom of speech. The CERD Committee reminded the German judiciary that freedom of speech is there to protect people against states and not to protect people who disseminate racist ideology.

Using UN Complaint Mechanisms Without State Ratification

Some countries, such as the United States, rarely ratify UN conventions; others, such as India, ratify conventions but not their complaint mechanisms. Not ratifying a convention or a complaint mechanism obviously makes it impossible to make a complaint against this state, but this does not mean that the complaint mechanisms are of no use for civil society members in these countries. Jurisprudence against others states can be handled as "soft law" and be used as an argument to also pressure states for their shortcomings. Social workers, for example, can easily apply any of the successful complaints mentioned previously to their own cases and use the outcome to pressure local courts or police. In addition, once a UN treaty body has declared a practice to be a human rights abuse, this applies to all countries. So, for example, the case *Lecraft v. Spain* can be used around the globe when dealing with the issue of racial profiling. In this case the human rights committee declared racial profiling to be a practice that negatively affects the dignity of the persons concerned (United Nations Human Rights Committee, 2009). After this decision one can undeniably argue that racial profiling is a human rights violation. The same applies to concluding observations in other countries, such as the situation of intersex people in Germany, which can be taken as setting a precedent for understanding that intersex people have experienced inhuman, cruel, or degrading treatment by states.

In addition to the passive use of jurisprudence and the concluding observations, the Universal Periodic Review and the protection provided by UN special rapporteurs can be of great relevance for civil society members. This is especially the case in countries such as the United States where states try to avoid the UN protection system by not ratifying conventions, because these two complaint mechanisms apply to all member states and a submission does not require any form of consent by the state involved.

Consequences for Universities

An understanding of social work as a human rights profession, which "facilitates social change and development, social cohesion, and the empowerment and liberation of people" (IFSW & IASSW, 2000, para. 1) implies that students of social work need to learn methods that enable them to challenge structural injustices with or in the name of their service users. Public relation skills, advocacy, and the use of the UN human rights protection system are indispensable methods and at the same time very powerful and effective tools to use when confronting structural social injustice.

As members of academic institutions we are entitled to submit complaints, and we can therefore support students who want to pass on their research or other findings as complaints to the United Nations. An excursion to Geneva or New York for a thematic debate, a constructive dialogue, or the presentation of a report of a UN special rapporteur can be more than informative. For example, the report of the UN Special Rapporteur on the Right to Health (2010) examining the relationship between the right to the highest attainable standard of health and the criminalization of homosexuality masterfully described the significance of the debate between universalism and cultural relativism. In the report the Special Rapporteur effectively challenged arguments by many states that homosexuality, being a western phenomenon, has no relevance for them.

The UN produces a lot of material on human rights abuses around the globe, but it is seldom used in class as literature. For example, the report "Multiple and Intersecting Forms of Discrimination and Violence Against Women" by the UN Special Rapporteur on Violence Against Women (2011) is an excellent report that can easily be used as literature in class when issues of intersectionality are debated. But all reports of treaty bodies on each and every country are very rich sources of information for classes of international social work.

Universities and social work associations can also use their structural power to protect social workers in the field if they want to report findings to the UN but are afraid to do so. University professors can submit this information, offering people in the field protection, which unfortunately is often required. Teaching the use of complaint mechanisms of UN treaty bodies as a tool in international social work practice is a very challenging subject, but one that usually excites students because they feel they are learning skills that enable them to confront states with structural injustices and offer options to service users who belong to groups with minimal access to justice or state protection. I hope these issues will be given more attention in future, especially in social work classes by social work educators.

References

Aduhene, Claudia, and Agyeman, Daniel v. Germany. (2008). Communication No. 1543/2007. CCPR/C/93/D/1543/2007.

Advocates for Human Rights. (2013). 10 steps to writing a shadow report. Retrieved from http://www.ushrnetwork.org/sites/ushrnetwork.org/files/10 _steps_to_writing_a_shadow_report_-_iccpr.pdf

Alice Salomon University of Applied Sciences. (2013). *International master program: Social work as a human rights profession.* Berlin, Germany: Alice Salomon University of Applied Sciences.

Arendt, H. (1951/2009): *Elemente und ursprünge totaler herrschaft*. Munich, Germany: Piper.

Ban Ying (2003). *Female domestic workers in the private households of diplomats in the Federal Republic of Germany. Information collected for the CEDAW Committee to open an inquiry procedure according to Article 8 OP/ CEDAW.* Retrieved from http://www.ban-ying.de/downloads/cedaw%20engl.pdf

Bayefsky, A. (2002). *How to complain to the UN human rights treaty system.* The Hague, The Netherlands: Kluwer Law International.

Brillat, R. (2013). *Keynote Speech*, ENSACT Conference. Istanbul, 19 April 2013.

Edwards, A. (2011). *Violence against women under international human rights law.* Cambridge, UK: Cambridge University Press.

Healy, L. (2008). *International social work: Professional action in an interdependent world.* New York, NY: Oxford University Press.

Healy, L., & Link, R. (2011). *Handbook of international social work: Human rights, development and the global profession.* New York, NY: Oxford University Press.

Ife, J. (2001). *Human rights and social work: Towards rights-based practice.* Cambridge, UK: Cambridge University Press.

International Federation of Social Workers & International Association of Schools of Social Work. (2000). *Definition of social work.* Retrieved from www.ifsw.org

International Federation of Social Workers & International Association of Schools of Social Work. (2004a). *Ethics in social work: Statement of principles.* Retrieved from www.ifsw.org

International Federation of Social Workers & International Association of Schools of Social Work. (2004b). *Global standards for the education and training of the social work profession.* Retrieved from http://cdn.ifsw.org/assets/ifsw_65044-3.pdf

International Federation of Social Workers, International Association of Schools of Social Work & International Council on Social Welfare. (2012). *The global agenda for social work and social development.* Retrieved from www.iassw-aiets. orgInternational Federation of Social Workers European Region. (2010). *Standards in social work practice meeting human rights.* Retrieved from http://cdn.ifsw.org/assets/ifsw_45904-8.pdf

Intersexuelle Menschen e.V. (2011). *Parallel report to the 5th periodic report of the Federal Republic of Germany on the Convention Against Torture.* Retrieved from intersex.shadowreport.org/pubic/Association_of_Intersexed_People_Shadow_Report_CAT_2011.pdf

Mohamed Musa Gbondo Sama v. Germany. (2009). Communication No. 1771/2008. CCPR/C/96/D/1771/2008.

Office of the United Nations High Commissioner for Human Rights. (2008). *Working with the United Nations human rights programme: A handbook for civil society.* Retrieved from http://www.ohchr.org/EN/AboutUs/CivilSociety /Documents/Handbook_en.pdf

Reichert, E. (2003). *Social work and human rights: A foundation for policy and practice.* New York, NY: Columbia University Press.

Reichert, E. (Ed.). (2007). *Challenges in human rights: A social work perspective.* New York, NY: Columbia University Press.

Staub-Bernasconi, S. (2009). Human rights and their relevance for social work as theory, education and practice. In C. Dorrity & P. Herrmann (Eds.), *Social professional activity: The search for a minimum common denominator in difference* (pp. 29–46) New York, NY: Nova Science Publisher.

Staub-Bernasconi, S. (2010). *Human rights—facing dilemmas between universalism and pluralism/contextualism, international perspective.* In D. Zavirsek, B. Rommelspacher & S. Staub-Bernasconi (Eds.), *Ethical dilemmas in social work* (pp. 9–24). Ljubljana, Slovenia: University of Ljubljana, Faculty of Social Work.

Turkish Union in Berlin/Brandenburg v. Germany. (2013). Communication No. 48/2010. CERD/C/82/D/48/2010.

United Nations (UN). (1965). *International convention on the elimination of all forms of racial discrimination.* G. A. Res. 2106 (XX). Retrieved from http:// www.ohchr.org /Documents/ProfessionalInterest/cerd.pdf

United Nations (UN). (1966a, December 16). *International covenant on civil and political rights.* G.A. Res. 2200A (XXI). Retrieved from http://www.ohchr.org /Documents/ProfessionalInterest/ccpr.pdf

United Nations (UN). (1966b, December 16). *International covenant on economic, social, and cultural rights.* G.A. Res. 2200A (XXI). Retrieved from http://www .ohchr.org/EN/ProfessionalInterest/Pages/CESCR.aspx

United Nations (UN). (1979, December 18). *Convention on the elimination of all forms of discrimination against women.* G.A. Res. 34/180. Retrieved from http://www.ohchr.org/Documents/ProfessionalInterest/cedaw.pdf

United Nations (UN). (1984, December 10). *Convention against torture and other cruel, inhuman or degrading treatment or punishment.* G.A. Res. 39/46. Retrieved from http://www.ohchr.org/Documents/ProfessionalInterest/cat.pdf

United Nations (UN). (1989, November 20). *Convention on the rights of the child.* G.A. Res. 44/25. Retrieved from: http://www.ohchr.org/Documents /ProfessionalInterest/crc.pdf

United Nations (UN). (1990, December 18). *International convention on the protection of the rights of all migrant workers and members of their families.* G. A. Res. 45/158. Retrieved from http://www2.ohchr.org/english/bodies/cmw/cmw.htm

United Nations (UN). (2006, December 16). *Convention on the rights of persons with disabilities.* G.A. Res. A/RES/61/106. Retrieved from http://www.ohchr.org/EN/HRBodies/CRPD/Pages/ConventionRightsPersonsWithDisabilities.aspx

United Nations (UN). (2008). *Selected decisions of the Committee against Torture* (vol. 1). Geneva, Switzerland: Author.

United Nations (UN). (2010). *Convention for the protection of all persons from enforced disappearance.* Retrieved from http://www.ohchr.org/Documents/ProfessionalInterest/disappearance-convention.pdf

United Nations (UN). (2012). *Selected decisions of the committee on the elimination of racial discrimination* (vol. 1). Geneva, Switzerland: Author.

United Nations Centre for Human Rights. (1994). *Human rights and social work: A manual for schools of social work and the social work profession* (Professional Training Series No. 1). Retrieved from http://www.ohchr.org/Documents/Publications/traininglen.pdf

United Nations Committee Against Torture (UN CAT). (2011, December 12). *Consideration of reports submitted by states parties under Article 19 of the convention, concluding observations of the Committee Against Torture: Germany.* CAT/C/DEU/CO/5. Retrieved from http://tbinternet.ohchr.org/_layouts/treatybodyexternal/Download.aspx?symbolno=CAT/C/DEU/CO/5&Lang=En

United Nations Committee on the Elimination of Discrimination Against Women (UN CEDAW). (1992). *CEDAW general recommendations Nos. 19 and 20, adopted at the eleventh session, 1992* (contained in Document A/47/38), 1992, A/47/38). Retrieved from http://www.refworld.org/type,GENERAL,CEDAW,,453882a422,0.html

United Nations Committee on the Elimination of Discrimination Against Women. (2007a, August 6). Communication No. 5/2005. *Şahde Goekce (deceased) v. Austria.* CEDAW/C/39/D/2005 Retrieved from http://www.iwraw-ap.org/protocol/doc/Sahide_Goekce_v_Austria.pdf.

United Nations Committee on the Elimination of Discrimination Against Women (UN CEDAW). (2007b, October 1). Communication No. 6/2005. *Fatima Yildirim (deceased) v. Austria.* CEDAW/C/40/D/2005. Retrieved from http://opcedaw.files.wordpress.com/2012/01/yildirim-v-austria.pdf

United Nations Committee on the Elimination of Racial Discrimination
(UN CERD). (1999). Communication No. 10/1997. Ziad Ben
Ahmed Habassi v. Denmark. CERD /C/54/10/1997 Retrieved from
http://tbinternet.ohchr.org/_layouts/treatybodyexternal/Download.
aspx?symbolno=CERD%2fC%2f54%2fD%2f10%2f1997&Lang=en

United Nations Committee on the Elimination of Racial Discrimination (UN
CERD). (2013). Communication No. 48/210, TBB - Turkish Union in
Berlin/Brandenburg, CERD/C/82/D/48/2010. Retrieved from http://www2
.ohchr.org/English/bodies/cerd/docs/CERD-C-82-D-48-2010-English.pdf

United Nations Committee on Economic, Social and Cultural Rights.
(2009, July 2). *General comment no. 20 on non-discrimination in
economic, social and cultural rights*. (E/C.12/GC/20). Retrieved from
http://tbinternet.ohchr.org/_layouts/treatybodyexternal/Download.
aspx?symbolno=E%2fC.12%2fGC%2f20&Lang=en

United Nations Committee on Economic, Social and Cultural Rights. (2011, May
20). *Consideration of reports submitted by States parties under Articles 16 and 17
of the covenant concluding observations of the Committee on Economic, Social and
Cultural Rights Germany*. E/C.12/DEU/CO/5. Retrieved from http://www
.refworld.org/docid/52d664a24.html

United Nations Committee on the Elimination of Discrimination Against
Women. (1989). *CEDAW general recommendation no. 12: Violence against
women*. Retrieved from http://www.refworld.org/docid/52d927444.html

United Nations Committee on the Protection of the Rights of all Migrant
Workers and Members of Their Families. (2011, February 23): *General comment
no. 1 on migrant domestic workers*. (CMW/C/GC/1). Retrieved from
http://tbinternet.ohchr.org/_layouts/treatybodyexternal/Download.aspx
?symbolno=CMW%2fC%2fGC%2f1&Lang=en

United Nations Human Rights Committee. (2004). Communication no.
931/2000. *Hudoyberganova v. Uzbekistan*. ICCPR, A/60/40. Retrieved from
http://ccprcentre.org/doc/ICCPR/AR/A_60_40_vol.I_E.pdf

United Nations Human Rights Committee. (2009). Communication No.
1493/2006. Williams Lecraft v. Spain. Retrieved from http://ccprcentre.org
/doc/ICCPR/AR/A_64_40%28Vol%20I%29_Eng.pdf

United Nations Special Rapporteur the Right to Health. (2010, April 27). *Report
of the special rapporteur on the right of everyone to the enjoyment of the highest
attainable standard of physical and mental health, Anand Grover*.

A/HRC/14/20. Retrieved from http://www2.ohchr.org/english/bodies
/hrcouncil/docs/14session/A.HRC.14.20.pdf

United Nations Special Rapporteur on Violence Against Women. (2011, May
2). *Report of the special rapporteur on violence against women, its causes and
consequences, Rashida Manjoo.* A/HRC/17/26. Retrieved from http://www2
.ohchr.org/english/bodies/hrcouncil/docs/17session/A-HRC-17-26.pdf

Wronka, J. (2008). *Human rights and social justice: Social action and service for the
helping and health professions.* Thousand Oaks, CA: SAGE.

WSK-Allianz. (2011). *Parallel report of the alliance for economic, social and cultural
rights in Germany, complementing the 5th Report of the Federal Republic of
Germany on the International Covenant on Economic, Social and Cultural Rights
(ICESCR).* Retrieved from http://www.wsk-allianz.de/index-Dateien
/Doku/20110321%20ParallelReportWSKAllianz%20eng.pdf

Endnotes

1 Cases taken to the European Court of Human Rights have not been considered here because
these cases can only be filed by lawyers, which gives social workers a very passive role.

2 One of these exceptional cases is *MS. N.S.F v. The United Kingdom of Great Britain and
Northern Ireland*, CEDAW/C/38/D/10/2005.

3 These include the International Covenant on Civil and Political Rights (United
Nations, 1966a); International Covenant on Economic, Social and Cultural Rights
(United Nations, 1966b); the International Convention Against the Elimination of
All Forms of Racial Discrimination (United Nations, 1965); the Convention on the
Elimination of All Forms of Discrimination Against Women (United Nations, 1979);
the Convention against Torture and Other Cruel, Inhuman or Degrading Treatment
or Punishment (United Nations, 1984); the Convention on the Rights of the Child
(United Nations, 1989); International Convention on the Protection of the Rights
of All Migrant Workers and Members of Their Families (United Nations, 1990);
Convention on the Rights of Persons with Disabilities (United Nations, 2006); and
Convention for the Protection of All Persons from Enforced Disappearance (United
Nations, 2010).

4 For insights into the shadow reporting process in the United States (which is relevant
for other countries as well) see Advocates for Human Rights (2013).

9 | Integrating Human Rights into the Jamaican Social Work Curriculum

Sandra Chadwick-Parkes

Human rights is increasingly being incorporated into the andragogical curriculum due to its potential to prevent human rights violations, foster respect for rights, and realize the United Nations' (UN's) human rights goals (Teleki, 2007). Several social work bodies, including the International Federation of Social Workers (IFSW) and the International Association of Schools of Social Work (IASSW), deem it critical that the discipline be imbued with the "values and awareness of equality and human rights" (IFSW 2012a, para. 1) despite its inherent social justice and rights principles. This shift from "needs orientation" (p. 5) to "rights affirmation" p. 3) is prompted by the conviction that social work educators and practitioners must have a "clear and unreserved commitment to the promotion and protection of human rights and to the satisfaction of fundamental social aspirations" (UN Centre for Human Rights, 1994, p. 3). However, the world of the social worker does not always conform to that of textbooks. Given that socialization is the primary basis for students' view of the world when they enter academia, it is insufficient to merely familiarize them with human rights values. It is also critical that they be resocialized so that they become professionals genuinely committed to human rights, can translate these values into practice, and thereby contribute to a human rights culture in society.

This chapter highlights some of the ways in which faculty in the Social Work Unit (SWU) of the University of the West Indies' (UWI) Jamaica campus actively incorporate human rights into their curricula to challenge and reshape students' perceptions so they may internalize these new values, inculcate them into practice, and thereby promote societal change. The chapter begins with a brief description of human rights, followed by a discussion of whether human rights are separable from social work values and ethics. It then juxtaposes some Jamaican anti–human rights perceptions, attitudes, and behaviors against the UN Conventions to which the country is a signatory. This serves to alert the reader to students' socialization when they enter academe. This discussion leads into some of the teaching strategies for incorporating human rights into the curriculum. The chapter concludes by emphasizing that the assimilation of human rights values requires more than the use of human rights documents in the social work classroom.

Defining Human Rights

Human rights standards were first embodied in the 1948 UN Universal Declaration of Human Rights (UDHR; UN, 1948). Human rights are those rights that belong to everyone by virtue of being a human being. Regardless of age or sex, these rights are universal, inalienable, and "embody basic standards" whereby people "realize their inherent human dignity" (University of Minnesota Human Rights Resource Centre, Part I, n.d.). The UDHR established 30 articles of common freedoms and rights that are

> indivisible, whether they be civil and political rights, such as the right to life, equality before the law and freedom of expression; economic, social and cultural rights, such as the rights to work, social security and education, or collective rights, such as the rights to development and self-determination, are indivisible, interrelated and interdependent. The improvement of one right facilitates advancement of the others. Likewise, the deprivation of one right adversely affects the others. (Office of the UN High Commissioner for Human Rights [OHCHR], n.d. para. 6)

According to the OHCHR these standards are rooted in three primary human rights conventions to which all UN member states are signatories and which are legally binding once ratified. Collectively called the International Bill of Human Rights, they comprise the UDHR 1948; the International

Covenant on Civil and Political Rights 1996 and its two Optional Protocols; and the International Covenant on Economic, Social and Cultural Rights (University of Minnesota Human Rights Resource Centre, n.d, para. 6). These instruments precipitated other human rights treaties which all countries that have ratified must implement via appropriate legislation (para. 6).

Upholding rights and freedoms does not automatically result from ratification, particularly in societies acculturated to human rights abuses, violence, and religious fervor, such as former slave colonies. Therefore, a readily defined human rights violation elsewhere may be acceptable in that context. This translates into a degree of apathy toward or sanctioning of negative behaviors and attitudes or the selective upholding of rights. Further complications arise from according rights to actions deemed illegal, such as recognizing gay unions where male intimacy is punishable by statute. However, change is inevitable and "increasing integration" is now leading to the

> globalization of human rights [whereby] the growing ideology of human rights is taking hold of international systems and international law [rendering] many traditional practices endemic to the fabric of particular societies or cultures—from religious ... to esoteric practices—now... being called into question, challenged, forbidden or even outlawed (Rhoads, 2006, p. 8)

This quote highlights the importance of resocialization in reshaping local values and practices in harmony with human rights.

Social Work: Definition and Core Purposes

The call to incorporate human rights into social work begs the question of whether human rights are mutually exclusive from the values and ethics of social work. The following definition by the IFSW and IASSW reflects the intimate relationship between the two:

> [T]he social work profession promotes social change, problem solving in human relationships and the empowerment and liberation of people to enhance well-being. Utilizing theories of human behavior and social sys-

tems, social work intervenes at the points where people interact with their environments. Principles of human rights and social justice are fundamental to social work (IFSW, 2013, para. 4)

The organization further articulates the following 10 of 15 core and multi-faceted purposes of social work:

- inclusion of the marginalized, socially excluded, at-risk and vulnerable;
- addressing societal inequities and injustices;
- enhancing the well-being of people, communities and organizations;
- awareness raising of services and resources;
- promoting human rights and development, and fostering social stability via policies and programs that do not undermine human rights;
- effecting change through social policy and economic development;
- promoting respect for non-mainstream cultures, religions, and beliefs;
- fostering harmonious, respectful societies without human rights violations;
- protecting those unable to protect themselves (IFSW, 2012b, para. 4)

Hence, human rights—be they social, political, economic, or cultural—are at the forefront of the social work purpose. Moreover, the core social work values and ethics are based on principles of social justice, which is itself rooted in human rights.

An example of the connection between social work ethics, social justice, and human rights is illustrated in the Code of Ethics of the British Association of Social Workers (BASW), which incorporates the definition of *social work* from the IFSW and the IASSW in 2000. This code leaves little doubt that human rights are integral to social justice, which includes:

- The fair and equitable distribution of resources to meet basic human needs;
- Fair access to public services and benefits to achieve human potential;
- Recognition of the rights and duties of individuals, families, groups and communities;

- Equal treatment and protection under the law;
- Social development and environmental management in the interests of present and future human welfare;
- The pursuit of social justice by advocating strategies that address structural disadvantage (BASW, 2012, p. 8).

The aforementioned discussion demonstrates that human rights are inextricably intertwined in the purpose, values, and ethics of social work. Hence, social work educators implicitly instill future practitioners with the values and awareness of equality and human rights.

Why then is there a need for conscious human rights awareness-raising to be incorporated into the social work curricula? Blennberger (2006) argues that social workers make client decisions founded in their own ethical judgments and values. Hence, if these judgments and values are not framed within a rights based orientation, how can social work educators be certain they are producing social work professionals? Moreover, although Jamaica is a signatory to and has passed laws to implement international conventions, human rights violations occur in Jamaica that are rooted in negative perceptions and attitudes about and behaviors toward distinct groups. These groups include inner city residents, women, children, persons with disabilities, nonheterosexuals, and persons living with HIV/AIDS (PLWHA). Undoubtedly, incoming social work students are likewise socialized.

Jamaica and Human Rights
Issues and (Mis)Perceptions

Like its Caribbean counterparts, Jamaica has made significant strides in human development. Figure 1 illustrates Jamaica's key 2012 human development indicators. The Human Development Index (HDI) is an average measure of long-term progress in basic human development, that is (a) life expectancy (a long and healthy life); (b) mean years of schooling for adults 25 years and older, and expected years of schooling for children of school entrance age (access to knowledge); and (c) gross national income (GNI) per capita in constant 2005 dollars or standard of living (United Nations Development Programme, 2013).

Figure 1   **Human development indicators for Jamaica, 2012**

Life expectancy at birth	73.3 years
Expected years of schooling	13.1 years
Mean years of schooling	9.6 years
Gross national income	US$6,701[a]
Maternal mortality ratio	110/100,000 live births
Adolescent fertility rate	69.7
Female seats in parliament	15.5%
Population with at least secondary education	74% (female); 71.1% (male)
Labor force participation rate	56% (female); 71.8% (male)

[a]Compared to US$10,300 for LAC region.
Source: UNDP, 2013

As is evident, Jamaica is well ahead of many other developing countries in life expectancy and education. In 2012 it ranked 85 of 187 states on the Human Development Index or HDI (UNDP, 2013). However, its HDI is lower than the benchmark for high human development countries and below the average for the Latin America and the Caribbean region (UNDP, 2013). Moreover, the HDI masks inequality, and the Jamaica HDI drops 19.1% when discounted for societal inequality (UNDP, 2013).

The 2010 Jamaica Survey of Living Conditions reveals that 47.1% of households are headed by women and consist of more adult females and children than households headed by men (Planning Institute of Jamaica, 2010). On average, 17.6% of the Jamaican population lives below the poverty line, with the highest poverty rates (14.4%) occurring in the urbanized Kingston Metropolitan Area. The 2010 adult equivalent poverty line was approximately US$12,440 or J$124, 408.34 (H. Ricketts, personal communication, October 17, 2013). However, this figure is unrelated to social welfare payments. Rather, it is used to calculate the poverty line by indicating how much money a family of four requires annually to meet its basic needs. The Jamaica Programme of Advancement Through Health and Education (PATH) targets indigent households with children and the vulnerable elderly, but insufficient resources mean that only 53.8% of all households applying to the program actually receive benefits (Planning Institute of Jamaica, 2011).

Compared to most Caribbean islands, Jamaica lacks adequate social safety nets despite PATH. With unemployment rates of 20%–50%, unemployed persons across the region are forced to fend for themselves by "pimping, hustling, pushing, scrunting, prostitution, violence and wretchedness" (Pryce, 2007, p. 9). These strategies demonstrate the lack of social and economic rights of the most vulnerable, which in turn gives rise to other human rights abuses. A few are discussed in the following paragraphs.

Crime and Violence

In stark contrast to its idyllic setting, the Caribbean region had one of the highest homicide rates in the world in 2004: 30 per 100,000 persons (United Nations Office of Drugs and Crime/World Bank, 2007; Muggah & Krause, 2008). With a population of approximately 2.7 million (Planning Institute of Jamaica, 2011), Jamaica has a higher homicide rate than the death rate in many war zones. Homicides have steadily increased since 1989; from 439 in that year to 1,682 in 2009 (Levy, 2005; McLean, 2009). Although the figure began declining thereafter to 1,125 by 2011 (United Nations Office of Drugs and Crime, 2012), the 2011 Economic and Social Survey of Jamaica noted a corresponding increase in reported rapes and robberies (Planning Institute of Jamaica, 2011).

Much of this violence originates in the links between partisan politics and unionism of the 1940s, but escalated from the 1970s. Working class Kingston neighborhoods became divided along political affiliation. Now known as *garrison* or inner-city communities, each community is populated by supporters of one or the other political party where differing political hues do not mix. These political borders have given rise to intercommunity conflicts reinforced and perpetuated by political patronage.

Geography is a more recent contributor to crime and violence. The Caribbean archipelago serves as a transshipment point for drug flows between producers in South America and consumers in North America and Europe (United Nations Office of Drugs and Crime/World Bank, 2007). Jamaica also is a cannabis producer and exporter. Specific features make the islands ideal transshipment ports, including high unemployment and underemployment among male youth, high poverty levels, a large informal cash economy, significant unpatrolled borders, good air and sea communication links, ports, modern telecommunications infrastructure, and fiber-optic links to the rest of the world (Edwards, 2013). Drugs are accompanied by arms, resulting in criminals having more sophisticated weapons than members of security forces (United Nations Office of Drugs and Crime/World Bank, 2007).

Although politics and patronage remain important to community identity and local conflict in Jamaica, Mogensen (2005) argues that most of the violence is now less political and more aligned to increasing drug-related organized crime, protection and extortion rackets, and gang warfare. The situation is compounded by political corruption and links to criminal elements, police brutality and crime involvement, school delinquency, and drug use (Deosaran, 2007).

Pryce (2007) depicts Caribbean development as a system of exploitation that enriches a few and dispossesses the masses. The high crime and violence rates are no surprise; it has been demonstrated that violence is fueled by high levels of inequality and social exclusion (Buvini , Alda, & Lamas, 2005). The following description of Jamaican inner-city life confirms this:

It is the existence of an inner city of black people suffering huge unemployment, poverty, often derelict infrastructure, few social services but considerable social stigma, and a justice system characterized by vigilante or trigger-happy police, over-long court proceedings and over-crowded prisons. This inner city concentrates the very communities at "war" so that middle class politicians can acquire and hold onto political power and the mostly lighter-skinned middle and upper classes can be secure behind their grills (Levy, 2005, pp. 2–3).

Turf control and expansion in the garrisons add to the violence. Garrison communities have become increasingly fragmented as intracommunity conflict now pits street against street or one housing block against the other (Chadwick-Parkes, 2012). These borders are established by youths as young as 15 years old who are generally illiterate and seek to carve out and control a piece of turf to gain respect (Ferreira-Sutherland, 2010).

These narrow demarcations place tight restrictions on freedom of movement with implications for human, social, and economic development in these areas. The boundaries prevent school attendance, hamper daily activities, and deter provision of public services including garbage disposal and sanitation to the communities (Ferreira-Sutherland, 2010). Lack of social interaction has caused and is caused by violence, mistrust, insecurity, and high levels of illiteracy, but especially poverty. For one inner-city resident life means

> hunger, vengeance/retaliation, conflict and unemployment/low economic status.... To [incur] change [you] have to change social conditions... better housing, plumbing, schools... economic conditions. Livin(g) in one room, you gotta take up a gun. There's no other way. Persons hungry! You change the social condition you affect people's thinking, behavior (Mogensen, 2005, p. 13).

This quote illustrates the abject poverty and poor social, economic, and infrastructural conditions, as well as the stigmatization, marginalization, and ostracism faced by inner-city residents (Harriott & Chadwick, 1999). Educational attainment is generally low despite access to schools. Additionally, hunger and disruptions from sporadic violence deter attendance. Respect is important to Jamaicans, including inner-city residents, and entails citizens living by a code of silence: "minding your own business and keeping your mouth shut" (Chadwick-Parkes, 2012, p. 35). Indeed, even the police accord respect to the community Don, trusting him to deal with internal community issues.

The Don or garrison "community leader," a peculiarity of Jamaican politics, is akin to the Italian Mafia Don, who determines life and death yet is also protector and disburser of economic spoils and justice in his community. Dons emerged in the 1960s as armed political enforcers who assured votes in return for political largesse to their communities. Although political affiliation remains strong, drug trade money and ammunition have reduced political control over the Don. Some communities remain internally cohesive under the rule of a single Don. But most tend toward internal fragmentation, thus paving the way for youths as young as 14 to establish themselves as corner

Dons with accompanying corner gangs or crews that exist alongside community Dons (and community gangs) and criminal gangs, thereby adding multiple layers of violence to the inner city and Jamaican society (Chadwick-Parkes, 2012).

The violence has resulted in the marginalization and ostracism of inner-city residents to the extent that they are unable to secure employment. Children witness murders, including that of male family members, and boys as young as 8 years regard killing someone as their rite of passage. Those deported from other countries are stigmatized and blamed for spiraling crime rates and young girls are victims of sexual exploitation.

The State of Children

The Jamaica Coalition on the Rights of the Child was established in November 1989 on the heels of the 1989 adoption of the United Nations Convention on the Rights of the Child (UNCRC) and prior to the country becoming a party to the convention in 1991. The rights of children can be summed up as "provision, protection and participation" (Hammarberg, 1990, as cited in Barrow, 2001, p. xv). Barrow (2001) makes the point that although previous declarations had a "restricted, paternalistic view" of child development, the 1989 UNCRC "acknowledges autonomy of the child and the accompanying principles of social inclusion, self-determination and empowerment" (p. xv). Furthermore, the UNCRC shifts the emphasis "from protection to autonomy, nurturance to self-determination and from welfare to justice" (Freeman, 1992, p. 3 as cited in Barrow, 2001, p. xv).

In 2004 Jamaica passed the Child Care and Protection Act, established the Office of the Children's Advocate and appointed a Children's Advocate in 2006 to protect the rights and best interests of its children (UNICEF, 2006). In addition, the country is home to a multiplicity of institutions dealing with child related issues. Examples include the Child Development Agency, the Early Childhood Commission, Caribbean Child Development Centre, Jamaica Coalition on the Rights of the Child, the Office of the Children's Registry, the Planning Institute of Jamaica, the Ministry of Education, and the United Nations International Children's Emergency Fund (UNICEF) and other UN agencies. UWI also hosts a biennial Child Rights Conference. Along with the rest of the Caribbean, Jamaica formulated the Belize Commitment to Action on the Rights of the Child (1996), the Kingston Accord (1997) that articulated strategies to implement the Belize Commitment to Action, and the Lima Accord to reduce infant mortality rates (Williams, 2002).

Despite all this, child rights remain precarious. Although many islands have reformed birth status, McDowell (2001) argues that legal differentials still exist in the treatment given to children born out of wedlock in terms of inheritance, child support, and birth registration. In some islands the father of an out-of-wedlock child can register the birth only if the mother is deceased or cannot be located. This has negative implications for inheritance (Thompson-Ahye, 2004), especially given the high incidence of out-of-wedlock births.

Moreover, many children continue to be abused in spite of the protection rights outlined in Article 32 of the UNCRC. They are often involved in trafficking (Singh, 2001); armed conflict; prostitution; and hazardous work as domestics, street vendors, or beggars (Office of the Child Advocate, 2011). Singh (2001) goes on to note that although the voting age is 18, a child aged 7 to 12 can be held criminally responsible. Furthermore, in the face of a lack of "resources and alternatives," a growing number of "juveniles and 11–14" year olds are imprisoned with adults in facilities where "remand prisoners are held with convicted persons and petty offenders held with murderers" (Singh, 2001, p. 44). This reinforces the observation by Brown (2001) that "the concept of child rights remains alien to Caribbean society and provokes resistance, especially from parents" (p. xix).

Sexual Assault and Minors

The UNCRC identifies four articles that are the basis of implementing all the rights articulated in the Convention: (1) Article 2, nondiscrimination; (2) Article 3, the best interests of the child; (3) Article 6, the right to life, survival, and development; and (4) Article 12, respect for the views of the child. There were 6,330 reports of child abuse in 2008 and 6,778 cases in 2009. Further, sexual assault was the most prevalent reason for children being taken to the hospital in Jamaica. Those aged 10 years and under constituted 17% of all sexual assault, whereas those aged 10–19 accounted for 57% (U.S. Department of State, 2010).

Almost half (48%) of the young women participating in the 2008 Reproductive Health Survey in Jamaica reported their first sexual experience as forced or pressured (Serbanescu, Ruiz, & Suchdev, 2010, p. 247). This is consistent with a previous study by Halcon et al. (2003), which found that 48% of adolescent Caribbean females were subject to forcible sexual initiation. More concerning is that some Dons, male caregivers, and fathers view it as their right to initiate the girls' first sexual experience (U.S. Department of State, 2010). In some instances child sexual abuse is rooted in the belief that sexually transmitted diseases (STIs) are cured through intercourse with a virgin. Along with impunity, social ills such as overcrowding and poverty contribute to abuse.

Persons With Disabilities

Of particular interest to Jamaica is Article 23 of the United Nations Convention on the Rights of the Child (United Nations, 1989), which urges all states to recognize that a mentally or physically disabled child should enjoy a full and decent life, in conditions that ensure dignity, promote self-reliance, and facilitate the child's active participation in the community (UNICEF, 1989).

The disabled are excluded primarily because of stigmatization but also through infrastructure deficits. Some parents deem the birth of a disabled child a supernatural event. In a 2012 UNICEF study, 40% of parents with disabled offspring believed that the child was sent by God, whereas 18% attributed the disability to evil spirits, punishment for a sin, or looking at a disabled person during pregnancy (UNICEF, n.d., para. 7).

There are still persons who believe that disabilities are contagious and hence oppose their "normal" children being seated next to a disabled child at school, regardless of the disability. In seeking to protect disabled children against stigmatization, some parents refuse to send them to school despite the availability of special needs institutions. In the past such misperceptions resulted in disabled children being abandoned at rehabilitative or other state institutions; this practice is changing to children now being cared for at home. These children continue to be disadvantaged as adults.

PLWHA

The first documented Jamaican HIV/AIDS case was in 1982. By 2012, 1.7% of the adult population (32,000 people) was living with the disease. Next to homicides, it is the leading cause of death among 15–49 year olds (Ministry of Health [MOH], 2012). The MOH estimates a higher prevalence in men who have sex with men (MSMs) of 32.8%, homeless persons accounting for 12%, and sex workers for 4.1% (2012). Since 1986, a national HIV/STI program has been in operation for the care, treatment, and support of infected and affected persons. Thereafter, the rights-based National HIV Strategic Plan 2012–2017 was developed to reduce stigma and create an enabling environment for HIV/AIDS responses.

The epidemic is fueled by negative gender norms and behaviors and practices including male dominance/female submission, cross generational sex, multiple partners, early sexual debut, high levels of transactional sex, commercial sex, inadequate condom use, gender based violence, stigma and discrimination, and homophobia (UNAIDS, 2012). Homophobia and the association of HIV/AIDS with homosexuality result in bisexuals hiding their orientation, whereas MSMs refuse to be tested. A poignant example of homophobia is a 2011 government initiative to reduce HIV/AIDS transmission among prison inmates by distributing condoms. A riot ensued because implicit in the initiative was that all male prisoners were homosexuals. Socioeconomic conditions that render women dependent on males for financial support erode their ability to negotiate condom use. Moreover, a request to use a condom is tantamount to an accusation of infidelity. Despite antiretroviral distribution, elimination of mother-to-child transmissions, and a reduction in deaths, PLWHA are ill-treated and sometimes rendered homeless due to fears that HIV/AIDS is contagious outside intimacy. Orphans who are free of the infection are similarly ostracized.

Reproductive Health

In the 1979 Convention on the Elimination of Discrimination Against Women (UN, 1979), Article 12 deals with women's rights in the field of health care, including information and advice on family planning. Although the Jamaican government provides direct support for contraception, the Offenses Against the Person Act of 1864 subjects anyone who procures, intends to procure, or provides a miscarriage to life imprisonment with or without hard labor (UN Department for Economic and Social Affairs, n.d.). The church deems abortion immoral, whereas human rights groups advocate against its legalization due to their pro-life stance on behalf of the fetus.

Abortions are illegal except to save the life of the woman or to preserve her physical or mental health. In these cases the consent of the spouse is required. However, the abortion policy does not allow abortions for rape, incest, fetal impairment, economic or social reasons, or on request. In the case of mental health, fetal impairment, rape, or incest, the approval of two specialists must be obtained and the woman must be referred for the abortion by a judge or law enforcement official before the procedure can be undertaken. Moreover, a woman cannot have more than one abortion in her lifetime, even when the pregnancy results from a criminal act. Yet approximately 30,000 illegal abortions are performed annually (Pregnancy Resource Centre of Jamaica, n.d.). Despite attempts to review the legislation, the church and high levels of religiosity thwart reform. Hence, Jamaican women are discriminated against and denied the right to choose their own best interest. Induced and botched back-room abortions account for the high maternal mortality rate shown in Figure 1.

Sexual Orientation

Human rights groups label Jamaica as the most homophobic place on earth (Padgett, 2006). The Offenses Against the Person Act of 1864 remains on the statute books and sentences those convicted to 10 years in prison for engaging in "acts of gross indecency," interpreted as any physical intimacy between men in public or private, men and women in public, and bestiality (Gays in Jamaica, n.d.). It is possible that intimacy between women was not anticipated in 1864 and hence was excluded from the law. Heterosexual couples can also be charged for engaging in intimacy in public spaces. The degree of intimacy is not specified, but whether due to statute or culture, it is extremely unusual for Jamaican couples to hold hands in public, let alone kiss. It must be emphasized that despite being a signatory to every UN convention, there is no treaty that "expressly states that homosexuality must be regarded as lawful" (Richards, 2012). In a country described as having a church on every corner, homosexuality is deemed a sin, an abomination unto God, and as going against Christian values. The antigay, violence-inciting lyrics of Jamaican dancehall music are renowned; gay activists are murdered; lesbians are subjected to corrective rape, ostensibly to turn them back into normal women; and the police are accused of ignoring evidence in antigay hate crimes. In such a context, sexual orientation not only challenges social workers' values but also renders them liable when dealing with gay clients because the 1864 Act remains in force.

The Human Rights Imperative: Integrating Human Rights Into the UWI Social Work Curriculum

The previous sections illustrate a few examples of how human rights abuses and impunity are ingrained in Jamaica. It goes without saying that social work students are similarly socialized when they enter academia and will also have to contend with and counter these negative values from future clients. Hence, to transform students into social work professionals, social work educators must develop classroom resocialization strategies that enable students to assimilate human rights values, apply these values to daily practice, and become human rights champions and activists.

There are four social work programs taught by the SWU: certificate, diploma, bachelor, and graduate. The graduate program has four specializations: clinical, community, advanced generalist, and administration and management. Although each has distinct ethical issues, cultural values also warrant inclusion of context-specific material germane to human rights. Social work students are indoctrinated in the rights-based approach on entering academia, but those from other disciplines enrolled in social work electives often harbor values counter to human rights.

The SWU uses various teaching tools to incorporate human rights into the curriculum. Some courses have a dedicated human rights module that includes documents on human rights conventions, international treaties, and regional and national statutes and agreements. Students use these documents as a frame of reference when analyzing topical issues in the media that constitute human rights breaches. For example, students in the Disability Studies course ascertain how international conventions and national statutes specific to the rights of persons with disabilities actually affect the disabled. Given that the Jamaican Education Act 1982 (Jamaica Government Printer, 1982) enshrines the right and access to education for every child, students are asked to discuss such issues as how the Act relates to education for disabled children in the face of limited resources for children with disabilities and the cultural factors that impinge on their access to education. Of course, Law and Human Services draws on the expertise of human rights specialists from the legal community.

Important to human rights education is raising awareness of rights and violations across the region. One course, Caribbean Social Issues, examines problems such as poverty, crime and violence, human trafficking, child abuse, marginalization, aging, and PLWHA. Like other social work courses it draws on multidisciplinary and multilevel expertise from academia, nongovernmental organizations (NGOs), and the public sector. Issues are discussed in the context of international conventions, the Millennium Development Goals, and national and regional statutes and policies, all of which help shape national policy.

Other tools include role playing, scenarios, videos, and discussions of the relationship between human rights and social work practice. Courses such as Community Organization and Social Planning and Project Design integrate an inductive, experiential approach that combines teaching, learning, community participation, and the use of participatory learning approaches that involve community residents in resolving longstanding issues. Students learn the importance of and respect for local knowledge and voice. Additionally, students gain first-hand knowledge of societal issues in a real-life setting and can apply their learning through interacting with marginalized and stigmatized persons.

The interaction helps to change students' preconceived notions of poor inner-city residents. The students also draw up contracts among themselves about appropriate behaviors in the community and with each other. The community is empowered by the process, knowledge created, and capacity building exercises, which later enable them to acquire funding to address issues.

Another core course, Ethics and Professional Development, challenges students on various ethical and human rights issues. The assignments include an ethics audit of a human services entity, case studies on ethical dilemmas, and the social worker–client power differentials in seemingly mundane issues such as the facilities provided to clients. These exercises provide students a holistic understanding of human rights and help shape their client relationships. This is not a smooth process; students initially resist if they believe they are being forced to condone behaviors such as gay lifestyles that counter their own value systems.

The Human Behavior in the Social Environment course indoctrinates students to the child rights approach. They examine trauma from a variety of sources, including community violence, sexual abuse, or parental migration. Again, UN documents and case studies are used, including those highlighted in the media. The problems are analyzed in relation to child rights and how those rights have or have not been met, and the class concludes with proposed policy and interventions. In the past, students have developed an advocacy project, but this has since fallen victim to budget cuts.

These examples of how the SWU incorporates human rights into the social work curriculum are not exhaustive. The SWU also plays a pivotal role in raising awareness and the institutionalization of human rights in Jamaica. The Office of the Child Advocate was the brainchild of a social work graduate who lobbied for its establishment (see Chapter 19). Faculty launched the Children's Lobby in conjunction with an interdisciplinary group of child services practitioners from 1984–1988. Among its achievements are advocacy for a metropolitan school bus system and investigation of child prostitution and child pornography when it surfaced in the society (Claudette Crawford-Brown, personal communication, October 11, 2013).

The SWU was also directly involved in the establishment of Hibiscus House, which provides support to deportees, particularly women and their families (K. Boyce-Reid, personal communication, April 22, 2013). These organizations are now established NGOs. The SWU continues to assign practicum placements to these agencies to ensure students' involvement in human rights issues. These examples illustrate that the faculty members serve as role models and can draw on these examples to "cultivate a human rights culture in the classroom" (IFSW, 2012(a), para. 3).

The course offerings and student assignments of the social work curriculum as well as the advocacy roles played by the SWU faculty embody the IFSW recommendations that

> The most effective method of teaching ethics and human rights involves integrating ethics and human rights into all courses, as well as offering separate courses on these topics. Students need to learn about values, personal, societal, cultural and professional, to explore where there are similarities and where there are areas of conflict. Social workers everywhere should be familiar with the major international human rights declarations and conventions and their implications for social policy and social work practice. National codes of ethics, as well as international codes on ethics and human rights, should be included in the curriculum. These documents, however, should not be presented as abstractions, but rather applied to relevant case examples. Students should have the opportunity to analyze these documents in terms of their strengths and limitations. Finally, students must learn to recognize ethical and human rights dilemmas that arise in practice, as well as models of ethical decision-making that can help in resolving these dilemmas (IFSW, 2013, para. 3-4).

The earlier sections of this article demonstrate that SWU integrated human rights education into its curriculum long before it was mandated by the IFSW and IASSW. However, it is readily acknowledged that more needs to be done. It is imperative that incoming social work students be made aware of society's values and perceptions as well as their own. Additionally, students need to evaluate and interrogate how their perceptions and values affect their decision-making role in clients' lives. Finally, students should reflect on how to avoid stereotyping at-risk groups who seek social services. Social work educators must help students examine and challenge their values for these to be reshaped and rooted in a rights-based approach that is in the interest of both clients and society at large. Hence, apart from incorporating human rights documents into the curriculum, a human rights culture also needs to be created that will be translated into practice.

Conclusion

As this chapter demonstrates, Jamaica is a signatory to every UN convention and has implemented laws and interventions to meet these obligations and foster development. However, a large cross-section of the citizenry is socialized in ways that counter human rights. Moreover, Caribbean social workers have a significant number of issues to deal with that do not surface in the sterile environment of a classroom or which are not covered in texts. Hence, regardless of the intimate relationship among social justice, human rights, and social work, societal problems and culture warrant that human rights be made explicit in teaching and learning. To this end, SWU has consciously incorporated human rights into its curriculum in a number of innovative ways.

This chapter demonstrates that fostering a human rights culture in social work education goes beyond the use of international conventions and treaties. Although these documents are essential human rights teaching and learning tools, it is equally necessary to open up issues for discussion, force students to interrogate their values and how these affect their clients, enable them to set aside prejudices and exorcise their own antirights socialization. This is to help students view all clients as deserving of respect and service equality by being human beings. Equally critical is to broaden students' understanding of human rights beyond resolving client problems to examine their general treatment and advocate for societal change—in other words, teaching them to take a person-first approach and not focus on the clients' lifestyle. This enables the practitioner to focus on the issue at hand rather than allowing personal values to further marginalize clients.

Currently, the incorporation of human rights into the social work curriculum is conducted on an individual basis. Although human rights is incorporated into social work teaching and learning, the inclusion of designated human rights modules into social work courses is based on the discretion of individual faculty members. However, the faculty has acknowledged that incorporating human rights into the curriculum requires a systematic approach to ensure that the many facets of human rights are addressed, because gaps and duplication may occur with this individual approach.

It would be remiss of this author to limit the discussion to the social work programme given that non-social work students comprise the majority of the student body. Therefore, it is recommended that the teaching of human rights be adopted as an institutional and collaborative approach. Thus, the design and delivery of human rights modules should be expanded for the understanding of the legal and other environments in which human rights are located. In short, it highlights a need to teach across the disciplines to infuse human rights throughout the university curricula and reshape the social fabric to one of respect for and adherence to human rights principles.

References

Barrow, C. (2001). *Introduction: Child rights and the Caribbean experience.* In C. Barrow (Ed.), *Children's rights: Caribbean realities* (pp. xiii–xxxv). Kingston, Jamaica: Ian Randle Publishers.

Blennberger, E. (2006). *Ethics in social work: An ethical code for social work professionals.* Stockholm, Sweden: Swedish Association of Graduates in Social Science.

British Association of Social Workers (BASW). (2012). *The Code of ethics for social work: Statement of principles.* Birmingham, UK: Policy, Ethics and Human Rights Committee. Retrieved from http://cdn.basw.co.uk

Brown, J. (2001). Parental resistance to child rights in Jamaica. In C. Barrow (Ed.), *Children's rights: Caribbean realities* (pp. xiii–xxxv). Kingston, Jamaica: Ian Randle Publishers.

Buvinić, M., Alda, E., & Lamas, J. (2005). *Emphasizing prevention in citizen security: The Inter-American Development Bank's contribution to reducing violence in Latin America and the Caribbean.* Washington, DC: Inter-American Development Bank. Retrieved from http://idbdocs.iadb.org

Chadwick-Parkes. S. (2012). *Youth armed violence interventions: Jamaica and its Toronto diaspora.* Research report prepared for Project Plousghshares, Waterloo, Ontario, Canada.

Deosaran, R. (2007). A Caribbean portrait of crime, justice and community policing. In R. Deosaran (Ed.), *Crime, delinquency and justice: A Caribbean reader* (pp. 241–264). Kingston, Jamaica: Ian Randle Publishers.

Edwards, A. (2013). *Caribbean drug trends.* PowerPoint presentation to Caribbean Social Issues Course, University of the West Indies, March 2013.

Ferreira-Sutherland, V. (2010). *Strengthening understandings of how borders and boundaries affect lives of women and men in the Lyndhurst/Greenwich Park Community.* Report prepared for the Women Resource and Outreach Centre and UNIFEM. Retrieved from http://www.iansa-omen.org/sites/default/files /newsviews/jamaica-borders-and-boundaries-wroc-2010.pdf

Gays in Jamaica. (n.d.) *The Jamaica Gleaner.* Retrieved from http://jamaica -gleaner.com/pages/gay/sexandthelaw.html

Halcon, L., Blum, R. W., Beuhring, T., Pate, E., Campbell-Forrester, S., & Venema, A. (2003). Adolescent health in the Caribbean: A regional portrait. *American Journal of Public Health, 93,* 1851–1857. Retrieved from http://people.stfx.ca/ibertsch/Grenadareadings/Halcon_et_al.pdf

Harriott, A., & Chadwick, S. (1999). *Impact of the activities of the Kingston Restoration Company (KRC) on community development, crime control and community policing within inner city areas in Kingston.* Study conducted on behalf of the Kingston Restoration Company, Kingston, Jamaica.

International Federation of Social Workers (IFSW). (2012a). *Teaching and learning about human rights.* Retrieved from http://ifsw.org/resources/ publications/human-rights/teaching-and learning-about-human-rights

International Federation of Social Workers (IFSW). (2012b). *Global standards for the education and training of the social work profession.* Retrieved from http://ifsw.org/policies/global-standards

International Federation of Social Workers (IFSW). (2013). *Policies.* Retrieved from http:www.ifsw.org/policies/

Jamaica Government Printer. 1982. *The Acts of Jamaica passed in the year 1982: Jamaica Education Act.* Kingston, Jamaica: Government Printer.

Levy, H. (2005). *Jamaica: Homicides and the peace management initiative.* Retrieved from www.un.org/esa/socdev/sib/egm/paper/HoraceLevy.pdf

McDowell, Z. (2001). Birth status, domestic law and the United Nations Convention on the Rights of the Child (UNCRC): A commonwealth Caribbean experience. In C. Barrow (Ed.), *Children's rights: Caribbean realities* (pp. 22–42). Kingston, Jamaica: Ian Randle Publishers.

McLean, A. (2009). Assessment of community security and transformation programmes in Jamaica. Kingston, Jamaica: Government of Jamaica. Retrieved from http://www.jm.undp.org/files/Community%20Security%20Assessment %20Report.pdf.

Ministry of Health. n.d. *The Jamaica National HIV/STI Control Programme.* Retrieved from http://www.jamaica-nap.org/hiv_jam

Ministry of Health (MOH). (2012). HIV Epidemic Update: Facts & Figures 2012. Retrieved from http://www.nhpjamaica.org/hiv-epidemic-update-facts -figures-2012

Mogensen, M. (2005). *Corner and area gangs of inner-city Jamaica: Children in organized armed violence.* Retrieved from http://www.coav.org.br/publique /media/ReportJamaica.pdf

Muggah, R., & Krause, K. (2008). *Framing contexts and responses to armed violence: Perspectives from Latin America and the Caribbean.* Paris, France: OECD-DAC Network on Conflict, Peace, and Development Co-operation. Retrieved from http:///www.genevadeclaration.org/fileadmin/docs/regional- publications /Framing-Contexts-and-Responses-to-Armed-Violence-Perspectives-from -Latin-America-and-the-Caribbean.pdf

Office of the Child's Advocate. (2011). *Office of the children's advocate 2009–2010 annual report.* Kingston, Jamaica: Author.

Office of the United Nations High Commissioner for Human Rights. (n.d.). *What are human rights?* Retrieved from http://www.ohchr.org/EN/Issues/pages /WhatareHumanRights

Padgett, T. (2006, April 12). The most homophobic place on Earth? *Time Magazine.* Retrieved from http://content.time.com/time/world/article /0,8599,1182991,00.html

Planning Institute of Jamaica (PIOJ). (2010). *Jamaica survey of living conditions 2010.* Kingston, Jamaica: PIOJ.

Planning Institute of Jamaica (PIOJ). (2011). *Economic and social survey of Jamaica 2011.*Kingston, Jamaica: PIOJ.

Pregnancy Resource Centre of Jamaica. (n.d.). *Information sheet.* Retrieved from http://yesprogramme.org/uploads/PRCJ_Information_Sheet.pdf

Pryce, K. (2007). Towards a Caribbean criminology. In R. Deosaran (Ed.), *Crime, delinquency and justice: A Caribbean reader* (pp. 3–18). Kingston, Jamaica: Ian Randle Publishers.

Rhoads, R. A. (2006). University reform in global times: Opportunities and challenges. *Chung Cheng Educational Studies, 5,* 1–24. Retrieved from http://globalhighered.com/articles/rhoads_global_times.pdf

Richards, S. (2012, December 19). Jamaica's buggery law no violation of human rights, international obligations. Retrieved from http://jamaica-gleaner.com /gleaner/20121219/cleisure/cleisure4.html

Serbanescu, R., Ruiz, A., & Suchdev, D. (2010). *Reproductive health survey Jamaica 2008: Final report.* Retrieved from http://stacks.cdc.gov/view/cdc/8254

Singh, W. (2001). Imprisonment and Caribbean youth. In C. Barrow (Ed.), *Children's rights: Caribbean realities* (pp. 43–59). Kingston, Jamaica: Ian Randle Publishers.

Teleki, K. (2007). *Human rights training for adults: What twenty-six evaluation studies say about design, implementation and follow up.* Research in Human Rights Education Paper Series. Human Rights Education Associates. Retrieved from http://www.hrea.org

Thompson-Ahye, H. (2004, November). *The rights of the child and the Caribbean: Prospects and challenges for the 21st century.* Presentation at the Child Rights Convention, Bahamas.

United Nations. (1948). *Universal declaration of human rights.* G.A. Res. 217 A (III). Retrieved from http://www.refworld.org/docid/3ae6b3712c.html

United Nations. (1979). *Convention on the elimination of all forms of discrimination against women.* G.A. Res. 34/180. Retrieved from http://www.ohchr.org /Documents/ProfessionalInterest/cedaw.pdf

United Nations. (1989). *Convention on the rights of the child.* G.A. Res. 44/25. Retrieved from http://www.ohchr.org/Documents/ProfessionalInterest/crc.pdf

UNAIDS. (2012). *Country progress report: Jamaica.* Retrieved from http://www .unaids.org/en/dataanalysis/knowyourresponse/countryprogressreports/2012 /ce_JM_Narrative_Report[1].pdf

UNICEF. (n.d.). *Situation analysis on excluded children in Jamaica Update 2006.* Retrieved from http://www.unicef.org/jamaica/resources_3950.htm

UNICEF Jamaica. (2006). Jamaica. *Jamaica gets its first children's advocate.* Retrieved from http://www.unicef.org/jamaica/promoting_child_rights_2990 .htm

United Nations Centre for Human Rights. (1994). *Human rights and social work: A manual for schools of social work and the social work profession* (Professional Training Series No. 1). Retrieved from http://www.ohchr.org/Documents /Publications/traininglen.pdf

United Nations Department for Economic and Social Affairs. (n.d.). *Jamaica.* Retrieved from www.un.org/esa/population/publications/abortion/docjamaica .doc

United Nations Development Programme (UNDP). (2013). *Human Development Report 2013: The rise of the south: Human progress in a diverse world.* New York, NY: Author.

United Nations Office of Drugs and Crime. (2012). *Homicide statistics 2012.* Retrieved from http://www.unodc.org/unodc/en/data-and-analysis/homicide .html

United Nations Office of Drugs and Crime/World Bank (2007). Crime, violence and development: Trends, cost and policy options in the Caribbean. Joint Report No. 37820. Retrieved from http:// www.unodc.org/documents/data -and-analysis/Caribbean-study-en.pdf

University of Minnesota Human Rights Resource Centre. (n.d). *The human rights education handbook: Effective practices for learning, action and change.* Retrieved from http://www1.umn.edu/humanrts/edumat/hreduseries/hrhandbook

U.S. Department of State. (2010). *Jamaica.* Retrieved from http://www.state.gov /documents/organization/160168.pdf

Williams, S. (2002). The effects of structural adjustment programs on the lives of children in Jamaica. In N. Hevener Kaufman & I. Rizzini (Eds). *Globalization and children: Exploring potentials for enhancing opportunities in the lives of children and youth* (pp. 151–160). New York, NY: Kluwer Academic Publishers.

SECTION II

Policy, Research, and Social Justice

S
ection II explores human rights in the macro context. Individuals, families, and communities experience extreme social and economic marginalization often as a result of structural and institutions failing to meet their social, economic, civil, and political rights. This section raises critical questions about how one would operationalize human rights in social work education to continue the mission, values, and priorities of social work. To that end, policy, research, and social justice requires an understanding of economic and political justice to effect and advocate for change in communities and nation states around the globe. Social work education must provide opportunities for students to analyze and develop knowledge and skills through experiential preparation and practice. Using the human rights framework, social work's role is to challenge the structures that continue to sustain inequalities and provide pathways for access by challenging power and privilege. It must not adhere to the status quo.

Michael Reisch raises points of contention or discourse between complementary goals of human rights, social justice, and multiculturalism. He postulates that there is indeed agreement that human rights provides a conceptual framework that addresses people's multidimensional needs and encourages greater political participation. In fact, both the National Association of Social

Workers and the Council on Social Work Education (CSWE) have affirmed this position by advocating ethical principles that promote social justice; in the accreditation standards CSWE has mandated inclusion of content that teaches students about social policy and services from an international perspective and to recognize the global interconnectedness of oppression. The critique Reisch makes lies in the extent and/or the capability of the social work profession to apply the human rights framework when the emphasis of social work practice is on needs rather than on rights. Other areas of concern among scholars include the practical and conceptual difficulties of integrating a human rights perspective into social work education. Therefore, Reisch draws attention to the need to take a critical view of the human rights framework to continue to advance the social justice mission of social work in the context of existing infrastructure, institutions, power, privilege, historical conditions, diverse cultural traditions, and context.

Louise Simmons' chapter demonstrates that social justice and economic justice are inextricably intertwined, particularly as these intersect with class, race, and gender. Economic inequalities are the basis of many social problems experienced by individuals, families, communities, and nation-states. All students of social work must understand the interplay between economic justice and the broad understanding of social justice and how it fits into the human rights framework. Simmons' chapter identifies methods of injecting economic justice concepts into social work education.

Students become active learners by engagement, practice, modeling, and participating. Rebecca Thomas, Christina Chiarelli-Helminiak, and Brunilda Ferraj present a model of using student researchers and working in a team employing a rights-based approach to conducting program evaluation of a social integration project with newly arrived immigrants and refugees. This approach provides students an opportunity to connect human rights to research throughout various steps of the evaluation and research process. This team approach provides a beneficial collective environment for learning and professional development. Rosemary Barbera provides another example of learning by doing, discussing how her university integrates action for human rights and social and economic justice into its curriculum through two capstone courses. In these courses students design, implement, and evaluate their projects to advance social and economic justice and human rights. Shirley Gatenio Gabel provides an alternative model for teaching policy practice based on the application of human rights principles. Her chapter outlines a new framework for developing social programs based on their intended outcomes rather than on financial eligibility criteria or type of benefit. Students use the human rights principles of participation, accountability, nondiscrimination, and equality as an alternative method of policy analysis.

In the final chapter in this section, Viviene Taylor discusses the challenges faced by South Africa 20 years after the end of the apartheid era. The democratically elected government faces the daunting task of addressing the inequalities that exist because of a sustained institutionalized racial discrimination, social inequalities, poverty, and economic exploitation. Social work education that aims to advance human rights must address the realities of an unjust system that affects the everyday life of individuals.

10 The Boundaries of Social Justice:
Addressing the Conflict Between Human Rights and Multiculturalism in Social Work Education

Michael Reisch

Since the adoption of the Universal Declaration of Human Rights (UDHR) in 1948 (United Nations, 1948), a human rights framework has been widely employed to promote social justice agendas, particularly in the West. Until recently human rights literature was dominated by lawyers (Steen & Mathiesen, 2005); however, increasingly social work educators have called for the incorporation of a human rights framework into all areas of social work practice (Reisch, Ife, & Weil, 2012; Wronka, 2008). The language of international human rights offers a "moral grounding for social work's more complex interpretations of social justice, equality, and empowerment" (Dewees & Roche, 2001, p. 137). Although a human rights framework can serve as a bridging concept, its underlying cultural biases may prevent it from providing the conceptual glue that would bind together increasingly fractious and multicultural societies. This chapter discusses some of the issues that create actual or potential conflicts among the seemingly complementary goals of human rights, social justice, and multiculturalism.

Social work proponents of human rights assert that they provide a comprehensive conceptual framework that addresses people's multidimensional needs and encourages greater political participation within the profession (Healy, 2008). The National Association of Social Workers' (NASW's) ethical imperative that social workers "promote social justice" (1996, p.1) provides additional professional reinforcement for this position. The Council on Social

---

This article is based on a paper presented at a seminar "Advancing Human Rights in Social Work Education," at the University of Connecticut, School of Social Work, May 16, 2013.

Work Education's (CSWE's) Educational Policy and Accreditation Standards (EPAS; CSWE, 2008) also requires programs to include content on the "global interconnectedness of oppression" and teach students about social policy and services from an international perspective (see also NASW, 2013). Hawkins and San Marcos (2009) argue further that the linkage of human rights and social justice within social work education promotes a focus on empowerment rather than individual pathology by enabling students to integrate knowledge, empathy, and action.

Most social work critics of a human rights framework have not challenged these premises. Instead, they have focused on the extent to which the profession has actually applied this framework or is capable of doing so within the context of established institutions, particularly those that emphasize human needs rather than human rights (Murdach, 2011). They have pointed out the fundamental distinction between the fulfillment of rights (which implies legal and/or moral obligation) and the fulfillment of needs, which can be viewed "as one of many compartmentalized options identified in [the] assessment of … clients' situations" (Dewees & Roche, 2001, p. 139).

Other critics have expressed concerns about the practical and conceptual difficulties of integrating a human rights perspective into social work education. These concerns include the conflict between the indivisibility of human rights and opposition to certain human rights tenets in the United States (Dewees & Roche, 2001); contested definitions of human rights and social justice (Reisch, 2002); faculty members' and students' lack of intellectual preparation to engage effectively with these complex issues (George, 1999); students' resistance to the political action implied by a human rights agenda because of their individually oriented perspective on change (Reisch & Jani, 2012); the paucity of social work theories that are compatible with human rights (Payne, 2005); the disjuncture between universalist human rights framework and the cultural relativism embodied in social work practice principles (Reisch, 2007); the belief that by focusing on the victims of oppression and disadvantage social work educators have already implicitly adopted a human rights perspective (Steen & Mathiesen, 2005); and the gap between the idealism of universal human rights and the reality of persistent inequality and oppression (Douzinas, 2000). Despite these critiques, for the past several decades human rights and social justice have been treated as complementary, if not equivalent concepts in the social work literature (Reisch et al., 2012).

The appeal of a human rights framework for a justice-oriented profession is obvious. Human rights perspectives assume that all human beings are entitled to certain inalienable social and economic protections and civil rights. Yet although human rights provisions may appear consistent with dominant understandings of social justice, they are not equivalent. Although the concept of human rights has a complex and frequently contested history,[1] U.S. scholars have rarely closely examined the compatibility of human rights, social justice, and other core social work values such as multiculturalism.

Human Rights, Social Justice, and Multiculturalism in U.S. Social Work

Social workers first used the term *social justice* more than a century ago as part of an effort to replace hierarchical charitable principles with universal standards of decency, enforced by the state and rationalized by social science research (Elshtain, 2002; Wise, 1909). This view of social justice synthesized religious ideas and secular principles of liberalism and social democracy (Reisch & Andrews, 2001). Over the past century oppressed groups modified this universal definition to fit their particular circumstances and aspirations. Their struggles transformed the debate about social justice—from the elimination of legal discrimination to the establishment of multiculturalism—and underscored the contradictions between the profession's stated commitment to justice principles and its practice (Reisch, 2008).

For example, it proved difficult to balance social work's inclusive rhetoric with selective approaches to social and economic problems or to resolve the tensions between individually based services and those rooted in collectivist perspectives on social justice and rights, such as the mutual aid societies created by Chicanos, African Americans, and European and Asian immigrants (Gordon, 1991; Rivera, 1987). These populations tended to view social justice through a skeptical cultural lens that rejected the rhetoric of "the general welfare" (Beito, 2001; Lai, 2004). In contrast, by assuming that social justice could only be achieved through assimilation, even sympathetic social work reformers subtly denigrated the survival mechanisms immigrants developed (Hammond, 1920). They had difficulty embracing full social equality because most social service agencies were physically and socially segregated (Iglehart & Becerra, 2013).

Consequently, racial minorities rejected compulsory or coerced assimilation presented under the banners of social justice and human rights because they feared it would lead to the loss of their cultural heritage (Wright, 1920). They have used specific issues, from lynching in the South a hundred years ago to racial profiling in the North today, to illuminate the often hidden dimensions of injustice (Alexander, 2010). Sometimes their discourse emphasized self-determination and self-help (Carson, 1993; Dubey, Miranda, & Turner, 1969); at other times it combined a critique of capitalism, feminist ideas, and elements of "racial uplift" (Owen & Randolph, 1920). This produced what Hamilton and Hamilton (1997) called a "dual agenda."

Although the development of welfare state policies between the 1930s and 1970s enhanced the prospects of achieving social justice and human rights on a national scale, the gap between policy rhetoric and practice persisted and even widened (Katz, 2001). The United States took few steps toward racial or gender justice until the resurgence of the civil rights and feminist movements after World War II, a period coinciding with the introduction of human rights discourse into social work. Postwar efforts to promote human rights and social justice, however, focused primarily on eradicating discrimination not on structural change (Valien, 1949, 1951). Meanwhile, the professionalizing impulse among social workers and a hostile political climate encouraged a search for universalist theories and largely ignored or pathologized the particular issues racial and ethnic minorities and women confronted (Kluckhorn, 1951).

Social work curricula emphasized a broad examination of class, ethnicity, and culture rather than race or gender (Rohrer, 1957). Social work research reinforced the tendency to view racial minorities and women through different lenses and to regard their deviance from dominant cultural norms as distinct from class, ethnic, or religious differences (Barrabee, 1954). These assumptions provided the conceptual foundation for the 1960s War on Poverty, which focused on fixing cultural deficiencies instead of addressing systemic inequalities (Quadagno, 1996). Scant references to racism and sexism appeared in social work literature until the 1970s (Dodson, 1970; Shannon, 1970) and even fewer references to sexual orientation or ability status (Lee, 1972). The profession framed its focus on rights, therefore, in narrow rather than universal terms (Berry, 1963).

The new social movements of the 1960s and 1970s highlighted the contradictions between social justice rhetoric and the realities of social work practice and education and challenged their benign underlying assumptions (Young, 1990). Consequently, by the 1970s the profession's language began to change. Publications on ethnic sensitive practice, cultural competence, and bicultural models appeared (Lum, 2007; Devore & Schlesinger, 1996; Gibson, Gomez, & Santos, 1973). An alternative vision of social justice—a "multiple melting pot"—imagined a future U.S. society "in which separation is neither required nor forbidden but is to be tolerated with sympathy" (Olan, 1971, pp. 31, 40).

These emerging theoretical frameworks ultimately revised the meaning of social justice in social work education (Morris, 2002). Yet their analyses of social issues through the lens of group rather than individual characteristics inadvertently undermined efforts to establish a universal human rights framework and rationalized conservative attacks on social justice goals (Mead, 1992).[2] Thus, the profession's historic failure to incorporate the concerns of excluded populations into mainstream theoretical constructs about rights and justice created parallel discourses within social work. One focused on the uncritical adoption of universal human rights principles, the other emphasized group-specific inequalities and oppressions rooted in social identity (Chestang, 1970; Morales, 1978).

In the late 1970s the term *multiculturalism* first appeared as part of an effort to fuse these approaches. Initially it signified an attempt to go beyond ethnic sensitivity by incorporating insights from postmodernism (Leonard, 1997), critical race theory, new wave feminism (Hill Collins, 2000), social constructivism, and queer theory into prevailing conceptual frameworks (Ramakrishnan & Balgopal, 1995). Proponents of multiculturalism also encouraged marginalized groups to define their identities outside the influence of the dominant culture and to preserve their heritages, traditions, and languages. Like earlier critiques of assimilation, this perspective represented a fundamental challenge to professional hegemony (Keyes, 1991).

By the 1990s, however, the widespread use of the term *multiculturalism* began to obscure its relationship to social justice and human rights (Gould, 1996). Some social workers interpreted multiculturalism as a means to promote the distinct needs of specific racial and ethnic groups, not in terms of collective goals (Delgado, 1994). Broadening the concept to include class, gender, age, sexual orientation, and ability status made its meaning increasingly diffuse and weakened efforts to create an overarching conceptual framework for practice (Yellowbird, Fong, Galindo, Nowicki, & Freeman, 1996). This led to growing concern among social workers that multiculturalism would morph into cultural relativism, romanticize cultural differences, and ignore "the internal variations in traditional culture" (Goldberg, 2000, p. 13; Potockey, 1997).

Contemporary literature on multiculturalism continues to eschew a structural analysis aimed at universal rights and social justice goals in favor of what would formerly have been regarded as separatist practice (Schiele, 2011). This has produced a still unresolved "conflict between respecting the contents of all cultures versus supporting basic human rights" (Goldberg, 2000, p. 13). Van Soest and Garcia (2003), however, assert that a focus on oppression is inextricably linked to nine core human rights values: life, freedom and liberty, equality and nondiscrimination, justice, solidarity, social responsibility, evolution, peace and nonviolence, and reciprocal relations between humankind and nature (pp. 65–67). Despite such efforts, debates over the relationship among human rights, social justice, and multiculturalism have become increasingly contentious, particularly in the international arena (Caputo, 2000).

Implications for Practice and Education

Thus, although social justice, human rights, and multiculturalism have been normative components of U.S. social work for decades, their meaning and implications remain ambiguous (Reisch, 2002). This ambiguity largely emerges from the conflict between universalist views of social justice and rights and those that focus on achieving justice and rights for specific groups. Attempts to resolve this conflict have included reliance on a version of modern liberalism (Rawls, 2001), an updated expression of social democracy (Gil, 1998), a postmodern emphasis on socially just processes (Prigoff, 2003), and the application of the capabilities perspective (Nussbaum, 2011). In most Western social work discourse, social justice is still equated with human rights; both are presumed to be consistent with multiculturalism (Caputo, 2000; Finn & Jacobson, 2008). However, Yee and Dumbrill (2003) argue provocatively that by "essentializing and circumscribing people's social identities ... multiculturalism maintains oppressive structures, undermines efforts to generate social action, and ignores the historical context that produces various forms of injustice" (pp. 108–110).

These conflicts also persist because proponents of the symmetry among human rights, social justice, and multiculturalism base their arguments on several debatable propositions. First, they assert that the attainment of social justice and human rights merely requires the creation of a more egalitarian society with principles that reflect "the subordination of market price" (Marshall, 1992, p. 40). This assumption is increasingly challenged by the realities of globalization and the pursuit of human rights, such as marriage equality, that do not require fundamental changes in market-oriented institutions (Reisch, 2013b).

A related assumption—that the establishment of individual rights is complementary, if not essential, to the attainment of social equality—has been undermined by racially based attacks on legal entitlements to social welfare benefits and efforts to roll back civil rights through both judicial and legislative means (Piven, 2002). A third assumption, that a socially just society is one in which both "economic and *social differences* between social classes and groups are markedly reduced" (Jansson, 2005, p. 24, emphasis added) presumes that all groups regard the reduction of such differences as desirable because they share a common definition of social justice. Persistent controversies over LGBTQ rights, the status of women, and the role of religion in social services are merely the most vivid illustrations of divergent conceptions of social justice in the United States today.

Another persistent issue directly relevant to the introduction of a human rights framework into social work education involves the relationship between individual and group identity and rights. Social justice in the United States has often been equated with the application of color-blind meritocratic principles. The emphasis on multiculturalism during the past several decades has been, in part, a reaction against both the ideal and the reality of a color-blind society (Young, 2011). This issue is closely related to the definition of citizenship, which involves not only the establishment of legal rights but also the balance between the attainment of universal ideals of life and liberty and the preservation of cultural distinctions regarding the meaning of "the pursuit of happiness" (Foner, 1999).[3]

Thus, achieving a balance between group-specific interests and universal ideals of social justice remains an intellectual and political challenge. Social workers agree that systemic injustices must be addressed and the effects of structural inequities on specific groups should be analyzed.[4] Yet the persistence of selective approaches to socioeconomic problems and the focus on cultural rather than systemic factors inadvertently reinforces longstanding social divisions by essentializing concepts such as race and gender (Longres, 1997), thereby undercutting a basic premise of universal human rights.

Critiques of the Human Rights Framework

The most common criticisms of the human rights framework involve its Eurocentric bias. Although many non-European traditions were represented when the Universal Declaration of Human Rights was drafted, its philosophical foundations are clearly rooted in French and Anglo-American conceptions of individualism, democracy, and citizenship (Foner, 1999). Both before and after its ratification nations as diverse as Saudi Arabia and Brazil criticized the document for assuming that individualism and democracy constituted the cornerstones of international human rights doctrine (Ignatieff, 2001).

A second source of criticism emerged within the West itself, based on perspectives as diverse as Marxism, postcolonial critiques of imperialism (Said, 2000), and postmodern arguments against the "universalizing pretensions of Enlightenment thought" (Ignatieff, 2001, p. 105). A common theme of these critics is that human rights language resonates solely within a small number of nations, which share a historical commitment to liberal individualism, human agency, freedom, and a civic conception of citizenship (Foner, 1999). These critics argue that human rights doctrine is another mechanism of Western cultural and political hegemony, which eliminates local sources of knowledge and cultural practices and promotes a vision of modernity and progress consistent with Western values and goals.

The division between proponents of social justice and human rights has intensified in recent years as a consequence of economic globalization and the spread of a neo-liberal worldview that stresses individual agency rather than collective responsibility (Reisch, 2013a). This problem has particular resonance within U.S. social work, which has increasingly focused on individually oriented rather than communal problem definitions and solutions (Reisch & Jani, 2012). As Merry and Levitt (2008) state

> Human rights ideas produce a new consciousness of entitlement that allows people to stand up for themselves and ultimately generate actions that we might call emancipatory. But as they emphasize individual choice rather than collective responsibility, they promote understandings of the self compatible with capitalism. They help to acclimate people to the idea that ... [individuals], and not society or the state, are thus responsible for their failures as well as their successes. (p. 4)

East Asian critiques of human rights similarly frame their arguments within a communitarian perspective that emphasizes family and community well-being over individual rights, freedom, and democracy. Some Asian critics even question whether the linkage between social justice and universal human rights should be used as the foundation for social welfare policies (Akimoto, 2007). They regard human rights claims as an "alien, Western import not suited to local normative systems" (Merry, 2006, p. 38).

Another source of contestation results from the distinctions in human rights doctrine among political and individual freedoms, so-called negative rights that protect individuals from the tyranny of the state; positive rights, which emphasize protections to ensure an adequate standard of living; and collective rights that promote intergovernmental cooperation between nations and peoples in the pursuit of peace, economic and social development, and environmental protection. Other conflicts have emerged due to the prominence of two major concepts within the human rights paradigm: universalism and indivisibility. The former refers to the universal applicability of human rights protections regardless of group membership. This premise has been challenged on philosophical grounds for assuming that individualism and democracy should be the foundation of international human rights doctrine (Akimoto, 2007). The latter asserts that no single human right is more or less important than any other and that certain rights must be realized to facilitate the enjoyment of other rights. This concept has been questioned on grounds of feasibility and, in practice, has rarely been realized. Civil rights have often been ignored in developing nations, whereas rights relating to economic and social well-being have been systematically subordinated to political and civil rights, particularly in the West (Wronka, 2008).

A final challenge to the linkage between human rights and social justice stems from the conceptual and practical problems related to enforcement and accountability. A human rights framework was originally envisioned as a tool to protect individuals from governmental tyranny. In practice a focus on human rights has generally relied on voluntary compliance by governments to enforce various protections (negative rights) and to create the conditions possible to realize so-called positive rights. As many social justice advocates have pointed out, this position is largely unenforceable because national governments can and do perpetrate human rights violations against vulnerable groups with impunity (Reisch et al., 2012).

Therefore, the practical challenges to the implementation of human rights principles are significant, not least because, in the absence of social mobilization, promoting human rights claims often requires access to the legal system and the assistance of attorneys and managerial elites (Armaline, Glasberg, & Purkayastha, 2011; Merry, 2006). This kind of advocacy from above raises issues about the institutions and policies this approach generates and the extent to which it actually produces socially just outcomes in practice and education.

Conclusion

These critiques underscore how an uncritical adoption of a human rights framework may not advance the social justice mission of social work as its proponents contend. Although human rights principles are consistent with the profession's goal to improve the life conditions of vulnerable and disadvantaged populations, in practice it is difficult if not impossible to operationalize these principles in ways that do not reinforce and reproduce the dominant order under current conditions. A social justice orientation to social welfare and social work in the 21st century would recognize the relationship between people's complementary needs for economic assistance and nonmaterial supports. It would also address issues of power and privilege and challenge prevailing assumptions about the existence of universal human needs that frequently underlie the profession's view of justice (Jani & Reisch, 2011). It might even question the assumption that a universal idea of social justice exists and produce a revised conception of social justice and human rights that recognizes the implications of global interdependence and increasing demographic and cultural diversity.

This approach to incorporating human rights into social work education would also recognize that definitions of social justice and human rights are strongly influenced by historical conditions, diverse cultural traditions and belief systems, the effects of religious or secular ideas, and the existence of institutions to implement or thwart the attainment of social justice goals. In some circumstances, such as the South African liberation struggle, the establishment of civil or political rights was considered a prerequisite for the attainment of social and economic justice. In other places, such as India, overcoming hegemonic cultural norms and values that had been imposed by colonial or imperial powers took priority (Chakrabarty, 2006).

Context also plays a critical role in shaping how different societies articulate their conceptions of justice. Latin American narratives, for example, which are expressed most vividly through poetry and the visual arts, synthesize indigenous myths and a hybrid form of Catholicism (Petrella, 2005). In Africa, justice concepts have used a new vocabulary (such as *negritude*) and are frequently depicted through traditional songs and stories (Le Baron, 1966).

Asian conceptions of social justice borrow heavily from Hindu, Buddhist, and Confucian philosophy and are often reflected through the use of educational aphorisms (Chew, 2004; Green, 2004).

Cultural and contextual influences also shape how societies implement concepts of human rights and justice through laws, institutions, customs, and traditions. This underscores the importance of education and consciousness-raising, of providing people not only with basic skills but also with new ways of thinking about themselves and their role in the world. It also stresses the need for people to regain control of the physical environment and develop sustainable forms of economic self-sufficiency.

Finally, many contemporary struggles for human rights and justice frame their arguments in group rather than individual terms, reflecting the collectivist orientation of the cultures in which they emerged. Although many non-Western justice movements use the language of universal rights to promote their causes, they often reject the application of a universal human rights framework to their specific contexts on the grounds that it fails to respect their unique cultural values and traditions and is merely another symbol of Western hegemony. These differences have been most clearly expressed around such issues as the separation of church and state, the role of women, the concept of private property, and the meaning of political democracy.

As a solution, Ife (2010) proposes a model for "human rights from below" that would preserve social work's longstanding commitment to end exploitation and inequality yet would avoid the imposition of hegemonic Western standards and goals. He suggests using existing human rights doctrine as a starting point, which can then be deconstructed and critiqued because "universalism need not mean uniformity" (p. 94). This vision of justice would reflect local sources of knowledge and traditional cultural norms. Although the application of this vision to social work practice and education presents complex and abundant challenges, it may be more suitable as a guide to "doing justice" in the rapidly changing and complex economic and demographic environment of the future than a set of detailed prescriptions that ignore the effects of culture, context, and history.

References

Akimoto, T. (2007, April 20). Social justice and social welfare policies: Beyond national boundaries: What should we question? In *Human Rights and Social Justice: Rethinking Social Welfare's Mission*. Seoul, Korea: Korean Academy of Social Welfare.

Alexander, M. (2010). *The new Jim Crow: Mass incarceration in the age of colorblindness*. New York, NY: New Press.

Armaline, W. T., Glasberg, D. S., & Purkayastha, B. (Eds.) (2011). *Human rights in our own backyard: Injustice and resistance in the United States*. Philadelphia, PA: University of Pennsylvania Press.

Barrabee, P. (1954). How cultural factors affect family life. *Proceedings of the National Conference on Social Welfare* (pp. 17–30). New York, NY: Columbia University Press.

Beito, D. (2001). *From mutual aid to the welfare state: Fraternal societies and social services, 1890–1967*. Chapel Hill, NC: University of North Carolina Press.

Berry, M. (1963). Civil rights and social welfare. *Proceedings of the National Conference on Social Welfare* (pp. 84–96). New York, NY: Columbia University Press.

Brown v. Board of Education, (1954). 347 U.S. 483, 74 S. Ct. 686, 98 L. Ed. 873.

Caputo, R. (2000). Multiculturalism and social justice: An attempt to reconcile the irreconcilable within a pragmatic liberal framework. *Race, Gender, and Class, 7*(4), 161–182.

Carson, E. D. (1993). *A hand up: Black philanthropy and self-help in America*. Washington, DC: Joint Center for Political Studies.

Chakrabarty, B. (2006). *Social and political thought of Mahatma Gandhi*. Abingdon, Oxon, UK: Routledge.

Chestang, L. W. (1970). The issue of race in casework practice. *Social Work Practice*, 14–26.

Chew, L. (2004). Reflections on Buddhism, gender and human rights. In K. M. Tsomo (Ed.), *Buddhist women and social justice: Ideals, challenges and achievements* (pp. 35–44). Albany, NY: State University of New York Press.

Council on Social Work Education (CSWE). (2008). *Educational policy and accreditation standards*. Retrieved from http://www.cswe.org/File.aspx?id =41861

Delgado, G. (1994) *Beyond the politics of place: New directions in community organizing in the 1990s*. Oakland, CA: Applied Research Center.

Devore, W., & Schlesinger, E. G. (1996). *Ethnic-sensitive social work practice* (4th ed.). Boston, MA: Allyn and Bacon.

Dewees, M., & Roche, S. E. (2001). Teaching about human rights in social work. *Journal of Teaching in Social Work, 21*(1/2), 137–155.

Dodson, D. (1970). Institutionalized racism in social welfare agencies. *Proceedings of the National Conference on Social Welfare* (pp. 88–98). New York, NY: Columbia University Press.

Douzinas, C. (2000). *The end of human rights: Critical legal thought at the turn of the century.* Oxford, UK: Hart.

Dubey, S. N., Miranda, M., & Turner, J. B. (1969). Black unity and self-determination: Social welfare implications. *Proceedings of the National Conference on Social Welfare.* New York, NY: Columbia University Press.

Elshtain, J. B. (2002). *Jane Addams and the dream of American democracy: A life.* New York, NY: Basic Books.

Finn, J., & Jacobson, M. (2008). *Just practice: A social justice approach to social work* (2nd ed.). Peosta, IA: Eddie Bowers.

Foner, E. (1999). Who is an American? In E. Foner, *Who owns history: Rethinking the past in a changing world* (pp. 149–166). New York, NY: Hill & Wang.

George, J. (1999). Conceptual muddle, practical dilemma: Human rights, social development and social work education. *International Social Work, 42*(1), 15–26.

Gibson, G., Gomez, E., & Santos, Y. (1973). Bilingual-bicultural service for the barrio. *Proceedings of the National Conference on Social Welfare.* New York, NY: Columbia University Press.

Gil, D. (1998). *Confronting injustice and oppression: Concepts and strategies for social work.* New York, NY: Columbia University Press.

Goldberg, M. (2000). Conflicting principles in multicultural social work. *Families in Society, 81*(1), 12–20.

Gordon, L. (1991). Black and White visions of welfare: Women's welfare activism, 1890–1945. *Journal of American History, 78*(2), 559–590.

Gould, K. H. (1996). The misconstruing of multiculturalism: The standard debate and social work. In P. L. Ewalt, E. M. Freeman, S. A. Kirk, & D. L. Poole (Eds.), *Multicultural issues in social work* (pp. 29–42). Washington, DC: NASW Press.

Green, P. (2004). Transforming conflict, transforming ourselves: Buddhism and social liberation. In K. L. Tsomo (Ed.), *Buddhist women and social justice:*

Ideals, challenges and achievements (pp. 73–88). Albany, NY: State University of New York Press.

Hamilton, D. C., & Hamilton, C. V. (1997). *The dual agenda: The African American struggle for civil and economic equality.* New York, NY: Columbia University Press.

Hammond, L. H. (1920). *Interracial cooperation: Helpful suggestions concerning relations of white and colored citizens.* New York, NY: National Board of the YWCA.

Hawkins, C., & San Marcos, T. X. (2009). Global citizenship: A model for teaching universal human rights in social work education. *Critical Social Work, 10*(1). Retrieved from http://www1.uwindsor.ca/criticalsocialwork /global-citizenship-a-model-for-teaching-universal-human-rights-in-social -work-education

Healy, L. M. (2008). Exploring the history of social work as a human rights profession. *International Social Work, 51*(6), 735–748.

Hill Collins, P. (2000). *Black feminist thought: Knowledge, consciousness, and the politics of empowerment* (2nd ed.). New York, NY: Routledge.

Hendricks, H.A. (1937). Social needs of Indian children, *Social Service Review,* 11(1), 52-65.

Ife, J. (2010). *Human rights from below: Achieving rights through community development.* New York, NY: Cambridge University Press.

Iglehart, A., & Becerra, R. M. (2013). *Social services and the ethnic community* (2nd ed.). Boston, MA: Allyn and Bacon.

Ignatieff, M. (2001). The attack on human rights. *Foreign Affairs, 80*(6), 102–116.

Jani, J. S., & Reisch, M. (2011). Common human needs, uncommon solutions: Applying a critical framework to perspectives on human behavior. *Families in Society, 92*(1), 13–20.

Jansson, B. (2005). *The reluctant welfare state* (5th ed.). Belmont, CA: Brooks /Cole.

Katz, M. B. (2001). *The price of citizenship: Redefining the American welfare state.* New York, NY: Henry Holt.

Keyes, P. R. (1991). Ethnic and multicultural concerns in social work. *Journal of Multicultural Social Work, 1*(1), 1–6.

Kluckhorn, F. R. (1951). Dominant and variant cultural value orientations. *Proceedings of the National Conference on Social Welfare* (pp. 51–67). New York, NY: Columbia University Press.

Lai, H. M. (2004). *Becoming Chinese-American: A history of communities and institutions*. Walnut Creek, CA: AltaMira.

Le Baron, B. (1966). Negritude: A Pan-African ideal. *Ethics, 76*(4), 267–276.

Lee, R. D. (1972). Mental health and gay liberation. *Proceedings of the National Conference on Social Welfare*. New York, NY: Columbia University Press.

Leonard, P. (1997). *Postmodern welfare: Reconstructing an emancipatory project*. Thousand Oaks, CA: Pine Forge Press.

Longres, J. (1997). The impact and implications of multiculturalism. In M. Reisch & E. Gambrill (Eds.), *Social work in the twenty-first century* (pp. 39–47). Thousand Oaks, CA: Pine Forge Press.

Lum, D. (Ed.) (2007). *Culturally competent practice: A framework for understanding diverse groups and justice issues* (3rd ed.). Belmont, CA: Thompson/Brooks Cole.

Marshall, T. H. (1992). *Citizenship and social class*. London, UK: Pluto Press.

Mead, L. (1992). *The new politics of poverty*. New York, NY: Basic Books.

Merry, S. E. (2006). Transnational human rights and local activism: Mapping the middle. *American Anthropologist, 108*(1), 38–51.

Merry, S. E., & Levitt, P. (2008, April). *Law, human rights and social movements: Exploring the justice scaffold*. Unpublished paper presented at Women and the Law seminar, University of Michigan, Ann Arbor.

Morales, A. (1978). Institutional racism in mental health and criminal justice. *Social Casework, 59*(7), 387–395.

Morris, P. M. (2002). The capabilities perspective: A framework for social justice. *Families in Society: The Journal of Contemporary Human Services, 83*(4), 365–373. doi: 10.1606/1044-3894.16

Muller v. Oregon. (1908). 208 U.S. 412, 28 S. Ct. 324, 52 L. Ed. 551.

Murdach, A. D. (2011). Is social work a human rights profession? *Social Work, 56*(3), 281–283.

National Association of Social Workers (NASW). (1996). *Code of ethics* (revised ed.). Washington, DC: Author.

National Association of Social Workers (NASW). (2013). *Working for equal opportunity in the U.S. and internationally*. Washington, DC: Author.

Nussbaum, M. C. (2011). *Creating capabilities: The human development approach*. Cambridge, MA: Belknap Press.

Olan, L. A. (1971). Aspirations for ethnic minorities. *Proceedings of the Annual Forum of the National Conference on Social Welfare* (pp. 28–40). New York, NY: Columbia University Press.

Owen, C., & Randolph, A. P. (1920, August). The new Negro: What is he? *The Messenger*, 73–74.

Payne, M. (2005). *Modern social work theory* (3rd ed.). Basingstoke, UK: Palgrave MacMillan.

Petrella , I. (Ed.). (2005). *Latin American liberation theology: The next generation.* Maryknoll, NY: Orbis Books.

Piven, F. F. (2002). Welfare policy and American politics. In F. F. Piven, J. Acker, M. Hallock, & S. Morgen (Eds.), *Work, welfare and politics: Confronting poverty in the wake of welfare reform* (pp. 19–33). Eugene, OR: University of Oregon Press.

Potockey, M. (1997). Multicultural social work in the United States: A review and critique. *International Social Work*, *40*(1), 315–326.

Prigoff, A. W. (2003). Social justice framework. In J. Anderson & R. W. Carter (Eds.), *Diversity perspectives for social work practice* (pp. 113–120). Boston, MA: Allyn and Bacon.

Quadagno, J. (1996). *The color of welfare: How racism undermined the war on poverty.* New York, NY: Oxford University Press.

Ramakrishnan, K. R., & Balgopal, P. R. (1995). Role of social institutions in a multicultural society. *Journal of Sociology and Social Work*, *22*(1), 11–28.

Rawls, J. (2001). *Justice as fairness: A restatement.* Cambridge, MA: Belknap Press.

Reichert, E. D. (Ed.). (2007). *Challenges in human rights: A social work perspective.* New York, NY: Columbia University Press.

Reisch, M. (2002). Defining social justice in a socially unjust world. *Families in Society: The Journal of Contemporary Human Services*, *83(4)*, 343–354.

Reisch, M. (2007). Social justice and multiculturalism: Persistent tensions in the history of U.S. social welfare and social work. *Studies in Social Justice*, *1*(1), 67–92.

Reisch, M. (2008). From melting pot to multiculturalism: The impact of racial and ethnic diversity on social work and social justice in the U.S. *British Journal of Social Work*, *38*(4), 788–804.

Reisch, M. (2013a). Social work education and the neoliberal challenge: The U.S. response to increasing global inequality. *Social Work Education*, 32(6), 217–233.

Reisch, M. (2013b). What is the future of social work? *Critical and Radical Social Work*, *1*(1), 67–85.

Reisch, M., & Andrews, J. L. (2001). *The road not taken: A history of radical social work in the United States.* Philadelphia, PA: Brunner-Routledge.

Reisch, M., & Jani, J. S. (2012). The new politics of social work practice: Understanding context to promote change. *British Journal of Social Work, 42*(6), 1132–1150.

Reisch, M., Ife, J., & Weil, M. (2012). Social justice, human rights, values, and community practice. In M. Weil, M. Reisch, & M. Ohmer (Eds.), *Handbook of community practice* (2nd ed.) (pp. 73–103). Thousand Oaks, CA: SAGE Publications.

Rivera, J. A. (1987). Self-help as mutual protection: The development of Hispanic fraternal benefit societies. *Journal of Applied Behavioral Science, 23*(3), 387–396.

Rohrer, J. (1957). Sociocultural factors in personality development. *Proceedings of the National Conference on Social Welfare* (pp. 193–211). New York, NY: Columbia University Press.

Said, E. W. (2000). *The Edward Said reader.* M. Bayoumi & A. Rubin (Eds.). New York, NY: Vintage Books.

Schiele, J. H. (Ed.). (2011). *Social welfare policy: Regulation and resistance among people of color.* Los Angeles, CA: SAGE Publications.

Shannon, B. E. (1970). Implications of White racism for social work practice. *Social Casework, 51*(5), 270–276.

Specht, H., & Courtney, M. (1994). *Unfaithful angels: How social work abandoned its mission.* New York, NY: Free Press.

Steen, J. A., & Mathiesen, S. (2005). Human rights education: Is social work behind the curve? *Journal of Teaching in Social Work, 25*(3/4), 143–156.

United Nations. (1948). *Universal declaration of human rights.* G.A. Res. 217 A (III). Retrieved from http://www.refworld.org/docid/3ae6b3712c.html

Valien, P. (1949, 1951). Racial programs in social work. In M. B. Hodges (Ed.), *Social work year book, 1949, 1951.* Albany, NY: Boyd Printing.

Van Soest, D., & Garcia, B. (2003). *Diversity education for social justice: Mastering teaching skills.* Alexandria, VA: Council on Social Work Education.

Wise, S. S. (1909). The conference sermon: Charity versus justice. *Proceedings of the National Conference of Charities and Corrections* (pp. 20–29). Fort Wayne, IN: Fort Wayne Printing.

Wright, R. R. (1920). What does the Negro want in our democracy? *Proceedings of the National Conference of Social Work* (pp. 539–545). New York, NY: National Conference.

Wronka, J. (2008). *Human rights and social justice: Social action and service for the helping and health professions.* Newbury Park, CA: SAGE Publications.

Yellowbird, M., Fong, R., Galindo, P., Nowicki, J., & Freeman, E. M. (1996). The multicultural mosaic. In P. L. Ewalt, E. M. Freeman, S. A. Kirk, & D. L. Poole (Eds.), *Multicultural issues in social work* (pp. 3–13). Washington, DC: NASW Press.

Yee, J. Y., & Dumbrill, G. C. (2003). Whiteout: Looking for race in Canadian social work practice. In A. Al-Krenaw & J. R. Graham (Eds.), *Multicultural social work in Canada: Working with diverse ethno-racial communities* (pp. 98–121). Don Mills, Ontario: Oxford University Press.

Young, I. M. (1990). *Justice and the politics of difference*. Princeton, NJ: Princeton University Press.

Young, I. M. (2011). *Responsibility for justice*. New York, NY: Oxford University Press.

Endnotes

1 In the introduction to her book on social work and civil rights, Reichert (2007) cites the NASW 2003 policy statement on the subject of human rights:

> Social work…is the only profession imbued with social justice as its fundamental value and concern. But social justice is a fairness doctrine that provides civil and political leeway in deciding what is just and unjust. Human rights, on the other hand, encompass social justice, but transcend civil and political customs, in consideration of the basic life-sustaining needs of all human beings, without distinction. (p. 4).

2 Ironically, liberal precedent for such arguments existed in the use of Kenneth Clark's research to support the plaintiffs' case in the 1954 *Brown v. Board of Education* decision and even as far back as 1908 in the testimony women settlement house leaders provided in the landmark case of *Muller v. Oregon* (1908).

3 Unfortunately, recent scholarship continues to be plagued by definitional ambiguity and conflicting principles. A content analysis of documents in the field of social welfare conducted by the author unearthed no fewer than 25 terms that have been used, in one form or another, as synonyms for *multiculturalism*. Each of these terms, however, has different nuances of meaning and serves different purposes.

4 The recurrence of this criticism throughout U.S. social welfare history, in slightly different form, is remarkable. See, for example Specht and Courtney (1994). What is equally remarkable is that little has been done to address these concerns.

11 | Economic Justice, Social Work Education, and Human Rights

Louise Simmons

Social work educators are accustomed to depicting oppression with terms such as *race, class, gender*, and other identities. They are also accustomed to asserting that social justice is a goal of social work practice, and among the elements of social justice we often include economic justice. Yet how do social work educators understand economic justice, particularly as it intersects with class, race, and gender? How does this understanding relate to embracing human rights in social work education? I argue in this chapter that to embrace the goal of economic justice, it is critical to understand the contemporary economic climate and how it affects individuals, communities, the nation, and the globe. This is essential for community organizing and macro practice but also important for micro practice. Economic inequality is at the root of many problems social workers and their constituents encounter. Economic issues have major effects on families in terms of stress, family breakdown, and relationships among family members. Thus, for all students, concepts of economic justice should be incorporated into a broad understanding of social justice, as well as social work education and practice. This chapter identifies methods of inserting economic justice concepts into social work education, mainly for the U.S. context, but also with implications internationally. It also discusses how education related to economic justice fits within a human rights framework.

Economic Literacy

One approach to incorporating economic justice themes into the curriculum is by cultivating economic literacy among students. This involves integrating economic concepts into courses so that students grasp the sources of contemporary economic inequality. These include concepts such as globalization, neoliberalism, economic restructuring, privatization, precarious and low-wage work, outsourcing, immigration trends, and urban restructuring, to name a few. Having a grasp of these issues can help students understand economic and social dynamics in locales that affect communities and individuals. It is also important for students to understand that these economic policies have not emerged from some invisible hand of the market that is detached from human beings and their intentions, but are the products of decisions made by individuals in governmental and economic institutions to facilitate the accumulation of wealth by financial elites at the expense of poor, working class, and middle class communities.

As a case in point, many students understand from their own life experiences how their prospects for attaining economic stability differ substantially from previous generations. But do they understand why this is so, and why social work faces huge challenges in maintaining social protections and social programs in which current students may want to find employment? Why are government interventions to address social problems under such attack? To answer these questions, we would argue that comprehending neoliberalism, associated globalization, and the neoliberal agenda is critical.

Neoliberalism

There is a wide array of literature on neoliberalism that includes analysis from a number of academic disciplines. For our purposes here and to put it as succinctly as possible, neoliberalism encompasses a stage of capitalism in which capital is globally mobile and can locate operations in areas of the world with the lowest labor costs, fewest regulations, and greatest profit maximization possibilities; a system in which the role of government moves away from providing programs to protect vulnerable citizens and mitigate the harshest effects of the private market to a government that facilitates maximum profits for the private sector; a social ethos that elevates individualism and individual responsibility for one's fate while denigrating social solidarity and responsibility; and a system in which an ongoing assault on collective action on behalf of the vulnerable and exploited, particularly labor unions and the welfare state, minimizes the possibility for economic advancement for the majority of the population, and where widespread inequality is accepted as "the new normal."[1]

Globalization

Several related phenomena important in social work need to be understood in relation to neoliberalism. The first is how we understand the concept of globalization. In the U.S. context globalization is often associated with the movement of jobs from the United States to low wage countries and the development of technology that facilitates communication with and transportation to distant areas of the globe. The Internet; satellite communication; jet travel; and global exchange of information, goods, and services are generally thought of under the rubric of globalization. Under neoliberalism much of this capacity serves the interests of multinational capital, but these technological capacities can also be harnessed for social advancement and social equity projects. Thus, there is the counter narrative of *globalization from below*, a phrase adopted in the titles of books, journal articles, other scholarly discussion, and popular mobilization.[2] One has only to think of 1999 protests accompanying the meeting of the World Trade Organization in Seattle, WA, or to the development of the World Social Forum to understand this nonhegemonic globalization movement, often described as antiglobalization. Additionally, the work of many nongovernmental organizations (NGOs) is part of this emerging tradition.

Immigration

The second related phenomenon is that of immigration or migration. Again, in the U.S. context this is often associated with the movement of people from Latin America and increasingly from Asia to the United States, often without legal authorization to enter the United States, creating a status of undocumented worker for millions of individuals who live in constant fear and are vulnerable to exploitation, wage theft, and a more general insecurity in their lives. Most social work educators know that immigration to the United States emanates from all parts of the globe and has a multiplicity of causes. Yet this phenomenon has to be contextualized so that it is clear that trade agreements, international agribusiness, unscrupulous employers, and government policy on immigration, among other factors, contribute to the complexities of immigration within the United States. Moreover, immigration and migration are global phenomena that manifest in complicated arrangements between sending and receiving countries around the world. In particular for social work, the vulnerability of economic immigrants that results in human trafficking and other exploitive employment is of great concern.

Work and the Labor Market

A third phenomenon associated with neoliberalism is the changing nature of the work and labor markets. Social work students are quite aware of the insecurity associated with less than full-time positions, minimal benefits, and dubious job security. Typically, we think of the changing nature of employment in the manufacturing sector—the shrinking number of jobs, the exporting of jobs to low wage areas, and the extraction of concessions from unionized manufacturing workers—as associated with a changing labor market. Critically important here is understanding that manufacturing jobs are no more intrinsically better paying than other jobs, but that collective struggle and unionization—with an important and under-appreciated history—made these jobs the "desirable" or "good jobs" whose decline is lamented. The concurrent rise of low-wage, largely nonunionized service sector employment, part-time and temporary employment, low benefit levels and lack of economic mobility are realities that those seeking work in myriad sectors face. These labor market trends have been accompanied by a fierce assault on the labor movement and worker organizing that has resulted in the lowest degree of unionized private sector workers in close to a century at 6.6% (Greenhouse, 2013; U.S. Bureau of Labor Statistics, 2013). The most robust unionized sector, the public sector, was at 35.9% in the most recent report (U.S. Bureau of Labor Statistics, 2013); however, this is a decrease from the previous year's level of 37%. These public sector unionization percentages, even with the decrease, approximate the highest level of unionized private sector workers back in the 1950s, which is considered the apex of union power in the U.S. private sector. Thus, the unionized public sector is now the target of the neoliberal agenda, with the startling attack on public sector unionization in Wisconsin, Indiana, Michigan and other states, often considered union strongholds.

Effects in Communities and on Individuals

All of these trends profoundly affect communities and individuals. At the community level, once vibrant manufacturing centers suffer abandonment; there is erosion of tax bases and resulting municipal fiscal crises and cuts in local services; limited opportunities for economic advancement of residents; and, in some instances, depopulation. In terms of individuals and families, economic stress may contribute to family instability and violence, lack of supervision of children as parents must piece together several part-time jobs with multiple scheduling complexities to make ends meet, and personal problems such as substance abuse. Increases in incarceration rates often coincide with increases in unemployment, and this takes a huge toll in communities of color across the United States who disproportionately bear the brunt of incarceration.

The Assault on the Welfare State

Finally, at the very time when social programs are most needed, the neoliberal agenda undertakes to shrink government programs that would cushion the blows of the economy. The conservative intellectual infrastructure churns out model legislation that is circulated to state legislatures to curtail social service spending and exerts influence on federal legislation and policy-making. Ostensible education reforms have largely involved high stakes testing and privatization schemes for public education, even capturing support from heretofore progressive and community-oriented constituencies. Privatization of public services is offered as a means of cutting government inefficiencies, whereas in reality these schemes siphon off precious public resources as profit for the firms involved. The public sector is starved for fiscal resources while the private sector plays an increasing role in service delivery of formerly public services. One alarming example is the increase in private prisons and the ever widening prison industrial complex that contributes to the school (dropping out)-to-prison pipeline for most marginalized segments of communities of color.

Effects for Social Work

These developments have significant consequences for social work practice, social work education, and social workers as workers. In comparison to other highly developed western economies, the U.S. experiences one of the highest levels of inequality, and this inequality is increasing over time. In comparison to other Organisation for Economic Co-Operation and Development counties, the United States has the second highest Gini coefficient, behind only Mexico. The Gini coefficient is a measure of inequality that ranges from zero (when everybody has identical incomes) to 1 (when all income goes to only one person), and the United States experienced extraordinary growth in its Gini coefficient between the mid-1980s and the mid-2000s (Organisation for Economic Co-Operation and Development, 2011). Inequality generates huge problems for those at the low end of the income and wealth scale who are most affected, and those most likely to use public programs. It also affects the middle income population in myriad ways, from rising costs of higher education and associated student debt to insecurity for those in retirement as pensions disappear (if they exist) and private investments vacillate with market fluctuations. Social workers will face this insecurity in the lives of their clients and communities, and even in their own careers and working lives as social workers.

Yet, despite the dire picture painted by these trends and statistics, resistance is being mounted in many ways. These are also crucial developments for social workers and social work education to consider and participate in. Moreover, one way to situate the resistance is by incorporating human rights themes into the analysis and demonstrating that another world is indeed possible.

The Human Rights Frame—The Added Value

By nesting these issues within a framework of human rights, a number of advantages can be gained on the basis of social work ethics and principles and on the basis of accountability. Within the U.S. context, what is taken as the new normal of economic insecurity for the many and extravagant wealth and opulence for the few, a human rights framework can call into question just how normal this all is or, more important, should be. By comparing our practices to human rights standards through having students read the Universal Declaration of Human Rights (United Nations, 1948) and then thinking about the reality of many exploited and vulnerable populations in the United States, the value of employing human rights standards to ameliorate economic exploitation becomes apparent. One could go farther and compare the United States to other highly developed countries on such issues as access to health care, rights on the job, access to education, and other social benefits.

Using the human rights framework also helps to locate the U.S. situation within the international arena. We can look at how U.S. policies with regard to trade and immigration create a climate ripe for human rights abuses, particularly in the economic realm, but with consequences that relate to racism, sexism, human trafficking, environmental degradation, and other abuses (Armaline, Glasberg, & Purkayastha, 2011).

Finally, we can insert into the conversation some of the possible means by which to hold the United States accountable. Understanding why America is so reluctant to sign international treaties and conventions that would hold it to greater accountability on economic human rights would help reveal those forces that want to thwart economic human rights for their own gain. This could point the way toward campaigns to solve the problems of exploited low wage and vulnerable workers. It could compel us into action and involve our students in the pursuit of human rights.

Resistance

As throughout human history, oppression breeds resistance, and resistance to the oppressive forms of this neoliberal order materializes in many settings and spawns new kinds of social movements on a global scale. These developments are also vitally important for social workers and social work education. These movements implicitly or explicitly embrace or are consonant with a human rights frame and serve as exemplars of human rights as motivation for action. They offer hope and inspiration for affected individuals and communities and for students and practitioners. The issues and movements address multiple levels of policy-making—global, federal, state, and local government—and employ diverse strategies and tactics. A brief survey of issues and movements is offered in following paragraphs. This is not an exhaustive list, but rather an illustration of some the dynamism of new models of organizing for economic justice. Following this section I discuss how to incorporate them into social work education.

Raising the Minimum Wage in the United States

Given overwhelming evidence that existing minimum wage rates, both federal and state, do not provide adequate income, legislation has been or will be introduced to raise minimum wage levels at state and Congressional levels. There is fierce resistance from the corporate lobby and many politicians, but there is huge support from labor, faith-based, and community constituencies.

Paid Sick Days

In several states laws are being enacted that guarantee workers paid sick days each year. Proponents argue that these laws make workplaces healthier, allow caretakers to tend to sick relatives, and are long overdue. Again, fierce opposition is encountered from business lobbyists.

Living Wage Laws and Ordinances

Across the United States, Canada, the United Kingdom, and elsewhere, local movements press municipal governments, and sometimes universities, county, regional, or state/provincial entities, to require that in exchange for contracts (e.g., security, janitorial, food preparation), development permits, tax abatements, or other assistance, firms agree to pay wage rates that are higher than minimum wage so that public dollars do not result in employment at poverty level wages. In some cases, different rates apply when health insurance coverage is provided, and in some limited instances, firms must agree not to hinder unionization efforts.

Immigrants Rights and Immigrant Workers Rights

A number of movements and campaigns press for immigrant rights:
- Development of immigrant worker centers to assist and develop immigrant worker leaders so that they can fight for decent working

conditions and standards, particularly for day laborers, but also for other sectors such as the garment industry, landscaping, plant nurseries, and other areas (see Fine, 2006; Peck & Theodore, 2012; Theodore, Valenzuela & Melendez, 2006). A particularly important aspect of decent working conditions is the campaigns against wage theft in which unscrupulous employers exploit immigrant workers by not paying them all (and sometimes any) of the wages they have earned.

- Passage of state and federal Dream Act legislation to allow undocumented youths to pay in-state tuition rates at public universities and to enjoy the rights of other young people (Wong et al., 2012).

- Monitoring police behavior toward immigrants and pressuring local governments to halt police harassment of immigrants, restrain police from collaborating with immigration officials, and to exploit the vulnerability of many immigrants.

Extension of Rights to Organize and Enforce Workplace Standards

Certain jobs and industries are exempt from the National Labor Relations Act and therefore do not have the protections it offers, such as the right to organize (agricultural workers, domestic workers, and other categories); other workers who are classified as independent contractors also face difficult hurdles to assert control over their working conditions (taxi drivers) or are tipped workers whose minimum wage rates are lower than regular minimum wage rates. Organizations representing these different groups of workers are combining efforts to press for protections and rights to organize and coalesced in 2010 under the auspices of the Excluded Workers Congress. A report, *Unity for Dignity: Expanding the Right to Organize to Win Human Rights at Work* (United Workers Congress, 2010), detailed the concerns of workers in the following sectors: day laborers, domestic workers,[3] farmworkers, formerly incarcerated people, guest workers, restaurant workers, workers in right-to-work states, taxi drivers, and workfare workers.

Now known as the United Workers Congress, this important alliance is devising new campaigns to develop working class power and is a source of inspiration to the entire labor movement.[4] In their vision statement (United Workers Congress, n.d.) is the following sentence that explicitly embraces a human rights framework:

> The United Workers Congress believes that all people who work have the human right to organize and deserve working conditions of respect and dignity, regardless of the temporary nature of their work, their lack of a fixed workplace, their immigration status, any previous criminal convictions, whether they currently have a job or not, how they are classified or misclassified, or their lack of a traditional collective bargaining structure.

Community-Labor Organizations and Coalitions

Now common in many parts of the United States and Canada and employing different models and organizing strategies, unions, community organizations, and often faith-based groups have been working together on numerous campaigns in local and regional areas. They have worked on issues such as responsible development through creation of community benefits agreements, living-wage campaigns, safe ports, job creation, union organizing drives, strike support, political and legislative campaigns, and more (see Dean & Reynolds, 2009; Simmons & Harding, 2010b; Figueroa, Grabelsky & Lamare, 2013). These kinds of coalitions began to form in the 1980s (see Brecher & Costello, 1980) when neoliberalism was emerging and now are more widely embraced by organized labor, the AFL-CIO, and local community forces.

Unionization of Low-Wage Workers and New Strategies of Organizing

In the context of unrelenting assaults on unions, the labor movement is coming to terms with the necessity of adopting new methods of organizing and reaching out to a wider constituency that embraces the diversity of the American workforce of the 21st century. AFL-CIO leadership is imploring unions to embrace this new sense of urgency and to consider different strategies for incorporating new workers in sectors previously considered too difficult to organize. Several developments illustrate this: Worker centers can now affiliate with central labor councils and state labor federations so their concerns are incorporated into labor's agenda. Organizing efforts are taking place in such hard-to-organize sectors as the car wash industries in New York and Los Angeles; fast-food and chain restaurants in New York, Chicago, and elsewhere; and among warehouse workers at Walmart, a notoriously antiunion corporation.

Protecting Public Sector Workers' Rights to Have Unions and Collective Bargaining

Since the attempt to roll back public sector workers' rights to have unions and engage in collective bargaining in Wisconsin, Ohio, Michigan, and other states, massive responses have erupted that included occupation of the state capitol in Madison, WI, and Ohio's successful campaign to maintain collective bargaining rights for public employees. Some instances, such as the campaign to recall Wisconsin Governor Scott Walker, were unsuccessful. There are several interpretations of why this was so, but issue campaigns such as that of Ohio were able to convince voters to overturn anti-worker legislation. This should be of extreme concern to social workers, many of whom are public sector workers, and who are likely to see impossible working conditions and decreasing quality of public services should these sharp examples of the neoliberal agenda succeed.

Occupy Wall Street (OWS)

Regardless of how one assesses the efficacy of this movement, OWS was a singular "movement moment" (Hartmann, 2013), facilitated by modern technology but also employing creative nontechnological techniques (e.g., "the people's microphone") that focused on the huge inequality within the United States. "We are the 99%" continues to resonate globally with myriad constituencies and readily illustrates the unfairness that people experience in their daily lives. This movement and whatever successors it generates tap deep sentiments and potentially serve to inspire mobilization and action. That it came up suddenly and unexpectedly provided a teachable moment that hopefully was incorporated into social work education.

National and International Gatherings and Associations

A variety of venues exist to share strategies and developments among popular movements, create academic exchanges, and develop national and international campaigns. Within the United States many are familiar with the Seattle protests in 1999 to mark resistance to the meeting of the World Trade Organization. Other venues include the World Social Forum, the U.S. Social Forum, international academic conferences, networks of activist scholars, and international cooperation among trade unions that address global corporations. The participation and voices of social work educators and practitioners in these venues can provide needed insights as to the social dimensions of the problems under consideration and opportunities for social workers to engage with other disciplines and kindred spirits.

Implications for Social Work Education

The aforementioned list embodies the yearning for the realization of human rights as well as many vehicles to achieve greater degrees of human rights. Moreover, it provides rich opportunities within social work education. For example, much of this content could be incorporated into existing macro practice courses, macro theory courses, human behavior and the social environment courses, courses on social work values and ethics, and social policy courses. Moreover, as mentioned above, the entire sphere of work and its relationship to mental health, health, and family issues are relevant to clinical courses or micro practice and theory courses. This content can also be addressed through short workshops, continuing education, special seminars, programs, or various combinations of educational opportunities.

Other opportunities involve courses that specifically address economic justice. In this arena, courses on social movements for economic justice, labor movements, labor and social work connections, human rights, international social work, immigration, and other topics are relevant. In an elective course offered at the University of Connecticut School of Social Work titled Economic Justice, Labor and Social Work, one of the first activities is to examine the Universal Declaration of Human Rights and review Articles 22 through 25 concerning economic rights, as well as to examine the NASW Code of Ethics and review its relevant areas. This course examines the range of issues under the rubric of economic justice including economic inequality, the role of the labor movement in achieving economic justice, and how social workers participate in unions and other movements for social and economic justice. The course draws on the leaders and activities of the labor and economic justice movements in Connecticut but could be replicated in other locales and incorporate local economic justice struggles in the respective communities.

From an international perspective, student learning could be enhanced by examining other international conventions and treaties besides the Universal Declaration of Human Rights and offer opportunities to compare economic rights within the United States to other national contexts. Additionally, for educators the International Association of Schools of Social Work and International Federation of Social Workers *Definition of Social Work* (2000) provides ample opportunity to consider economic rights and economic justice within social work education and practice.

Field placements and class projects offer additional opportunities in which economic justice can be formulated. Placements in community organizations that work on economic rights, with labor unions who organize low wage and immigrant labor or who organize social service workers, and with advocacy organizations who take up economic issues are all possibilities. If anti–sweat shop organizations or fair trade organizations exist in the locales of schools and departments of social work, these organizations are concerned with economic justice and human rights. Clinical and micro placements in employee assistance programs, union-sponsored worker assistance settings, and occupational health and safety organizations should be considered. Class projects that involve research on these topics and other related areas can be extremely meaningful to students. Additionally, comparative work on the United States and other countries in terms of economic issues, including economic rights and protections, can offer interesting contrasts.

Concretely, at this author's institution several students have been placed for field work at labor unions that represent public sector social workers and other health care workers. Placements include those in the nursing home sector, which is comprised largely of women of color and immigrant women. In another union-based placement, students were working to help create collective bargaining rights for home child care providers. Students have also been placed at community–labor coalitions working on corporate responsibility, universal health care campaigns in Connecticut, community benefits agreements, and other economic rights oriented groups. These are not the typical field placement, even for community organizing students, and students who have been in these settings find the experiences to be inspiring, rewarding, and a means of opening new options for careers. Several MSWs who graduated and have developed careers in labor organizing within the area have been able to serve as field instructors. For a class project in an urban policy class that I teach, students worked with a labor-community organization to increase voter turnout in local neighborhoods that had previously been largely disengaged in elections.

Finally, embracing teachable moments such as OWS or other local struggles provide invaluable opportunities for learning. OWS offered students some actual experience in creating a new model of a social movement, as well as an opportunity to consider the pros and cons of the so-called leaderless style and other OWS characteristics. (These discussions continue in various classroom settings currently.) During the fall 2011 semester when OWS was underway, several students participated in the local encampment and with the protests and marches organized by the local OWS group, and one student decided to participate in civil disobedience (this was on his own and not related to any course assignments). In 2003 the Immigrant Workers Freedom Ride, a remarkable national mobilization that took immigrant workers all over the country to develop awareness of their struggles, was another such moment. Students who participated were inspired by the courage of these workers to caravan around the country, despite the undocumented status many of them endured. When there have been local strikes, strikers have been brought in as guest speakers at the University of Connecticut's School of Social Work, and students have gone to join their picket lines as class projects. Many were incredibly moved to hear the stories of strikers. Other students might be inspired by the stories of immigrant workers and may decide to find ways to support these groups. Through connections within local communities by students and faculty members, these issues will make themselves apparent. One does not have to look too far—perhaps in the cafeterias, janitorial staffs, or investments and licensing decisions of our own institutions—to find economic justice issues that need attention.

Conclusion

There are innumerable ways to cultivate awareness of economic justice and economic human rights within social work education. As social work educators, we need to use creativity and convey a sense of urgency about these issues and movements. We need to show the interaction of macro and micro aspects of economic justice issues. Most important, we need to find the ways to relate to local issues and local organizations that undertake to address the myriad economic problems and human rights abuses that human beings encounter in the neoliberal age. Social work students should come away from social work education with the knowledge and skills to address these problems on a large stage and on the smaller stages of everyday life.

References

Armaline, B., Glasberg, D. S., & Purkayastha, B. (Eds.). (2011). *Human rights in our own backyard: Injustice and resistance in the United States.* Philadelphia, PA: University of Pennsylvania Press.

Armstrong, E. (2004). Globalization from below: AIDWA, foreign funding, and gendering anti-violence campaigns. *Journal of Developing Societies, 20*(1–2), 39–55. doi: 10.1177/0169796X04048302

Benton-Short, L., Price, M. D., & Friedman, S. (2005). Globalization from below: The ranking of global immigrant cities. *International Journal of Urban and Regional Research, 29*(4), 945–959. doi: 10.1111/j.1468-2427.2005.00630.x

Brecher, J., & Costello, T. (Eds.). (1980). *Building bridges: The emerging grassroots coalition of labor and community.* New York, NY: Monthly Review Press.

Brecher, J., Costello, T., & Smith, B. (2000). *Globalization from below: The power of solidarity.* Boston, MA: South End Press.

Dean, A., & Reynolds, D. (2009). *A new new deal: How regional activism will reshape the American labor movement.* Ithaca, NY: ILR Press.

Figueroa, M., Grabelsky, J., & Lamare, J. (2013). Community workforce agreements: A tool to grow the union market and to expand access to lifetime careers in the unionized building trades. *Labor Studies Journal,* 38(1), 7–31.

Fine, J, (2006). *Worker centers: Organizing communities at the edge of the dream.* Ithaca, NY: ILR Press.

Ginsburg, L. (2013).Understanding Baltimore's United Workers: An interview with Todd Cherkis. *Social Policy 43*(2), 25–29.

Greenhouse, S. (2013, January 23). Share of the work force in a union falls to a 97 year low, 11.3%. *New York Times.* Retrieved from http://www.nytimes.com/2013/01/24/business/union-membership-drops-despite-job-growth.html?_r=0

Hartman, C. (2013, April 4). "The meaning of protest movement for cities." Remarks at panel presentation, Urban Affairs Association Annual Meeting, San Francisco, CA.

International Federation of Social Workers & International Association of Schools of Social Work. (2000). *Definition of social work.* Retrieved from www.ifsw.org

Organisation for Economic Co-Operation and Development. (2011). *Growing income inequality in OECD countries: What drives it and how can policy tackle it?* Paris, France: OECD.

Peck, J., & Theodore, N. (2012). Politicizing contingent work: Countering neoliberal labor market regulation... from the bottom up? *South Atlantic Quarterly, 111*, 741–761. doi: 10.1215/00382876-1724165

Portes, A. (1996). Globalization from below: The rise of transnational communities. In W. P. Smith & R. P. Korczenwicz, (Eds), *Latin America in the world economy* (pp. 151–168). Westport, CT: Greenwood Press.

Simmons, L., & Harding, S (Eds.) (2010a). *Economic justice, labor and community practice.* New York, NY: Routledge.

Simmons, L., & Harding, S. (2010b). Community-labor coalitions for progressive change. In P. Kurzman & P. Maiden (Eds.), *Union contributions to labor welfare policy and practice* (pp. 103–116). New York, NY: Routledge/Taylor & Francis.

Theodore, N., Valenzuela, A., & Melendez, E. (2006). La esquina (The corner): Day laborers on the margins of New York's formal economy. *Working USA, 9*, 407–423.

United Nations. (1948, December 10). *Universal Declaration of Human Rights.* G.A. Res. 217 A (III). Retrieved from http://www.refworld.org/docid/3ae6b3712c.html

U.S. Bureau of Labor Statistics. (2013). Union members, 2012. Retrieved from http://www.bls.gov/news.release/pdf/union2.pdf

United Workers Congress. (2010). Unity for dignity: Expanding the right to organize to win human rights at work. Retrieved from www.unitedworkerscongress.org

Vega, C. A. (2011). Globalization from below and its political regulation forms. *Revue Tiers Monde, 208*, 103–119.

Wiest, D. (2007). Globalization from below: Transnational activists and protest networks. *International Journal of Comparative Sociology, 48*(5), 433–437.

Wong, K., Shadduck-Hernández, J., Inzunza F., Monroe, J., Narro, V., & Valenzuela, A. (Eds.). (2012). *Undocumented and unafraid: Tam Tran, Cinthya Felix, and the immigrant youth movement.* Los Angeles, CA: UCLA Labor Center.

Endnotes

1 For an extended discussion of these trends as they relate to social work and community practice, see the special issue of the *Journal of Community Practice* on Economic Justice, Labor and Community Practice, Volume 17, Numbers 1-2, also available as a book: *Economic Justice, Labor and Community Practice*, edited by Simmons and Harding (2010a).

2 For a sampling of the hundreds of articles and books employing this theme see Armstrong (2004); Benton-Short, Price, and Friedman (2005); Brecher, Costello and Smith (2000); Portes (1996); Vega (2011); and Weist (2007). Several hundred citations result from searches of academic databases when one uses the term "globalization from below."

3 Recently several states have passed or are considering domestic workers' bills of rights that enumerate work standards and rights for domestic workers.

4 See Ginsburg (2013) for an interview with a leader of a Baltimore organization that grew from a homeless shelter to encompass advocacy and organizing for workers' rights and community benefits from development, all while employing a human rights framework.

12 | A Case Study in Immigrant Civic Engagement Research: Linking Human Rights to Social Work Education

Rebecca L. Thomas, Christina M. Chiarelli-Helminiak, and Brunilda Ferraj

The concept of human rights is demanding more attention in social work education. In response to students' growing interest in human rights and the addition of human rights to the Council on Social Work Education's (CSWE's) Educational Policy and Accreditation Standards (2008), social work educators need to develop ways to integrate human rights throughout the curriculum. Although it may seem intuitive to add human rights content to practice or policy courses, how does one successfully integrate human rights into research education? This chapter highlights how students have been engaged in the program evaluation of a project focused on civic engagement in the immigrant community and implications for human rights-focused research.

Social Work Research Education

Research is an essential component of social work education, as evidenced by inclusion of research in several standards for BSW and MSW curricula in the United States (Council on Social Work Education, 2008). CSWE's Educational Policy 2.1.6 states that students should be engaged in practice that is informed by research and research that is informed by practice. Educational Policy 2.1.10 mandates that students engage, assess, intervene, and evaluate at multiple levels of practice. Although social work educators tend to see the value of research in the curriculum, students may exhibit different dispositions.

A common challenge faced by social work educators is engaging students in the research process. The literature suggests social work students' resistance may be related to higher levels of anxiety and a general lack of interest in research, especially when compared to students in other majors (Adam, Zosky, & Unrau, 2004; Green, Bretzin, Leininger, & Stauffer, 2001). When given the option, students may delay taking research until the end of their educational program. Unable to see the connection between social work practice and social work research, students are limiting the value research has on providing quality client-care.

Maschi et al. (2007) suggest social work students' satisfaction with the research process affects their interest. Certain social work knowledge and skills are better learned though experience; therefore, innovative approaches to teaching research are needed that directly engage and connect students to real life situations (Harder, 2010). Providing students with the opportunity to engage in the research process, including the dissemination of findings, will not only benefit students' learning experience, but will further research and practice within the profession. Students engaged in the research process will be more likely to use research in practice and possibly conduct research after graduation. Through this process, research becomes a natural part of social work practice (Witkin, 1993).

Integrating a Human Rights Framework

Social workers are intuitively engaged in practice that promotes human rights, because these issues have been at the heart of the social work profession since its conception (Healy, 2008). With the recent emphasis on integrating human rights into the social work curriculum, the natural area for inclusion seems to be in practice courses, or as Steen and Mathiesen (2005) suggest, into electives and core courses. Integrating human rights into research education can be more of a challenge.

The authors and publishers of social work research textbooks have been slow to incorporate human rights. For example, Rubin and Babbie (2011) do not even make mention of human rights in their popular text, *Research Methods for Social Workers*. Orme and Combs-Orme's (2012) *Outcome-Informed Evidence-Based Practice*, part of the publisher Pearson's *Advancing Core Competencies Series*, only reference human rights in one case study at the beginning of a chapter. For students, the limited reference to human rights in research texts further contributes to a lack of connection between practice and research.

There are some examples of social work educators integrating human rights and research. Maschi and Youdin (2011) have woven human rights throughout their recent research text, *Social Worker as Researcher*. The text provides connections between the history of social work, human rights, practice, and research. The authors suggest employing a human rights framework to identify the research problem and question(s), select an appropriate method of inquiry, analyze the context of the problem, apply social work research ethics, and disseminate findings. Witkin (1993) suggests three ways of integrating human rights into social work research:

> by adopting the protection and advancement of fundamental human rights as explicit research goals, by using the protection and advancement of fundamental human rights as evaluative criteria, and by conducting research that respects and fosters the human rights of participants. (p. 246)

Limited resources in this area of the social work curriculum present a challenge for educators.

Human Rights and Immigrant Civic Engagement

Recognizing that the social work educator must find creative ways to engage students in the research process while promoting human rights, the evaluation of a project based on the engagement of immigrants in civic activities provided such an opportunity. Employing tenets of social capital, the evaluation focuses on building networks of trusting relationships between community partners, program participants, and even the evaluators. The project advances the human rights of immigrants by combating social exclusion and promoting social inclusion, facilitating participation in democracy, as well as civil and political activities.

Social exclusion refers to the inability of an individual or population to fully participate in economic, social, and civic activities that directly affect their lives. The process of social exclusion is multidimensional and dynamic, influenced by the norms, attitudes, and behaviors of community members, institutions, or policies, among other factors. Although any group may be at risk for social exclusion, disadvantaged or marginalized populations such as racial and ethnic minorities have historically experienced social exclusion (United Nations Development Programme, 2011).

Exclusion from civic and political life can be measured through traditional political indicators such as voting in elections, running for office, writing letters to government officials or participating in party-based politics. Although these are essential activities, other valuable community-based actions are also considered civic in nature, including active participation in local associations, voluntary organizations, councils, discussion forums, or other community building efforts (Putnam, 2000). In Hartford, Connecticut, as well as other communities throughout the United States, there is limited participation of immigrants in broader community building groups and decision-making circles (Ramakrishnan & Lewis, 2005).

For immigrants, integration into an adopted country is a complex process. They face the reality of having left behind what was familiar and known in their homeland, while at the same time encountering new societal norms and customs (Bhattacharya, 2011; Segal, Elliot, & Mayadas, 2010). After their arrival, immigrants may form or join ethnic enclaves. Membership in such enclaves provides immigrants with access to valuable information and resources, which help them navigate the institutions of the receiving community. One example of this phenomenon is the emergence of rotating credit associations within the tightly knit Cuban community in Miami, which give newly arrived and resourceless immigrants and refugees an immediate line of credit (Portes & Sensenbrenner, 1993). Yet, as immigrants increasingly rely on their own enclaves for support, they are invariably less inclined to engage with the broader community (Portes, 1998; Portes & Sensenbrenner, 1993). Portes and Sensenbrenner (1993) provide several noteworthy examples of how immigrant enclaves restrict communication and integration into the broader community, including the restrictions imposed among Latinos in South Florida by the Spanish-language media and the strong political power wielded by the Korean Consulate General in New York.

Newly arrived immigrants are also less likely to participate in civic activities due to barriers concerning language, a lack of knowledge regarding local programs and organizations, discrimination and stigma, disempowerment, mistrust and fear of authorities, or lack of income (United Nations, 2014). Considering that integration is a two-way process, it is important to note that receiving communities may not be equipped with the resources, knowledge, or desire to facilitate the integration of newly arrived immigrants into the community. This may intensify the boundary between the two populations, furthering immigrants' exclusion from civic life.

Barriers to inclusion infringe on immigrants' basic human right to participate in civic activities and take part in the decisions that directly affect their lives. The human right to participate in civil and political activities is upheld by the international human rights framework. Magdalena Sepulveda Carmona, Special Rapporteur on Extreme Poverty and Human Rights, highlights international documents in which such rights are enshrined:

- Universal Declaration of Human Rights (Articles 21 and 27);
- International Covenant on Civil and Political Rights (Article 25);
- International Covenant on Economic, Social, and Cultural Rights (Articles 13.1 and 15.1);
- Convention on the Elimination of All Forms of Discrimination Against Women (Articles 7, 8, 13(c), and 14.2);
- International Convention on Elimination of All Forms of Racial Discrimination (Article 5(e)(vi));
- Convention on the Rights of the Child (Articles 12 and 31);
- International Convention on the Rights of All Migrant Workers and Members of their Families (Articles 41 and 42.2);
- United Nations Declaration on the Right to Development (Articles 1.1, 2, and 8.2); and
- United Nations Declaration on the Rights of Indigenous Peoples (Articles 5, 18, 19, and 41). (United Nations, 2014)

Participation in civic life is based on fundamental human rights principles, including the respect for dignity, the exercise of autonomy and self-determination, nondiscrimination, and equality. Through active participation, individuals may voice their concerns and contribute to the decision-making processes that directly affect their lives, thus allowing them to be recognized as human beings and active agents in their own lives. Through participation in civic activities, an individual may acquire access to resources or information available to the broader community, allowing decisions to be made based on their own desires and well-being. Thus, the right to participation is linked to the human rights principle of autonomy in which an individual is able to direct his or her own life.

The right to participate is also based on the human rights principles of equality and nondiscrimination, which imply that all individuals have an equal opportunity to be active members of society. The inability to participate in civic activities perpetuates a cycle of powerlessness in which key decisions regarding programs or policies are made by individuals in power who may not understand others' experiences or have their best interests at heart. Participation in community building efforts and civic activities can be a vehicle for traditionally marginalized populations to challenge power structures that can deny one's agency and self-determination (United Nations, 2014). In this way, the realization of participation in civic activities as a human right can be a catalyst to reclaiming other rights.

It is also important to note that participation in civic activities provides individuals with an opportunity to build social capital. For the purposes of this chapter, *social capital* refers to the connections between individuals that are acquired through group membership. These connections are based on the social norms of trust, respect, and reciprocity and may provide individuals with access to new resources and information. In this way, social capital is a valuable resource for marginalized populations who may lack other forms of capital (Portes, 1998). Communities endowed with a rich stock of social capital exhibit increased trust, resiliency, and solidarity; thus, they are in a stronger position to confront poverty and vulnerability, address disputes, take advantage of opportunities, and reclaim rights (Putnam 2000; Woolcock & Narayan, 2000).

Immigrant Civic Engagement Project

Recognizing that relationship-building is one of the fundamental principles for best practices in newcomer civic participation in the United States, the Hartford Public Library secured funding through the National Leadership Grants awarded by the Institute of Museum and Library Services to develop and implement the Immigrant Civic Engagement Project (the project). As facilitators of knowledge, resources, and information, libraries face a set of unique challenges in communities with large immigrant populations that may experience high levels of information illiteracy, language barriers, social exclusion, or high poverty rates (Bourke, 2005). Libraries are well-equipped to participate in the process of community building by being sensitive to issues of equity, access, and representation among residents in the communities they serve. The ability to form partnerships with other community organizations, tap into local networks, and develop creative, engaging programs contributes to the opportunity for libraries to be "visible and active in their communities, constantly looking for new ways to build bridges to the excluded and marginalized" (Bourke, 2005, p. 74).

The Immigrant Civic Engagement Project facilitated civic engagement and built social capital between immigrants and receiving community members through two complementary and interconnected goals:

1) Facilitate the transition of newly arrived immigrants into the community and build social capital by establishing a cultural navigator program to match immigrants with local community members who volunteer to serve as guides, mediators, advocates, and friends.

2) Engage better-established immigrants and receiving community members in civic activities and increase involvement in broader community building efforts through the implementation of community dialogues, which are structured, facilitated, small group discussions.

From the organization and structure of meetings to the social space provided by the library, many aspects of the project provided a supportive environment for the development of social capital. The project's flexible structure was able to respond to the unique context of the community and needs of receiving and immigrant members. This dynamic approach enabled participants to engage in multiple activities at multiple levels that facilitated civic engagement and relationship building.

In regard to relationship development among participants in the cultural navigator program, interviews with cultural navigators and immigrant participants illustrate that cross-cultural learning occurred. Cultural navigators began by sharing information about their own interests or introducing participants to culture in the United States. As immigrant participants became more comfortable with cultural navigators, they, too, shared information about their home cultures, creating strong bonds between navigators and immigrant participants that often last beyond the life of the project. Cross cultural learning and the development of bonded relationships offers evidence that social capital was developed between immigrant and receiving community members through the cultural navigator program.

By using the community dialogue model, the library brought together immigrant and receiving community members to participate in a series of community building events. Through these relationship building opportunities, community members formed a neighborhood welcoming committee to facilitate social inclusion within their own community. The stated purpose of the welcoming committee is to identify local community strengths and resources that can be used to improve the neighborhood and orient incoming community members, focusing special attention on the immigrant population and the unique barriers they may encounter.

One unexpected outcome of the project was the establishment of the Hartford Commission on Immigrant and Refugee Affairs. The advisory commission was initiated to address concerns that the immigrant voice was not adequately represented throughout the community. The goals of the city commission are to legitimize and elevate the issues of new arrivals, to hear and understand immigrants, and to civically engage immigrants. Various immigrant groups are represented on the commission charged with addressing issues pertaining to policy, education, communication, and connections between groups and organizations. The commission is responsible for (but not limited to) advising the city government on the needs and status of the immigrant community; advocating for the interests of immigrants; analyzing existing or proposed policies and actions that impact immigrants; promoting the resources and skills that immigrants bring to the community; and educating the receiving community about immigrants, their concerns, and their rights. The commission's charter designates that a greater proportion of immigrants than nonimmigrants make up the commission, with seats also available for noncitizens, who previously had been prohibited from serving on a city commission. The establishment of such a commission provides an example of how the project is working toward the social inclusion and civic engagement of immigrants within the city's governance.

Evaluation Team Model

An innovative program evaluation team model was developed to integrate human rights into social work research as a learning tool. Over the course of 3 years the evaluation team conducted a process and outcome evaluation of the Immigrant Civic Engagement Project. The evaluation team structure included a principal investigator (social work faculty), research coordinator (social work doctoral candidate and instructor of research methods), and research assistants (MSW students).

A total of eight MSW students were part of the program evaluation team. Involvement on the project was voluntary, and the students did not receive academic credit for participation. Work-study money was leveraged to pay for the students' employment. The students' commitment to the overall goals of the project drove their dedication to the research process. In return, the student researchers gained valuable insight beyond the classroom about what the research process entails.

The evaluation team model demonstrates how social work educators can engage students in community-based research with a human rights focus as a way to prepare for professional social work practice. The team model focused on building social capital within the group. The model recognized that each member of the team had a unique knowledge-base and capitalized on the team's strengths. The team was encouraged to take new risks that enhanced their learning and growth while finding comfort in knowing that the evaluation team was available for support.

Through conscious planning and effort, the principal investigator created an environment of mutual respect and cohesion among the team by building and sharing knowledge and experience. All members were encouraged to engage in dialogue during the weekly team meetings, which stimulated new ideas and conceptualizations about the project. Over time, relationship building occurred, accountability was expected, and group expectations became familiar. These principles reflect the ideals of a human rights culture (Wronka, 2008). Such structure speaks to what Wronka calls the "importance of socialization" (p. 13), in which students are being introduced to a model of faculty–student collaboration not typical in research universities.

Acting as participant observers, student researchers gained knowledge of the research process through engagement in the program evaluation at multiple levels. Evaluation team members attended numerous project-related meetings and community activities, conducted interviews with key informants, administered surveys, and engaged with representatives from various stakeholder groups including immigrants, community organizers, service providers, educators, government and public employees, as well as project administrators. Taking part in the development and implementation of a community-based program evaluation provided students with the opportunity to develop research skills and increase knowledge of immigrant rights issues. Through engagement in the project, student researchers were able to identify potential human rights violations within their own community and beyond and actively participated in a project intended to address such violations. This process provided students a more localized perspective of human rights.

The research design, a mixed methods evaluation, assisted in meeting the goals of increasing and fostering opportunities in relationship building and civic engagement. Because the goals are to create a lasting effect on the community through a sustainable program, relationship building with stakeholders, volunteers, and immigrant participants was vital. Data were triangulated through surveys, interviews, observations, researcher notes, meeting agendas, minutes, and other documents related to the project.

Recalling Witkin's (1993) suggestions for integrating human rights into social work research, the evaluation team adopted research goals that sought to protect and advance social inclusion of immigrants within the community. Research questions focused on immigrant rights and the social inclusion and participation of immigrant residents. Discussions during team meetings and debriefing sessions helped to ensure that all aspects of the research respected and fostered the human rights of participants. This demonstrates the power social work research has to cultivate human rights within the context of community practice (Ife & Fiske, 2006).

A feedback loop was incorporated into the evaluation model to ensure validity. Because a participatory model of evaluation is gaining recognition as a valuable approach to relationship building within communities, evaluators solicited feedback concerning evaluation findings from members of the project leadership team biannually. The leadership team provided the opportunity to share feedback concerning the evaluators' annual report. This resulted in the development of trusting and reciprocal relationships between the evaluation team and project administrators, highlighting another venue where social capital was built.

The evaluation team was active in presenting on the research model and disseminating findings on the Immigrant Civic Engagement Project evaluation. Abstracts were successfully submitted to various conferences, and the team has presented internationally (Joint World Conference on Social Work and Social Development), nationally (Council on Social Work Education Annual Program Meeting, Fordham University Human Rights, Social Justice, and Qualitative Methods Conference, and Society for Social Work Research), locally (University of Connecticut School of Social Work Research and Scholarship Exhibition and Central Connecticut State University Social Justice Conference), and to other community partners (Hartford Immigrant Advisory Group and University of Connecticut School of Social Work, Social Workers for Global Justice). The team also prepared manuscripts, such as this one co-authored by a recent MSW graduate, doctoral degree recipient, and faculty member. Through this process, student researchers recognized that the task of conducting research does not end with report writing, but that findings must be shared through presentations and writing scholarly articles.

Such engagement with students, despite being involved and complex, is an excellent learning tool and encourages the development and application of critical thinking crucial for research. It provides a forum for rights-based discussion, advocacy, and engagement, because as Wronka (2008) points out, knowledge is powerful. The synergy that occurred during meetings forced the team to be thoughtful, meticulous, and tease out ideas grounded in a human rights framework. Students recognized that being a social work researcher requires discipline, advanced knowledge, and continuous learning.

The members of the evaluation team seamlessly incorporated the theories of social capital, social inclusion, and civic engagement into their papers and practice. This indicates that the theories were not mere abstract concepts but something students have integrated into their thinking. Interest in this topic has had a trickle-down effect into other school-wide and community-based ventures in which the students are involved.

As student researchers integrated theory and engaged into the practice of conducting research, they became viewed as student leaders in the school's research community. The student researchers have been invited by social work instructors to present in research methods and evaluation courses. The presentations focused on information about the project, the student's role, and evaluation findings. The shared learning and teaching opportunities affirmed and solidified student researchers' practice experience. Additionally, the presentations encouraged other students to see the link between research and social work practice. The meaningful dialogues with peers encouraged other students to explore research opportunities to advance their own research questions and be less intimidated by the process.

As part of an assignment for a community organization course, one of the student researchers invited library staff and other partners to discuss the goals and organizing strategies of the project. The student's project was instrumental in raising other students' awareness about immigrant issues within Hartford and the goals of the project. Other student researchers have fostered activities focusing on immigrant issues within the school through the Social Workers for Global Justice, a student group to enhance students' understanding of global social issues.

Over time, the student researchers have created their own networks and have begun to organize, mobilize, and take action to address immigrant issues with the ultimate goal of effecting change in the broader community. Student researchers spurred on by the issues and concerns of immigrants have joined community organizing and social movements in the greater Hartford area. Student researchers have also participated in lobbying and advocacy activities, demonstrating they are knowledgeable and articulate about the topic. Two students of the evaluation team provided public testimony on proposed legislation concerning immigrants' rights, analyzing the issue through a human rights perspective. Such examples illustrate what Wronka (2008) terms "moving from the mind to the heart to the body" (p. 15), as the students are actively engaged in working toward the realization of human rights within the community.

Conclusion

Since the implementation of the Immigrant Civic Engagement Project, four student researchers have graduated with MSW degrees and have used the experience on the project to expand their professional networks and secure employment. Each of the students involved with the project has something unique to include in his or her résumé as they begin their careers as a professional social workers. Most students plan to continue to work in the area of international social work, including one who plans to continue her practice in research and pursue a doctoral degree. Cameron and Este (2008) point out that more funders are now requiring evaluation of programs, highlighting the value this experience will have in the students' future careers.

The principal investigator continues to work in the capacity of a consultant with the Hartford Public Library. She provides input and guidance on other projects related to immigrant engagement and social inclusion in Hartford. This ongoing relationship demonstrates the bonds of social capital that were built during the course of the project evaluation.

The Immigrant Civic Engagement Project has had a lasting effect on the Hartford community. The Hartford Commission on Immigrant and Refugee Affairs aims to address concerns that the immigrant voice was not adequately represented throughout the community. This commission provides an avenue for Hartford immigrants and refugees to voice their concerns and suggest areas for growth and opportunity. The institutionalization of such a permanent infrastructure provides a mechanism for civic engagement and participation in coalition building and policy development. In addition, immigrant and receiving community members have formed a Welcoming Committee. This stemmed from participants' desire to organize a community hub where all residents in the neighborhood gather to welcome new arrivals into the community and help guide the process of integration. The Welcoming Committee also serves as a clearinghouse for the community's assets and residents' skills, allowing residents to connect to one another to obtain neighborhood-based services. These activities continue to promote dialogue and action to advance the human rights of immigrants, including social inclusion and civic participation.

Given the challenge of engaging students in research while also integrating a human rights framework in social work curriculum, a multimethod teaching approach is recommended (Dewees & Roche, 2001; Krain & Nurse, 2004). The evaluation team model was presented as an innovative way to engage students in the social work research process, while raising awareness of human rights and the immigrant experience. Engaging students in faculty research enabled them to connect with real life situations. Benefits of such a model are realized from student, faculty, and community perspectives. Providing students with a comprehensive understanding of immigrant civic engagement has enhanced students' ability to connect human rights to social work practice at multiple levels of intervention.

References

Adam, N. N., Zosky, D. L., & Unrau, Y. A. (2004). Improving the research climate in social work curricula: Clarifying learning expectations across BSW and MSW research courses. *Journal of Teaching in Social Work*, 24(3/4), 1–18.

Bhattacharya, G. (2011). Is social capital portable? Acculturating experiences of Indian immigrant men in New York City. *Journal of Intercultural Studies, 32*(1), 75–90.

Bourke, C. (2005). Public libraries: Building social capital through networking. *Aplis, 18*(2), 71–75.

Cameron, P. J., & Este, D. C. (2008). Engaging students in social work research education. *Social Work Education, 27*(4), 390-406.

Council on Social Work Education. (2008). *Educational policy and accreditation standards*. Retrieved from http://www.cswe.org/File.aspx?id=13780

Dewees, M., & Roche, S. E. (2001). Teaching about human rights in social work. *Journal of Teaching in Social Work, 21*(1–2), 137–155. doi: 10.1300 /J067v21n01_09

Green, R. G., Bretzin, A., Leininger, C. & Stauffer, R. (2001). Research learning attributes of graduate students in social work, psychology, and business. *Journal of Social Work Education, 37*, 333–41.

Harder, J. (2010). Overcoming MSW students' reluctance to engage in research. *Journal of Teaching in Social Work, 30*, 195–209.

Healy, L. (2008). *International social work: Professional action in an interdependent world*. New York, NY: Oxford University Press.

Ife, J., & Fiske, L. (2006). Human rights and community work. *International Social Work, 49*(3), 297–308. doi: 10.1177/0020872806063403

Krain, M., & Nurse, M. (2004). Teaching human rights through services learning. *Human Rights Quarterly, 26*(1), 189–207.

Maschi, T., Bradley, C., Youdin, R., Killian, M., Cleaveland, C., & Barbera, R. (2007). Social work students and the research process: Exploring the thinking, feeling, and doing of research. *Journal of Baccalaureate Social Work, 13*(1), 1–12.

Maschi, T., & Youdin, R. (2011). *Social worker as researcher: Integrating research with advocacy*. Upper Saddle River, NJ: Pearson.

Orme J. G., & Combs-Orme, T. (2012). *Outcome-informed evidence-based practice*. Boston, MA: Pearson.

Portes, A. (1998). Social capital: Its origins and applications in modern sociology. *Annual Review of Sociology, 24*, 1–24.

Portes, A., & Sensenbrenner, J. (1993). Embeddedness and immigration: Notes on the social determinants of economic action. *American Journal of Sociology, 98*(6), 1320–1350.

Putnam. R. (2000). *Bowling alone: The collapse and revival of American community*. New York, NY: Simon & Schuster.

Ramakrishnan, S. K., & Lewis, P. G. (2005). *Immigrants and local governance: The view from City Hall*. San Francisco, CA: Public Policy Institute of California.

Rubin, A., & Babbie, E. (2011). *Research methods for social work* (7th ed.). Belmont, CA: Brooks/Cole.

Segal, U. A., Elliot, D., & Mayadas, N. S. (2010). *Immigration worldwide: Policies, practices, and trends*. New York, NY: Oxford.

Steen, J. A., & Mathiesen, S. (2005). Human rights education. *Journal of Teaching in Social Work, 25*(3–4), 143–156. doi: 10.1300/J067v25n03_09

United Nations. (2014). *Report of the special rapporteur on extreme poverty and human rights, Magdalena Sepulveda Carmona*. Retrieved from http://www .ohchr.org/EN/Issues/Poverty/Pages/AnnualReports.aspx

United Nations Development Programme. (2011). *Beyond transition: Towards inclusive societies*. Bratislava, Slovakia: UNDP Regional Bureau for Europe and the Commonwealth of Independent States.

Witkin, S. L. (1993). A human rights approach to social work research and evaluation. *Journal of Teaching in Social Work, 8*(1/2), 239–253.

Woolcock, M., & Narayan, D. (2000). Social capital: Implications for development theory, research, and policy. *World Bank Research Observer, 15*(2), 225–249.

Wronka, J. (2008). *Human rights and social justice: Social action and service for the helping and health professionals*. Thousand Oaks, CA: SAGE.

13 | Human Rights, Social Welfare, and Questions of Social Justice in South African Social Work Curricula

Viviene Taylor

South Africa's political and social struggle prior to the 1990s was based on the principle that democratic change would lead to an improvement in the overall quality of life for all, especially the disenfranchised majority (Taylor, 1997). Two decades after coming to power, the most important challenge of the democratically elected government remains the need to address the legacy of racial discrimination, social inequalities, poverty, and economic exploitation. Experiences since 1994 reveal that overcoming these structural conditions alongside new risks and vulnerabilities spawned by neoliberal globalization are a complex and daunting task. At every level and in every sphere of society the policy rhetoric focuses on the need to unify a country deeply fragmented along race, class, gender, language, and many other divides.

Central to overall transformation of society is the question of how to ensure that South Africans begin to transcend their differences, develop a shared identity, and work together to achieve the common objectives of eradicating poverty and addressing social inequality within a human-rights based constitution (Constitution of the Republic of South Africa, 1996, Act 108). What is the role and place of social work and social development in the broader processes of transformation and change in South Africa? Can social work education and professional practice reclaim its relevance through critical theorizing and reflexive practice as part of the process of advancing human rights? Do theories of social change and social justice inform discourses on curricula design and social development within the fields of social work? Which knowledge systems inform social work and social development curricula, are these contextually relevant, and do they advance human rights and social welfare? This chapter engages with some of these questions in a social work and social development[1] terrain that remains professionally contested.

Social work practice and social work education in South Africa, despite the country's checkered apartheid history, has a central role in ensuring that basic social welfare rights are accessible to all. Making human rights a reality for the millions of historically disenfranchised people is part of a transformative[2] social work agenda. Some argue that the intellectual traditions of social work and its historic vocation are more consistent with an approach that is reactive, piecemeal, and ameliorative (Lee & Raban, 1988) rather than transformative and emancipatory. Is this because social work as a profession serves to integrate individuals, families, and communities into existing unequal structures and systems? Is the social integration role of social work designed to reproduce inequities in access to resources, power, and privilege?

In South Africa educational processes and content that do not engage with why the majority of people remain excluded from social, economic, and political structures and systems run the risk of reproducing past inequities. Educational processes and the content of education require a critical understanding of the history, politics, and economics that lead to privileging a few and marginalizing the majority. This is essential in understanding the type of social change that should be promoted while ensuring that individual and collective rights of all are upheld. Understanding the policies, the controls, rules, and forms of social discipline that constrain democracy and human rights enables social work educators to better apply alternatives that are contextually relevant and results in empowering social work professionals and the people served.

Assumptions that social work education and social development processes are designed to advance human rights and protect the most vulnerable and exploited are debatable given the current context of huge inequalities and deprivations. Unequal power relations, structural inequities, and economic and social exclusions that deny access and equitable distribution of public goods and services are important considerations in designing curricula on the role and place of social work in advancing human rights. Moving away from the intellectual roots and the historical vocation of social work in apartheid South Africa requires critical theorizing of social work to change curriculum content for professional practice. This is especially significant in light of social work and welfare services being socially constructed to promote policies and practices approved by the pre-1994 apartheid state that reinforced race-based inequities and exclusions. Advancing human rights, social welfare, and issues of social justice in South Africa is crucial to the transformation of social work education and social work as a profession if human well-being and collective social welfare is to be achieved. Even more important is the need to engage with how social workers, social service professionals, and others perceive issues of human rights and social justice and how they link such issues within social work curricula.

Advancing human rights and social justice is especially difficult in a dynamic national and regional context influenced by complex political and economic forces underpinned by neoliberal capitalism promoted through globalization processes. Just as globalization is presently—slowly, unevenly, but inexorably—transforming our understanding of ethics itself, the Universal Declaration of Human Rights also did this when it was first proclaimed on December 10, 1948 (United Nations, 1948). At the time, the recently established United Nations was responding to issues in the wake of World War II that included massive attacks on civilians that amounted to genocide. The proclamation of the Universal Declaration of Human Rights began a new era in global ethics at the time (Lane, 2001). Contemporary debates about the meaning of rights and their enforcement in the context of globalization and the erosion of human well-being reinforce the need for an understanding of how ethical obligations of states that are signatories to related conventions and treaties can be reinforced. Human rights violations affect people's welfare in multiple ways and require a rethinking of the role and place of social workers in response to these violations.

Educating social service workers within a human rights framework provides a basis for them to make a difference in the lives of people who are excluded from the benefits of development. It is evident that the intentions of educators and policymakers to promote human rights are seldom matched by action today. For example, take the situation in South Africa. Despite the policy rhetoric of social transformation and the promise of basic welfare rights for all (African National Congress [ANC], 1994), social work has not had as much of an impact as it should. Is this because the shadow of apartheid's history still looms over the profession? What are some of the processes that constrain social work and social workers from robustly advancing human rights within social work and social development?

South Africa's history requires us to take a somewhat different analytical approach if we are to understand the role and place of social work in bringing about change from an unjust system to a social welfare system that is transparent, accountable, and gives expression to human rights. Such a different approach has its basis in critical theory and links this to a political economy framework to review what has changed and what remains to be done to advance human rights in social work education and practice in South Africa. A critical political economy framework provides the impetus for theorizing about social work in South Africa's historical context of economic and social privilege in which White people were regarded as citizens and Black people were disenfranchised and dispossessed. South Africa as a country was characterized by disequilibria and was dysfunctional for the majority. In this chapter I argue that we need to make sense of the factors that shape social welfare and the factors that influence processes of change. We need to adopt principles and values that underpin a vision of transformed social welfare and social work. These aspects are part of a conceptual framework (Figure 1) that links elements of a critical political economy framework for social change and transformation in social work curricula by embedding constitutional and human rights principles to advance social justice.

Figure 1 **Conceptual framework for advancing human rights and social justice in social work**

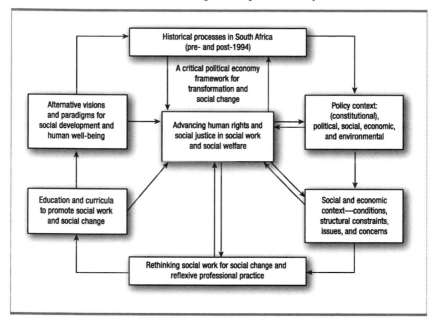

Historical Background: From the Political Economy of Apartheid to Constitutional Democracy Within a Human Rights Framework

Evolving in the context of colonialism, racialism, and distorted patterns of development, social work historically mirrored divisions along race, gender, class, and spatial lines. Social work was experienced by the majority of South Africans (categorized as Black Africans)[3] as a handmaiden of the apartheid state. Social welfare and social work benefits and services (systems) were fragmented along discriminatory racial, spatial, and economic divisions, and were characterized by inequities and a low or nonexistent standard of services for the Black majority. Discriminatory practices and inequities existed in all social services, including social work, education, health, access to basic services such as water and sanitation, housing, and access to income support such as social security. This places an obligation on educators to introduce antidiscriminatory social work and social development education and professional practice. The majority of people experienced the brutality of the state in many ways. The denial of full citizenship to Black[4] people along with the denial of human rights was part of a deliberate apartheid political and economic strategy designed to exclude Black people from access to resources and at the same time to exploit their labor. Social workers were viewed with suspicion because they were identified as professionals who carried out state regulations that were specifically designed to control and discipline Black people using apartheid laws and regulations.

Despite the suspicion, there were progressive and concerned social workers who led resistance against discriminatory and oppressive social welfare and social work legislation and practices from within the nongovernmental social work sector (Patel, 1992). At various times individual social workers became part of social movement activism and also mobilized against the brutality of the state as part of the broader struggle for democracy and human rights. As these progressive social workers engaged in resistance, they were at the same time part of the official system of state sanctioned racially differentiated social welfare. Some scholars argue that social welfare—and, by extension, social work—was designed historically as a system of services to control and coerce people into compliance with a discredited state regime (Rycroft, 1988). This did create tension about how to relate to a state that was seen as authoritarian, illegitimate, and punitive while at the same time engaging in professional practice that was theoretically understood to empower and enable individuals, families, and communities to overcome dehumanizing social conditions.

Mobilization against oppressive and paternalistic aspects of social work led to tensions and struggles within the profession. Fractures and fissures within the profession of social work were evident in debates about how social work is conceptualized and its role, place, and aims in a democratic developmental South African state. Debates and discourses on the elements of a transformed social welfare system and the role of social work in such a system are on-going. This is not unique to South Africa. Writing on a paradigm for radical[5] practice in the United Kingdom decades earlier, Leonard (1975) explored the aims of radical social work within existing social welfare systems in that context. As he put it,

> the aims of education, systems linking and counter-systems building account for much of the activity of the radical worker, but we must also

identify the aims in providing those direct services—material, psychological and sometimes coercive for which the official welfare system was developed. (p. 58, as cited in Bailey & Brake, 1975)

Although contradictory processes emerge in many contexts, what is unique to South Africa is that institutionalized exclusion, oppression, and exploitation of the majority had to be dismantled at the same time as continuity with many elements of the former regime were retained (Taylor, 2001). For example, the institutional arenas within which social work education and professional development are being offered retain many aspects of traditional social work[6] while at the same time undergoing processes of organizational restructuring.

Assumptions that such restructuring is part of the process to make education accessible to all and to make the content of education align with constitutional and developmental agendas do not take into account a constraining macro-economic agenda fashioned on neoliberal capitalism. Restructuring of universities and other institutional arenas is driven by competing and contradictory processes. There is also the drive to achieve greater efficiencies given financial constraints arising from budget cutbacks and the adoption of a business management approach to educational endeavors. On the other hand, there is the South African imperative of widening access to tertiary education especially focusing on those previously denied access, redirecting resources to greatest need and transforming curricula to achieve the mandates of a human-rights based constitution. It is in the design and redesign of social work curricula within complex institutional spaces that contestation and critical discussion emerge about what changes are necessary and how best to achieve these within a constrained macro policy environment.

The transformation of social policy and the entire social welfare system in South Africa thus remains an on-going project. In the next section some processes that led to changes in the characteristics and the values of social work are discussed. Issues that relate to policy and legislative coherence with social work and social development are discussed within the framework of the South African Constitution.

The Constitution: Policy and Legislative Coherence in Social Work and Social Development

Between 1990 and 1994 the democratic movement under the leadership of the ANC assembled a wide range of policies as part of a program of reconstruction and development of the country. In the social welfare policy arena, consultations took place with social workers, communities, and progressive formations. Progressive formations involved in redefining social welfare included women's organizations, youth and civic movements, and a range of trade unions. Arising from these processes, a National Social Welfare and Development Plan (ANC, 1994a) was developed to clarify the role of social welfare and social work in a democratic state. This plan included the values and principles that would inform social service provision and the restructuring of the welfare system.

The aims of the National Social Welfare and Development Plan were to ensure that in a future democratic society, a social welfare system can be developed that has its basis in values and principles such as equity, social justice and the protection of human rights and fundamental freedoms of all South Africans (Taylor, 1994, as cited in the ANC National Social Welfare and Development Plan, 1994). The values and principles adopted by the democratic government and that influenced changes in social work were also made explicit in the first State of the Nation address by President Nelson Mandela (1994) when he said,

> My Government's commitment to create a people-centered society of liberty binds us to the pursuit of the goals of the freedom from want, freedom from hunger, freedom from deprivation, freedom from ignorance, freedom from suppression and freedom from fear. These freedoms are fundamental to the guarantee of human dignity. They will therefore constitute part of the centrepiece of what this government will seek to achieve, the focal point on which our attention will be continuously focused. (p. 10)

The founding provisions of the Constitution of the Republic of South Africa of 1996 (Act 108) focus specifically on the importance of values of human dignity, the achievement of equality, and the advancement of human

rights and freedoms as well as nonracialism and nonsexism. The supremacy
of the Constitution is explicit, and all laws or conduct inconsistent with the
Constitution are invalid. Chapter 2 of the Constitution is the Bill of Rights,
and in Clause 7 (2) the state's role is identified as to "respect, protect, promote
and fulfill the rights in the Bill of Rights." This clause reflects the intention of
a strong role for the state in protecting and promoting the rights of citizens.
Such a role does not place limitations on what the state should and should
not do in relation to private markets in the social development arena, nor
does it leave social work and social development to the nonprofit sector. The
case for change from a race based, narrow, fragmented system of social work
services to a comprehensive social welfare system is supported by the South
African Constitution, the imperatives of the social and economic context of
extreme hardship and deprivations of the majority, and increasing levels of
social inequality.

Social and economic rights in South Africa are justiciable and have the same
status as civil and political rights. Importantly, the South African Constitution
mandates the right of access to health care, food, water, and social security under
Chapter 2 of the Bill of Rights. Specifically, Section 27 (1)(c) states that everyone
has the right of access to social security, including, if they are unable to support
themselves and their dependents, "appropriate social assistance." Subsection 27
(2) states that "The state must take reasonable legislative and other measures,
within its available resources, to achieve the progressive realization of each of
these rights" (Constitution of the Republic of South Africa, 1996, p. 13).

The progressive realization of socioeconomic rights contained in the
Constitution distinguishes South Africa as a developmental state, because it
reflects the aim of systematically advancing a rights agenda over time with a
predetermined plan that gives programmatic effect to the realization of human
rights. Although the Constitution provides support for social and economic
rights, a political mandate also exists for the realization of social rights. In
1994 the ANC campaigned for political power under an election manifesto
that included welfare rights for all. In addition, the Reconstruction and
Development Programme policy framework of the tripartite alliance[7] launched
that same year (ANC, 1994b) identified a main goal of a developmental social

welfare program as "the attainment of basic social welfare rights for all South Africans, irrespective of race, colour, religion, gender and physical disability, through the establishment of a democratically-determined, just and effective social delivery system" (ANC, 1994b, p. 52).

South Africa became a signatory to the Universal Declaration of Human Rights (1948) and is also obliged to ensure access to social and economic rights for its citizens. The South African government clearly has the firm historical base, political mandate, and constitutional and normative imperatives to develop a social welfare system that is responsive to peoples' needs and grounded in human rights. Such normative and constitutional imperatives require us to interrogate the role of social work, the curricula, and knowledge systems that inform the education of social work professionals in social development and to do this while maintaining existing welfare services and even increasing service provision for all.

The challenge for social work professionals and for educators is that of translating these rights and values into tangible outcomes in the design of curricula, in placements where work integrated learning occurs, and in the professional services that people receive. The adopted values and principles of the democratic social welfare system include principles of equality, equity, access, user involvement, empowerment, and public accountability (ANC, 1994a, p. 52). To address the challenges of poverty and inequality, the democratic government adopted an integrated developmental vision of social welfare policy. The aim is to promote human development, economic inclusion, and social stability. As expressed in the South African White Paper on Social Welfare (1997), "social welfare is understood as a comprehensive, integrated system of social services and benefits acting as a redistribution mechanism to bring about progressive change in the social, economic, political, cultural and physical conditions of people, especially the poorest" (Republic of South Africa [RSA], 1997). This definition of social welfare has two central components: a recognition of structural inequalities and the need for equitable redistribution of benefits and services and the prioritization of the needs of those most deprived.

Giving effect to constitutional, policy, and legislative mandates in a society that is undergoing multiple transitions in the midst of social crises spawned by internal (apartheid and racial capitalism) and external (neoliberal economic globalization) factors is particularly difficult. The next section discusses some of the key trends and indicators that influence the social and economic context within which the majority of South Africans live and social work and social development services are located.

Socioeconomic Context and Social Work: The Search for Contextual Relevance

Poverty and social fragmentation are not sudden occurrences in society. The roots are complex and intertwined. Poverty and social fragmentation in South Africa, primarily resulting from a racially and class divided society, continues to have a determining effect on the country's human development status and growth prospects. Apartheid influenced human development in many negative ways for Black South Africans. The institutional and psychological costs are evident in human development indicators and in the breakdown of social institutions of society. A migrant labor system and a system of labor reserves in homelands, usually far from urban centers, destroyed family life, eroding the social institution of the family and the social support systems of Black people. Among many social challenges facing the social development sector, interpersonal violence ranks as South Africa's second leading cause of morbidity.

Poverty reduction was embedded in the policies, strategies, and programs that framed debates on the transformation of the social welfare system. The poverty concept that signposted the theme of eliminating poverty and reducing inequalities was a broad based, holistic, and operational concept. Although poverty reduction, inequality, and equitable development were included in the transformational script and post-1994 narratives that unfolded, they have yet to be translated into significant social welfare outcomes. Indicators reflect that many South Africans (close to 30%) are unable to find paid work, and more than 40% of the population are living below a poverty line of R450 per month (Statistics South Africa, 2012).

Markers of structural inequities are evident in levels of economic participation of the majority of the population and the racial dimensions of such participation rates. As a result of recession and other factors, Black African participation rates are much lower than other race groups; participation rates declined 6.2% between 2001 to 2010. Low participation rates of Black people, especially women, in the economy mirror patterns of unemployment, which according to a wide definition is estimated at close to 36% (Development Bank of South Africa [DBSA], 2011). The links between people's ability to participate in economic activity through employment opportunities, their levels of poverty, and deprivations in health and education are direct. Unemployment and poverty as a result of structural barriers to participation affect individuals, households, and communities. The effects are multidimensional and intergenerational.

The content and curricula of social work should include a history of social work, the distinctions with social development, and courses that focus on the links between macro social and economic policy processes and how these interact to influence social development outcomes for people. Courses designed to introduce social work students to knowledge of social and economic policy interactions and the structural barriers that keep people trapped in poverty and socially marginalized are crucial in how change is theorized in social work.

Advancing Human Rights and Building Human Capabilities: A Continuum in Educating for Social Change

The combination of poor and inadequate state services in social welfare and high levels of poverty and inequality produces social problems and high risk behavior that undermines human development and social cohesion. High levels of domestic violence are exacerbated by poverty and unemployment. Alcohol and drug abuse are other factors that are both causes and manifestations of stresses in households and communities. Poor social services and ineffective safety and security reinforce the sense of powerlessness in poor communities. Poor quality education limits social mobility, further straining basic social relations that many societies take for granted. The effects of youth unemployment and HIV/AIDS have worsened matters. Statistics show that only 23% of African children are raised by both their parents. The remaining 77% live with a single parent, in a skip generation (with one or two grandparents) household, in a child-headed household, in foster care, or in extended family arrangements (Statistics South Africa, 2012). These are explosive phenomena that could derail efforts to build a successful, cohesive, and democratic society.

Statistics paint a disturbing picture of increasing violence, increasing numbers of income-poor households, and other social determinants, but they do not expose the full picture (National Planning Commission, 2012). Social surveys reveal rising levels of addictions and related alcohol substance disorders; increasing criminality among young people; high levels of gang related violence in schools and communities; and sexual violence against children and women, especially in economically deprived areas (Statistics South Africa, 2007). Households without working adults, without parents, without access to social support systems, and without access to effective social services are not functioning; evidence reveals high risk behavior especially of young people in economically deprived areas (Rapp-Palicci, Roberts, & Wodarski, 2002; Statistics South Africa, 2012). Race, gender, income, and spatial inequalities, combined with weak and ineffective social institutions, reinforce social fragmentation and alienation. Education, health, and social welfare are key determinants of individual and household earning capacity and development; but the type and quality of education, health care, and social welfare services are also critical to building an inclusive society.

South Africa's human development as measured by education and health outcomes shows continuing inequalities. Education outcomes in relation to critical areas such as mathematics and science reveal that 62.5% of White sixth grade learners can do mathematics, compared with only 0.1% of Black sixth grade learners. Race-based inequalities in learning outcomes are particularly prevalent in higher education levels, especially at universities. Black student enrollments have increased since 1994 because access to education is widening, but the retention rate of Black students is far lower because of the social and economic hardships that the majority still experience (DBSA, 2011). As the DBSA finds: "of the entire cohort of black children entering school in any one year, the education system can only convey approximately five percent to graduation—from Grade 1 to the completion of an undergraduate degree"

(DBSA, 2011, p. 27). According to the same research report, the life chances of Black children contrasts starkly with that of White children, who have a 60% chance of graduating with a degree from a university.

An important feature of the higher education landscape is that in social sectors where teachers, health care professionals, and social workers dominate, the curricula do not take as much account of the needs identified in the social and economic contexts, the gaps in service provision for those who were historically excluded, and their social and economic locations in local and global systems of production. These issues have particular relevance for the design of university qualifications for social work and social development professionals. Careful attention in the design of such qualifications has to take account of the environmental contexts from which students are drawn, the learning and psychological and social needs of students, as well as the core and generic disciplinary knowledge that is required to ensure professional competence in changing local and global contexts. Changing social work educational curricula and methods to ensure contextual relevance and to increase the capabilities of social workers can lead to the strengthening of social institutions and individual and community capacities of those who are being served.

Deprivations in education and in health undermine the capacities of social work students and the communities where they work. Indicators of health deprivations are evident in infant mortality rates; from 1993 to 1998, deaths per live births increased from an average of 45.5 to 69 in 2005. Of equal concern is the increase in maternal mortality rates from 200 per 100,000 live births in 2000, to 400 per 100,000 in 2008 (DBSA, 2011). Despite significant policy and legislative changes that widen access to education, health, and essential services and that make opportunities accessible, the life chances for Black citizens are far from just and equitable. Inequities in the distribution of social development services remain a significant challenge. For example, in health the government (public health care) provides R99 billion to provide health care to 85% of the population, whereas the private sector spends R93 billion to provide health services to 15% of the population (DBSA, 2011).

Huge income differentials between the rich who can pay for services through the private sector and the poor who rely on the public sector result in differences in the types and quality of services provided to people. Such income and wealth differentials also influence the numbers of social service workers who can be employed in the public sector and the conditions (including wages, professional development, and career paths) under which they work. These issues influence the status of the profession and undermine efforts to improve the education of professionals. The numbers of social workers who graduate and go into the public sector are inadequate given the increasing demand for social care and welfare services across the country (Taylor, 2009).

Besides deprivations in health and education, interpersonal violence as a result of social inequalities in South Africa contributes to morbidity. Unacceptably high instances of violence against women and children are conditions that destroy human lives, as well as trust and social cohesion. These social pressures undermine economic development, civic responsiveness, and democratic processes. Social workers and other social service professionals work in a context in which individual, household, and community resilience is being eroded. Rethinking social work so that it is responsive to human well-being and can enhance social welfare requires a rethinking and reorganizing of institutional capabilities within principles that build individual and collective capacities for social change and equitable development. Social service professionals, especially social workers, function as catalysts for social change, as interrupters in the chain of events that leads to poverty and inequalities. They are part of a continuum in the educational endeavor that enables social service professionals to contribute to wider processes of social change. Other parts of the continuum include processes designed to enhance individual, collective, and institutional capabilities that together create an environment for the promotion of human rights and development.

Conditions that are uniquely South African and that shape South Africans' experiences in social development include the institutional violence of the apartheid system. South Africa's Truth and Reconciliation Commission (TRC) has exposed the horrors of the past. Creating a process through which people could ask for information about their own experiences and what happened to those close to them has had a shattering effect. It has revealed in harrowing detail just a few of the experiences of the victims of the war against apartheid. In some instances it led to some perpetrators of violence being given opportunities to confront their decisions and to take responsibility for their actions. A significant consequence of the hearings held by the TRC is that they broke the culture of silence on political violence and the various forms of discrimination people experienced.

Despite these positive outcomes of the TRC, there remains a lack of acknowledgment and information on the whereabouts of the bodies of hundreds of liberation fighters who were part of the just war against the apartheid. Families of those who fought for freedom and died live in the long shadow of apartheid and have yet to receive reparations and other forms of assistance through the TRC process. Clearly, the trauma of individuals, households, and communities in reliving the past and coming to terms with their pain will remain a part of the psyche of the nation for some time and is influencing the process of nation building and democratization. Such painful experiences lay bare the fractures of our society and the extent of alienation in South Africa. This especially occurs among those who are part of the economically and socially disaffected.

These processes and their outcomes distinguish South Africa's current development path from that of other countries in Africa. At times they have laid bare the soul of the nation and left a chasm that cannot be adequately captured when expressed simply as the legacy of apartheid. The importance of the TRC's work in this context is that it underlines the need for South Africa's Constitution to become a framework of human rights that is understood, lived, and experienced by all its citizens. Even more pertinent is the role of social welfare and social work in the process of healing, reconciliation, and nation building—the building of individual and collective capabilities. The consequential effects of state based political violence, economic marginalization, and exploitation and the systematic breakdown of social institutions highlights the absence of adequate social welfare services to respond to the range of complex social conditions that persist today. This is the complex social development context in which it is essential to rethink the role and place of social work education in South Africa.

Changing Social Work Education and Curricula
Rethinking Social Work Within the Framework of Social Development

I concur with Hettne (1982) that there is no fixed and final definition of development but that there are suggestions of what development should imply in particular contexts. His view is that development necessarily involves structural transformation, which implies political, social, and economic changes. This type of transformation should lead to equitable distribution of rights, benefits, and services in society. In practical programmatic terms, how do social welfare, social development, human rights, and human well-being relate to each other? This is an obvious and complex question to begin with, but it is useful to frame it in this way to identify the unique and common elements the concepts bring to the study of social work in the context of development. Social welfare at individual, family, and community levels is a critical component of social development and social inclusion. Social development links economic and social goals through macro policies in ways that influence what people are able to do in micro development settings (Sen, 1999).

This understanding of social development fits well with the Universal Declaration of Human Rights of 1948 and its 30 articles, which form the basis for international human rights law. The South African Constitution of 1996 is also consistent with the Universal Declaration of Human Rights. The *White Paper on Social Welfare of 1997* (RSA, 1997) includes values and principles consistent with social development, the Universal Declaration of Human Rights, and with the vision of a socially just, equitable, and sustainable society that promotes antidiscriminatory practices and social inclusion.

Central to achieving such a vision is the training and education of social work professionals. Problems exist in the supply of qualified social service professionals and are linked to the funding of higher education institutions, poor working conditions, and lack of employment opportunities (despite great needs). Efforts to increase the supply of professionals led to the South African government declaring social work a scarce skill. However, higher education institution graduates of social work, community development, and social development, as well as specialists such as clinical social workers, are also influenced by changes in social work curricula, standards, and other factors (Taylor, 2009).

Social work education is provided through 17 university institutions across South Africa. At the university level an undergraduate generic bachelor of social work degree is available to those who enter the profession. This degree (content and quality) has to comply with the South African Council for Higher Education (CHE) qualifications framework and also with the South African Council for Social Service Professions (SACSSP). Both bodies are statutory. Whereas the CHE regulates the quality of the curricula and approves social work degrees within higher education, the SACSSP regulates the terms in which social workers can practice the profession. This ensures the ethical requirements for professional practice are in place.

Social work education providers must comply with regulations established by the Standard Generating Body (SGB) for Social Work in line with the CHE and the South African Qualifications Authority (SAQA) requirements. These regulations are approved by the SACSSP, the statutory body that provides accreditation of social service professionals and without which no social worker can practice. The SACSSP operates under the Social Service Professions Act 110 of 1978 as amended. The Minister of Social Development is responsible for oversight of the implementation of this Act (Taylor, 2009).

The SACSSP works closely with the social work SGB to set standards for education and professional development of social work professionals. SGBs, operating under the auspices of the SACSSP, ascertain that the educational programs offered to their members are accredited by the SAQA and are registered on the National Qualifications Framework. The White Paper on Social Welfare Services (RSA, 1997) also recognizes the different roles of various occupational groups (social development workers, child and youth care workers, community development workers, probation workers, and correctional practice workers) in effective social service delivery. The education and professionalization of various social service occupations is an evolving and contested process. Issues that emerge in this process relate to who can practice and under which conditions, how admission criteria into social work educational programs is determined, and aligning curriculum design with minimum standards for academic programs and a significant field practice instruction component as well as with the national and local social contexts.

Specialist (as distinct from generic) social work services in the fields of social development, social policy and management, probation and correctional practice, and clinical social work are offered at the University of Cape Town at the postgraduate level (honors and master's degrees). The University of Cape Town also offers postgraduate doctoral programs in social development and in social work (University of Cape Town, 2013).

Estimates are that the country requires close to 55,000 social service professionals (including social workers) to provide a minimum level of social development services to respond to the country's social welfare needs and to address social fragmentation and dislocation. Approximately 15,000–17,000 social workers are registered with the SACSSP, and we can assume that they register to practice as social workers (Taylor, 2009). However, many social work graduates find employment outside the social work profession because of the poor working conditions, poor remuneration, and low status of the profession.

Ensuring Contextual Relevance and Building Capabilities

Demographic trends and human development indicators point to a country with significant levels of social fragmentation, unacceptable levels of social alienation, and the breakdown of social institutions in South Africa (Statistics South Africa, 2012). In the absence of fully functioning families, households, communities, and neighborhoods, social welfare institutions in most countries step in to provide services to improve the social functioning of members of society and enhance social integration. Yet without building the capabilities of people, institutions, and communities, social welfare responses will remain ameliorative rather than transformative. Social work educators and social service providers are using democratic spaces that have opened up since 1994 to promote the rights of people at an individual and collective level.

Advancing Human Rights and Social Justice in Social Work Curricula

How does social work navigate this complex context and give real content to human rights and social justice? One option is to take a human development and freedom centered approach (Nussbaum & Sen, 1993; Sen, 1999) to social welfare. This would include a focus on the social and economic development of individuals, families, and communities as well as advancing a social justice agenda that reduces inequalities and eliminates poverty. The approach requires the use of methods and techniques to raise the awareness of government and community sectors to social conditions that require change. In addition, the knowledge and techniques required to link social and economic processes that build capacities of professional social service workers and institutions are essential to ensure human well-being. The inclusion of such knowledge and techniques in social work curricula will enable social workers to identify and focus on the links between micro level experiences and structural inequities.

Reinforcing Knowledge That Links Micro and Macro Development Processes

Responses in the social work field include early intervention through community development strategies and statutory intervention such as residential and alternative care arrangements for those found to be in need (such as orphaned and vulnerable children, survivors of violence, and those with health conditions). Within the public and nongovernmental sectors the professional response also includes the treatment, rehabilitation, and reintegration of ex-offenders, recovering substance abusers, and alcoholics into families and society. Active citizenship is most visible through the work of nongovernmental welfare organizations, advice offices, civic organizations, and faith-based organizations in such responses. As significant as their roles are, they are unable to respond to the scale and complexities of South Africa's social fragmentation, lack of social support systems, and poverty. Increasingly the burden of care falls on women, the elderly, and the poorest communities. The coping abilities and resilience of these households and communities is stretched, with their own needs compromised. In many instances they are being reduced to a sense of powerlessness and social isolation, thereby increasing their own vulnerabilities.

Linking Individual Welfare and Capabilities With Human Well-Being and Distributive Justice in Welfare Provision

The distribution of public and private social welfare services remains skewed along racial and income lines, with the wealthy having access to quality private services and the poor having limited access to generic state social welfare services that are concentrated in urban areas. The government has adopted a partnership model of service provision and relies mainly on nongovernmental welfare organizations to provide professional social services to those in need. However, the funding of nongovernmental welfare and development organizations has declined steadily since 1994, which has reduced the range of services available and compromised the quality of services provided. At the same time, the demand for such services has increased as social conditions worsen due to epidemiological crises such as HIV/AIDS, migration, and internally displaced groups, including refugees (Taylor, 2009).

The demand for social work and social development services is most critical for social integration and human development. The current model—shifting the burden of care, treatment, rehabilitation, and building social capital to the nongovernmental sector and poorest communities—does not address structurally embedded inadequacies. Within the social work profession as well as in broader society it cannot be assumed that there is agreement about the type of society to be achieved and the type of structural change that would promote social justice. South African social work education has many unacknowledged values and theoretical assumptions that contribute to disciplinary ambiguity for educators and professionals in practice. False binaries are perpetuated about the therapeutic, preventive, or developmental roles of social work. Consequently, the place and values of the discipline become constrained by an ideological impasse that either privileges individual welfare over collective well-being or vice versa. For example, current debates on social work education and curricula focus either on the need to address structural inequities using a developmental approach to human well-being or on the need to provide therapeutic interventions to promote individual and family well-being.

South Africa's social work and social welfare system, with its historical basis in oppressive and discriminatory policies, requires changes to enable it to contribute to social transformation of society within a rights based framework. To be sure, this poses certain fundamental questions about how to change curricula in ways that enable professionals to serve both statutory functions as well as the social needs of society to promote social change for human well-being. How is curricula designed to enable critical theorizing and reflective social work practice? Other questions include whether the specificity of human rights and social justice in different contexts is given conscious expression in the design of social work and social development. Further, in embedding human rights and social justice in social work curricula, can social work education adequately reflect an intellectual and theoretical rupture with a past characterized by colonialism, patriarchy, and apartheid? Further, can this lead to critical reframing of social work to advance human rights in the present?

Even more important is how to distinguish the characteristics of a critical social work curriculum that is specific for its time and place in Africa from a curriculum that is orthodox, positivist, promotes a pathology orientation to the study of social work, and reproduces existing patterns of privilege and power within the social work educational environments as well as the profession at large. Designing curricula within a critical theorizing of social work, especially in South Africa, requires an analysis of the epistemology of different sources of knowledge and understanding of why some knowledge systems count and others do not.

Conclusion

South Africa's contemporary context provides a renewed urgency to translate issues of human rights and social justice into policy outcomes that matter for people whose daily lives are characterized by poverty and multiple deprivations. Clearly, what is meant by *human rights* and how to advance social justice and human rights within a global, regional, and national context of huge inequalities remains a complex problem. Access to rights and entitlements matters; but who decides how citizens claim their rights, under which conditions, and how social justice can be achieved are issues that foreground measures to change curricula that would in turn enable professionals to work to eliminate poverty, reduce inequality, and advance social equity.

The challenges of contemporary societies demand an approach to social justice that anchors ethical and moral arguments in people's everyday lives. In other words, quality of life concerns demand knowledge systems that place the socially excluded at the center of the approach. Systems that do not promote human flourishing and that are unjust and repressive require more than a theoretical and philosophical debate (Nussbaum & Sen, 1993). Social work educators in South Africa aim to advance human rights and demand a focus on contextual realities and practical evaluative aspects of people's lives. Finally, as Sen (1999) argues, social work focuses on what people are capable of doing and the space within which they are able to make choices.

References

African National Congress. (1994a). *National social welfare and development plan.* Cape Town, South Africa: Southern African Development Education Programme.

African National Congress. (1994b). *The reconstruction and development programme.* Johannesburg, South Africa: Umanyano Publications.

Bailey, R., & Brake, M. (Eds.) (1975). *Radical social work.* London, UK. Edward Arnold.

Constitution of the Republic of South Africa. (1996). Act 108 of 1996. Cape Town, South Africa: Constitutional Assembly of the Republic of South Africa.

Development Bank of Southern Africa (DBSA). (2011). *Prospects for South Africa's future* (Development Report 2011). Pretoria, South Africa: Development Planning Division.

Hettne, B. (1982). *Development theory and the third world* (SAREC Report Number 2). Stockholm, Sweden: SAREC.

Lane, M., (2001). [Globalization and human rights]. Unpublished meeting notes.

Lee, P., & Raban, C. (1988). *Welfare theory and social policy: Reform or revolution?* London, UK: SAGE Publications.

Leonard, P. (1975). *Towards a paradigm for radical practice.* In R. Bailey & M. Brake (Eds.), *Radical social work* (pp. 46–61). London, UK: Edward Arnold.

Mandela, N. (1994, May 24). *State of the nation address.* Cape Town, South Africa: Government of the Republic of South Africa.

National Planning Commission. (2012). *National development plan: Vision 2030.* Pretoria, South Africa: The Presidency in the Government of Republic of South Africa.

Nussbaum, M. C., & Sen, A. (1993). Capability and well-being. In M. C.
Nussbaum & A. Sen (Eds.), *The quality of life* (pp. 1–29). Oxford, UK:
Clarendon Press.

Patel, L. (1992). *Restructuring social welfare: Options for South Africa.*
Johannesburg, South Africa: Ravan Press.

Rapp-Paglicci, L. A., Roberts, A. R., & Wodarski, J. S. (Eds.). (2002). *Handbook
of violence.* New York, NY: John Wiley & Sons.

Republic of South Africa (RSA) (1997, August). *White paper for social welfare.*
Pretoria, South Africa: Department of Welfare/Government Printer.

Rycroft, A. (1988). "Social pensions and poor relief in South Africa: An exercise in
social control." Unpublished paper presented at the ASSA Sociology of Health
Conference, South Africa.

Sen, A. (1999). *Development as freedom.* Oxford, UK: Oxford University Press.

Social Service Professions Act, 110 (1978). Retrieved from http://www.dsd.gov.za
/dmdocuments/Social_Service_Professions_Act_1978.pdf

Statistics South Africa. (2007). *General household survey, 2007.* (Report Number
P0318). Pretoria, South Africa: Author.

Statistics South Africa. (2012). *Social profile of vulnerable groups in South Africa,
2002 to 2012.* (Report No. 03-19-00). Pretoria, South Africa: Author.

Taylor, V. (1997). *Social mobilisation: Lessons from the mass democratic movement.*
Cape Town, South Africa: University of the Western Cape.

Taylor, V. (2001). *Relating human development to economic growth: The human
development report 2000.* (New Agenda, Issue 2). Cape Town, South Africa:
Institute for African Alternatives.

Taylor, V. (2009). "Social work education in the Western Cape: Responding to
contextual realities in South Africa." Paper prepared for the Consortium of
Higher Education in the Cape, Cape Town, South Africa, University of Cape
Town.

United Nations. (1948, December 10). *Universal declaration of human rights.*
G. A. Res. 217 A (III). Retrieved from http://www.refworld.org/docid
/3ae6b3712c.html

University of Cape Town. (2013). *Faculty of humanities' handbooks, 2013.* Cape
Town, South Africa: University of Cape Town.

Endnotes

1   A social development perspective recognizes that barriers to human well-being are not only economic but also social, political, military, and environmental. Within this perspective the links among social and economic policy goals are understood as important for individual and society well-being. Social work curricular interventions that focus on human welfare by linking structural barriers to human development to macro policy analysis and change work within a social development paradigm. Addressing issues that affect individual welfare, household, and community well-being and addressing social inequalities are part of the social development terrain within which social workers practice.

2   Transformative social work curricula embed principles of human rights and social justice into content and practice.

3   Racial categories such as Black African, colored or mixed race, Asian, and White were used to provide differential and discriminatory access to resources and power under the apartheid state pre-1994. These categories (sometimes referred to as population groups) are still in use administratively to identify gaps in provision and introduce measures to ensure equity in allocation of resources and access to opportunities.

4   In this sense I use *Black* to denote all people of color, not only those categorized as African. In the 1970s, during the period defined as "an era of Black consciousness" under the leadership of Steve Biko, a conscious attempt was made to redefine all those who experienced oppression under the collective term *Black* to build unity against apartheid and reaffirm being Black.

5   Radical social work practice in Bailey and Brake (1975) and as I understand it has its basis in social justice, egalitarianism, social solidarity, and social change that promotes human well-being. It is the antithesis to individualism, competitiveness, social and economic exclusions, and social isolation.

6   The use of the term *traditional social work* in this context denotes social work methods and approaches that evolved in the period of early industrialization and that had basis in a medical or clinical assessment and intervention treatment model of individuals, families, and groups. This differs from interventions that are responsive to structural conditions that prevent individual and collective human well-being as well as those that deal with specific vulnerabilities and psychosocial conditions that affect human beings.

7   The tripartite alliance at the time included the ANC, the South African Communist Party, and the Congress of South African Trade Unions. On specific issues this alliance included in various forums the South African National Civic Organization and Women's Organizations.

Learning by Doing: Integrating Social and Economic Justice and Human Rights Into Social Work Practice

Rosemary A. Barbera

Social work's explicit commitment to social and economic justice is well-documented. The U.S. based National Association of Social Workers and Council on Social Work Education (CSWE), as well as the International Federation of Social Workers (IFSW), include this commitment to social and economic justice in their mission statements. The IFSW also articulates an explicit commitment to human rights. Schools and departments of social work in the United States are mandated by CSWE to include content on social and economic justice in their curricula. But we must ask ourselves, if social work students and practitioners are learning about social work practice from a social and economic justice and human rights perspective, why have inequalities not only persisted but increased? Why does much social work practice still rely on methods that blame the victim/exploited? Why do many social workers work in isolation with individual cases rather than examining, analyzing the causes of, and demanding changes in the unjust structures that perpetuate human rights violations and exacerbate social and economic injustice? Although students and practitioners report theoretical knowledge of these concepts, frequently they do not understand how to operationalize human rights and social and economic justice in their practice.

Using a Latin American human rights framework, this chapter will discuss how one social work program integrates action for human rights and social and economic justice into its curriculum through two capstone courses. Students design, implement, and evaluate projects to advance human rights. These projects go beyond charity to address, as much as possible, the structures that perpetuate injustice and human rights violations. This experience helps students learn how to do social work from a human rights framework that advances social and economic justice, so they can later practice social work integrating these concepts and values into their practice.

Social Work and Human Rights—A View From the South

For many in Latin America, "the practice of social work is committed to the values that define how we live together: solidarity, justice, and freedom" (Sánchez, 1989, p. 20). These values are communal values and not individualistic values, which are more pervasive in the United States. These values express the commitment to work together collectively to create the conditions in which the human rights of all humans are respected. These include civil, political, economic, cultural, social, and collective human rights. These rights reflect the multifaceted nature of human life and together, if respected, would ensure that all humans have a standard of living that meets basic needs and promotes dignity and health.

At the very core of social work is a commitment to the dignity of all humans as well as a commitment to improving the living conditions of the most exploited and vulnerable groups and persons in society. Work toward the attainment of the human rights of all persons is critical because "human rights are intimately linked to the idea of 'quality of life'" (Cáceres, 2000, p.19). In this way, "social work and human rights have a very close relationship" (Eroles, 1997, p.56) that calls on social workers to be active in the construction of a new society based on human rights where the needs of all are met with dignity. It is not enough to only have knowledge of and a commitment to human rights, however:

It is not enough for social workers to speak the language of human rights and democracy; before they can even engage in social service work, they have to have in their hearts the conviction that all human beings are worthy. (Eroles, 1997, p. 19)

This supposes two things: one, that social workers are committed to relationships based on democracy and partnerships and not on hierarchical relationships of professional and client; and two, that social workers know how to put human rights into practice in their ongoing practice. The continued emphasis on the professionalization of social work has led social workers away from a practice that is democratic and perpetuates a society based on categories of worthy and unworthy. Even the use of the terms *client* and *consumer* stresses the differences between the social worker and the person in client status rather than focusing on their common humanity and a commitment to attaining the common good in a democratic manner, as social work pioneer Bertha Capen Reynolds (1963) enjoined early social workers in the United States.

Further, social work's commitment to the most vulnerable is clearly in concert with practicing social work from a human rights perspective.

Social work from a human rights perspective helps us attain the very basis of our professional principles: the preoccupation for serving, for being useful, more than anything, to the weakest members of society; to intervene specifically confronting social problems until we are able to assure that the necessary conditions which guarantee that all basic necessities are met. (Sánchez, 1989, p. 21)

Therefore, a commitment to the most vulnerable of society necessitates action that ensures that the human rights of these vulnerable persons are respected. This implies a commitment to a social work practice that addresses social and economic injustice and aims to eliminate, not ameliorate, the conditions that perpetuate injustice and exploitation. Therefore, social workers are called to make a *preferential option with the poor* (Farmer, 2005; see also Gutiérrez, 1973), a phrase used widely in Latin America to articulate the commitment people of privilege have to fight for social and economic justice in partnership with the most affected. This option necessitates that "social work (must) revise itself according to the present reality" (Colectivo, 1989, p. 9), as in Latin American social work.

This analysis of the present reality as a way to improve upon social work practice requires a theoretical base that gives us a framework for action; action in both the popular/grassroots and professional arenas; and, an organization ideology with three elements: 1) a commitment to basing our work in the knowledge of the people; 2) an ethical commitment to work in partnership with the most affected to ensure human rights; and, 3) interaction with other social actors towards a practice oriented towards social change. (Eroles, 1997, pp. 28–29)

In other words, we have to "know how to integrate human rights into our practice" (Sánchez, 1989, p. 28), going beyond a verbal commitment to action. Likewise, "we have to change our educational models so that they integrate theory and practice in human rights. We must generate a style of work that is participative and active" (Sánchez, 1989, p. 28). For "social workers, human rights should be the basis of our action and our work. They are non-negotiable" (Johansson, 1989, p. 34), not just a passing fad.

Finally, it is important to note that our colleagues in Latin America do not envision human rights in individualistic terms as is common in the Northern hemisphere. Human rights are inherently collective; therefore, solidarity is critical. And as social workers we must recognize the social element of human rights; social work practice that focuses on individual strategies is diametrically opposed to the idea of social work with its emphasis on the social. In this way, the struggle for human rights requires social workers to work collectively, with people in client status taking the lead, to make change. This is the essence of human rights practice, a practice centered on those most affected by injustices. As Sánchez (1989) points out: "with the introduction of human rights into the daily work of social workers, the profession became much more meaningful" (p. 20).

Implications and Applications of Social Justice and Human Rights for Social Work Practice

The School of Social Work at Monmouth University is committed in its mission to "prepare its graduates for professional practice with a commitment to advancing human rights by implementing social and economic justice, improving the quality of life of vulnerable families, individuals, organizations, communities and nations on the local, national, and international levels" (Monmouth University, 2014). To that end, students read and discuss the Universal Declaration of Human Rights (United Nations, 1948) adopted by the United Nations in 1948 and various codes of ethics of social work organizations in their early classes in the BSW and MSW programs. Students are asked to reflect on the social and economic justice and human rights implications for most assignments, ranging from psychosocial, a paper on policy analysis, or an analysis of human behavior theory.

At the MSW level, however, they are asked to go further. All students are required to take a two-course sequence that is described as the Advanced Core of the MSW program. These courses are Implications of Social Justice and Human Rights for Social Work Practice and Applications of Social Justice and Human Rights for Social Work Practice. Students take these classes at the concentration level so that they can use the knowledge and skills from class in their practice, and they can apply their practice to the material in these classes.

Both courses ask students to understand the mechanisms of oppression in society that maintain and perpetuate suffering and exploitation. The members of the classes engage in conversation about issues related to the advancement of human rights using a number of human rights documents to guide them. They are also asked to locate their own human rights documents and apply them to their work. They can choose to focus on an international treaty such as the Convention on the Rights of the Child (United Nations, 1989); or they can look at something more local such as the Foster Child Bill of Rights (1973; see National Foster Parent Association, 2014); they also can choose a document that is particular to their field or work site such as a Residents' Bill of Rights.

Special emphasis in these classes is placed on Article 25 of the Universal Declaration of Human Rights as a charge to the profession of social work. It states that (1) everyone has the right to a standard of living adequate for the health and well-being of him- or herself and of a family, including food, clothing, housing and medical care, and necessary social services, and the right to security in the event of unemployment, sickness, disability, widowhood, old age, or other lack of livelihood in circumstances beyond the person's control; and that (2) motherhood and childhood are entitled to special care and assistance. All children, whether born in or out of wedlock, shall enjoy the same social protection (United Nations, 1948).

One of the key elements discussed is the need to understand human rights in a context larger than the individual. To really understand the dynamics at play that keep people oppressed, it is necessary to look at individuals as part of communities and societies. We must situate human rights in the collective experience of all, because we need to "understand all human rights as having both individual and collective aspects" (Ife & Fiske, 2006, p. 299). Human rights abuses are structural. As such, only collective expressions and movements can effect change for the recognition of and respect for human rights. This necessitates discussions that are counter-cultural and asks us to look beyond the individualistic notion that is so prevalent in mainstream U.S. society, and in much of social work practice and education, to embrace a fuller understanding of a society in which our lives are interdependent.

Implications of Social Justice and Human Rights for Social Work Practice

The first course focuses on the development of a deeper knowledge of principles and theories related to social and economic justice and human rights. Students are asked to analyze these theories and principles and their relationship to a social work practice that is committed to advancing human rights. Students begin with readings that discuss the definition and practice of social justice and then move into a similar discussion on human rights. Some of the resources are David Gil's (2013) book *Confronting Injustice and Oppression: Concepts and Strategies for Social Workers*; Jim Ife's *Human Rights and Social Work: Towards Rights-Based Practice* (2008); Finn and Jacobson's (2008) *Just Practice: A Social Justice Approach to Social Work;* and articles/book chapters by Joseph Wronka, the Center for Economic and Social Rights, the National Association of Social Workers, the IFSW, and Paul Farmer (2005). Students also engage in a discussion that applies the concepts of social and economic justice and human rights to a variety of issues/social problems that affect social work practice.

After this introduction to the concepts the class takes an in-depth look at some theories or paradigms that help us understand social and economic justice and human rights, principally, the work of John Rawls, feminist theory, and liberation perspectives. The course looks at theory as bell hooks (hooks as quoted by Finn & Jacobson, 2008) talks about it:

I came to theory because I was hurting—the pain was so intense that I could not go on living. I came to theory desperate, wanting to comprehend— to grasp what was happening around and within me. Most importantly, I wanted to make the hurt go away. I saw in theory a location for healing. (p. 163)

The course uses theory/paradigms to help students understand what is going on and to make sense of it, to the extent possible. It also ask students to use theory in their project proposals, and our discussions in class help them choose a particular theory or paradigm that is relevant to their work.

The work of John Rawls is presented and discussed with a focus on distributive justice and the social contract. Discussion of this theory also includes a critique of it because of its underlying assumptions. For example, it comes out of a worldview that is Northern and male-oriented. It is also comes from a worldview that is steeped in individualism to neglect of the commons. As Farmer (2005) mentions, "according to Gustavo Gutierrez is that 'liberal doctrines' about human rights presuppose 'that our society enjoys an equality that in fact does not exist'" (p. 221). And this theory is critiqued because it makes assumptions that are not accurate in U.S. society today. Specifically, it assumes that although all citizens may have equal opportunities for education and work, people who are long-term welfare recipients lack the institutional conditions and resource supports to allow them to acquire these opportunities and face many more personal, interpersonal, and structural barriers to capability development than others (Banerjee, 2005, p. 53).

Feminist theories, with a focus on the Feminist Ethic of Care, are also presented, as a critique of Rawls and as a tool to organize our thinking on social and economic justice. The work of Iris Marion Young (1990) is particularly useful in this regard. Finally, we present a paradigm that we call liberation perspectives. This draws on the work of a variety of persons from the Global South, including Paulo Freire, Ignacio Martín-Baró, and Dawn Belkin-Martínez. The strength of this perspective is that it situates both knowledge and power in those who are most affected by social and economic injustice and human rights abuses.

Within the first month of the class students are asked to discuss a social issue of their choosing. This could be something from their field placement, their work, or their community. They get feedback and ideas from their professor and their student colleagues. Students begin to develop proposals for projects they will design, carry out, and evaluate during the two semesters. Their projects can be based in their field placement agency or in another organization. If they choose to do their projects in an agency, they must include persons in client status in the planning and facilitation of the projects as much as possible. The goal is to work in partnerships, but it is recognized that not all agencies permit that form of alliance. A project can also take the form of a creative original work or a minithesis. The course syllabus explains that "building on the School of Social Work theme of strengths based empowerment practice, students are directed to examine the pathologies of power and structural violence which shape social conditions and access to human capabilities" and that cause and exacerbate human suffering (Farmer, 2005).

These projects help students develop alternatives to neoliberal social work. That dominant model does not permit us to do real social work (Ferguson & Lavalette, 2006) because it reduces us to "the core tasks [of] rationing and surveillance" (Jones, 2007, p. 192). The projects help students understand that wherever and however they choose to practice social work, they can integrate a human rights framework, which always necessitates some form of action. As Farmer (2005) discusses, the poor do not ask for more studies to be carried out on their poverty. Therefore, the role of the academy is not to do more research but to work in partnership to act for change (Farmer, 2005). We must begin to model that action in the social work curriculum, or it will not persist in practice. This also helps us bridge the chasm that some students believe exists between social workers in clinical settings and those in community settings. They begin to understand that all social work at the master's level requires an understanding and application of advanced generalist practice.

Throughout the semester students are asked to read and reflect on the meanings of social justice, economic justice, and human rights. They engage in weekly discussions on the course's Web page, and they pick an issue of interest to them and present it to the class. For their presentation they are asked to reframe the issue from a human rights perspective; that is, what would change if this issue were seen through a human rights lens? How might using a human rights framework in society affect the issue and those most affected by it? They are also asked to discuss ways they could educate others on the issue and its human rights implications. At the end of the semester they make a formal proposal to the class that includes what they plan to do and their goals for the project.

Applications of Social Justice and Human Rights for Social Work Practice

The second half of this sequence of the courses asks students to apply the concepts and theories of social and economic justice and human rights. The syllabus states that the course "guides students in the practice and application of social justice and human rights theories within their concentration-specific engagement with social work. Within this course students undertake the implementation of a project that advances social justice and human rights as appropriate to their concentration area and practice interests."

The course is designed to help students develop the skills necessary to engage in social work practice that is consistent with a commitment to advancing social and economic justice and human rights. It focuses on guiding "students in their synthesis and application of professional knowledge, values and skills as they apply the principles of social justice and human rights to their practice of social work. (SW 669 syllabus, 2013)

Most of this course is focused on an in-depth study and analysis of various human rights organizing examples from across the United States.[1] These efforts include a variety of issues and serve as case studies of how social workers can make significant social change to improve the lives of vulnerable and oppressed communities. Cases are taken from a variety of realms of U.S. society. For example, students have studied the Liberation Health method employed by practitioners in Boston. This model integrates the work of Paulo Freire into clinical practice to create methodologies for clinician activists (Belkin Martínez, 2014).[2] It uses the process of praxis, as described by Freire (1970), so that we can engage in partnerships with the persons with whom we work to see, reflect, and act on in practice. In this process, which is repeated as much as necessary, people are able to gain a sense of self-efficacy and begin to understand how and where they can intervene to improve their life conditions.

A variety of other cases are examined during the semester. These include the right to a living wage, conditions for women in prison, domestic violence, Gray Power, the Poor People's Economic Human Rights Campaign, organizing in the face of racism, the rights of indigenous persons, immigrants and human rights, gender and sexual identity discrimination, and environmental justice. In each case students are asked to reflect on the situation lived by the protagonists. They are then asked to point out how the organizations took actions to improve the quality of their lives. Finally, they are asked to name how they could integrate some of the methods used in each case in their social work practice at various levels of intervention.

It is not always easy to get students to see the connections between many of these cases and the work that they do. They can easily identify the human rights abuses, but it becomes more difficult when they are asked to reimagine their social work practice using some of the methods used in the case. It gets easier with practice.

Also during this semester students are implementing, evaluating, and planning the next steps for their projects to advance social and economic justice and human rights. They give progress reports to the class early in the semester and receive feedback from their school colleagues on how to carry out their projects more effectively. At the end of the semester they give final reports on the projects to the class.

The Projects

Projects for these classes can take many forms, but they all have one thing in common: They cannot be based on charity. That is, students must move beyond temporary, top-down fixes to addressing structural issues that include those most-affected in the articulation of the situation and its potential solutions. This is not always easy, because many field placements operate from a temporary charity mentality. This means that at times students must look elsewhere for a site to do their projects. Students are encouraged to use course readings to think about how their projects advance social and economic justice and human rights as a way of helping them move beyond charity to justice. They must choose a human rights document to help guide their work.

Over the years there have been some creative, profound, and impressive projects. Some of them have changed the lives of the students and the people with whom they worked. Below is a brief sampling of some of these projects. It is worth mentioning that the three projects highlighted here were carried out by students studying in the clinical concentration.

US Uncut New Jersey

One student set out to do a creative option project to educate about issues of economic justice and injustice in U.S. society. She began a blog and a series of open online discussions to educate people she knew about the ever-increasing economic inequality in the United States. This student came from a rather conservative background and had a difficult time at first setting aside her biases to consider the new information she was learning about injustice in the United States. Between the course readings and research she did on her own, she began to understand the structural aspects of the vast inequality in the United States. She wanted to find a way to help others also unlearn the lies and deconstruct the mainstream portrayal of poverty and those living in poverty. She began to understand poverty as structural injustice and planned exploitation (Farmer, 2005; Gil, 2013).

Her motivation for this project was finding herself surrounded by friends and family who were blaming the poor for their poverty, which was not consistent with what she was learning in class and on her own. She did not set out to join/form a social movement. But during her project she found out about the organization UK Uncut, which was formed to protest the profound cuts to social care in the United Kingdom in fall 2010. US Uncut began soon after. This student started US Uncut New Jersey after she learned about the U.S. movement.

This organization planned events, actions, and flash mobs to call attention to the cuts to necessary services that were occurring in New Jersey and across the country. The group planned coordinated actions at Bank of America to call attention to the fact that while funding for education, housing, health and food were being cut, Bank of America was not paying any taxes and making windfall profits. At these activities group members handed out flyers with information about corporations earning millions of dollars in profits while services for people living in poverty were being drastically cut. These flyers gave specific information, citing reliable sources, and included some ideas for action. The group also planned flash mobs on campus to educate the campus community about these cuts by using creative theater. On campus the group connected the issue of economic injustice to social work practice at all levels. Members of the group also began to integrate information learned into discussions in their classes, particularly in the clinical concentration. As a result, they were able to make connections between social work practice at the clinical level with issues of social and economic injustice, which was not always apparent.

To reach a wider audience, US Uncut New Jersey began a presence on social media, which remains active in its third year. The organization uses social media to plan events, share resources, and educate followers about what is happening regarding economic justice and injustice in the United States. When the Occupy movement began, US Uncut New Jersey linked to that movement and joined forces with other organizers to continue to educate about injustice and create actions designed to create a movement for change.

Bullying and the Theater of the Oppressed

On separate occasions Monmouth students worked with children in local middle schools to write and carry out plays about bullying, a social injustice issue. These were students who were interning at middle schools and found themselves often working with middle school students who were bullied, left out, and abused by other students. Sometimes the abuse was subtle and at other times it was obvious. All the time, however, it had the effect of significantly affecting the quality of life for those students who were bullied. These survivors of bullying often reached out to school administrators, teachers, and parents for help, but found the adults did not understand how devastating it could be to be bullied.

The Monmouth students, often assigned to run groups as part of their field placements, worked with the students to discuss what was happening in the school and learn the effects of bullying on these children's lives. They decided to use the method of the Theater of the Oppressed, created by the Brazilian Augusto Boal, to see, reflect, and act on reality as experienced and articulated by the middle school students themselves. This process, also called praxis, was implemented in the groups the Monmouth students ran to help the middle school students articulate what was going on and what this meant to them.

After articulating and reflecting on the situation, they decided to take action to improve the lives of the bullied students and of others who were also being bullied but not coming forward about it. They decided that the most effective thing was to educate adults in students' lives about bullying through performing plays. They included information about the signs of bullying in the play.

Using the Theater of the Oppressed methodology—based on local knowledge and participation—the students invited all participants to join the process by coming up with solutions to the problem of bullying in their schools. They had some ideas about what adults could do to stop bullying and support children who had been bullied, but they also wanted the wisdom of the collective to be shared. In conversations after their performances they found out that although many adults had theoretical knowledge about bullying, they did not feel competent to actually address it. They were grateful to the middle school students for their leadership on this issue.

The Monmouth students and the schools where they were interning were pleased with the results of these projects. The schools thought they had been addressing bullying because they were implementing a curriculum related to bullying in the schools. What they realized is that they neglected to include those who were most affected by bullying in the planning and implementation. The Monmouth students understood how they could integrate social and economic justice and human rights into their social work practice. These students had difficulty at the beginning of the two-course sequence understanding how these concepts could be integrated into social work practice at the clinical level, but the projects made it real to them.

Kids From the System Telling the System What They Need

This project worked with young adults who had aged out of the foster care system in New Jersey but had difficulty adapting to independence. Many of them felt they had been abandoned without necessary knowledge and resources. Additionally, they found themselves living in poverty without assistance to help them establish themselves as adults. The Monmouth student had worked with these young adults when they were in foster care. The student heard how their lives became increasingly difficulty when they left the foster care system because they were not prepared to fend for themselves educationally, economically, and in the labor arena.

The Monmouth student decided to debrief with these young adults about how they could have been better supported by the local child welfare office. They met regularly to talk about their situations and to support one another. They found they had a lot in common, and their experiences could serve as guidance for other youth aging out of the system. As a result they decided to compile their experiences and suggestions and share them with the child welfare workers. They were scared to do this so they held mock presentations and learned skills in public speaking. They then went to different offices of the state agency that oversees foster care and presented to the workers and supervisors. After the presentations the group continued offering suggestions and working with the agency to provide better support for young people. They also used the New Jersey Foster Care Bill of Rights to guide their work and shared with the agencies the importance of this document.

These are just three examples of the projects that students have carried out. At the end of the second semester the students wrote papers evaluating the projects and discussed the outcomes. However, the students were asked to use the bulk of the paper to reflect on what they learned about how to include social and economic justice and human rights into their social work practice, regardless of the setting or population. They used the methodology of praxis as developed by Paulo Freire (1970) to reflect on what occurred, the new knowledge and insights they gained, and made plans for action based on their reflection and new knowledge. They were asked to come up with concrete ideas about how they would continue to advance social and economic justice and human rights as they move forward with their careers. They also articulated the difference between having an intellectual commitment to social and economic justice and human rights and being able to operationalize these concepts in their own practice.

In the evaluation of the projects most students discuss how the project affected their vision of the world and how it has influenced the way they want to practice social work. As a class we share the ideas that students have developed for integrating what they learned into their practice. We also develop more ideas, and we discuss how the limitations of certain social service agencies might get in the way of practicing social work from this perspective. This leads to a further discussion of the need to actively engage in change in the agency and in the world. This part of the discussion is guided by the principles of solidarity and the need for collective action as articulated by our Latin American colleagues.

Students understand that to be agents of change, we need to work together and support one another, not as social worker and client—a typically hierarchical relationship—but as partners in the process. They understand that the people with whom we work, even if they are just in middle school or have grown up in foster care, are the experts in their own lives. They also learn that people could be protagonists in their own lives, if the exploitive systems in society did not rob people of being protagonists. Some of these systems include well-meaning social service agencies. Likewise, they learn that we can use the knowledge we have, which comes from our great privilege of being able to pursue higher education, to make sure that those people who have been limited because of structural violence, oppression, and exploitation can have their voices heard and their lives improved.

Conclusion

Eroles (1997) points out "The IFSW and IASSW consider it imperative that social workers clearly commit themselves to the promotion and protection of human rights without reservation" (p. 119). We have to reflect that if this were the case, if social workers were to use their powerful collective voice to demand respect for human rights, then change would have to occur. But so often social workers perpetuate the problems because they do not question the problematic practices that have come to dominate the field; rather, they go along with said practices. If social workers were educated from a human rights framework, they would be able to engage in more complete structural analysis to understand how the various forms of human rights violations are interconnected. Further, they would empower themselves to engage in social work practice based on human rights.

Social workers have a clear role to denounce violations of human rights (Sánchez, 1989) because we interact daily with those who are surviving despite social and economic injustice. We know that human rights are violated each day in insidious ways in the United States. The time for social workers to be human rights workers is now. Social workers have "as their task the transformation of societal conditions" (Eroles, 1997, p. 26), which is an ethical imperative and commitment. This means we have to go beyond models that are based on charity, pathology, and blame. We also have to move beyond a model of practice that keeps people in isolation and help people who are experiencing injustice to join together. They can be the protagonists of their own lives, but often social services get in the way.

In the end, we are also fighting for the soul of social work itself because the neoliberal model has reduced what social workers can do to a shadow of its former self. It is no accident that as cutbacks in services have increased, the conditions of work for most social workers have declined. Ferguson and Lavalette (2006) make the assumption that there is a project called social work worth fighting for because it can improve people's lives. They talk about colleagues who have said, "I didn't come into social work for this!" (p. 309) as well as the "growing mismatch between what social workers feel they are trained to do and what they are required to do" (p. 309). We have to be able to make the connections between increasing inequality in society and harsher working conditions for social workers, and understand that using a human rights framework for practice not only improves the lives of those with whom we work but also has the potential to improve our own working conditions and lives.

Of course, all of this is counter-cultural. We have to be willing to take risks and be questioned. We have to be willing to not only know, but to understand. As Chilean economist Manfred Max-Neef (cited in Smith & Max-Neef, 2011) says, when

> we realize knowledge is not the road that leads to understanding because the port of understanding is on another shore and requires a different navigation, we will then be aware that we can attempt to understand only that of which we become a part. That understanding is the result of integration, whereas knowledge has been the result of detachment; understanding is holistic, whereas knowledge is fragmented. (p. 17).

Therefore, it is necessary that we create communities of support so that we do not feel marginalized and we can build a human rights culture. "The challenge is to create a socially just world in which one's lived awareness of human rights principles is known not only cognitively but in one's heart" (Wronka, 2008, p. 9) and, by extension, in one's practice. This is the task ahead of us. Monmouth University believes that this two-course sequence in Implications and Applications of Social Justice and Human Rights for Social Work Practice gives emerging social workers the tools necessary to see, analyze, and act (Freire, 1970) for social change.

References

Banerjee, M. M. (2005). Applying Rawlsian social justice to welfare reform: An unexpected finding for social work. *Journal of Sociology & Social Welfare, 32*(3) 35–57.

Belkin Martinez, D. (2014). *Therapy for liberation: The Paulo Freire methodology.* Retrieved from http://liberationhealth.org/documents/freiresummarysimmons .pdf

Belkin Martínex, D., & Fleck Henderson, A. (Eds.). (2014). *Social justice in clinical practice: A liberation health framework for social work.* London UK: Routledge.

Cáceres, E. (2000). Building a culture of rights. *NACLA Report on the Americas, 34(1),* 19–24.

Colectivo de Trabajo Social. (1989). *Trabajo social y derechos humanos: Compromiso con la dignidad. La experiencia chilena* [Social work and human rights: A commitment with dignity. The Chilean experience]. Buenos Aires, Argentina: Editorial Humanitas.

Eroles, C. (1997). *Los derechos humanos: Compromiso ético del trabajo social* [Human rights: An ethical imperative for social work]. Buenos Aires, Argentina: Espacio Editorial.

Farmer, P. (2005). *Pathologies of power: Health, human rights, and the new war on the poor.* Berkeley, CA: University of California Press.

Ferguson, I., & Lavalette, M. (2006). Globalization and global justice: Towards a social work of resistance. *International Social Work, 49*(3), 309–318.

Finn, J., & Jacobson, M. (2008). *Just practice: A social justice approach to social work* (2nd ed.). *Just thinking: Theoretical perspectives on social justice-oriented practice.* Peosta, IA: Eddie Bowers.

Freire, P. (1970). *Pedagogía de los oprimidos* [Pedagogy of the oppressed]. New York, NY: Continuum.

Gil, D. (2013). *Confronting injustice and oppression: Concepts and strategies for social work* (2nd ed.). New York, NY: Columbia University Press.

Gutiérrez, G. (1973). *La teología de la liberación* [A theology of liberation]. Maryknoll, NY: Orbis Books.

Ife, J. (2008). *Human rights and social work: Towards rights-based practice* (Rev. ed.). Cambridge, UK: Cambridge University Press.

Ife, J., & Fisk, L. (2006). Human rights and community work: Complementary theories and practices. *International Social Work, 49*(3), 297–308.

Johansson, C. (1989). Los derechos humanos no se transan en el mercado de valores [Human rights cannot be compromised by the market]. In Colectivo de Trabajo Social (Colectivo) *Trabajo social y derechos humanos: Compromiso con la dignidad. La experiencia chilena* [Social work and human rights: A commitment with dignity. The Chilean experience] (pp. 31–36). Buenos Aires, Argentina: Editorial Humanitas.

Jones, C. (2007). What is to be done? In M. Lavalette & I. Ferguson (Eds.). *International social work and the radical tradition* (pp. 189-195). Birmingham, UK: Venture Press.

Monmouth University. (2014). *About the School of Social Work.* Retrieved from www.monmouth.edu/socialwork

National Foster Parent Association. (2014). *National foster child bill of rights.* Retrieved from http://nfpaonline.org/page-1105707

Reynolds, B. C. (1963). *An uncharted journey: Fifty years of growth in social work.* New York, NY: Citadel Press.

Sánchez, M. D. (1989). Trabajo social en derechos humanos: Reencuentro con la profesión [Social work in human rights: A reunion with the profession]. In Colectivo de Trabajo Social (Colectivo), *Trabajo social y derechos humanos: Compromiso con la dignidad. La experiencia chilena* [Social work and human rights: A commitment with dignity. The Chilean experience] (pp. 17–30). Buenos Aires, Argentina: Editorial Humanitas.

Smith, P. B., & Max-Neef, M. (2011). *Economics unmasked: From power and greed to compassion and the common good.* Devon, UK: Green Books.

United Nations. (1948). *Universal declaration of human rights.* G.A. Res. 217 A (III). Retrieved from http://www.refworld.org/docid/3ae6b3712c.html

United Nations. (1989). *Convention on the rights of the child.* G.A. Res. 44/25. Retrieved from: http://www.ohchr.org/Documents/ProfessionalInterest/crc.pdf

Wronka, J. (2008). *Human rights and social justice: Social action for the helping and health professions.* Thousand Oaks, CA: SAGE Publications.

Young, I. M. (1990). *Justice and the politics of difference.* Princeton, NJ: Princeton University Press.

Endnotes

1 Two excellent free resources can be downloaded: (1) T. Coke & The U.S. Human Rights Fund, *Perfecting Our Union: Human Rights Success Stories Across the United States,* New York, NY: U.S. Human Rights Fund, 2010. Retrieved from http://www.publicinterest-projects.org/wp-content/uploads/downloads/2010/05/Perfecting-Our-Union.pdf; (2) Ford Foundation, *Close to Home: Case Studies of Human Rights Work in the United States,* New York NY: Ford Foundation, 2004. Retrieved from http://www.fordfoundation.org/pdfs/library/close_to_home.pdf

2 See the book of case studies based on this work by Belkin Martinez (2014).

15 | Analyzing Social Policies From a Rights-Based Approach

Shirley Gatenio Gabel

This chapter outlines an alternative model for teaching policy analysis to social work students. Social policies have the potential to play key roles in transforming our current societies into more equitable and just ones. Yet we tend to fall back on implementing social policies that most resemble the ones we have, policies that far too often lack evidence of their effectiveness, and ones that value efficiency and development more than human dignity, freedom, equity, and equality, both in the process and outcomes. The policy analysis framework introduced here is based on human rights standards and principles and can be used to establish policy goals whether related to local, national, or global issues. Four main human rights principles are used to guide the analysis: participation, accountability, nondiscrimination, and equality. Indicators drawing on international and national standards, laws, governance processes, social policy choices and implementation, populations reached, and participation are used to assess progress toward rights-based realization. This rights-based approach to social policy analysis provides a value-based analysis of public programs that pays particular attention to the marginalized and vulnerable groups in a population. This alternative approach is illustrated using child marriage as an example.

Models of Social Policy Analysis

As Bardach (2005) said, "policy analysis is more art than science" (p. xiv). A variety of frameworks on social policy analysis have been developed (e.g., Bardach, 1996; Chambers, 2000; DiNitto, 2011; Dobelstein, 1990; Dolgoff,

Portions of this chapter appear in *A Rights-Based Approach to Social Policy and Analysis*, by Shirley Gatenio Gabel, Springer International Publishing © 2015.

& Feldstein, 2009; Gilbert & Specht, 1986). Each is rooted in the rationalist approach initially embraced by social planners, emphasizing a different aspect of analysis and intent of social policy and sometimes confounding the policy process with policy analysis. Current policy analysis tends to consist of consideration of policy choices; evaluating the achievement of a policy goal; or sometimes the political, social, and technical processes in policy formulation (Stone, 2002). Rarely do analyses account for policy choices, evaluation of selected goals, and the processes involved simultaneously—a departure from the generally more holistic approaches of social work practice. Social policy goals tend to be treated as finite ends, most often related to meeting the unmet needs of a population. Often dominated by economics, policy analyses tend to favor efficiency over other values, thereby driving, as Myrdal noted in 1968, "values underground, to make analysis appear more scientific by omitting certain basic assumptions from the discussion" and in so doing confining social policy to rationality in decision making and its subsequent evaluations (as cited in Gilbert & Specht, 1986, p. 49). Gilbert and Terrell (2005) argue that although less recognized, social values do underlie policy analyses and typically define the range of alternatives seen as available and are embedded in the theories or assumptions justifying the choices.

Here an alternative approach is offered, one that openly places a normative framework to sit prominently in analyses and to guide an ongoing process of reflection, choices, and understanding.

Rights-Based and Needs-Based Approaches to Social Policy Analysis

A rights-based approach (RBA) guides social workers on how to integrate human rights principles into social work practice with the goal of developing long- and short-term responses to current social issues that further human rights. Human rights are integral to the enjoyment and safeguarding of human life, the achievement of human progress, the protection of human dignity, and the advancement of human security.

Most societies have long pursued a basic-needs approach, that is, an approach based on identifying the basic requirements of human development and advocating within societies in favor of their fulfillment. Some human rights are based on needs such as food, safety, and housing, but a human rights approach differs from the basic needs approach in critical ways. A key difference is that the basic-needs approach does not necessarily identify or imply responsibility for the need being met, whereas in an RBA a right is assigned to rights-holders who claim their rights from duty-bearers.

Rights entail obligations, whereas needs do not. Duty-bearers have a clear-cut duty to meet needs, and if they do not, they are violating the rights of rights-holders. In a needs-based approach, needs are often satisfied through benevolent or charitable actions. Actions based on a human rights approach are based on legal and moral obligations to carry out a duty that will actualize one's right. In a needs-based approach it is assumed that the person with power/authority to allocate resources knows what is needed and how best to deliver resources deemed necessary. This is quite different in a rights-based approach, in which rights-holders and duty-bearers ideally contribute throughout the decision-making process and its implementation.

Rights-holders or their representatives should participate in well-informed ways in the formulation, implementation, and monitoring of policies and programs and should be fully consulted in developing other state actions. This participatory process is empowering and contributes to rights-holders' understanding of relevant issues and their capacity for self-determination. In this way, RBAs seek to transform societies by reallocating power and decision-making. This is an outcome that is not inherent in needs based approaches. Another key difference in approaches is that the basic-needs approach may or may not recognize patterns of historical marginalization, whereas an RBA aims to directly overcome marginalization by more equitable sharing of resources and power.

A needs based approach typically establishes policy or program goals, and the success of an intervention or method of practice often is measured by the attainment of these goals. In an RBA, the success of policy or program interventions is measured against the progressive realization of human rights. The decisions, actions, and conduct of political, economic, social, and institutional systems and actors are evaluated by their contribution to the realization of rights. Rights based social policy analysis also differs from needs based approaches in that an RBA may focus on a particular set of rights, but it recognizes that a range of rights will need to work in tandem for a right or set of rights to be realized. Although there is no hierarchy of rights (indivisibility), some human rights are progressive, whereas others are immediate. For example, the right to life, the right to equal expression before the law, and freedom to express oneself are immediate. Many of the social and economic rights, however, require the input of state resources and are implemented progressively based on available resources. States have the obligation to improve the realization of social, economic, and cultural rights, such as working toward quality education for all children or the highest standard of health for all, and at minimum, to satisfy the essential level of each right. By nature then, the RBA calls for the measurement of outcomes over time not just at one point in time and recognizes the interrelatedness of multiple efforts.

In an RBA to analysis of social policies the goal is to move to a higher level of rights realization, recognizing that policy goals are provisional and subject to change because as we understand the fullness of issues and rights, our interpretations of rights realization may change and our practices may need to be modified accordingly.

Traditional indicators need to be reconsidered because of the different emphasis that an RBA brings to policies and programs. An RBA measures both the process and outcome of social work efforts; it relates human rights principles, including nondiscrimination, equality, participation, and accountability, and seeks to measure the transformative change between the right-holders and duty-bearers.

Furthermore, up until now efforts to apply an RBA to social policy analysis have been limited (Ife, 2008; Reichert, 2011; Wronka, 2008). Efforts by United Nations (UN) agencies to do so tend to focus on standard setting, implementation, and monitoring. International agencies have devoted energies to the establishment of standards that have overemphasized western interpretations of human rights, including civil and political rights. The overemphasis on civil and political rights has often narrowed the human rights remit and restricted accurate diagnoses of human rights within states at the cost of emphasizing individual over collective rights and neglecting efforts to increase social inclusion, and moderate inequalities (Ife, 2008; Reichert, 2011; Wronka, 2008). States have then been left to implement these international standards that may conflict with cultural, social, economic, and political contexts of countries and may also create defensive postures for states when monitored by international evaluators who tend to focus disproportionately on rights violations over rights based solutions.

Social Policies and Human Rights

Although social security has played an integral role in many states for decades, in the last two decades social policies and programs have been recognized for the role they play in stabilizing countries politically and economically, particularly in developing countries, and in supporting development. Increasingly, social policies and programs, often referred to as social protection systems, are viewed as an effective response to poverty and vulnerability in developing countries and as an essential component of economic and social development strategies (Devereux & Sabates-Wheeler, 2004). The last decade has seen a growing number of entities integrate RBAs into their work, and among UN agencies this has long been led by the International Labour Organization (ILO). An RBA moves social protection from a policy option to an obligation for states and international governance structures (van Ginneken, 2003). Article 22 of the Universal Declaration of Human Rights (UN, 1948) articulates the right to social security as a basic human right:

> Everyone, as a member of society, has the right to social security and is entitled to realization, through national effort and international co-operation and in accordance with the organization and resources of each State, of the economic, social and cultural rights indispensable for his dignity and the free development of his personality.

This right is echoed in the International Covenant on Economic, Social and Cultural Rights (UN, 1966) and other major UN human rights documents and was reaffirmed at the ILO Conferences in 2001 and 2008.

In April 2009 the UN Chief Executives Board introduced a social protection floor initiative as one of its nine initiatives to cope with the global economic crisis beginning in 2008. The UN Social Protection Floor takes an RBA by obligating governments to ensure that all persons have the availability, continuity, and geographical and financial access to essential services such as water and sanitation, food and adequate nutrition, health, education, housing, and other social services such as asset saving information. It obligates states to provide a minimum income and livelihood security for poor and vulnerable populations such as children, people in working age groups with insufficient income, and older persons. The Social Protection Floor mandates UN agencies and partners to "facilitate and accelerate the introduction or strengthening of sustainable context-specific social protection systems…by offering high-quality/low-cost technical assistance to countries through a mechanism of increased interagency collaboration" (ILO & World Health Organization, 2009, p.3).

The 2009 mandate obligates UN agencies to incorporate RBAs into their social protection efforts as a means of promoting human rights while recognizing that the realization of rights is progressive and constrained by the resources available. The 2010 UN Millennium Summit acknowledged the contribution of social protection in achieving progress toward the Millennium Development Goals (MDG), and support for social protection was echoed at the 2011 Cannes Summit Final Declaration (G20, 2011). The MDG Summit adopted by the UN General Assembly declared that national Social Protection Floors should include at least the four social security guarantees (UN, 2010):

1) guaranteed access to goods and services constituting essential health care, education and other social services;
2) basic income security for children with the aim of facilitating access to nutrition, health, education, care and any other necessary goods and services;
3) basic income security for non-retired persons unable to earn a sufficient income; and
4) basic security income for persons in old age.

UN agencies have moved away from an exclusive needs-based justification to embrace an RBA, including key development nongovernmental organizations Oxfam, Save the Children, and World Vision (Gatenio Gabel, 2012). And although support and acknowledgement for the contributions of social protection has grown, social protection and human rights outcomes have largely not been integrated into development reports. The exception to this is the Special Rapporteur's report on human rights and cash transfer programs, noncontributory pensions, MDGs, gender-related issues, and regarding recovery from economic crisis (Sepulveda & Nyst, 2013).

RBA to Social Policy Analysis

The RBA offered here incorporates some of the steps of traditional social policy analyses but goes beyond this to analyze social policies and programs on several dimensions from the perspective of how policies and programs affect or are expected to affect the realization of rights. The analysis should begin with a definition of the social issues/problem from a rights perspective, including the use of international, regional, and country-specific laws and instruments that articulate rights to identify violations. The analysis also should account for country-specific efforts and statements on policies and programs that have been designed to address or that affect the social issue/problem identified.

An RBA does not prescribe specific social protection programs. Rather, it evaluates policies and programs according to standards specified in human rights laws and instruments adopted by a country. The responsibility for implementation of social protection programs ultimately rests with the sovereign country. The framework presented here (see Figure 1) suggests that social policy and programs be analyzed according to cross-cutting human rights principles while keeping in mind the obligation states have regarding social, economic, and cultural rights to give priority to the most marginalized and vulnerable groups. Drawing from work for the UN Human Rights Council's Special Rapporteur (Sepulveda & Nyst, 2013), four cross-cutting human rights principle-based dimensions are identified as participation in the decision-making process, accountability, nondiscrimination, and equality. For each of these principles, relevant dimensions are suggested as the basis for analysis, and examples of the types of indicators that may capture the realization of rights are suggested.

Because the analysis seeks to measure the progressive realization of rights, a baseline should be established from which negative, positive, and nonmovement can be measured. For example, have any human rights instruments been ratified since the baseline or have new laws incorporating the instruments been enacted? Have new facilities been built to increase access? Have local councils been established to increase citizen participation in policymaking? Depending on the type of social issue being examined, the dimensions and types of indicators used will be modified. Furthermore, new indicators of rights realization are called for, which in some circumstances incorporate existing policy indicators.

Figure 1 **Guidelines for a rights-based approach to social policy analysis**

A. Identify the social issue/problem

    1. Identify the rights violated or compromised by the social issue, using

        i. International and regional human rights laws and instruments

        ii. National constitutions, laws, and regulations

        iii. In-country policies addressing or affecting social issue

    2. Formulate the social issue/problem from a rights based frame

B. Contextualize the social issue/problem

    1. Identify the stakeholders, rights-holders, and duty-bearers and their roles.

    2. Who benefits from the policy as it exists? Who loses?

    3. How have policies affecting rights-holders marginalized the population?

C. Analysis of the dimension or dimensions according to cross-cutting human rights principles of participation, accountability, and nondiscrimination and equality.

Participation

Social protection programs should strive to ensure that rights-holders and duty-bearers are heard at every stage of the social protection process, from identifying the social issue through evaluation of the program. Special effort should be used to give voice to those who are historically marginalized due to ethnicity, gender, language, or ability and institutionalizing forums for expression so that power relations can be transformed by both the process of formulating policies and their implementation. It is important to consider how rights-holders participate in the policymaking process and how the voices of rights-holders are excluded in the policymaking process.

Accountability

Policymakers, administrators, and others involved in policy formulation and allocation of resources must be held accountable for their decisions and actions with clearly defined processes for persons to seek redress when they believe their rights have been violated regarding social protection efforts.

Two questions should be considered: (1) If citizens feel they have unfairly been denied assistance, is the process to challenge the decision documented and without repercussions? (2) Are accountability mechanisms in place with responsibility of implementation clear and open to input from all citizens?

Nondiscrimination and Equality

These principles require the state to ensure that laws, policies, and practice relating to social protection are nondiscriminatory and that priority is given to protect the most vulnerable segments of the population. Social protection programs should be accessible to all persons including women, children, persons with disabilities, and/or those living with HIV/AIDS, older persons, and ethnic minorities without stigmatizing beneficiaries and at all stages of the program (from design through the selection of beneficiaries).

Questions to be considered are how the policy might be discriminatory or socially unjust and whether benefits are accessible, affordable, and adequate to all persons.

RECOMMENDATIONS

Develop policy recommendations to resolve the social issue/problem identified that will further the realization of the human rights principles of participation, accountability, nondiscrimination, and equality.

Case Example

The example of child marriage is used to illustrate how the suggested RBA might be used with students to identify and frame a social issue, causality, and possible solutions.

Child marriage occurs when at least one partner in a marriage is under the age of 18 years. This definition of child is used by the Convention on the Rights of the Child (CRC) (UN, 1989). Girls or boys may be affected by child marriage, but the majority of such marriages occur between a girl who is under 18 years old and a man who is over 18. One-third of the world's girls are married before the age of 18, and one in nine are married before the age of 15 (International Center for Research on Women, 2007).

Research findings indicate that the consequences of girls marrying before they are the age of majority tend to be more severe than if they marry as adults (UN Population Fund, 2012). Girls who marry before age 18 are more likely to experience abuse, violence, and exploitation than those who marry as adults. Bearing and delivering children prematurely may impair reproductive organs and the health of the young mother and her child. An example of this is obstetric fistula, a condition that leaves 2 million females leaking urine or feces due to prolonged labor and injury to the birth canal and is especially common among physically immature girls (UN Children's Fund [UNICEF], 2009). Approximately 15 million females between the ages of 15 and 19 years give birth each year, and girls under the age of 15 are five times more likely to die during pregnancy or childbirth than women in their 20s (UNICEF, 2009). Children born to adolescent mothers are 60% more likely to die than infants born to mothers older than 19 years (UNICEF, 2009). Girls who marry young typically leave school and are subject to isolation from family and friends, leaving them unprepared for the psychosocial and emotional consequences they are forced to confront. Young girl brides are more likely to be abused and be victims of domestic violence than women who marry when they are older (International Planned Parenthood Federation and the Forum on Marriage and the Rights of Women and Girls, 2006). For young brides, leaving an abusive home is often not seen as an option because of economic pressures and cultural expectations. Young brides who have left their marriages have been reported to suffer from social and economic stigma, be punished or killed by close male kin for bringing shame on the family, or be left to fend for themselves with little legal recourse (International Planned Parenthood Federation and the Forum on Marriage and the Rights of Women and Girls, 2006).

Unlike traditional policy analyses that might frame child marriage as a social problem because it removes girls from school or that initiates a pattern of dependency, RBA first looks to international and national human rights instruments to frame this social issue. In this case, the Universal Declaration of Human Rights states that all persons have a right to "free and full consent" to a marriage and acknowledge that partners who are not fully mature may not be in a position to make a fully cognizant decision. The Convention to Eliminate Discrimination Against Women (UN, 1979) specifies in Article 16 that "the betrothal and marriage of a child shall have no legal effect and all necessary action, including legislation, shall be taken to specify a minimum age of marriage." The UN Committee on the Elimination of Discrimination Against Women (1994), General Recommendation 21, states that 18 should be the minimum age for marriage for men and women.

Interestingly, the CRC does not explicitly address marriage, although child marriage may be a violation of children's other rights articulated in the CRC such as Articles 12 and 13 (the right to express one's views), Articles 19, 34, 35, and 36 (the right to be protected from exploitation and abuse), and Article 24 (the right to be protected from harmful practices). Child marriage often curtails a child's education and relocates girls to live in isolating and/or abusive situations that may violate related rights such as education, information, rest and leisure, health, and protection from physical and mental violence and abuse and from being separated from their parents against the child's or parent's will (see CRC Articles 9, 17, 19, 20, 24, and 28–32).

The CRC General Comment 4 notes that all states are obligated to protect adolescents from all traditional practices that are harmful to children's health (UN Committee on the Rights of the Child, 2003). The next step would be to consider whether there are regional human rights instruments that address the social issue. For example, the African Charter on the Rights and Welfare of the Child (1990) prohibits marriage for persons under age 18 years and requires countries signing the charter to incorporate this into their laws.

Before proceeding to national law, it is critical to check which relevant international and regional human rights instruments have been ratified by the country. If a country has ratified the relevant international and regional human rights instruments, it is obliged to integrate the content and spirit of the convention or treaty into national law. The analysis that follows would capture how effectively this and the implementation of law has been. For example, in the case of child marriage it would be important to identify national (and state) laws governing marriage with specific attention paid to gender bias, minimum age of marriage, forcible marriage and rape, and dissolution of marriage. Depending on the country, knowing whether birth registration and marriage registration is compulsory may be relevant, as well as how effectively the law is enforced, if one exists.

If a country has not ratified the relevant international or regional document, the analysis should include the country's reasons for not participating in international or regional normative standards and how existing national laws violate or uphold the international and regional standards. These steps will allow for the social issue to be framed from a rights based perspective, either as a violation of rights or identifying the less than full realization of relevant rights. One may further explore whether the country has made general or specific reservations to the international human rights instruments it has ratified with regard to gender, age, traditional law, or religion, or whether reservations have been made to the definition of a child in CRC.

The next step is to contextualize the social issue by understanding the cause or causes underlying the issue, the consequences of the social issue, who and what contributes to its perpetuation, and who is affected by the social issue (stakeholders). In the example of child marriage, household poverty and discriminatory cultural practices are at the root of the practice. Girls are seen as economic burdens to families in some cultures because they are expected to leave their birth families when they marry and contribute to the welfare of their husband's family. This often occurs in cultures that attribute higher social, economic, and cultural status to males and tend to minimize the ability of women to participate in decisions affecting themselves, their children, the family, and the community. Too often, women's livelihood and status in society depends entirely on their marital status and/or male guardianship. Economic hardship of the household then might be the root cause; cultural factors may exacerbate and reinforce the continuation of child marriage.

The stakeholders in this issue vary depending on the country and the cultural context, but generally speaking they will include child brides and grooms, the fathers or male guardians responsible for negotiating marriages, mothers or female guardians who sometimes reinforce societal expectations or take issue with the practice, other relatives who may act as gatekeepers for the family honor, and community practices that may dictate standards for bride prices or dowries depending on the age and status of the bride. Following the identification of stakeholders, a discussion of the ways in which each stakeholder benefits or loses from child marriage should follow. Examples include economic gains and losses to families, the benefits and losses to the child bride or groom (education, physical or emotional abuse, labor division, securing a socioeconomic position within a society), and the benefits and losses to the community (social and economic development, reinforcing patriarchy and cultural practice, etc.). The duty-bearers may include the parents, the husband, the in-laws, the community, the government, and possibly the media and other opinion makers who consciously shape public opinion on child marriage.

The next step is to consider how child marriage affects one or all four of the human rights principles of participation, accountability, nondiscrimination, and equality. In the case of child marriage, the principles of nondiscrimination and equality are violated because the practice has differential effects on women and men, girls and boys. Boys may also be forced into child marriages, but the prevalence is much higher among girls. Many countries legally recognize the marriage of males at age 18 and females at age 16. Girls are more likely to suffer physically because they may be encumbered with heavy physical tasks that are damaging, forced to have sexual relations prematurely, and may experience lifelong physical suffering from bearing children early and continuously. Young girls who marry older men are at a higher risk for physical and mental abuse and are more likely to contract sexually transmitted infections such as HIV/AIDS. As a result of marriage, girls may forfeit their education (United Nations Population Fund, 2012). The community and family may offer girls who marry young few options for recourse. The analysis in this section would demonstrate the gender bias that is perpetuated by this social issue.

Another dimension to be considered in the analysis is how women and children participate in decisions affecting child marriage practices at the family, community, and legislative levels. There is no standard method for measuring children's participation in society. A good place to begin is to review the legal provisions within a country for children to participate in decisions affecting their well-being and the inclusion of children's participation in marriage decisions. The analysis may include an evaluation of the children's minimum ages of consent; confidential mechanisms offered for children to express their own opinions, conscience, and religion in accordance with evolving capacities; their legal entitlements to be involved in decision-making processes affecting their lives and legal proceedings; and obligations to involve children in decisions affecting them. If these mechanisms do exist, the analysis may explore the methods for making children aware of their legal rights and the mechanisms available to them, including the process for children to exercise their rights. More generally, consideration should be given to opportunities available for children to influence local and national government legislation, policies, services, and resource allocations. Similarly, because child marriage overlaps with women's rights, an analysis of women's opportunities to participate and the effectiveness of these efforts may also be conducted.

Accountability is closely related to access to remedy, a critical element in the human rights framework. In the event of a violation or denial of rights, an RBA emphasizes the need to have available and appropriate means to seek and support redress, including invoking the right to remedy and due process and the right to information. The existence of mechanisms for redress should be included in an analysis as well as accessibility, availability, and affordability of these mechanisms. What structures and processes are in place for a child spouse to seek redress for rights violations in a marriage? Can a child present directly in court, or must a representative be appointed for the child? Who and how is this representative appointed? Are procedures in place to assure the neutrality of the representative and safeguard the child from further repercussions? How are children made aware of the availability of such services? Are these processes transparent, and if not, how do they impede redress regarding child marriage?

Policy recommendations flowing from this analysis should seek to address the violations or denial of rights identified in the first part of the analysis with consideration given to the stakeholders and their roles as duty-bearers. The recommendations must identify the root cause of child marriage and responsibility for rectifying the rights violated by child marriage. If economic hardship is at the root of child marriage, the policy recommendations should consider alternative methods for securing household income that may reduce reliance on child marriage as an income source. In doing so, the recommendations should address how infringements of the human rights principles analyzed will be remedied by the proposed responses. Will laws be modified to address the discrimination revealed and unequal opportunities that result from the discriminatory practices? Will legislation be introduced to prohibit child marriage? What mechanisms will be introduced to enforce prohibition against child marriage? What will the response be to the likely resistance by some stakeholders? Do laws need to be introduced prohibiting gender-based violence and/or defining family violence? Do existing laws mandate minimum levels of education for children, and do they need to be amended? Are mechanisms needed for redress to be accessible, available, and affordable to children who seek to end their marriages? If social protection programs are introduced to increase household livelihoods or human capital, the anticipated consequences on child marriage should be made clear and tied to the concerns identified by the analysis of the principles.

Discussion

This case example yields information on the causes of child marriage and frames the issue in a way that calls for progressive responses that will further the realization of rights, not just attend to the immediate causes of the problem. The approach used in this chapter relies on legal frames to identify specific and interrelated violations of rights. To develop policy recommendations that are responsive to the root causes requires a solid contextual understanding of the issue, the stakeholders involved and their perspectives, and a clear definition of the duty-bearers. A deepened understanding of the social issue can be derived from analyses of how the issue compromises the four basic human rights principles: participation, accountability, nondiscrimination, and equality. By proposing policy recommendations that are responsive to the violations or denials of human rights principles, the recommendation should further the realization of rights.

To conduct a full analysis would no doubt be time-consuming and require a solid understanding of the topic. The exercise can also be used in class with supporting documents to further the understanding of rights-based approaches to policy analysis and to stimulate discussion. A comparison of the policy responses yielded by the RBA to those developed using more conventional methods might also spur interesting class discussions regarding the purpose of social policies.

It seems likely that the indicators needed for the proposed RBA may not always be available and accessible, and their accuracy may be questionable in some countries. Although frustrating, this may challenge us to develop new indicators that incorporate rights realization instead of using existing indicators to approximate the realization of rights.

The RBA to social policy analysis proposed here asks social workers to reinsert the value base that our profession was built on by placing the furthering of human dignity and elimination of human suffering at the center of our practices. New solutions to old problems can only be achieved through innovative ways of understanding social issues and consequent alternative approaches.

References

African Charter on the Rights and Welfare of the Child. (1990). OAU Doc. CAB/LEG/24.9/49.

Bardach, E, (1996). *The eight-step path of policy analysis (A handbook for practice).* Berkeley, CA: Berkeley Academic Press/Odin Readers.

Bardach, E. (2005). *A practical guide for policy analysis* (2nd ed.). Washington, DC: CQ Press.

Chambers, D. (1992). *Social policy and social programs: A method for the practical public policy analyst* (2nd ed.). New York, NY: Macmillan.

Devereux, S., & Sabates-Wheeler, R. (2004). Transformative social protection. (Institute of Development Studies Working Paper 232). Brighton, UK: IDS. Retrieved from http://www.ids.ac.uk/files/dmfile/Wp232.pdf

DiNitto, D. (2011). *Social welfare: Politics and public policy* (7th ed.). New York, NY: Allyn and Bacon.

Dobelstein, A.W. (1990). *Social welfare: Policy and analysis.* Chicago, IL: Nelson-Hall.

Dolgoff, R., & Feldstein, D. (2009). *Understanding social welfare* (8th ed.). Boston, MA: Allyn and Bacon.

G20. (2011). Cannes Summit final declaration: Building our common future: renewed collective action for the benefit of all. Retrieved from https://www.g20.org/sites/default/files/g20_resources/library/Declaration_eng_Cannes.pdf

Gatenio Gabel, S. (2012). Social protection and children in developing countries. *Children and Youth Services Review, 34,* 537–545. doi: 10.1016/j.childyouth.2011.10.013

Gilbert, N., & Specht, H. (1986). *Dimensions of social welfare policy* (2nd ed.). Englewood Cliffs, NJ: Prentice-Hall.

Gilbert, N., & Terrell, P. (2005). *Dimensions of social welfare policy* (6th ed.).Boston, MA: Pearson/Allyn and Bacon

Gilbert, N., Specht, H., & Terrell, P. (1992). Dimensions of social welfare policy (3rd ed.). Englewood Cliffs, NJ: Prentice Hall.

Ife, J. (2008). Human rights and social work. Revised edition. Cambridge, UK: Cambridge University Press.

International Center for Research on Women. (2007). Child marriage factsheets. Retrieved from http://www.icrw.org/publications/child-marriage-factsheets

International Labour Office (ILO) & World Health Organisation. (2009). *Social Protection Floor Initiative: Manual and strategic framework for joint UN country operations.* Retrieved from http://www2.ilo.org/gimi/gess/ShowRessource.action?ressource.ressourceId=14484

International Planned Parenthood Federation & Forum on Marriage and the Rights of Women and Girls. (2006). Ending child marriage: A guide for global policy action. Retrieved from http://*www.ippf.org/system/files/ending_child_marriage.pdf*

Reichert, E. (2011). *Social work and human rights: A foundation for policy and practice,* (2nd ed.). New York, NY: Columbia University Press.

Sepulveda, M., & Nyst, C. (2013). *The human rights approach to social protection.* Enwiko Oy, Finland: Ministry for Foreign Affairs of Finland. Retrieved from http://www.ohchr.org/Documents/Issues/EPoverty/HumanRightsApproachToSocialProtection.pdf

Stone, D. (2002). *Policy paradox: The art of political decision making*. New York, NY: Norton.

United Nations (UN). (1948). *Universal declaration of human rights*. G.A. Res. 217 A (III). Retrieved from http://www.refworld.org/docid/3ae6b3712c.html

United Nations (UN). (1966). *International covenant on economic, social, and cultural rights*. G.A. Res. 2200A (XXI). Retrieved from http://www.ohchr.org/EN/ProfessionalInterest/Pages/CESCR.aspx

United Nations (UN). (1979). *Convention on the elimination of all forms of discrimination against women*. G.A. Res. 34/180. Retrieved from http://www.ohchr.org/Documents/ProfessionalInterest/cedaw.pdf

United Nations (UN). (1989). *Convention on the rights of the child*. G.A. Res. 44/25. Retrieved from http://www.ohchr.org/Documents/ProfessionalInterest/crc.pdf

United Nations (UN). (2010). *Keeping the promise: United to achieve the Millennium Development Goals*. A/65/L.1. Retrieved from http://www.un.org/en/mdg/summit2010/pdf/ZeroDraftOutcomeDocument_31May2010rev2.pdf

United Nations Children's Fund (UNICEF). (2009). *The state of the world's children 2009: Maternal and newborn health*. Retrieved from http://www.unicef.org/sowc09/docs/SOWC09-FullReport-EN.pdf

United Nations Committee on the Elimination of Discrimination Against Women. (1994). *General recommendation No. 21 (13th Session): Equality in marriage and family relations*. (Document A/49/38). Retrieved from http://www.un.org/womenwatch/daw/cedaw/recommendations/recomm.htm#recom21

United Nations Committee on the Rights of the Child. (2003, July 1). General comment no. 4: Adolescent health and development in the context of the convention on the rights of the child. CRC/GC/2003/4. Retrieved from daccess-dds-ny.un.org/doc/UNDOC/GEN/G03/427/24/PDF/G0342724.pdf

United Nations Population Fund. (2012). Marrying too young: End child marriage. Retrieved from http://www.unfpa.org/public/home/publications/pid/12166

Van Ginneken, W. (2003). Extending social security: Policies for developing countries. *International Labour Review, 142*, 277–294.

Wronka, J. (2008). *Human rights and social justice: Social action and service for the helping and health professions*. Thousand Oaks, CA: SAGE.

Travel Study and Exchange Models to Promote Human Rights Education

Section III examines four models of social work travel study or exchange, in Uganda, Costa Rica, Malawi, and Jamaica. Social work educators describe the process of educating graduate students to analyze and apply human rights principles in the context of health challenges, and women's and child welfare concerns. The authors explore the use of service learning modalities, university exchange models, and other pedagogical advances to examine such themes as the development of effective international partnerships to address health disparities affected by globalization, educating students to promote human rights, working as part of interprofessional teams, and professional exchange.

Hugo Kamya's chapter illustrates how a human rights approach to health can be taught to masters' level social work students through a service-learning model. Kamya reflects on ethical and other challenges related to introducing U.S. social work students to the pandemic of HIV/AIDS on the ground in a travel-study experience in Uganda. The program he describes was developed through the Simmons College Graduate School of Social Work. Students study the effects of social problems on health, mental health, and human rights over 3 weeks through interactions with Ugandan agencies and nongovernmental organizations. Kamya describes the preparation students undergo in advance of the study-trip and how each conducts an ethnographic inquiry into a topic of their choice while in Uganda with host community groups who are equal partners in the learning process.

Jody Olson and Anusha Chatterjee examine a 6-week long student research project in Malawi involving interdisciplinary graduate student teams from the University of Maryland's professional schools of social work, dentistry, law, medicine, nursing, and pharmacy. The teams explore human rights as it relates to health outcomes through an interprofessional approach. Olson and Chatterjee illustrate the positive contributions that social work students can make to these interdisciplinary teams by describing a 2012 project focused on evaluating interventions and making policy recommendations through a human rights lens designed to reduce maternal mortality and morbidity in southern Malawi.

Dennis Ritchie and Laura Guzman Stein analytically describe a model of educating undergraduate and graduate American social work students about sustainable human rights and development through a short-term, intensive, study-abroad course in Costa Rica. This field-based course is the result of a partnership between George Mason University in Virginia, USA, and the University of Costa Rica. Global and comparative perspectives are use to examine health and human rights in Costa Rica versus the United States with an emphasis on women's and children's rights. The authors use students' personal reflections on their learning to discuss course goals and outcomes and provide recommendations for similar offerings.

Barris Malcolm explores the contributions made to advancing the human rights of children in Jamaica by a long-term university-to-university exchange program between the Social Work Unit of the Department of Sociology, Psychology, and Social Work at the University of the West Indies Mona Campus in Jamaica and the University of Connecticut School of Social Work. Malcolm examines how this international partnership and collaboration in social work education addressed the effects of poverty and tradition and contributed to advancing the protection of child rights in Jamaica. Additionally, the chapter reflects critically about the effects of the extended international collaboration and partnership model.

16 | Developing Global Partnerships in Social Work: HIV/AIDS and the Case of Uganda

Hugo Kamya

The importance of developing effective global/international partnerships in social work practice cannot be overstressed. Cox and Pawar (2006) describe the concept of international social work as the "promotion of social work education and practice and locally [to] respond appropriately and effectively in education and practice terms to the various global challenges [affecting] the world's population" (p. 26). The local is becoming increasingly global just as the global is becoming local. It is not uncommon to find more and more populations that were often thought of as a world away to be part of the neighborhood in which social work students practice. Immigrant populations represent this increasingly shrinking world. Therefore, it is of great importance for social work education to develop programs that address this need. The establishment of a Commission on Global Social Work Education by the Council on Social Work Education underscores recognition of the need to include global content in the curriculum for social work students.

Healy (2008) identified four areas in which international social work action as a profession thrives: internationally related domestic practice and advocacy, professional exchange, international social work practice, and international policy development and advocacy. One innovation and outcome of this emphasis in social work is an increasing attention to study-abroad programs in which students are introduced to and participate in service learning projects. Simmons College Graduate School of Social Work in Massachusetts has pioneered one such project with Ugandan agencies and nongovernmental organizations. This chapter explores some of the lessons, ethical struggles, challenges, and rewards of this project.

Service Learning and Social Work

Jacoby (1996) defines *service learning* as "a form of experiential education in which students engage in activities that address human and community needs together with structured opportunities intentionally designed to promote student learning and development" (p. 5). Service learning is an attempt to overcome modern trends of diminishing social cohesion and responsibility to create community solidarity (Murphy & Rasch, 2008). By engaging students in partnerships with communities, service learning integrates academics with practical actions that meet expressed community needs, which often are linked to human rights (Brodeur, 2013). According to Cox and Pawar (2006), the service-learning project is conceived as an integrated perspectives approach that includes global, ecological, social development, international education and practice, and human rights perspectives.

Rather than a charity or volunteer model, which emphasizes the transfer of goods or services from those who have to those who have not (Jacoby, 1996), or a practicum-based model that prioritizes student goals and learning (Tapp & Macke, 2011), service learning is distinct in its emphasis on community development and social solidarity (Murphy & Rasch, 2008). Service learning is distinguished from other community service and volunteer programs by the centrality of relationship-building, cooperation, student reflection, and reciprocity with the community partners involved (Jacoby, 2000; Tapp & Macke, 2011; Murphy & Rasch, 2008).

Service learning has been shown to be an effective pedagogy in K-12, collegiate, and postgraduate education (Acauave & Edmonds Crewe, 2012; Billig, 2000; Billig, Root, & Jesse, 2005; Tapp & Macke, 2011). Service learning provides opportunities for students to "utilize and gain recognition for strengths not typically valued within academic settings" (King, 2004, p. 122). Additionally, service learning allows students to become more deeply involved in an agency or community, develop and use leadership skills, provide a service to the community, think critically, and gain knowledge and skills (Tapp & Macke, 2011).

Students who participated in some type of service learning had more civic knowledge, felt more attached to their communities, showed increased academic engagement (Billig et al., 2005), and had positive changes in their attitudes toward people of different races and socioeconomic backgrounds (Tapp & Macke, 2011). They showed greater maturity in ethical decision-making and the ability to work collaboratively (Gammonley, Smith Rotabi, Forte, & Martin, 2013). Participation in service learning has been shown to increase measures of personal and social responsibility, self-esteem, empathy and cognitive complexity, acceptance of cultural diversity, civic engagement, academic performance, and to reduce behavioral problems (Billig, 2000).

Boateng and Thompson (2013) found that international service learning enhances cultural sensitivity and competence, increases self-awareness, and enhances personal and professional development. Students who participated in service-learning programs abroad showed greater gains in self-reported skill development than those who remained in the classroom (Greenfield, Davis, & Fedor, 2012). International service learning can foster the development of greater critical thinking and problem-solving skills, plus an awareness of culture and social issues (Acauave & Edmonds Crewe, 2012). Even short-term service-learning programs abroad have been shown to improve students' flexibility and openness to new experiences, personal autonomy, and emotional resilience, or the ability to effectively regulate one's emotions in changing environments (Mapp, 2012). Further, international experiences prepare students to live and work in an increasingly globalized society (Acauave & Edmonds Crewe, 2012); give students greater ethnic sensitivity and awareness; increase awareness and insight into students' own culture and values; and increase critical thinking about culture, social problems, and social service systems (Boateng & Thompson, 2013). However, Billig et al. (2005) found that positive outcomes of service learning were strongly related to teacher-reported service-learning program quality. Poorly implemented programs showed no benefit over traditional classroom-based learning experiences (Billig et al., 2005).

Although many outcome measures focus on personal changes in student participants of service-learning programs, very little research has been done regarding community outcomes (Cruz & Giles, 2000; Murphy & Rasch, 2008; Sandy & Holland, 2006). The lack of available research and program administrators' frequent failure to understand the community perspective may cause service-learning programs to struggle or fail (Sandy & Holland, 2006).

Many service-learning programs fail to make a distinction between other pedagogical approaches such as volunteering (Tapp & Macke, 2011). This may lead to a one-way service paradigm in which a person perceived to be more competent aids a less competent person or community (Jacoby, 2000). Service-learning programs often fall into the traps of focusing on student needs without considering community needs and approaching community members in a condescending manner that fails to recognize their expertise (Brodeur, 2013). Such programs may be perceived as exploitive (King, 2004) and may end up providing services that meet no actual need in the community or perpetuate a state of need rather than addressing the causes of inequality (Jacoby, 2000). Murphy and Rasch (2008) suggested that in the planning of service-learning projects, "many times the community is all but forgotten" (p. 71). Programs that lack a true sense of mutuality between learners and the community reinforce what Freire (2000) called a dichotomy between subject and object in which the object—the community partner—becomes a power-less recipient of the subject's, or service-learner's, expertise.

Without adequate collaboration, service-learning programs may actually reinforce prejudices and perpetuate existing power imbalances between those providing and those receiving services (King, 2004). Poorly designed service-learning programs risk "reinforcing the dependency model… violating the empowerment of a people, further entrenching the effects of neoliberal economic models, or taking away opportunities for leadership at a local level" (Gammonley et al., 2013, p. 629). King (2004) found that greater difference in socioeconomic or cultural backgrounds between students and the community increased the likelihood of the relationship being perceived as paternalizing, patronizing, or racist. Sandy and Holland (2006) found that common challenges to successful partnerships between communities and service-learning programs in higher education included limited or conflicted interaction with faculty, unclear communication and a lack of standardized policies, an emphasis on completing hours that led to a community service rather than a service-learning approach, and short rather than longer-term commitments.

Service-learning programs that maintained successful community partnerships and were perceived to be beneficial by both students and the community had the common elements of solidarity, reciprocity, and reflection (Acauave & Edmonds Crewe, 2012; Billig, 2000; Brodeur, 2013; Jacoby, 2000; King, 2004; Sandy & Holland, 2006; Tapp & Macke, 2011). Successful service-learning programs met an "authentic community need" (Billig, 2000, p. 662) that was defined by community members (Jacoby, 2000). The community was involved in identifying the need and planning and implementing the program (King, 2004; Tapp & Macke, 2011). Successful projects were meaningful to students and community, rather than focused on helping students "feel good about their privileges or fulfill some academic requirement" (Murphy & Rasch, 2008, p. 71). These service-learning projects used a justice rather than a charity model; an approach to help make communities autonomous by leaving important skills in the community to enable self-determination, rather than simply providing a good or service (Murphy & Rasch, 2008).

Successful community partnerships were built on a sense of solidarity and equality between partners, in which students and community members united around their commonalities and a common cause, allowing them to "overcome the usual power differentials in establishing the donor/recipient relationship" (Tapia, 2010, p. 31). Intergroup contact has been shown to reduce prejudices toward minorities and out groups only when interactions occur among people who are perceived to be of equal status (Rodenborg & Boisen, 2013). Such an approach reflects the principles of human rights as well, in which fostering participation and solidarity in pursuit of social justice is regarded as a vital aspect of service learning (Amnesty International and Human Rights Education Associates, 2007).

The pedagogical principle behind service learning is that "learning and development do not necessarily occur as a result of experience itself but as a result of a reflective component explicitly designed to foster learning and development" (Jacoby, 2000, p. 6). Reflection is an essential part of a successful service-learning program; students consider not just the needs of the community, but also the role of power, privilege, inequality, and the larger historical, sociological, cultural, economic, and political context in which these needs exist (Brodeur, 2013; Jacoby, 2000). Reflection can take the form of journals, papers, or guided group discussion. Reflection and guided cognitive linking increases the likelihood that potential benefits of service learning will be actualized. Lee and Fortune (2013) found that participation in such activities led to greater student satisfaction with the learning experience. Reflection should be designed to advance course objectives and a broader understanding of community life, leadership, and civic responsibility (Tapp & Macke, 2011). Through reflection, students must be shown how service learning is not a one-directional transaction but a process through which they derive mutual benefit (King, 2004). King (2004) found that successful service-learning programs acted in a "destabilizing manner," which exposed students to contrasting information and experiences, and provided a space for them to reflect on current assumptions "in such a way that renders hidden tensions, inconsistencies, and inequalities available for scrutiny and critique" (King, 2004, p. 134).

The Uganda/ Simmons Project on HIV/AIDS

The Uganda/Simmons Project provides students opportunities to engage in a study abroad program with a strong service-learning component. This study abroad opportunity examines the effects of social problems with a focus on health, mental health, and human rights in Uganda and the role of the social work profession. It explores the use of various professional methods to promote self-sufficiency, social integration, social change, human rights, and justice in a developing country. In this 3 week study program, students examine the social problems and learn about the cultural context of delivery of human services. The service-learning project in Uganda has been framed by the issue of HIV/AIDS, a prominent health problem and human rights concern in Uganda.

The HIV/AIDS Situation in Uganda as a Human Right to Health

The recognition of a human right to health in the Universal Declaration of Human Rights (United Nations, 1948) is important for the consideration of HIV/AIDS as a human rights concern. However, considerable work has been done on the intersection of HIV/AIDS and the right to health, especially with the International Covenant on Economic, Social and Cultural Rights (ICESCR; United Nations, 1966), the World Health Organization, and the Joint United Nations Program on HIV/AIDS (UNAIDS). Integrating insights from these more specific initiatives in addition to the UDHR is crucial in the context of Uganda.

A human rights-based approach to HIV/AIDS must address both the human right to health and appropriate health care as well as human rights infringements that increase vulnerability to HIV among specific populations. International consensus on the human right to health is based on the Universal Declaration of Human Rights, which establishes the right to an "adequate standard of living," including medical care and security in the event of sickness or disability (United Nations, 1948, Article 25).

The ICESCR expands on these rights and clarifies the right to health as the right to "enjoy the highest attainable standard" of health, including the "prevention, treatment and control" of epidemic and endemic disease (United Nations, 1966, Article 12). The ICESCR also outlines the "right to enjoy the benefits of scientific progress and its applications" (Article 15). The Convention on the Rights of the Child entitles children to the opportunity to develop physically, mentally, and socially in a "healthy and normal manner" (United Nations, 1989). The International Conference on Population and Development expands health to include "a satisfying and safe sex life," access to contraception and appropriate pre- and postnatal health-care services, which are essential to HIV prevention (Barroso & Sippel, 2011, p. S250).

Although the Ugandan government has been lauded for dramatically reducing the prevalence of HIV/AIDS since the 1980s, current policy and implementation fail to fully provide this standard of health in regard to AIDS (UNAIDS, 2012). Uganda has been cited as an HIV-prevention success story for reducing the estimated adult prevalence of HIV from more than 30% in the early 1990s to 6.4% in 2009. This is attributable to a combination of reduced incidence of infection and high HIV-related mortality (Stover & Northridge, 2013; Strand, 2011). However, the 2012 UN Global AIDS Response Progress Report for Uganda describes the prevalence of HIV in Uganda as "still unacceptably high" (UNAIDS, 2012, p. 2). Slow implementation of policy, inadequate prevention services, lack of medication, and insufficient human resource capacity leave those who have been orphaned by the disease, people living with HIV/AIDS, and affected families and communities deprived of their right to an adequate standard of living (UNAIDS, 2012).

Cohen and Tate (2006) state that prevalence of abstinence-only prevention programs in Uganda deny the basic right to affordable, safe contraception and lead to increased risk of HIV infection. Atwine, Canton-Graae, and Bajunirwe (2005) report that Ugandan AIDS orphans had higher levels of psychological distress than nonorphans. Current resources are insufficient to mitigate the physical and mental health consequences of being orphaned and provide for healthy child development. Mental health care is insufficient and largely unavailable (Atwine et al., 2005). Makhlouf Obermeyer, Bott, Baye, Desclaux, and Baggaley (2013) suggest that the biomedical benefits of scientific advances in regard to HIV/AIDS have not been realized by most Ugandans due to barriers to testing and treatment, itself a violation of the right to health care.

Adequately confronting HIV/AIDS necessitates addressing other human right issues that create vulnerability to the disease (USAIDS & Office of the High Commissioner for Human Rights, 1998). Westerhaus, Finnegan, Zabulon, and Mukherjee (2008) suggest that contrary to the logic behind Uganda's "abstinence, be faithful, use a condom" approach to HIV prevention, HIV risk in the context of the armed conflict in northern Uganda is less a matter of personal choice and more a function of "exposure to physical, emotional, and structural violence" (p. 39). Risk avoidance and harm reduction paradigms that depend on behavior change and fail to acknowledge social determinants of HIV, including poverty, political instability, war, and gender equality will be ineffective and the disease will "continue spreading along societal fault lines" (Westerhaus et al., 2008, p. 40). Chopra and Ford (2005) argue that research has shown that an effective response must move beyond behavior modification and address issues of stigma, power, and social structure. Gender based violence is a key problem in Uganda, "which manifests itself in a wide range of human rights violations" (UNAIDS, 2012,

p. 36), including sexual abuse and assault, discrimination, intimate partner abuse, female circumcision, and the trafficking of women and girls.

Strand (2011) states that Uganda's antihomosexuality attitudes and legislation undermine efforts to prevent and address HIV/AIDS. Makhlouf Obermeyer et al. (2013) argue that political, cultural, and religious hostility toward men who have sex with men in Uganda creates barriers to HIV prevention, testing, and services; increases the risk of exposure; and decreases the likelihood of obtaining treatment for this population. To provide the "highest attainable standard" of health (United Nations, 1966), Westerhaus et al. (2008) argue that the Ugandan government must provide adequate services to meet the health and social needs of affected individuals, families, and communities; ensure access to scientific advancement; and seek to "reduce contextual vulnerability" to HIV by addressing issues of discrimination and human rights abuses (Westerhaus et al., 2008, p. 44). It is with this background on human rights violations contributing to HIV/AIDS epidemic in Uganda that the course unfolds for students. Several organizations in Uganda are engaged in work with children, women's groups, sexual minorities, domestic violence, and child welfare and serve as local partners for this service learning project. A unifying dimension to the services provided by most of these groups is HIV/AIDS.

The Scope of the Course

Several objectives are geared toward building knowledge, skills, and values in keeping with the Council on Social Work Education Educational Policy and Accreditation Standards competencies (2008). In addition to explicitly addressing rights in the objectives, the course addresses issues that link directly to human rights. Indeed, these issues can be framed as human rights issues. They include health care; security of persons; freedom from violence; and the right to an adequate standard of living, housing, and employment, to name a few. They are also linked to a rights-based practice.

In terms of knowledge objectives, the course addresses the following:

- To understand the relationship of political, social, and cultural realities of the country in its historical context

- To learn about HIV/AIDS and its relationship to problems such as poverty, domestic violence, illiteracy, malnutrition, sex trafficking, health, and the criminal justice system in Uganda
- To identify, critique, and evaluate the micro and macro interventions, methods of treatment, prevention programs, and policies that have been developed to respond to psychosocial needs of the people
- To identify concerns of certain groups—particularly children, women, the elderly and poor communities—that are especially at risk for psychosocial problems
- To learn about the organization and delivery of social services in a developing country and its implications in a global context
- To understand political realities and the relationship of economic development to social well-being and social disruption
- To develop awareness of and a responsible response to HIV/AIDS and issues of social inclusion and social exclusion and effects on well-being

The values objectives for the course are clearly linked to human rights principles as outlined in the Universal Declaration of Human Rights and core documents of the International Federation of Social Workers and International Association of Schools of Social Work (2004a; 2004b). These values objectives include the following:

- To respect cultural influences on behavior and values within and between cultures and societies
- To acknowledge the dignity and worth of all people
- To promote and protect human rights worldwide
- To make social institutions more humane and responsive to psychosocial needs
- To end oppression, poverty, and other forms of social injustice

Skills objectives for the course also are related to human rights. These include helping the student acquire competency in

1) analyzing organizational and social structures that affect individual and community well-being;

2) ethnographic research, including observation, interviewing, and analysis;

3) critical analysis of interventions that are responsive to the ethnic and cultural variations of individuals, families, and communities;

4) working with diverse cultures;

5) community organizing and advocacy; and

6) evaluating studies and evidence-informed practices with various populations.

Students are introduced to the context of international social work, including human rights law and practice, from the outset using an integrated approach for international social work and practice. Within this integrated perspectives approach, students are introduced to global, ecological, and social development perspectives and a human rights perspective within Ugandan cultural, historical, political, economic, religious, and social contexts. Specific issues that address health and mental health are explored as attention is paid to certain populations including women, children, gays and lesbians, and other sexual minorities.

A rigorous regimen of writing, self-examination, and debriefing is employed prior to the travel, during course work, and while abroad. The writing is in a form of individual and group journaling, Web postings, and academic papers. Students delve into personal and professional discourse as they struggle with entry into a different culture. Students are encouraged to enter into ethnographic research with their selected topics of inquiry.

Students are challenged to examine key assumptions that guide their worldview as they enter a new culture. Some of the struggles include a serious consideration of the solidarity they share with their host culture. They often need to debunk what they bring with them, including assumptions and myths about the new communities they encounter, to begin to engage in collaborative practices with the host communities. Therefore, attention to a sense of cultural curiosity that honors the local community knowledge and resourcefulness is essential. It is important to maintain a sense of accountability in which host communities are seen as equal partners in the learning process.

Some of the challenges that underline key lessons include building a sense of cultural humility. Students need to learn that the capital they bring to these communities does not in any way surpass the capital that these communities already have. Students need to learn that the host communities have as much to offer as they do. To achieve this effect, any learning should be based on common research interests. Such a stance helps address an academic arrogance that comes with knowing.

One of the challenges to meeting the course objectives is the students' lack of experience abroad. For many, this is the first trip they have taken outside of the United States. Their initial exposure to a new and different culture often presents them with a type of anxiety associated with a need to save the other and often leads them to act in patronizing ways. Such a stance often is riddled with academic arrogance that manifests itself as ignorance.

However, the students also enjoy certain rewards as part of this experience. One such reward is the fact that students participate in a stewardship of care. Students become stewards of the tradition out of which the profession has come. The context of HIV and AIDS reveals key human rights issues that affect populations affected by the disease. Stewardship concerns managing one's responsibility with proper regard to the rights of others. These rights include access to health care, due process rights, institutional rights, treatment rights, and civil liberties. The protection of these rights for people living with HIV/AIDS and the challenges that surround access to health care is a preservation of the community as a whole.

Another reward that students have gained from these experiences is the opportunity to experience compassion with those they encounter. Compassion is about being with another. No more powerful is the opportunity to be in solidarity with another than suffering with and being one with the other. When students enter the homes of the people they work with and experience the simplicity of their lives they come to learn the depth of experience that unites them as human beings.

Developing effective partnerships presents opportunities and challenges. Students learn as much from the communities as they give. This mutual learning becomes the bedrock of solidarity. Indeed, the relationship becomes one of mutual mentoring rather than leadership, one in which strengths are honored (Holm & Malete, 2010). One challenge for students is negotiating the academic demands of school and honoring host institutions as key partners in their learning. This challenge presents one of the sharpest ethical dilemmas for students. Another big challenge for students is the nature of involvement with these host communities, often seen as one-time brief interactions with no follow-up. Some students struggle with what it means to participate in opportunities such as these. They may ask questions such as "Are we really making a difference?", "Does this not feel like a drop in the ocean?", "Should we have stayed home and thought of here?", "How does work continue when we are gone?", "We have the choice to come and go, but do our host communities have that luxury?", and "How do we begin to explain to communities back home about the complexity of challenges?". These questions challenge students to examine their involvement in study abroad and their commitment to an ethic of care.

Ethic of Care

An ethic of care grounded in human rights and social justice helps to anchor the role of such a program in the lives of students. Some people have described this ethic of care as a "relational stance" (Madsen, 2007, p. 323), or an "emotional posture" (Griffith & Griffith, 1992, p. 6) or a "way of being in relationship with our fellow human beings, including how we think about them, talk with, act with, and respond to them" (Anderson, 1997, p. 94). It is about the way helping professionals position themselves as allies, culturally curious, and always seeking collaboration, partnerships, and engaging in accountable practices even in the absence of codes. An ethic of care presupposes no rules or codes to be followed. An ethic of care concerns being human with all other humans and acting in humane ways. Such humane ways pay respect to all human beings regardless of their social condition. An ethic of care encompasses attention to all aspects of human life, not just those that do no harm, but also those that enhance well-being. The challenge for a program such as this is to assist students to live the principles of helping grounded by an ethic of care.

The questions mentioned previously also have compelled a serious examination and evaluation of the program. From the Simmons perspective, students have been challenged to examine their assumptions. Through engaging in the program, students have reexamined their social work training in light of this experience of uncovering their own commitment to social justice and human rights. Indeed, some students have felt compelled to start social action groups at local, national, or international levels. For instance, one student launched a nonprofit organization to raise funds in support and awareness of children living with HIV/AIDS in Uganda.

Another student mobilized other students who graduated from this experience to start advocacy campaigns for people living with HIV/AIDS. For the host communities in Uganda, agencies have incorporated this learning experience into their programs. Every year they welcome students with whom they share their accomplishments. The opportunity to teach and learn from each new group gives them a sense of hope and possibility, thereby alleviating the sense of isolation that comes with living with HIV/AIDS. In two organizations students have worked with the agencies to help them develop their own internal review boards to act as informed gatekeepers around research. A few organizations also have developed evaluation criteria to assess the effects of their work and enhance their competitive grant writing skills.

Conclusion

Social work as a profession leans on a very rich tradition of rights and values as it reaches out to serve all peoples, including those living with HIV/AIDS. Such a call to service rests on the foundational values of the helping profession. These values have been variously embedded in charity and care; a commitment to social justice, service, the importance of human relationships, and human rights; and the empowerment and strengths perspectives. This legacy compels social workers and helping professionals to pursue a critical agenda for all persons, including people living with HIV/AIDS. Such a commitment propels helping professionals to work for social transformation, compassion, and hope and to witness as part of a larger context in the ethic of care. The case of Uganda and my work with students there has made this ethic of care even more apparent to social work education and practice. Indeed, when students engage in a program such as the one described here, they are immediately and intimately exposed not only to human rights issues but also to the challenges of engaging in a human rights based practice.

References

Acauave, L. A., & Edmonds Crewe, S. (2012). International programs: Advancing human rights and social justice for African American students. *Journal of Social Work Education, 48,* 763–784.

Amnesty International and Human Rights Education Associates. (2007). *Human rights and service learning: Lesson plans and projects.* Retrieved from http://www.hrea.org/pubs/AIUSA-HREA-ServiceLearning.pdf

Anderson, H. (1997). *Conversation, language, and possibilities.* New York, NY: Basic Books.

Atwine, B., Cantor-Graae, E., & Bajunirwe, F. (2005). Psychological distress among AIDS orphans in rural Uganda. *Social Science & Medicine, 61,* 555–564.

Barroso, C., & Sippel, S. (2011). Sexual and reproductive health and rights: Integration as a holistic and rights-based response to HIV/AIDS. *Women's Health Issues, 21*(6), S250–S254.

Billig, S. H. (2000). Research on K-12 school-based service-learning. *Phi Delta Kappan, 81,* 658.

Billig, S., Root, S., & Jesse, D. (2005). *The impact of participation in service-learning on high school students' civic engagement. CIRCLE working paper 33.* Center for Information and Research on Civic Learning and Engagement (CIRCLE), University of Maryland, College Park.

Boateng, A., & Thompson, A. M. (2013). Study abroad Ghana: An international experiential learning. *Journal of Social Work Education, 49,* 701–715.

Brodeur, D. R. (2013). Mentoring young adults in the development of social responsibility. *Australasian Journal of Engineering Education, 19*(1), 13–25.

Chopra, M., & Ford, N. (2005). Scaling up health promotion interventions in the era of HIV/AIDS: Challenges for a rights based approach. *Health Promotion International, 20,* 383–390.

Cohen, J., & Tate, T. (2006). The less they know, the better: Abstinence-only HIV/AIDS programs in Uganda. *Reproductive Health Matters, 14*(28), 174–178.

Council on Social Work Education. (2008). *Educational policy and accreditation standards.* Retrieved from http://www.cswe.org/File.aspx?id= 13780

Cox , D., & Pawar, M. (2006*). International social work: Issues, strategies and programs.* London, UK: SAGE Publications.

Cruz, N. I., & Giles, D. E. (2000). Where's the community in service learning research? *Michigan Journal of Community Service Learning*, Special Issue, 28–34.

Freire, P. (2000). *Pedagogy of the oppressed.* New York, NY: Bloomsbury Academic.

Gammonley, D., Smith Rotabi, K., Forte, J., & Martin, A. (2013). Beyond study abroad: A human rights delegation to teach policy advocacy. *Journal of Social Work Education, 49,* 619–634.

Greenfield, E. A., Davis, R. T., & Fedor, J. P. (2012). The effect of international social work education: Study abroad versus on-campus courses. *Journal of Social Work Education, 48,* 739–761.

Griffith, J. L., & Griffith, M. E. (1992). Owning one's own epistemological stance in therapy. *Dulwich Center Newsletter, 1,* 5–11.

Healy, L. (2008). *International social work: Professional action in an interdependent world* (2nd ed.). New York, NY: Oxford University Press

Holm, J., & Malete, L. (2010, June 13). Nine problems that hinder partnerships in Africa. *The Chronicle of Higher Education.* Retrieved from: http://chronicle.com/article/Nine-Problems-That-Hinder-P/65892/

International Federation of Social Workers & International Association of Schools of Social Work. (2004a). *Ethics in social work: Statement of principles.* Retrieved from www.ifsw.org

International Federation of Social Workers & International Association of Schools of Social Work. (2004b). *Global standards for the education and training of the social work profession.* Retrieved from www.iassw-aiets.org

Jacoby, B. (1996). *Service-learning in higher education: Concepts and practices.* San Francisco, CA: Jossey-Bass.

King, J. T. (2004). Service-learning as a site for critical pedagogy: A case of collaboration, caring, and defamiliarization across borders. *Journal of Experiential Education, 26*(3), 121–137.

Lee, M., & Fortune, A. E. (2013). Do we need more "doing" activities or "thinking" activities in the field practicum? *Journal of Social Work Education, 49,* 646–660.

Madsen, W. (2007). *Collaborative therapy with multi-stressed families.* New York, NY: Guilford Press.

Makhlouf Obermeyer, C., Bott, S., Baye, R., Desclaux, A., & Baggaley, R. (2013). HIV testing and care in Burkina Faso, Kenya, Malawi and Uganda: Ethics on the ground. *BMC International Health & Human Rights,13*(1), 6–19.

Mapp, S. C. (2012). Effect of short-term study abroad programs on students' cultural adaptability. *Journal of Social Work Education, 48*, 727–737.

Murphy, J. W., & Rasch, D. (2008). Service-learning, contact theory, and building Black communities. *Negro Educational Review, 59*(1), 63–78.

Rodenborg, N. A., & Boisen, L. A. (2013). Aversive racism and intergroup contact theories: Cultural competence in a segregated world. *Journal of Social Work Education, 49*, 564–579.

Sandy, M., & Holland, B. (2006). Different worlds and common ground: Community partner perspectives on campus-community partnerships. *Michigan Journal of Community Service Learning, 13*, 30–43.

Stover, G. N., & Northridge, M. E. (2013). The social legacy of HIV/AIDS. *American Journal of Public Health, 103*(2), 199.

Strand, C. (2011). Kill bill! Ugandan human rights organizations' attempts to influence the media's coverage of the anti-homosexuality bill. *Culture, Health & Sexuality, 13*, 917–931.

Tapia, M. N. (2010). Service learning widespread in Latin America. *Phi Delta Kappan, 91*(5), 31–32.

Tapp, K., & Macke, C. (2011). Competency-based capstone projects: Service learning in BSW field practica. *Journal of Baccalaureate Social Work, 16*(2), 75–91.

United Nations. (1948, December 10). *Universal declaration of human rights.* G.A. Res. 217 A (III). Retrieved from http://www.refworld.org/docid/3ae6b3712c.html

United Nations. (1966, December 16). *International covenant on economic, social, and cultural rights.* G.A. Res. 2200A (XXI). Retrieved from http://www.ohchr.org/EN/ProfessionalInterest/Pages/CESCR.aspx

United Nations. (1989). *Convention on the rights of the child.* G.A. Res. 44/25. Retrieved from: http://www.ohchr.org/Documents/ProfessionalInterest/crc.pdf

UNAIDS. (2012). *Global aids response progress report: Country progress report Uganda.* Retrieved from http://www.unaids.org/

USAIDS & Office of the High Commissioner for Human Rights. (1998). *HIV/AIDS and human rights: International guidelines.* (HR/PUB/98/1). Geneva, Switzerland: Author.

Westerhaus, M. J., Finnegan, A. C., Zabulon, Y., & Mukherjee, J. S. (2008). Northern Uganda and paradigms of HIV prevention: The need for social analysis. *Global Public Health: An International Journal for Research, Policy and Practice, 3*(1), 39–46.

17 | Educating U.S. University Students to Promote Human Rights:
A Study Abroad Field-Based Intensive Seminar in Costa Rica

Dennis J. Ritchie and Laura Guzman Stein

This chapter analytically describes a short-term intensive study abroad course targeting undergraduate and graduate social work students from the United States that is also open to students from other disciplines. Students learn about human development and human rights from a global and comparative perspective focusing on Costa Rica and the United States. This course, Sustainable Human Development and Human Rights: A Gender Perspective, was developed by the authors and has now been offered annually for the past 7 years. It has been a collaborative partnership between two public universities: George Mason University (GMU) in Virginia and the University of Costa Rica (UCR). The primary units involved are the Center for Global Education and the Department of Social Work from GMU and the Centro de Investigacion en Estudios de la Mujer (CIEM) [Women's Studies Research Center] of UCR. The course has always been co-taught by a GMU social work professor and a professor from UCR who is linked to CIEM. This Center contains social work and psychology faculty experienced in addressing a diversity of human rights issues from a gender perspective. This provided an additional opportunity for social work students to expand their visions and develop a better understanding of how women and men of different ages, social classes, ethnic groups, and countries are affected differently by gender.

The chapter first explains the need for this course in terms of the context of the lack of human rights education in the United States. It then discusses literature attesting to the value of study abroad in social work education. Next it describes the course: its objectives, content, and process along with a brief historical overview of its development and implementation. Finally, it presents course outcomes and results by sharing excerpts from participants' coursework and own words to document and exhibit what students attest to taking away from the overall course experience.

The Need for and Purpose of This Course

Human rights education has been largely absent from the formal educational system in the United States across all levels in primary, secondary, and higher education. This salient deficiency applies to education in the health, education, and human service professions as well. The authors believe that a number of factors contribute to this situation that all relate to the tendency of people in the United States not to embrace a holistic, global, and collective perspective.

Overwhelmingly, the U.S. view of human rights reflects its emphasis on individualism, competition, free market economy, and civil and political rights over economic, social, cultural, and collective rights. Furthermore, this limited conception of human rights appears to predominantly be viewed as the domain of the legal profession and not the concern of other professions and disciplines. The Human Rights Resource Center of the University of Minnesota (2000) presents a critical overview of the status of human rights education in the United States and supports the authors' contentions.

> In the United States human rights education is still in its beginning stages. Although virtually every high school in the country requires a course on the US Constitution and Bill of Rights, very few people study human rights in schools or even at the university or graduate level.... It remains to find an established place in the mainstream educational system. Instead it has flourished in alternative settings: non-profit organizations, extracurricular groups like Amnesty International's campus chapters, alternative educational settings, and communities of faith. (Human Rights Resource Center, University of Minnesota, 2000, Part I)

The United Nations (UN) World Programme for Human Rights Education recognizes and addresses this shortcoming. The UN General Assembly (UN,

2004) proclaimed the World Programme for Human Rights Education "to advance the implementation of human rights education programmes in all sectors." The Programme is divided into phases. The first phase was from 2005 to 2009 and focused on human rights education in primary and secondary schools. We are currently in the second phase, 2010 to 2014, which focuses on promoting human rights education in higher education and human rights training for teachers and educators, civil servants (including social workers), the military, and police (UN World Programme for Human Rights Education, 2014). Although many social workers in other parts of the world are aware of this initiative, very few U.S. social workers know of it.

Social work and other helping professions and academic disciplines in the United States have been slow to embrace a human rights perspective as a framework for education and practice. Colleagues in Latin America are much more advanced in conceptualizing the link between helping professions (for example, social work, psychology, and teaching) and human rights. This trend to incorporate a human rights perspective into social work curricula, national and international conferences, and social policies throughout Latin America began in the 1980s.

The profession of social work in the United States has been experiencing a relatively recent but rapidly increasing interest in refining its conceptualization of social work education and practice to incorporate global and human rights perspectives. This change is evidenced by the national accrediting organization, the Council on Social Work Education's (CSWE) current Educational Policy and Accreditation Standards (EPAS; 2008), and by a number of professional publications linking social work and human rights that have appeared over the past several years (see, for example, Healy [2008]; Mapp [2008]; Reichert [2007]; Wronka [2008]). The CSWE standards that were approved in 2008 mandate that all accredited social work programs prepare their graduates to master 10 competencies. It should be noted that human rights has now been given a prominent position in the required curriculum at both the baccalaureate and masters levels of social work education. Indeed, it is one of the 10 required competencies. As stated in the CSWE standards:

Educational Policy 2.1.5—Advance human rights and social and economic justice. Each person, regardless of position in society, has basic human rights, such as freedom, safety, privacy, an adequate standard of living, health care, and education. Social workers recognize the global interconnections of oppression and are knowledgeable about theories of justice and strategies to promote human and civil rights. Social work incorporates social justice practices in organizations, institutions, and society to ensure that these basic human rights are distributed equitably and without prejudice. Social workers

- understand the forms and mechanisms of oppression and discrimination;
- advocate for human rights and social and economic justice; and
- engage in practices that advance social and economic justice. (CSWE, 2008, p.5)

Although the U.S. social work profession now recognizes the need for all social workers to become competent at advancing human rights, the fact that human rights content has not been a part of the formal education of the vast majority of social work educators and practitioners in the United States serves as a critical obstacle to effectively fulfilling this mandate. Knowledge and understanding of the human rights field is simply lacking, and this poses a serious challenge to social work education programs' capacity to teach and incorporate this now required competency into their curricula. Many programs may simply add the words *human rights* to curriculum components that address social justice, without actually adding any new content or experiences that provide genuine human rights education.

Indeed, the very wording pertaining to human rights in the previously quoted Educational Policy 2.1.5 section of the EPAS provides further evidence of the U.S. social work profession's lack of knowledge about human rights. Note that it reads "Social workers…are knowledgeable about…strategies to promote human and civil rights" (CSWE, 2008, p. 5). Why are civil rights separated from human rights? Civil rights are human rights! Human rights include civil and political rights; economic, social, and cultural rights, and collective or solidarity rights. Further, one of the basic principles of human rights thinking is that all human rights are interrelated and inseparable with no single category of rights being more important than the others. It is also interesting to note that although the Educational Policy requires all social workers to be "knowledgeable about theories of justice," it calls for social workers to be "knowledgeable about…strategies to promote human and civil rights" (CSWE, 2008, p. 5). This then translates into the associated practice behavior stating that social workers "advocate for human rights and social and economic justice." How can one advocate for human rights without first learning and understanding the meaning, principles, categories or types, and the UN system and instruments or documents of human rights? It is necessary to know how the international and inter-American systems for the protection of human rights work.

Study Abroad and Social Work Education

A growing body of literature attests to study abroad programs' positive contributions to globalizing social work education in the United States. These programs can assume a variety of forms. A prevalent model is to arrange a field practicum abroad for U.S. social work students. Panos, Pettys, Cox, and Junes-Hart (2004) surveyed 446 baccalaureate and graduate social work programs throughout the United States and found that 21% had provided international field placements between 1997 and 2002. There is reason to believe that the number of international practicum opportunities and percentage of programs offering them have increased since the 2008 EPAS went into effect, demanding increased attention to a global perspective, social and economic justice, and human rights. In fact, CSWE Press published a guidebook on international field placements and exchanges (Lager, Mathiesen, Rodgers, & Cox, 2010).

Another common form of study abroad in social work is a short-term, faculty led, intensive immersion course in another country, typically lasting between 2 and 4 weeks (see, for example, Fairchild, Pillai, & Noble, 2006; Gammonley, Smith Rotabi, & Gamble, 2007; Greenfield, Davis, & Fedor, 2012; Jaoko, 2010). Such courses typically are offered either in the summer or during the intersemester break. Their short-term nature mitigates programs' concerns about fitting in a one or two-semester long practicum abroad while continuing to implement their rather rigid curricula designed to meet accreditation standards. It also addresses students' concerns regarding how to have a study abroad experience while juggling school, family, employment, and other financial responsibilities; in most cases, a short-term international experience is more practical and feasible.

The positive outcomes attributed to social work study abroad can assume various foci. Some authors claim a focus on social work values as the foundation for development and analysis of study abroad programs (Gammonley et al., 2007; Lindsey, 2005; Merrill & Frost, 2011). However, the vast majority of literature appears to focus on positive outcomes related to augmented understanding of the global context for social work practice and increased cultural competence: knowledge and skills necessary to effectively cross cultures and practice social work in a multicultural and diverse environment (Boyle, Nackerud, & Kilpatrick, 1999; Fairchild et al., 2006; Jaoko, 2010; Kreitzer, Barlow, Schwartz, Lacroix, & Macdonald, 2012).

The Course: Historical Overview, Content, Process, and Accomplishments

The study abroad course that is the focus of this chapter is a short-term faculty led seminar in Costa Rica. It provides students from the United States an opportunity to learn about human rights issues and principles; the international and inter-American systems of human rights (including major human rights instruments); and the value of adopting a human rights framework for critically reflecting on their own academic/professional disciplines and for analyzing and developing policies, programs, and services as a means of promoting human rights and advancing social and economic justice. It underscores the necessity of incorporating the concepts of power, participation, inclusion, and changing power relationships whenever conceptualizing and promoting empowerment practice. It emphasizes the need for a holistic view of human rights and human development and underscores the interrelatedness of these two concepts. Students also critically reflect on and discuss the difference between the concepts of equality and equity and are exposed to Costa Rican public policies and programs that promote equity and the advancement of human rights.

This course, Sustainable Human Development and Human Rights: A Gender Perspective, was developed by the authors and first offered in January of 2006. Over the past 7 years, 120 students have participated in the course. Although most participants have been social work students, we have had a diverse group of students in that a variety of majors, ages, and home universities have been represented. Course enrollment has been about equally divided between undergraduate and graduate students. The substantial majority have been full-time GMU students, although other home institutions have included George Washington University, American University, Washington University of Saint Louis, Wayne State University, University of Maryland, and Brown University.

The course is a 3-credit, 16-day, intensive field-based seminar in Costa Rica. Graduate and undergraduate students from the United States are provided a meaningful cross-cultural learning opportunity focusing on the interrelated themes of human rights (particularly women's and children's rights); sustainable human, social, economic, political, and community development; gender-based and community violence; poverty; and health and social services. Students critically examine policies and programs related to these themes and their implementation. Students learn about human development and human rights from a global perspective with a focus comparing Costa Rica and the United States. The course format combines predeparture reading and writing assignments with in-country lectures, active learning exercises, videos, and site visits to a variety of organizations. Students also write journal entries throughout the experience and a final integrative research paper after returning home to the United States.

All site visits and field trips are educational in nature. We have guided observation of cities and the countryside driving from site to site. We visit governmental and nongovernmental organizations that relate to the course theme and represent a variety of levels, such as intergovernmental, national government, community-based, and grassroots. Due to time constraints and logistical and financial reasons, a number of representatives from a variety of organizations and programs meet and give guest presentations to us at the university or our hotel.

All students are required to complete a substantial set of predeparture readings and an accompanying writing assignment prior to beginning the course in Costa Rica. This enables them to develop a crucial foundation of knowledge on which additional learning through the in-country lectures, active learning exercises, and site visits to a variety of organizations can be built. Students are provided a common base of knowledge regarding human rights and human development. This enables them to more effectively communicate with each other and critically reflect on the remaining course experiences and content while further refining their understanding of these related concepts.

The predeparture assignment includes the following topics and sources which are all accessible through the Internet. Students are required to write their critical reflections on these readings while responding to a set of questions from the instructors.

1) What is human development and what are the Millennium Development Goals? To answer this question, students read a number of the UN Development Programme's annual Human Development Reports (at least the summary or overview sections), which are all retrievable from its website (http://hdr.undp.org): Human Development Report 2000, *Human Rights and Human Development*; Human Development Report 2003, *Millennium Development Goals: A Compact Among Nations to End Human Poverty;* Human Development Report 2009, *Overcoming Barriers: Human Mobility and Development;* Human Development Report 2010, *20 Years on: Pushing the Frontiers of Human Development,* and Human Development Report 2011, *Sustainability and Equity: A Better Future for All.*

2) Human rights in development: Students access the UN Office of the High Commissioner for Human Rights Web page and read *Frequently Asked Questions on a Human Rights-Based Approach To Development Cooperation.* (www.ohchr.org/Documents/Publications/FAQen.pdf)

3) Social Watch reports related to human rights and social justice: Students go to the website of Social Watch, a network comprised by national coalitions of civil society organizations (www.socialwatch. org) and read *Social Watch Report 2012—Sustainable Development: The Right To a Future* and the *Social Watch Report 2008: Rights Is the Answer,* focusing on the sections "Rights in Times of Crisis," "Human Rights and the Economic System," and the national report for the United States (and any other countries they are interested in).

4) International human rights instruments (major UN human rights documents): Students can access all the major human rights instruments via the Office of the High Commissioner for Human Rights website (**www.ohchr.org**) under "human rights instruments." They are expected to familiarize themselves with the following instruments: the Universal Declaration of Human Rights (UN, 1948); the International Covenant on Civil and Political Rights (UN, 1966a); the International Covenant on Economic, Social and Cultural Rights (UN, 1966b); the Convention on the Elimination of All Forms of Discrimination Against Women (CEDAW; UN, 1979); the Convention on the Rights of the Child (CRC; UN, 1989); and the Declaration on the Right to Development (UN, 1986). They are further instructed to peruse the entire list and explore other documents and human rights instruments according to their particular interests.

5) The United States and its ratification of international human rights treaties: Students also acquaint themselves with the U.S. government's record regarding signature and ratification of the various instruments. (This information is available at www.hrw.org/en/news/2009/07/24/ united-states-ratification-international-human-rights-treaties).

6) *The State of the World's Children* (annual reports by UNICEF): Students are instructed to read *The State of the World's Children 2010: Child Rights* (www.unicef.org/sowc).

The social work students in the course are also expected to read Reichert's (2007) book, *Challenges in Human Rights: A Social Work Perspective.*

Outcomes and Results of the Program

As mentioned in the beginning of this chapter, the course is run as a collaborative partnership between GMU and UCR. It is offered as a GMU course, and students pay the course tuition and fees to earn credit from GMU. GMU has contracted with UCR and CIEM to help organize and deliver the course in Costa Rica. Although GMU could do this on its own, it made a purposeful decision to form this partnership with UCR and CIEM and to involve Costa Rican colleagues in the planning and delivery of the course content. This results in a number of benefits, including ensuring that the Costa Rican perspective is prominent, cross-cultural dialogue occurs, and students feel more immersed in the culture by being affiliated with UCR (and thereby do not feel as though they are tourists). Costa Rican colleagues serve as effective cross-cultural interpreters and provide insights into their reality that might otherwise be overlooked by faculty and students from abroad. The GMU faculty member who is the program director also firmly believes that it is essential for his university to provide resources—financial compensation—to the host institution so that the host country and institution gets something out of the relationship. Thus, the GMU faculty member feels that the U.S. institution and its course participants are not merely extracting resources and benefits from the country and institutions they are visiting and learning from. Rather, the intent is to establish and cultivate an ongoing collaborative partnership that is mutually beneficial, and that it is mutually rewarding to work and learn together. This vision of collaborative relations in a cross-cultural context is consistent with a human rights perspective grounded on mutual respect and recognition of cultural diversity as a necessary component in these relationships.

Costa Rica represents nations from Central America, Latin America, and the Global South. Generally speaking, these societies and cultures tend to be more collective and community-oriented compared to the United States, which is recognized as more individualistic-oriented. Exposure to and comparison of differing societal viewpoints and ideologies enables students to recognize how these differences can result in differing conceptualizations of social work and related concepts of human development, human rights, and sustainability. Students are also surprised to discover that Costa Rica's public and social policies, programs, and services are in many ways more progressive than those in the United States. In the words of an MSW student:

> One of the first things that surprised me when arriving in Costa Rica was cultural and society recognition of Human Rights. We noticed on the law school and on signs around campus words such as equality, solidarity, equity, and justice. This is in contrast to the United States, where individualism is valued, even to the detriment of society. If words like these were placed in a U.S. city, they would be decried as socialist, far-left propaganda. Additionally, we had a discussion about whether special attention should be given to certain groups. For example, are CEDAW and CRC really necessary when women and children are included in the UDHR (Universal Declaration of Human Rights)? I tied this in with the lecture at INAMU (National Institute for Women) about equity and equality. If a conversation about giving special preference or treatment to a certain group took place in the U.S., some groups would decry it as unfair and 'reverse discrimination.' This again shows the U.S. values of equality and individualism, which ignore equity and a critical analysis of the dominant power structures. So in many ways Costa Rica is more progressive than the United States on human rights issues.

As previously described, all students are required to complete a substantial set of predeparture readings and an accompanying writing assignment prior to beginning the course in Costa Rica. Although the predeparture assignment involves a real commitment of time and energy to complete, students recognize the importance of this assignment. The following student quote expresses this: "Starting from the beginning, the predeparture readings were a key aspect of my learning. Keeping in mind these readings throughout the whole trip is what allowed me to make connections between our different lectures and field visits."

Students have consistently attested to this being a meaningful educational experience that they never could have had without leaving home. They have referred to it as an "eye opening experience" that increased their knowledge and critical thinking about sustainable human development and human rights, the Central American context, and the role of United States government policies. Students perceive how holding the seminar in Costa Rica makes possible a learning experience that they could not have had at home. The immersion experience allows them to experience cross-cultural dialogue and increase self-awareness and understanding of a different culture and society expressed in macrosystem forces, microsystem relationships, policies, programs, and services. The following student quote expresses this view:

> During the entire academic Costa Rican experience, visiting the agencies, NGOs, and community based organizations was the most valuable learning experience. While I was interested in learning about the international human rights framework and Costa Rican legislation, those are all topics that I can teach myself about on the Internet. However, I can't fully learn about the work of groups on the ground if I am sitting at my desk back in the U.S. The site visits were the most unique to Costa Rica, and made me feel as if I were really getting to know what work was being done on the ground.

Our site visits and lectures have included presentations on programs to promote the human rights of children and adolescents. Some examples include a leading Costa Rican children's rights nongovernmental organization, Fundacion Paniamor; Programa Interdisciplinario de Estudios y Acción Social de los Derechos de la Niñez y la Adolescenia, a UCR-based interdisciplinary program focusing on child and adolescent rights; an overview of the work of the National Office for Women; an overview of the inter-American human rights system by the Inter-American Institute for Human Rights and the Inter-American Court for Human Rights; an analysis of the problem of and programs to address sexual exploitation of children and the tourism industry; the experience of a small women's organic farming and health products cooperative; and a grassroots women's organization of survivors of domestic violence. Other lectures have included critical reflections on the Central American Free Trade Agreement and presentations on the Annual Costa Rican State of the Nation

Report on Sustainable Human Development, human development and gender equity indicators, the Responsible Paternity Law, poverty, and migration. These lectures and site visits also contribute to the development of students' critical thinking and awareness of cultural differences among societies and diversity as a positive component in promoting social justice and human rights.

Another MSW student reflected on the differing societal views and how they affect views on human rights:

> Growing up in an individualistic culture such as that in the United States, it is so ingrained in us from a young age that an adequate standard of living is not guaranteed but must be *earned* through hard work and the quest for the 'American Dream.' This attitude is reflected in the fact that the United States has not ratified any of the Human Rights instruments that guarantee social, economic, and cultural rights, and I assume that this has a substantive impact on the dearth of human rights content in the U.S. educational system.

For the past 4 years we also have made a 2 day, 1 night visit to an eco-ethno tourism project of the Bribri indigenous community near the border with Panama, which turned out to be a highlight of the course for most of the students. We then spent 2 days and 2 nights at a Caribbean beach town in Limon Province. These two overnight trips outside San Jose exposed the students to issues concerning sustainable human development and human rights of the indigenous and Afro-Caribbean communities and their experiences of marginalization and exclusion. This brief but powerful experience introduced students to these issues from a gender perspective with power as a critical concept permeating societal relations at all levels.

A graduate student in International Development illuminates how comparing the Costa Rican context to the United States actually enhanced her understanding of U.S. and global contexts as well:

> Throughout the course, gender has been a theme that I have been thinking about a lot. Before, gender had been something that was just theoretical for me. Through this course, I felt that I was able to put this theory into a

specific context. Using specific examples from Costa Rica helped me appreciate how structurally ingrained gender roles are. I think that through this course I have reaffirmed my commitment to women and development. I want to work on gender issues, and I want to make a difference. I also want to work internationally, not make a career in Washington. I want to interact with the people I am helping and I want to be able to listen to their needs directly.

A number of students commented on power as a key concept and major theme of the course. An illustrative quote follows:

I believe that this U.S. emphasis on individualism is directly related to *power*, a concept that has been discussed in-depth during this trip. We have examined how patriarchal society reinforces male power over women, how dominant ethnic groups exert power over minority ethnic groups, and how traffickers exert power over their victims, among other power differentials. I also think the United States' avoidance of involvement in the Inter-American System and in other human rights treaties and conventions is a way to hold on to power by not allowing ourselves to be held accountable to any other nation or governing body. If the U.S. does not have to answer to anyone other than ourselves, then our image of our country as 'superior' and 'all-knowing' is not threatened or at risk of being shattered. This concept of accountability and responsibility (or avoidance of) was addressed, for example, in Costa Rica's Responsible Paternity Law. For the first time, men are being held accountable to women and children for their actions and are being *compelled* to take responsibility for their choices. This has put some long overdue power back in the hands of women and children in Costa Rica, and is an important step toward gender and age equity. I am wondering after these two weeks, however, when countries of privilege, like the United States, will be compelled to take responsibility for how citizens and other nations are treated and therefore be held accountable for their actions? I am a firm believer that with privilege comes responsibility—and one step the U.S. could take toward taking ownership of that responsibility would be ratifying important Human Rights documents and then putting those ideals into *practice.*

Several field trips were tourist-related but intended to educate students more about the Costa Rican and Central American context, the relationship between tourism and sustainable development, and the culture. These were very well received by the students because it also gave them a taste of the beauty of Costa Rica and why the country is such a mecca for ecotourism.

One student shared how an education-based immersion experience is different from visiting a country as a tourist:

> I am sad to see this trip come to an end. I really loved this experience. I have travelled to countries outside of the U.S. before, but I have never been on a study abroad trip. It is a really different experience. The educational aspect makes you learn about the country and culture on a much deeper level. By the end I felt like a part of the community there as a student instead of a tourist.

Students' final reflections on the course experience testify to the lack of human rights education throughout their educational career.

> What has stood out to me the most during these past 2 weeks is that, for the most part, this trip is the first time I have learned anything in-depth about human rights. Throughout my 4 years of undergraduate work in psychology, and my almost 3 years in master's level work in social work, I have only heard a minimal amount on human rights and absolutely nothing on the concept of sustainability.

Some skeptics, even social work educators, might question how much rigor and learning can be obtained in a 2-week study abroad opportunity. The authors believe that the student voices presented here do, indeed, verify that it is possible. The immersion experience is an intense one. It is like a reality TV show with all of us living, working, and traveling together 24/7 over the

2-week period. Additionally, the students complete a demanding predeparture assignment of readings and written critical reflections prior to departing for Costa Rica. They also research and write a final integrative paper when they return home following the time abroad.

Students consistently attest to the quality of the knowledge gained and of their personal and professional development, which has occurred in a relatively brief but intense period of time. The following two student quotes exemplify this:

Overall I had an amazing experience. The 2 weeks went by so quickly and yet we packed so much in. I feel like I learned an incredible amount for such a short period, I met some amazing and inspirational people, I visited some impressive organizations and I experienced the real culture of the country. I would definitely participate in another study abroad in the future.

Overall, this course has been the best learning experience of my educational career. I cannot believe how much I learned in just a 2 week period of time. I feel truly inspired and truly blessed to have this experience.

Student comments demonstrate that although the pedagogical strategy used in this course requires some changes, overall a great deal is accomplished in a relatively brief time, and student learning can be profound. The combination of predeparture readings; lectures with experts; group discussions grounded on critical questions addressing concepts, theories, and experience; journal writing; and cultural immersion activities provide the necessary instruments to advance understanding of the main concepts and issues addressed in the course. Students who register for this course are interested in influencing family and child social policies, as well as working in the future in international organizations focusing on the human rights of different populations, especially women and children. This experience prepares for a critical approach to issues, policies, and legislation from a human rights and gender perspective, as well as a cross-cultural understanding of U.S. and Latin American relations.

A large segment of the Latino population living in Virginia and Washington, DC, is of Central American origin. This course provides future practitioners with a broader understanding of the culture of these residents and facilitates incorporating a human rights perspective into social work practice. Students live a process of immersion that critically questions stereotypes, prejudice, myths, and concepts of social work practice grounded on asymmetrical power relations.

Outcomes Related to Women's and Children's Rights

Students from the United States, including the students in our course, typically are shocked to learn the United States is one of the only countries in the world that has not ratified either the CRC or the CEDAW. Furthermore, students from the United States are typically unaware of or unfamiliar with the international human rights system and all its relevant instruments or human rights documents. Some may have heard of the Universal Declaration of Human Rights but are not familiar with the CRC, CEDAW, or other human rights instruments. This clearly reflects the lack of human rights education, especially in the United States, and the need for the UN World Programme on Human Rights Education. Our course thus plays an important role in addressing this shortcoming in U.S. education.

Another important outcome of the course is that the students are challenged to critically reflect on and incorporate into their professional lens or framework the notion that possession of human rights for women, children, and others is not contingent on their nation state ratifying a treaty. The human rights literature and our seminar content and process all serve to reinforce that we are all born with these inalienable human rights, regardless of whether our governments, laws, policies, and programs recognize them.

Formal Course Evaluations

Consistent with a human rights framework, we used an alternative to the more traditional and typical numeric rating system for course evaluation. Ours was more person-centered, qualitative, ongoing, and participatory, emphasizing critical reflections on course and self, and it was formative in nature. Evaluation was oral and written and was cognitive and affective in nature. Students were asked to critically reflect on, analyze, and synthesize observations, learning, and questioning from the course content and process. Their critical reflections covered the entire course from orientation and predeparture reading assignments through the final integrative research paper completed after their return home. Students were also asked to address their experience of crossing cultures. Means of feedback included daily written journal entries while in Costa Rica; periodic participant and instructor group debriefing meetings at the end of the day; and a final meeting at the end of the seminar prior to departing Costa Rica to share experiences, learning, remaining questions, and provide feedback to each other and the instructors. Students also submitted along with their final paper an integrative final reflections paper on their overall course experience. It is the instructors'/authors' belief that this type of course evaluation becomes an instrument for promoting development of critical thinking, conceptual refinement, increased self-awareness, and purposeful use of self, as well as other skills needed to become an effective change agent to advance human rights and sustainable human development.

Next Steps and Challenges

Our critical reflections on our experience co-teaching this study abroad seminar leads us to the following list of next steps to build on successes and further improve the experience for participating students, faculty, and other collaborators. These steps can serve as guidelines to address further evolution and development of this and other study abroad offerings in the future.

- Include social work students from Costa Rica to guarantee a stronger cultural exchange. However, steps are required to build this participation with financial equity, because most Costa Rican students cannot pay the cost of GMU tuition.
- Guarantee an equitable distribution of benefits for both universities.
- Expand this experience to social work faculty members in the United States. Experiences of this nature can provide the instruments required to introduce changes in the curriculum according to the CSWE mandate.
- Enhance dialogue and transdisciplinary experiences between students and faculty.

- Include intensive voluntary service learning as a way of giving back to communities and organizations providing services to U.S. students.
- Build in a Spanish language study opportunity for those interested; perhaps make available an optional 2 to 4 week language immersion program immediately prior to or following the course.
- The course can become a platform for collaborative comparative faculty research and extension projects.

In sharing our experience and encouraging other social work programs to genuinely add a human rights framework into curricula, we propose the following questions to consider and help guide efforts to truly incorporate human rights content into the social work curriculum.

- Are students actually learning about the international human rights system and all the human rights instruments (declarations and binding treaties)?
- Are they learning a holistic view of human rights that perceives civil, political, economic, social, cultural, and collective rights as inseparable and that no single category or human right is more important than another?
- Are they learning about ways that a human rights framework has shaped policy and practice in much of the rest of the world and in some situations in the United States?
- Are they learning about the meaning and value added of moving from a needs-based to a rights-based conceptualization of social work, policy, programs, and services?
- Are they learning about the interrelatedness of human rights and human development?
- Are they learning about human development from a holistic and global perspective that moves beyond the typical focus on individual bio-psycho-social development across the various lifespan stages to one that embraces a human ecology viewpoint with a holistic view of persons and environment across all systems levels from the micro through

the macro, from the local through the global, while recognizing the interconnectedness among human development and social and economic and political development?

The authors would like to end with these exemplary words from a student revealing a number of the major course themes.

Over the past 2 weeks I have had some amazing experiences, and have learned so much about gender and about the importance of human rights in development. Prior to this trip, I had not made a real connection between human rights and development. I am interested in development because I want to help people have better lives. I think a lot of people are driven by this sort of "humanitarian impulse." While this is okay, it is more of a needs-based approach. We see people who have needs and want to help them. It is more like charity. A rights-based approach is based in the human right to development and the idea that individuals and states have an obligation to guarantee the rights of individuals. From this perspective, we can't do development just because we want to help. We have an imperative to assure people their rights and an obligation to eliminate poverty....Especially in the United States, we are not focused on human rights, and think of both social services and foreign assistance as charity. But the State has an obligation to its citizens, and because the global economy is so interconnected and we benefit economically from the exploitation of people in other countries, we have an obligation to people all over the world.

References

Boyle, D. P., Nackerud, L., & Kilpatrick, A. (1999). The road less traveled: Cross-cultural, international experiential learning. *International Social Work, 42,* 201–214.

Council on Social Work Education (CSWE). (2008). *Educational policy and accreditation standards.* Retrieved from http://www.cswe.org/File. aspx?id=13780

Fairchild, S. R., Pillai, V. K., & Noble, C. (2006). The impact of a social work study abroad program in Australia on multicultural learning. *International Social Work, 49*, 390–401. doi: 10.1177/0020872806063413

Gammonley, D., Smith Rotabi, K., & Gamble, D. N. (2007). Enhancing global understanding with study abroad: Ethically grounded approaches to international learning. *Journal of Teaching in Social Work, 27*(3/4), 115–135. doi:10.1300/J067v27n03_08

Greenfield, E. A., Davis, R. T., & Fedor, J. P. (2012). The effect of international social work education: Study abroad versus on-campus courses. *Journal of Social Work Education, 48*, 739–761. doi: 10.5175/JSWE.2012.201100147

Healy, L. (2008). *International social work: Professional action in an interdependent world.* New York, NY: Oxford University Press.

Human Rights Resource Center, University of Minnesota. (2000). *The human rights education handbook: Effective practices for learning, action, and change.* Minneapolis, MN: University of Minnesota Human Rights Center.

Jaoko, J. (2010). Study abroad: Enhanced learning experiences in cultural diversity. *College Quarterly, 13*(4). Retrieved from www.senecacollege.ca /quarterly/2010-vol13-num04/jaoko.html

Kreitzer, L., Barlow, C., Schwartz, K., Lacroix, M., & Macdonald, L. (2012). Canadian and EU social work students in a cross-cultural program: What they learned from the experience. *International Social Work, 55*, 245–265. doi: 10.1177/0020872811427047

Lager. P. B., Mathiesen, S. G., Rodgers, M. E., & Cox, S. E. (2010). *Guidebook for international field placements and student exchanges: Planning, implementation, and sustainability.* Alexandria, VA: CSWE Press.

Lindsey, E. W. (2005). Study abroad and values development in social work. *Journal of Social Work Education, 41*, 229–249. doi: 10.5175/JSWE.2005 .200303110

Mapp, S. (2008). *Human rights and social justice in a global perspective: An introduction to international social work.* New York, NY: Oxford University Press.

Merrill, M. C., & Frost, C. J. (2011). Internationalizing social work education: Models, methods and meanings. *Frontiers: The Interdisciplinary Journal of Study Abroad,* XXI, 189 – 210.

Panos, P. T., Pettys, G. L., Cox, S. E., & Jones-Hart, E. (2004) Research note: Survey of international field education placements of accredited schools of social work. *Journal of Social Work Education, 40*, 467–478.

Reichert, E. (Ed.). (2007). *Challenges in human rights: A social work perspective.* New York, NY: Columbia University Press.

United Nations (UN). (1948, December 10). *Universal declaration of human rights.* G.A. Res. 217 A (III). Retrieved from http://www.refworld.org /docid/3ae6b3712c.html

United Nations (UN). (1966a, December 16). *International covenant on civil and political rights.* G.A. Res. 2200A (XXI). Retrieved from http://www.ohchr.org /Documents/ProfessionalInterest/ccpr.pdf

United Nations (UN). (1966b, December 16). *International covenant on economic, social, and cultural rights.* G.A. Res. 2200A (XXI). Retrieved from http://www. ohchr.org/EN/ProfessionalInterest/Pages/CESCR.aspx

United Nations (UN). (1979, December 18). *Convention on the elimination of all forms of discrimination against women.* G.A. Res. 34/180. Retrieved from http://www.ohchr.org/Documents/ProfessionalInterest/cedaw.pdf

United Nations (UN). (1986, December 4). *Declaration on the right to development.* G. A. Res. 41/128. Retrieved from http://www.un.org/documents/ga/res/41 /a41r128.htm

United Nations (UN). (1989, November 20). *Convention on the rights of the child.* G.A. Res. 44/25. Retrieved from http://www.ohchr.org/Documents /ProfessionalInterest/crc.pdf

United Nations (UN). (2004). General Assembly proclaims World Programme for Human Rights Education, stressing its importance to the realization of all fundamental freedoms. (Press release) GA/13017. Retrieved from http://www .un.org/News/Press/docs/2004/ga10317.doc.htm

United Nations World Programme for Human Rights Education. (2014). *World programme for human rights education (2005-ongoing).* Retrieved from www.ohchr.org/EN/Issues/Education/Training/Pages/Programme.aspx

Wronka, J. (2008). *Human rights and social justice: Social action and service for the helping and health professions.* Thousand Oaks, CA: SAGE.

18 | Interprofessional Global Health Education: Human Rights and the Role of the Social Worker

Jody Olsen and Anusha Chatterjee

Health inequalities are a vital human rights and social justice issue that negatively affect social work and social development agendas around the world. The International Federation of Social Workers (IFSW) highlights the interface between inequitable distribution of health and the inequitable distribution of other valuable resources (IFSW, 2012). Bywaters, McLeod, and Napier (2009) stress the importance of understanding inequities in access to health care as powerful markers of social injustice standing in contravention to human rights, making it a vital social work issue. The IFSW statement on health urges social workers across borders to recognize health inequalities as a social work issue rooted in structural and institutional arrangements and policies that require change.

This chapter discusses the human right to health and the important role of interprofessional practice in fulfilling that right. To do this, the authors draw on the example of one particular model of international interprofessional health education experience, sponsored by the University of Maryland, Baltimore. The model is used to train social workers to practice in interprofessional global health settings. It discusses the social work student role in the global health project and implications for social workers interested in human rights and global health, whether in the United States or abroad.

Ten years ago, the World Health Organization (WHO) commissioned a group to "marshal the evidence on what can be done to promote health equity and to foster a global movement to achieve it" (World Health Organization Commission on Social Determinants of Health, 2008, p. 1). This Commission on Social Determinants of Health then published a report in 2008 that laid out a new global agenda for health equity and introduced a conceptual framework for social determinants of health and health inequities. The commission took a holistic view of social determinants of health when it indicated:

> Where systematic differences in health are judged to be avoidable by reasonable action they are, quite simply, unfair. It is this that we label health inequity. Putting right these inequities—the huge and remediable differences in health between and within countries—is a matter of social justice. Reducing health inequities is, for the Commission on Social Determinants of Health, an ethical imperative. Social injustice is killing people on a grand scale (WHO, 2008, as quoted in the unnumbered Executive Summary).

The commission's overarching recommendations, on which the conceptual framework is based, include the following:

- Improve daily living conditions
- Tackle the inequitable distribution of power, money, and resources
- Measure and understand the problem and assess the impact of action (WHO, 2008, p. 2).

This report and subsequent work have further framed the conclusions. Navarro indicated, "It is not the *inequalities* that kill people, as the WHO report states; it is *those who are responsible for these inequalities* that kill people" (Navarro, 2009, p. 423). Because of this WHO report, professionals in the global health community are seeing health inequality as a social justice or human rights issue. This offers important and expanded roles for the social work profession.

As the WHO Commission report states, some of the key determinants of health care are social and are linked to key human rights issues. Globally, access to health care is determined by social and economic conditions including socially constructed identities such as gender, ethnicity, and nationality (Bywaters et al., 2009). Larger macro-forces such as economic restructuring and globalization have also negatively affected chances for universal access to health care (Global Health Watch, 2005). Poor health care is closely associated with poverty. This is especially evident in countries where globalization and its associated factors have resulted in a shift from public to private health care services. In many cases, this implies high out-of-pocket expenditures leading to increased poverty, putting even basic health care out of reach for many. These complex socioeconomic and political drivers of health care have disadvantaged some individuals, communities, and countries more than others, making it a vital social justice and human rights issue. This is clearly indicative of why a multifaceted engagement with the pervasive ill-effects of health inequities through policy formulation, service design, research, and education is needed (Bywaters et al., 2009).

At the level of the individual, social workers in health and other settings play a key role in helping clients access health care and other resources, navigate health care systems, and manage their health conditions in ways that improve their overall well-being. In communities, social workers raise awareness on health related issues, focusing on the importance of prevention, promoting better health practices, and improving community attitudes and perceptions about certain diseases. At the policy level, the role of the social worker lies in advocating for necessary changes to make health care accessible to all.

The social worker's role in health settings globally is guided by the social work principle of respecting the inherent worth and dignity of all people (IFSW, 2012). The roots of this are clearly articulated in the IFSW and International Association of Schools of Social Work (2004) document *Ethics in Social Work: Statement of Principles*, which involves treating each person as a whole, respecting the right to self-determination, promoting the right to participation, and identifying and developing strengths.

Human rights are an integral value that informs social work education and practice. Staub-Bernasconi (2012) discusses that human rights should be a central regulative idea that informs the whole discipline and practice of social work. Health is an important human rights issue and social workers have an important role to play. The World Health Organization (WHO, 2013) lists ways in which human rights are linked to health with (1) the violations or lack of attention to human rights potentially leading to serious health consequences; (2) the design or implementation of health and social policies and programs promoting or violating human rights; and (3) the reduction of vulnerability by taking steps to respect, protect or fulfill human rights. Social work can play a vital role in all three aspects, attempting to reduce violations of human rights, advocating for better policies and programs that protect and promote human rights, and integrating elements into social work practice that facilitate the implementation of such policies.

Interprofessional Education and Global Health

Although understanding global health inequities is vital to social work training and practice, it is crucial for social workers to be able to work in interprofessional teams. The IFSW policy statement on health also discusses the need for social workers globally to engage with policy, education, research and practice in the field of health, working closely with members of different health and other disciplines (Bywaters et al., 2009). Research has shown that working "across disciplines is essential for effective, competent and culturally sensitive health care delivery" (Pecukonis, Doyle, & Bliss, 2008, p. 417).

The Institute of Medicine (IOM), at its workshop titled "Establishing Transdisciplinary Professionalism for Health," stated that a "new professionalism" is needed throughout health care and wellness that emphasizes cross-disciplinary responsibility to improve outcomes (IOM, 2014, p. xiv). In its conference statement of tasks the IOM defined transdisciplinary as "an approach to creating and carrying out a shared social contract that ensures multiple health disciplines, working in concert, are worthy of the trust of patients and the public" (IOM, 2014, p. 43). The IOM is leading efforts to bring interprofessional teams to the health related disciplines and professions, and social workers are being invited into these newer health service frameworks.

The importance of social workers to work in collaboration with professionals across other health and social care settings is echoed in the principles that guide interprofessional education and practice. The invocation of interprofessional education (IPE) by policy makers, educators, and social care professionals internationally (Department of Health, 1995) has resulted in a demonstrated positive effect on improving collaborative competencies of individuals across different professions, facilitating the development of greater knowledge and skills as well as improvement in care and service delivery (Hammick, Freeth, Koppel, Reeves, & Barr, 2007). IPE has been increasingly acknowledged as an important foundation in preparing professionals working in the area of health care, with WHO adding IPE to its global agenda and acknowledging it as a prerequisite for improved health care outcomes (Riva et al., 2010; WHO, 2010). The need for integration of the continuum of care and sustained integrated services is clear (Cashman, Reidy, Cody, & Lemay, 2004; Dieleman et al., 2004; European Public Health Associates, 2002; Howarth, Holland, & Grant, 2006). WHO (2004) has also focused on the importance of establishing integrated care that is available, accessible, comprehensive, and efficient in developing countries.

A Model of International Interprofessional Student Health Projects

Educators in the field of international social work acknowledge that international field placements have the potential to play a key role in helping students to develop broader cultural horizons and the necessary skills to practice in a globalized world (Lough, McBride, & Sherraden, 2012; Wehbi, 2008). However, these international placements are still relatively limited, and the role of social work students in international interprofessional field placements is even more limited.

However, social work students can have opportunities to participate in shorter field experiences as part of academic interprofessional global health projects. In these experience models, student academic credit is linked to course credit rather than field based credit, which offers more flexibility for the field experience. This type of student experience integrates social workers into global health projects, which also helps them build interprofessional skills for use later in more traditional health care professions.

The next section reports on one particular model of international interprofessional health education experience sponsored by the University of Maryland, Baltimore and offers the opportunity to train social workers to practice in global health interprofessional settings. The University of Maryland, Baltimore organizes a 6-week summer interprofessional research project in Malawi to provide students with practice experience in the field of global health. Students from the professional schools (dentistry, law, medicine, nursing, pharmacy, and social work) are selected for conducting a research project in the community with guidance and assistance from faculty from the different schools.

The program has been in place for 4 years and has focused on different areas, including access to health care for orphans and vulnerable children, access to health care for children with fevers, and maternal health and human rights, as well as how communities assess health care priorities. The latter used a community based Participatory Analysis for Community Action project design that includes community mapping, daily activity schedule, seasonal calendars, and priority ranking (Peace Corps Information Collection and Exchange, 2005).

During each summer program, faculty member responsibilities have included supporting the integrative model, ensuring research integrity, and encouraging student discussion of themes emerging from student observations and data collection. Funded by the University of Maryland Global Health Interprofessional Council (GHIC), the university's Institutional Review Board and the equivalent institutional review board mechanism in Malawi approved the projects.

The 6-week interprofessional projects draw on logistic support and health network knowledge from the university's in-country staff and faculty of its multiyear Malaria research programs in Blantyre, Malawi, to keep costs very low and have appropriate permission to work in the rural southern Malawi district. The GHIC, which sponsors these projects, has now set up the Malawi University of Maryland Partnership Fund to support very small-scale community initiated health center repairs in the communities where students conduct their work. Money is transferred through the University of Maryland malaria team, who can also ensure its proper distribution and use. For example, a new roof on the health clinic in the village of Mfera ensures continued care during rainstorms, previously not possible. The Mfera clinic health officer explained this critical need and its effects on women at the clinic to the UMB students, as it was not obvious to those there for only a short time.

The 2012 Malawi student project, the third of four summer projects, focused on maternal mortality and morbidity, and the research design used the WHO's Safe Motherhood Needs Assessment (WHO, 2001) to evaluate interventions related to safe motherhood in the Chikhwawa District of southern Malawi. This was a highly relevant topic because Malawi has 460 maternal deaths for 100,000 births, one of the higher ratios globally (WHO, 2010). These data reveal the failure to secure rights under Article 25(2) of the Universal Declaration of Human Rights, namely that "Motherhood and childhood are entitled to special care and assistance" (United Nations, 1948).

Before the students began the program in 2012, faculty members and students met in four 2-hour sessions over 2 months. These meetings included presentations on global health, maternal health, and ethics from a social work perspective and discussions about Malawi, culture, nonjudging observations and journal writing, and the project itself. This began the students' interprofessional team development before going to Malawi and helped them understand a country on a continent that only three of the 12 students had seen before.

Once in the country, students gathered data by surveying the 10 district maternal health clinics and two rural hospitals using nine assessment instruments included in the Safe Motherhood protocol. They reviewed and analyzed the results and prepared summary reports of their findings for each of the health clinics and for the district health director.

Data collection included reviews of medical charts; assessment of clinic equipment and supplies; and interviews of antenatal, health clinic staff, and traditional birth assistants. The students worked in mixed professional teams of two, rotating data gathering functions as they visited individual clinics to ensure that every discipline partnered with every other discipline at some point during the surveys and that every student participated in each of the nine data gathering functions. For example, the social work student reviewed medical charts with the nursing student at one center and then conducted antenatal interviews with the dental student at another center. This protocol encouraged students to understand the elements of maternal health care delivery through each other's professional perspectives and to appreciate how each delivery function contributes to the totality of maternal health care delivery.

The students worked during the final week to analyze data, prepare reports, report back to the health center directors with individualized report summaries, and prepare the final report as a group, always working across disciplines and asking all group members to read drafts being developed. For example, they discussed presenting their observations on traditional birth attendants' (TBAs') influences on antenatal clinic care; child delivery at clinics without access to water, electricity, or sterilized equipment; and access to health centers when mothers in labor are a 24-hour walk away. Students understood more clearly the complexities, specificities, and realities of trying to realize the right of women to maternal health care, which were first elaborated in the Universal Declaration of Human Rights in Article 25(2).

The students' presentation of the data to the 12 health clinic directors on the last day was important to their sense of project completion and, as one student said, to "giving back." Each project director received his own report summary from a student and saw from the barriers to health data that his clinic closely tracked data from the other clinics in the district. Clinic directors chose to share their individual reports with each other. Two directors volunteered at the end that no one had ever given them feedback before and how important this feedback was to them. They expressed the most comments back to the students about the data showing the appreciation the antenatal interviewees had for the health workers, particularly after the initial health center visit, an appreciation the health workers had not understood before (GHIC, 2012). This feedback reinforced their commitment to caring for the women despite poor facilities and limited equipment.

A Human Rights Approach

A section of the final report, drafted primarily by a social work and a law student, focused on the human rights perspective of maternal health. This topic was not previously familiar to most students and faculty members but was an acknowledged critical component of framing policy recommendations to save women's lives. The GHIC student report looked at "whether gaps in prevention and treatment of maternal mortality indicated a violation of women's and provider's human rights" (GHIC, 2012, p. 35). The students drew direct links between health clinic observations and a woman's human rights. They focused on life, health (including access to food, water, and shelter), dignity and privacy, gender discrimination, and culture.

Human rights encompass society values and behaviors and the variability of enforcement within societies is based on these values and beliefs. This was seen throughout the study. For example, at the national level, although Malawi has ratified the International Covenant on Social, Economic, and Cultural Rights (United Nations, 1966), the section of its own constitution promoting the right to health comes under Principles of National Policy. Thus, the constitution is a guide for making policy and not a guaranteed right (Constitution of the Republic of Malawi, 1995).

At the local level the intersection of human rights and beliefs is even more observable. Through the years village women relied on TBAs to assist in giving birth. TBAs' skills were passed down by tradition, not formal training. Currently, in Malawi 49% of births occur outside health centers, primarily with village based TBAs, although data are difficult to track (WHO, 2010).

The Ministry of Health has encouraged women to use the clinics, even making the use of the TBA illegal for a short time. Individual women in the student surveys expressed their initial fear of the health clinics and even of some clinic staff who had come from other tribes and regions of the country. They also expressed lack of access to the clinics and of little encouragement from others in the village, including their husbands.

Malawi's president, Joyce Banda, the second female president in Africa, has supported efforts to reduce maternal mortality. She has formed a national committee of senior village chiefs representing the three regions to help implement the WHO Safe Motherhood program. These chiefs meet regularly and in turn have invited the TBAs, whom the women trust, to be part of the program and are asking them to accompany women to health clinics for giving birth (GHIC, 2012).

The two social work students played important roles in helping the student team reach further into the data review, discussion, and recommendations and identify the human rights components of maternal health. They drew on their social work studies and previous international experiences (one had completed a 6 month vulnerable child project in Kenya; the other was a returned Peace Corps volunteer from Mozambique). They took the lead, with the law students, in identifying human rights health issues and then linking them to policy and social behavior actions.

This 2012 Malawi program was one of four 6 week summer programs, of which four of the five participating social work students had previous significant experience in Africa. Among the 31 participating students from all the schools during the 4-year period, about half had previous (at least a month) international experience but none had had experience in Malawi. Based on personal faculty observations of all four groups, having some members of an interprofessional global team with previous international experience is important in helping guide the group's integration into the new environment. In particular, the social work students, drawing on their own backgrounds, provided contextual dimension to student observations and questions. Faculty observations of the student groups suggest that the contextual discussions among the students were more effective when initiated by students themselves than when initiated by faculty members.

Building a team among the students before beginning actual travel is as important as having international experience. The previously mentioned preparation offered students a perspective on each other's discipline, a first step for the team. However, based on the GHIC faculty observations, more team building activities might have eased the group's in-country adjustment and early project preparation work (Rowthorn, & Olsen, forthcoming).

The influence team members had on each other through this Malawi program is illustrated in their comments in the last section of their paper. Their discussions and comments over the course of the summer were examples of seeing and assessing individual situations from each profession's perspective and then drawing on these individual observations to collectively frame the integrative macro perspectives.

[Medical student] Although I can now see how very connected this issue (domestic violence) is to maternal health, this topic never crossed my mind.

I think the social work approach really broadens the picture and gives a more holistic view and is an example of why I think interdisciplinary work is so important and the only way to truly help people. (GHIC, 2012, p. 47)

[Social work student] I knew hypertension and eclampsia were leading causes of maternal mortality, but I did not put all of the information together until the medical perspective was explained to me. This information helps me understand the importance of the protein test and I can now use this to help educate patients on an individual level and to influence the Ministry of Health to supply health centers with this test on a policy and macro-level. (GHIC, 2012, p. 46)

[Dental student] No physiological system in the body is isolated-everything interplays. While on this program I learned that pharmacy encompasses more than just drugs-supply chain changes and distribution. Law encompasses human rights and right to healthcare. Social work looks beyond the immediate issue and takes into account circumstances that exist beyond the focal problem. Nurses think about patients first and interact closely with them. Medicine focuses on treatment of pathology. Everyone has a different background-professionally and personally-and so collaboration creates an amalgam of ideologies that comes closer to understanding the macro issue. (GHIC, 2012, p. 44)

All five social work students participating in the Malawi programs have now begun careers related to their experience. Three are working for U.S.-based international nongovernmental organizations on health related projects, one is part of a U.S.-based international refugee settlement program, and one is integrating the social determinants model into local social work related training programs. They have been invited back to share their experiences with current social work students in classes and school-wide forums.

Based on the Malawi experience, in January 2014 an interdisciplinary student team, of which half were social work students, worked in partnership with Haifa University, Israel. The social work students observed health and social justice issues in West Haifa. The Haifa University social work students are planning to partner with an interprofessional University of Maryland, Baltimore team in 2015 to repeat the model in West Baltimore. This is only one of several examples of new faculty and student generated interprofessional international opportunities emerging from the Malawi model.

This Malawi model draws in non–health science professions such as social work and law and fully integrates them into global health policy and service delivery to foster broader interest (GHIC, 2010, 2011, 2012). Based on this model, the GHIC at the University of Maryland is now beginning to focus on developing an interprofessional skills domain to be added to existing global health education competencies. To further emphasize the importance of this domain, the president of the University of Maryland, Baltimore is linking the GHIC work with that of the IPE campus-wide council focused on interprofessional patient care. Returning Malawi student teams have presented their project results and their implications to domestic activity in Baltimore at campus forums and school specific gatherings.

The interprofessional global health competencies include valuing the role of different professions in global health practice; building strong team and communication skills; and furthering the ability to identify, frame, and address important health problems and issues that cut across disciplinary boundaries. The interprofessional competency domain should not be specific to a single profession and should be broad enough to incorporate students from fields that have been left out of traditional global health education initiatives (GHIC, 2013). Because this skills domain within interprofessional global health education can be articulated and codified, social work education will be able to claim a strong presence within global health and its human rights components (Rowthorn & Olsen, forthcoming).

Implications for International Social Work Practice

Koplan et al. (2009) posit the following description of global health:

> global health is an area for study, research, and practice that places a priority on improving health and achieving equity in health for all people world-

wide. Global health emphasizes transnational health issues, determinants, and solutions; involves many disciplines within and beyond the health sciences and promotes interdisciplinary collaboration; and is a synthesis of population based prevention with individual-level clinical care. (p. 1995)

The IFSW (2002) includes in its definition of social work that "social work intervenes at the points where people interact with their environments. Principles of human rights and social justice are fundamental to social work." As this chapter highlights, at the intersection of these two definitions is the opportunity for social workers to play critical roles in global health. Social workers train to work interprofessionally and increasingly are trained to work globally. They can and should be integrated partners in global health teams focused on care delivery, program and systems development, policy formulation, and advocacy for health as a basic human right.

As the implications of the WHO report on the social determinants of health reach further into the global health donor and organization implementation communities, health inequality as a human rights issue is becoming a more prominent issue across the disciplines. The social work profession should be an integral part of framing and implementing global health policy and practice nationally and globally.

References

Bywaters, P., McLeod, E., & Napier, L. (2009). *Social work and global health inequalities: Practice and policy developments.* Bristol, UK: Policy Press.

Cashman S. B., Reidy P., Cody K., & Lemay C. A. (2004). Developing and measuring progress toward collaborative, integrated, interdisciplinary health care teams. *Journal of Interprofessional Care, 18*(2), 183–196.

Constitution of the Republic of Malawi. (1995). Retrieved from http://www.icrc.org/ihlnat.nsf/162d151af444ded44125673e00508141/4953f2286ef1f7c2c1257129003696f4/$FILE/Constitution%20Malawi%20-%20EN.pdf

Department of Health. (1995). *Child protection: Messages from research.* London, UK: Author.

Dieleman, S. L., Farris, K. B., Feeny D., Johnson, J.A., Tsuyuli, R. T., & Brilliant S. (2004) Primary health care teams: team members' perceptions of the collaborative process. *Journal of Interprofessional Care, 18*(1), 75–78.

European Public Health Associates. (2002) *Integrated care in an international perspective.* Brussels, Belgium: Author.

Global Health Interprofessional Council (GHIC). (2010, September). *Reducing barriers to interdisciplinary professional training: The Malawi case study.* Poster session at Consortium of Universities for Global Health annual conference, Seattle, WA.

Global Health Interprofessional Council (GHIC). (2011, November). *Interdisciplinary healthcare access survey in rural Malawi.* Poster session at Consortium of Universities for Global Health annual conference, Montreal, Canada.

Global Health Interprofessional Council (GHIC). (2012). *Maternal morbidity and mortality in Chikhwawa Dsitrict, Malawi: An interprofessional assessment.* Retrieved http://global.umaryland.edu/ghic/documents/2012FinalMalawiPaper.pdf

Global Health Interprofessional Council (GHIC). (2013). *Events: Building a team.* Retrieved from http://global.umaryland.edu/ghic/event/fall2013conf.html

Global Health Watch. (2005). *Global health watch 2005–2006: An alternative world health report.* London, UK: Zed Books.

Hammick, M., Freeth, D., Koppel, I., Reeves, S., & Barr, H. (2007). A best evidence systematic review of interprofessional education: BEME Guide no. 9. *Medical teacher, 29*(8), 735–751.

Howarth, M., Holland, K., & Grant, M. J. (2006). Education needs for integrated care: A literature review. *Journal of Advanced Nursing, 56*(2), 144–156.

Institute of Medicine. (2014). Establishing transdisciplinary professionalism for improving health outcomes: Workshop summary. Retrieved from http://www.nap.edu/download.php?record_id=18398#

International Federation of Social Workers. (IFSW). (2002). Definition of social work. Retrieved from http://ifsw.org/policies/definition-of-social-work/

International Federation of Social Workers (IFSW). (2012, February 20). *Health.* Retrieved from http://ifsw.org/policies/health/

International Federation of Social Workers (IFSW) & International Association of Schools of Social Work. (2004). *Ethics in social work: Statement of principles.* Retrieved from www.ifsw.org

Koplan, J. P., Bond, T. C., Merson, M. H., Reddy, K. S., Rodriguez, M. H., Sewankambo, N. K., & Wasserheit, J. N. (2009). Towards a common definition of global health. *The Lancet, 373*(9679), 1993–1995.

Lough, B. J., McBride, A. M., & Sherraden, M. S. (2012). Measuring international service outcomes: Implications for international social work field placements. *Journal of Social Work Education, 48*, 479–499. doi: 10.5175 /JSWE.2012.201000047

Navarro, V. (2009). What we mean by social determinants of health. *International Journal of Health Services, 39*(3), 423–441.

Peace Corps Information Collection and Exchange (2005). *PACA: Participatory analysis for community action.* (Publication No. M0086) Retrieved from http://files.peacecorps.gov/library/M0086.pdf

Pecukonis, E., Doyle, O., & Bliss, D. L. (2008). Reducing barriers to interprofessional training: Promoting interprofessional cultural competence. *Journal of Interprofessional Care. 22*, 417–428.

Riva, J., Lam, J., Stanford, E., Moore, A., Endicott, A., & Krawchenko, I. (2010). Interprofessional education through shadowing experiences in multi-disciplinary clinical settings. *Chiropractic & Osteopathy, 18*, 1–5.

Rowthorn, V., & Olsen, J. (forthcoming). All together now: Developing a team competency domain for global health education. *Journal of Law, Medicine & Ethics.*

Staub-Bernasconi, S. (2012). Human rights and their relevance for social work as theory and practice. In L. M. Healy, & R. J. Link (Eds.), *Handbook of international social work: Human rights, development, and the global profession* (pp. 30–36). New York, NY: Oxford University Press.

United Nations. (1948, December 10). *Universal declaration of human rights.* G.A. Res. 217 A (III). Retrieved from http://www.refworld.org/docid/3ae6b3712c .html

United Nations. (1966, December 16). *International covenant on economic, social, and cultural rights.* G.A. Res. 2200A (XXI). Retrieved from http://www.ohchr .org/EN/ProfessionalInterest/Pages/CESCR.aspx

Wehbi, S. (2008). Teaching international social work: A guiding framework. *Canadian Social Work Review [Revue Canadienne de service social], 25*(2), 117–132.

World Health Organization (WHO). (2001). *Safe motherhood needs assessment (Version 1.1).* Geneva, Switzerland: Department of Reproductive Health and Research.

World Health Organization (WHO). (2004). *International plan of action on aging: Report on implementation. Report by the Secretariat.* (EB115/29). Retrieved from: http://www.who.int/gb/ebwha/pdf_files/EB115/B115_29-en.pdf

World Health Organization (WHO). (2010). *Women and health: Maternal mortality ratio by country.* Retrieved from http://apps.who.int/gho/data/node.main.214

World Health Organization (WHO). (2013). *Linkages between health and human rights.* Retrieved from http://www.who.int/hhr/HHR%20linkages.pdf

World Health Organization Commission on the Social Determinants of Health. (2008). *Closing the gap in a generation: Health equity through action on the social determinants of health. Commission on Social Determinants of Health final report.* Retrieved from http://whqlibdoc.who.int/publications/2008/9789241563703_eng.pdf?ua=1

19 Expanding Children's Rights in Jamaica Through an International Educational Partnership

Barris P. Malcolm

The Universal Declaration of Human Rights was adopted by the United Nations (UN) General Assembly on December 10, 1948 (UN, 1948) in Paris and translated into legally binding treaties in 1966 through the Covenant on Civil and Political Rights (UN, 1966a) and the Covenant on Economic, Social and Cultural Rights (UN, 1966b). Although the treaties are widely accepted in principle, for some countries that joined the treaties extenuating circumstances, mainly poverty, threaten the implementation, expansion, and monitoring of these rights. Often, among some lesser developed countries poverty has been identified as the most powerful suppressor of the advancement and monitoring of fundamental human rights. This appears to be the case in Jamaica. Pogge (2005) has established the important connection between poverty and human rights violations by stating that, "most of the current massive under fulfillment of human rights is more or less directly connected to poverty" (p.1).

This chapter is based on acceptance of the importance and relevance of social work as a human rights profession and the need for social work education to advance this perspective. The chapter discusses an international exchange partnership between the University of Connecticut School of Social Work (UConn) through its Center for International Social Work Studies and the Social Work Unit of the Department of Sociology, Psychology, and Social Work at the University of the West Indies (UWI) in Jamaica. It identifies ways in which the relationship strengthened understanding of human rights for both partners. Further, the chapter explores how an international partnership and collaboration in social work education helped in addressing and overcoming major challenges, including poverty and tradition, as serious threats to advancing and protecting certain human rights in Jamaica, with an emphasis on children's rights. Additionally the chapter reflects critically about the accomplishments in using the extended international collaboration and partnership model. Before discussing the effects of the collaboration, the partnership will be introduced and the context of human rights in Jamaica briefly summarized. Data were gathered for this chapter from a wide variety of sources, including journals, government reports, and newspaper articles, as well as anecdotal sources such as conversations and meetings.

The UWI-UConn Partnership

The partnership between the Social Work Unit of UWI and UConn was previously documented in publications including those by Maxwell and Healy, (2003); Healy, Asamoah, and Hokenstad (2003); and Healy, Maxwell, and Pine (1999). The two programs began to collaborate out of mutual interest. In the case of UConn, its location within the Greater Hartford area brought it in contact with large concentrations of immigrants from the West Indian Diaspora. Because Jamaicans constitute the largest population among this group in Greater Hartford, and with the intent of being more culturally competent and to learn more about immigration, UConn social work faculty members sought a connection with the Social Work Unit at UWI in Jamaica. According to Maxwell and Healy (2003), the initial formal contacts were made in 1992. Faculty exchange visits were made in 1993 and 1994 and a Memorandum of Agreement was signed in 1995. Since then, exchange visits and collaborative projects have continued for two decades.

Areas of mutual interest between the partners are migration, social welfare management, human rights, child welfare, HIV/AIDS, sickle cell disease, and field education (Healy, 2008). Human rights issues were present as a subtheme in most of the work of the partnership, including work on migration, HIV/AIDS, and child welfare. Activities and projects that have occurred include brief exchanges as well as more extended visits for lecture duties by faculty of the two institutions. Students of the institutions have also made brief visits, and several students have completed the field education practice requirement in a variety of Jamaican or Connecticut social agencies, respectively. Connecticut faculty and students have attended and participated in several regional conferences in Jamaica and other places in the West Indies, including a major co-sponsored conference in 1999. Joint publications have resulted, and the partnership also assisted in launching a peer-reviewed journal of social work for the Caribbean region (Maxwell & Healy, 2003). The partnership has been an active one and has been mutually beneficial to stakeholders in Jamaica, Connecticut, and beyond. From the outset the partnership was based on the principle of mutuality and was conducted in concert with human rights principles.

The following excerpt is from the UN *Human Rights Based Approach Statement of Common Understanding* and summarizes the required elements of policy development and service delivery using a human rights approach (Stamford Interagency Workshop on a Human Rights-Based Approach in the Context of UN Reform, 2003). The principles outlined are also highly applicable to collaborations in social work education, such as the one discussed here. They inform a human-rights based approach to partnerships.

1) People are recognized as key actors in their own development, rather than passive recipients of commodities and services.

2) Participation is both a means and a goal.

3) Strategies are empowering, not disempowering.

4) Both outcomes and processes are monitored and evaluated.

5) Analysis includes all stakeholders.

6) Programs focus on marginalized, disadvantaged, and excluded groups.

7) The development process is locally owned.

8) Programs aim to reduce disparity.

9) Both top-down and bottom-up approaches are used in synergy.

10) Situation analysis is used to identity immediate, underlying, and basic causes of development problems.

11) Measurable goals and targets are important in programming.

12) Strategic partnerships are developed and sustained

13) Programmes support accountability to all stakeholders. (Stamford Interagency Workshop on a Human Rights-Based Approach in the Context of UN Reform, 2003)

The Context: Social Work Programs of the Partners

It is in this context that a human rights-based approach to graduate level social work education is being developed at UConn and UWI. This pedagogical approach is intentional for preparing social work practitioners to be human rights advocates. For example, in its academic plan, UConn has established the connection between social work education and human rights as reflected by the following:

> The mission of the University of Connecticut School of Social Work is to provide professional master's and doctoral level social work education which will contribute to the promotion of social and economic justice, human rights, and the improvement of human wellbeing. (UConn School of Social Work, 2009, p. 3)

This fits well with the 2008 Educational Policy and Accreditation Standards adopted by the Council on Social Work Education (CSWE, 2008a). Educational Policy 2.1.5 mandates that social work education must address human rights and economic justice as well as elevate competencies among social workers to advocate for human rights. Intrinsically, social work education must also involve human rights education as a deliberate participatory practice aimed at empowering individuals, groups, and communities through fostering knowledge, skills, and attitudes consistent with internationally recognized human rights principles.

The academic plan adopted by UConn also outlines several goals and strategic steps for achieving this mission. The school has gained much attention as an institution that promotes social and economic justice and human rights and is a major source for MSW-qualified graduates in Connecticut. The school has a strong international program, and the curriculum has been enriched with more international content to prepare graduates with global perspectives for research, education, and practice. It offers an elective specialization in international issues and has had a Center for International Social Work Studies to expand credit and co-curricular programs since 1992. Notably, the courses include one on immigration and a course on human rights and social work. An important strategy is to strengthen interdisciplinary partnerships within the university and to broaden community collaborations, including international partnerships, to create opportunities for students to learn contemporary and emerging practice issues and applications (UConn School of Social Work, 2009).

With respect to UWI, most of the initial work in establishing the partnership was spearheaded by John Maxwell, then senior lecturer and head of the Social Work Unit. The mission of the Unit is expressed in the following:

We are dedicated to engendering a more just Caribbean Society by: Facilitating the lifelong, professional formation and development of students and staff; Strengthening the capacity of human service and social justice organisations that serve Caribbean people; and Fostering regional and international partnerships. (UWI, 2013)

The Unit states also that it will achieve its goals by using dynamic relevant teaching and learning practices, committed and competent social work educators, and leadership with a global perspective.

The Unit offers a BSW and an MSW, with foundational core courses, three fields of specialization, and an advanced generalist social work curriculum. Students may also choose to take two from the following list of electives: Community Economic Development for Social Change; Monitoring and Evaluation of Social Programmes; Sociology of Development; and Social Inequality, Inequity, and Marginalization. Among the core competencies of its field practicum is for students to "advocate, through professional and political means, for programs, services, and policies that promote economic and social justice and enhance the well-being of their clients and others in need of assistance." The Unit also provides students with an array of field practicum experiences in Jamaica and, through the Caribbean Internship Project, in other Caribbean nations. This is a collaboration among the three campuses of the UWI system in the assignment of student interns to social service agencies in various islands to assist regional development that is also cost-effective and that uses student internship to strengthen agencies in the region (UWI, 2013). Some students have also done their field practicum in Connecticut (for more on the UWI program, see Chapter 9).

The Context: Jamaica as Champion of Human Rights

Jamaica has been renowned historically as an early champion of human rights and social justice. Jamaica was at the forefront of the international campaign against apartheid in South Africa, even when Jamaica itself was a colony of Great Britain, and was the first country to declare a trade embargo against South Africa in 1957 (Walker, 1995). Since 1962, when it gained independence and full UN membership, Jamaica has been a strong advocate of human rights at the international level. Jamaica has consistently and unequivocally supported all UN decisions aimed at enhancing and protecting human rights. Jamaica's commitment to the principle of human rights and to a philosophy of international morality was exemplified by its stance on apartheid and racism (Ministry of Justice, 2006; Walker, 1995).

Jamaica gained international accolade and visibility in 1963, when Senator Hugh Shearer, in delivering Jamaica's maiden address to the UN General Assembly, proposed that 1968 be designated Human Rights Year to mark the 20th anniversary of the Universal Declaration of Human Rights (Walker, 1995). In making this proposal, Senator Shearer had two objectives in mind. The first was to bring new attention to the UN Charter and the Universal Declaration of Human Rights by setting aside a year for the world to highlight and focus on human rights; the second was to establish 1968 as the target year toward which the UN and its member states would work with renewed public commitment and benchmarks in enhancing and protecting fundamental human rights (Walker, 1995).

As members of the UN, many of the lesser developed countries or majority countries, such as Jamaica, have ratified treaties with the best intentions to abide by terms, requirements, and provisions. Jamaica acceded without reservation in 1991 with the Convention on the Rights of the Child (CRC). Jamaica has also actively participated in the work of the General Assembly and other international forums to promote women's advancement and was involved in the establishment of the United Nations Voluntary Fund for the United Nations Decade for Women and its successor organization, the United Nations Development Fund for Women (Walker, 1995).

Jamaican women, such as Sybil Francis and Dr. Lucille Mair, have also distinguished themselves in the work of the United Nations system. For example, Francis was a distinguished pioneer of social work services and training in Jamaica and the Caribbean. She was a member of the first UN delegation from Jamaica as an independent nation in 1963 and later chaired the National Council on Ageing and was a member of the Jamaican Delegation to the World Assembly on Ageing (Council on Social Work Education, 2008b). Dr. Mair served as secretary-general of the World Conference of the United Nations Decade for Women in Copenhagen in 1980 at the midpoint of the Decade for Women. Prior to that she was special adviser to UNICEF on Women's Development, and in 1983 she was invited to serve as secretary-general of the United Nations Conference on the Question of Palestine in Geneva. This conference was described as the most politically fraught conference in the history of the UN. In agreeing to organize the Palestine Conference, Dr. Mair became the first woman to hold the title of undersecretary-general of the UN (Walker, 1995). Thus, for a small country Jamaica has had an important effect on global human rights.

Recent Challenges to Human Rights in Jamaica

The Inter-American Commission on Human Rights (IACHR) is the principal organ of the Organization of American States responsible for promoting the observance and protection of human rights in Jamaica (granted by Article 41 of the American Convention on Human Rights).

Over the years the IACHR has consistently found that Jamaica has maintained a good record of human rights in several areas (IACHR, 2005, 2009, 2012). The country has an independent and impartial civil judiciary process, and there are no reports of political prisoners or detainees (U.S. Department of State, 2011). According to the IACHR (2012), there is freedom of speech and of the press. There are no government restrictions by Jamaica on access to the Internet or reports that the government monitored electronic mail or Internet chat rooms, and individuals and groups can engage in the peaceful expression of views via the Internet, including by electronic mail. The IACHR also found no government restrictions on academic freedom, and laws provide for freedom of assembly and association, and the government generally respects these rights in practice. The government generally cooperates with the Office of the UN High Commissioner for Refugees and other humanitarian organizations in assisting refugees and asylum seekers (IACHR, 2012).

However, since 2005 Jamaica has been receiving failing grades for other human rights violations by several international human rights monitoring agencies (e.g., Amnesty International 2005, 2012; Immigration and Refugee Board of Canada, 2007; Human Rights Watch, 2004; IACHR, 2005, 2009, 2012; Turner, 2008; U.S. Department of State, 2011; Why we should be outraged, 2010). In 2012 the IACHR stated that

> the profound social and economic marginalization of large sectors of the Jamaican population results in the poorest and most excluded sectors of the population being disproportionately victimized by the overall situation of insecurity. In the same way, the deep inequalities pervading Jamaican society are exacerbated by the State's inadequate measures to protect and guarantee the human rights of women, children and other vulnerable groups. (IACHR, 2012, p. 8)

Similar reports were made by several local human rights and civil society groups. In particular, the 2009 Country Reports on Human Rights Practices for Jamaica documented cases of erosion of human rights. Jamaican human rights agencies and civil society groups such as Jamaica Forum for Lesbians and Gays, Women for Women, and Jamaica AIDS Support for Life, have been critical of the country's record on the protection of human rights (Amnesty International, 2011; Brown, 2011).

It is of concern that a country such as Jamaica with an enviable history in support of human rights is now regarded as a villain or failed state due to its growing negative reports of human rights violations. Local nongovernmental organizations such as Jamaicans for Justice had focused on the issues of police impunity, extrajudicial killings, and excessive use of force by the police. Of major concern were reports of high rates of crime including gang violence, homicide, and abuse of women and children (Amnesty International, 2011; U.S. Department of State, 2011). The 2012 IACHR Report concluded that

although the government has undertaken certain constructive efforts to address the problem, these remain insufficient. They are hampered by inadequate resources, a failure to sufficiently address the severe shortcomings of the security forces and the judicial process, and the lack of integral, effective policies to ameliorate the social conditions that generate the violence. (p. 8)

The U.S. Department of Labor's 2008 report on the findings on the worst forms of child labor for Jamaica stated:

Commercial sexual exploitation of children is a problem in Jamaica, especially in tourist areas. Girls are recruited as barmaids and masseuses but then forced into prostitution. Boys who work on the streets of Kingston and Montego Bay are vulnerable to being trafficked. Boys working on the streets are also forced into selling drugs or becoming drug couriers. Girls in rural areas are sometimes recruited for domestic labor and then forced into servitude (U.S. Department of Labor, 2008; U.S. Department of State, 2011).

The allegations of the erosion and apparent violations of certain human rights by Jamaica gave cause for concern among social workers nationally and internationally and particularly among social work faculty of UWI and UConn.

Poverty as a Challenge to Human Rights

There are other contextual realities in which the partnership and collaboration between UWI and UConn faculty and students have occurred. Jamaica and

Connecticut share very few similarities. They have a similar total population (2.7– 3.0 million) and geographic area (4,400–4,800 square miles), but this is where similarities end. For whereas Connecticut is among the top three richest states in the United States, with income per capita in 2012 of $56,889, Jamaica is now among the poorer among lesser developed nations in the world, with an income per capita of $9,100, placing it at 117 in world rankings, which was lower than the rank for Cuba (111). A wide variety of sources concur that the Jamaican economy has experienced serious difficulties over the past 20 decades (Global Exchange, 2013; Heritage Foundation, 2013). The Jamaican economy is closely influenced by the U.S. economy, affecting the cost of living. The value of the Jamaican dollar has diminished severely during the past three decades. For example, in 1986 the rate was US$1 to J$4, but the rate has declined since then such that it was US$1 to J$67 by 2007, US$1 to J$89 in 2012, and US$1 to J$109 by 2013 (Jamaica Demographics Profile, 2013).

There have also been added demands for new and improved social services, but the bad economy that triggered restructuring as the terms for relief and loans from the World Bank and International Monetary Fund (IMF) have led to reduced social service programs. Jamaica is heavily indebted, and in 2013 owed the UN member agencies and projects an estimated $300 million, which has cost the country loss of technical assistance and voting rights on some committees. Jamaica also owes debts for the International Seabed Authority, created by the 1982 UN Convention on the Law of the Sea, of which Jamaica was a pioneer and offered to administer its headquarters, which is still located in downtown Kingston (Henry, 2013).

Children's Rights: An Area of Dynamic Change in Jamaica

In contrast, in children's rights, an area closer to social work, Jamaica has been making positive gains. Social work educators and practitioners have been powerful advocates in the campaign for social justice and human rights for children. The UWI–UConn partnership also played a role in expanding children's rights that went far beyond the original intent of sensitizing educators to the complexities and possible solutions of human rights issues. In retrospect, perhaps it should have come as no surprise when yet another Jamaican woman, who had graduated from the MSW program at UWI, became the one to take on the task of advancing and protecting fundamental human rights in Jamaica.

Over the 20 years of the partnership, there have been many exchanges of information, faculty, and students. One exchange had a particularly important effect on human rights and human rights education. It began in 1994, when two faculty members from UConn were invited to pilot a course for the newly established MSW program at UWI. Among the five students in the first cohort of the administration specialization was Mary Clarke, already a senior policy official at the Planning Institute of Jamaica. She maintained contact with UConn faculty over the years while she became increasingly involved in children's rights issues in Jamaica. She was a delegate to the World Summit for Children and also a member of Jamaica's official delegation to present their country report on compliance with the CRC to the treaty committee in Geneva. In these roles Clarke had access to experiences and materials not readily available to educators in the United States, few of whom are in such lead roles with human rights compliance at the government level. To expand UConn's capacity with regard to children's rights, Clarke was invited to give a keynote address on children's rights and to speak in several social work classes in 2004. Her talks helped Connecticut social work educators learn about the complexities of implementing, monitoring, and protecting human rights nationally and internationally.

While Clarke was in Connecticut, several agency visits were arranged for her by UConn. One of these was to the Connecticut Office of the Child Advocate, an autonomous advocate for children in the state government (Clarke, 2013; Center of International Social Work Studies, 2009, 2012). This contact was a pivotal one and resulted in an effectual relationship. Within 2 years of her visit Clarke was able to convince the Jamaican government to establish a similar office, and she was appointed as director of the Office of the Children's Advocate (OCA) on January 1, 2006, the first such position in Jamaica's history.

There had already been a shift in attitude toward children; in 1991 Jamaica ratified the International Covenant on Economic, Social and Cultural

Rights (UN, 1966b); the Convention on the Elimination of All Forms of Discrimination Against Women (UN, 1979); and the CRC (UN, 1989). The latter was the first international treaty to integrate the full range of human rights—civil, political, economic, social, and cultural—into a single document. Jamaica domesticated the CRC provisions of the convention by passing the Child Care and Protection Act in 2004 to implement the provisions of the CRC. This resulted in the creation of the Child Development Authority, located in the Ministry of Health, as the agency responsible for implementation of government programs to prevent child abuse and to promote and protect the well-being of all children. The country, assisted by nongovernmental organizations, made a number of advances in children's rights. Child protection laws, including mandatory reporting, were adopted. Workshops on parenting were developed to begin to address the widespread cultural acceptance of corporal punishment. In 2006 Jamaica established the OCA as a mandate and located it in the Child Development Authority.

The OCA was given broad responsibilities for reviewing laws, policies, practices, and government services affecting children; providing legal services and investigating complaints against the government; and publishing reports and issuing best practice guidelines concerning the rights or best interests of children. As children's advocate, Mary Clarke's charge was to effectively implement the Child Care and Protection Act. She was responsible for investigating and representing cases of violation of children's rights and various forms of crimes and abuses against children in Jamaica, and she reported directly to the Jamaica Parliament.

Traditionally in Jamaica, children have worked on plantations, farms, and construction sites, as well as in gardens, shops, and markets (U.S. Department of State, 2011). Children also work selling goods on the street and begging. In Jamaica there has been the societal pattern of physical abuse of children through spanking as a way to discipline and control bad behavior. A major challenge confronting the children's advocate was to change the adult view of children's rights as an option, favor, or kindness to children, or as an act of charity, to an understanding of children's rights as obligations and responsibilities that must be honored and respected by all. In the CRC, children's rights are described in 54 articles and two optional protocols that detail the basic human rights of children everywhere based on four core principles: (1) nondiscrimination; (2) devotion to the best interests of the child, protection from harmful influences, abuse, and exploitation; (3) the right to life, survival, and development to the fullest; and (4) respect for the views of the child and for the child to participate fully in family, cultural, and social life. The CRC also makes it clear that children's rights are human rights, and that these rights are not special rights, but rather the fundamental rights inherent in the human dignity of all people (UNICEF Jamaica, 2014a).

Critics of the CRC in Jamaica and other countries have raised concerns that its provisions undermine the rights of parents and allow the UN to dictate how parents should raise their children. However, the children's advocate has repeatedly emphasized the importance, role, and authority of parents in providing direction and guidance to their children. Until new laws were passed, the rights of children in Jamaica were ignored, and only the more egregious cases of violence against children were prosecuted.

Strengthening Children's Rights

As the first children's advocate, Clarke conducted needs assessments and engaged in research and evaluation to inform and educate the Jamaica populace about the realities that existed in the country. Applying social science research modalities, the OCA gathered data, completed analyses, and presented reports of results and findings (Clarke, 2013). Some results and reports presented first to the Jamaican parliament were far from flattering, and in the minds of many Jamaicans reports of violations of the human rights of children were embarrassing. Most Jamaicans seemed unaware of the extent and serious nature of the problems that affected children.

Statistics gathered by the OCA for the year 2008 give some examples of the magnitude of the problems. Between January and June 2008 the OCA received 1,592 reports of child abuse. In May 2008, when Jamaica celebrated Child Month, there were 200 reported cases of children under 10 treated for accident-related injuries and physical abuse, and 12 children were murdered (IACHR, 2009; U.S. Dept. of State, 2011). During the month of June 2008 the OCA reported 142 cases of physical abuse, 137 cases of sexual abuse, and 223 cases of neglect. In 2008 there also were 270 cases of care and protection violations, 17 cases of truancy, 102 cases of behavioral problems, seven cases of absconding, four of trafficking children, one of substance abuse, 23 of emotional abuse, and 13 cases of incest (IACHR, 2009). In August 2008 the Jamaica Information Service stated that the Office of the Children's Registry logged as many as 10 calls per day of child abuse. For the year 2007 it received 418 reports.

The OCA also expressed concern about the underreporting of incidents of child abuse and neglect. During 2008, there were 462 reported cases of carnal abuse (Jamaica Information Service, 2008). Statistics collected by OCA in 2008 showed also that the rate of school attendance was about 64% due to the expense of school uniforms, lunch, and books, coupled with lost wages for not working on family farms or selling items on the street. Other reports by the OCA for that year showed that many minor children had been expelled from schools in Jamaica for bad behavior or for involvement with the criminal justice system.

The OCA also brought attention to the large numbers of juvenile offenders held with adults in prisons for indefinite periods and the harsh and inhumane conditions under which they were being kept. The Reproductive Health Survey for 2008 found that half of all the young women reported that they had been pressured or forced into sexual intercourse at the time of their first sexual experience. Yet laws in Jamaica prohibit statutory rape, defined as sexual relations with a person less than 16 years old, the minimum age for consensual sex. Sexual relations by an adult with a child between the ages of 12 and 16 is a misdemeanor punishable by not more than seven years in prison; if the victim is younger than 12, it is a felony punishable by up to life imprisonment.

The OCA also addressed the problem of trafficking of girls and poor women, and the increasing numbers of boys being trafficked from rural to urban and mostly tourist areas of Jamaica. Research conducted by the OCA found that many children, especially teenage girls, were disappearing each year. For example, in the 2010 Annual Parliamentary Report, the children's advocate stated that between January and June 2010 a total of 1,144 children were reported missing, of which 959 returned home, 182 were still missing, and three were found dead. This report stated that girls accounted for the highest number of missing children, with 888 compared to 256 boys. Of the total number reported missing, 208 had been reported missing in June 2010 alone. Children who were 15-years old accounted for the highest number of missing children.

The OCA found that children trafficked within the country were being subjected to domestic servitude and forced labor. It was discovered that many minor victims had been lured by the promises of jobs and education. The OCA found that extreme cases of poverty were major contributors to abuse, trafficking, and truancy among urban and rural children. Research in the area further showed that some victims were being trafficked by family members, whereas others had voluntarily responded to employment advertisements not fully knowing what the offers entailed. For example, girls who were recruited in urban centers such as Kingston and Montego Bay were vulnerable to being coerced into selling or conveying illicit drugs by acting as couriers. Amnesty International reported that in January 2008, 10 Jamaicans, lured by the promise of work, had traveled to Curacao but on arrival were locked up and forced into prostitution by their sponsors. Later reports indicated that four of the victims had escaped, but no information was available on the remaining six (Amnesty International, 2009).

Success in Interventions

The achievements of the OCA for children in Jamaica have been significant. These efforts, shared through the educational exchange partnership, have also informed and influenced the Connecticut partners. Jamaica's efforts to take the CRC seriously and effectively pass and implement laws and programs to address children's rights has provided UConn educators with a successful example, demonstrating that treaties can create change. A particularly interesting aspect has been the achievement in child participation. Jamaica began by translating the CRC into children's books, educating children on their rights.

UNICEF had long set the example by partnering with local agencies in several countries to make children agents of change by having them participate in mock assemblies and students' cabinets to explore and discuss targeted issues and problems (UNICEF, 2011). Advocates in Jamaica adopted this concept and made children both motivators and catalysts of social change for human rights in Jamaica. Hearings with groups of children have been held on issues of concern to them, such as access to education.

This concept of making children agents of change has been particularly developed and implemented with the advent of the Caribbean Child Research Conference. The conference has been held annually since 2006 in Kingston, in the conference facilities of the UN Seabed Authority, with support from UNICEF and UWI. Faculty from UConn attended the 2011 conference, which was not simply about children, but has active and meaningful participation of children from Jamaica and other Caribbean islands. Hundreds of high school students are invited to actively participate in the children's sessions of the conference. Students conduct research on relevant topics and formally present papers that outline the research question, hypothesis, methodology, data collection, and analyses and results as researchers do at professional conferences. Each year also a prize is given to the outstanding child researcher. Children as young as 8 years old are in the audience and actively ask questions. There is also a preconference activity for teachers on the rights of the child based on the CRC and the Child Care and Protection Act of Jamaica. This Caribbean regional interdisciplinary conference covers a range of child-related themes with the goal of sharing research findings on issues related to children, strengthening the network of researchers on children's issues, and encouraging research in priority areas and in other important but neglected areas (UNICEF Jamaica, 2014b). The Connecticut observers learned from this model of child participation, an often neglected principle from the CRC, and have incorporated it into their teaching in various ways.

The OCA has achieved much in its short existence. In the case of minor children being expelled from schools for bad behaviors or involved in the criminal justice system, the children's advocate intervened to have students reinstated in schools or assigned lawyers to help children obtain bail. To address the problems of extreme poverty, abuse, trafficking, and truancy the OCA advocated for and was successful in getting the Jamaica Ministry of Social Security to establish a program to provide stipends to pay for educational expenses. Under Mary Clarke's leadership, the OCA advocated for children involved with the criminal justice system to be provided with psychological assessments, medical examinations, and individual and group counseling. The OCA also advocated for the housing of all juvenile offenders in facilities built exclusively for minors. To address the problem of sexual abuse against minors, Clarke first highlighted effects of the initial trauma among children who were abused and additional stress caused when asked to give evidence in court, which often resulted in perpetrators being let go. In response, Clarke proposed a more holistic multiple-agency approach by creating the Centre for the Investigation of Sexual Offences and Child Abuse. Additionally, the OCA was successful in getting laws passed making it the responsibility on all citizens to report suspected abuse and for a penalty of up to J$500,000 (US$5,600) for failure to report. Again applying social work principles, the OCA coordinated training sessions to familiarize police officers with the rights of children and to prepare them to enforce protection laws.

Conclusion

After 5 years of intense lobbying for better conditions for children in Jamaica, Mary Clarke retired as the children's advocate in 2011. "We have achieved a lot. Even across Jamaica, the level of awareness of child rights and the calls on the office indicated that persons know there is an office to promote, protect, and enforce their rights," she told the newspaper, *Jamaica Gleaner* (Hunter, 2011, para. 5). There are still serious concerns about the state of human rights in Jamaica. Yet despite poverty and lack of resources, when there was strong advocacy on the part of the OCA, attention was given and change implemented by the government and its agencies. The experience indicates that a country with serious human rights issues can draw on its heritage to make big strides in some areas. Through the contacts and experiences of an international exchange and integration of social work skills and human rights efforts, the OCA has become a prime protector and enhancer of human rights in Jamaica, of which Hugh Shearer would indeed be very proud.

On the other side of the partnership, educators and community agencies in Connecticut have gained a deeper understanding of the challenges and advances that can be made through implementation of the CRC. In particular, they have learned about prospects for engaging children directly in human rights awareness and advocacy. As the partnership continues, other human rights issues are being explored, including the rights of deportees and discrimination and stigma attached to lesbian, gay, bisexual, and transgender groups.

References

Amnesty International. (2005, May 25). *Jamaica*. Retrieved from http://www .refworld.org/docid/429b27e711.html

Amnesty International. (2009). *Jamaica: Stop the killings: Public security reforms and human rights in Jamaica*. (AMR 38/001/2009). Retrieved from http://www.amnesty.org/en/library/info/AMR38/003/2009/en

Amnesty International. (2011). *Amnesty International annual report 2011—Jamaica*. Retrieved from http://www.unhcr.org/refworld/docid/4dce155f3c. html

Amnesty International. (2012). *Amnesty International report 2012*. Retrieved fromwww.indexmundi.com/jamaica/demographics_profile.html

Brown, I. (2011, January 11). Cops get domestic abuse sensitivity training. *Jamaica Observer*. Retrieved from http://www.jamaicaobserver.com/news /Cop-get-domestic-abuse-sensitivity-training_8216800#ixzz1frckmfXU

Center of International Social Work Studies. (2009). International Korner. Retrieved from http://ssw.uconn.edu/wp-content/uploads/2010/03/CISWS -International Korner

Center of International Social Work Studies. (2012). Center of International Social Work Studies. Retrieved from http://ssw.uconn.edu/wp-content /uploads/2010/03/CISWS-brochure-2012.pdf

Clarke, M. (2013). Memories of a pioneer: Jamaica's first children's advocate. *Caribbean Journal of Social Work, 10*, 28–39.

Council on Social Work Education (CSWE). (2008a). Educational policy and accreditation standards. Retrieved from http://www.cswe.org/File.aspx?id =41861

Council for Social Work Education. (2008b). Annual social work day at the United Nations. Retrieved from http://www.cswe.org/File.aspx?id=25145

Global Exchange. (2013). Jamaica: Economy. Retrieved from http://www
.globalexchange.org/country/jamaica/economy

Healy, L. (2008). Exploring the history of social work as a human rights
profession. International Social Work, 51, 745-746.

Healy, L., Asamoah, Y., & Hokenstad, M. C. (Eds.). (2003). *Models of
international collaboration in social work education*. Alexandria, VA: Council on
Social Work Education.

Healy, L. M., Maxwell, J. A., & Pine, B. A. (1999). Exchanges that work:
Mutuality and sustainability in a Caribbean/USA academic partnership. *Social
Development Issues, 21*(3), 14–21.

Henry, B. (2013, March 3). More debt! Jamaica owes int'l bodies $794m. *Jamaica
Observer*. Retrieved from http://www.jamaicaobserver.com/news/More-debt
-3763419#ixzz2RsMzrj7F

Heritage Foundation. (2013). *2013 index of economic freedom: Jamaica economy*.
Retrieved from http://www.heritage.org/index/country/jamaica

Human Rights Watch. (2004). Hated to death: Homophobia, violence, and
Jamaica's HIV/AIDS epidemic. Retrieved from http://www.hrw.org/en
/node/11894/section/1

Hunter, N. (2011, February 19). Children's advocate Clarke retires. *The Gleaner*.
Retrieved from http://jamaica-gleaner.com/gleaner/20110219/news/news72.
html

Immigration and Refugee Board of Canada. (2007). Jamaica: Prevalence and
forms of child abuse; legislation governing the protection of abused children
and its implementation; availability of child protection services (2003–
2006), JAM101751.E. Retrieved from http://www.unhcr.org/refworld
/docid/46fa538023.html

Inter-American Commission on Human Rights (IACHR). (2005). *Inter-American
Commission on Human Rights 2005 Report on the situation of human rights in
Jamaica*. OEA/Ser.L/V/II.144 Doc. 12. Washington, DC: Organization of
American States.

Inter-American Commission on Human Rights (IACHR). (2009). Situation of
children in juvenile detention centers in Jamaica. Inter American Commission
on Human Rights Hearing, 137th Sessions. Retrieved from http://www.cidh.
oas.org/prensa/publichearings/Hearings.aspx?Lang=EN&Session=117

Inter-American Commission on Human Rights [IACHR] (2012). *Inter-American
Commission on Human Rights 2012 Report on the situation of human rights in
Jamaica*. OEA/Ser.L/V/II.144 Doc. 12. Washington, DC: Organization of
American States.

Jamaica Demographics Profile. (2013). 2013 Index: Mundi Country Facts. Retrieved from http://www.indexmundi.com/g/r.aspx?c=jm&v=67

Jamaica Information Service. (JIS). (2008). Minister Grange commits to facilitating dialogue on improving children's welfare. Retrieved from http://www.jis.gov.jm/information/html/20081024t100000-0500_17108

Maxwell, J. A., & Healy, L. M. (2003). Mutual assistance through an ongoing United States—Caribbean partnership: University of Connecticut and University of the West Indies in Jamaica. In L. Healy, Y. Asamoah, & M. C. Hokenstad (Eds.). *Models of international collaboration in social work education* (pp. 51–60). Alexandria, VA: Council on Social Work Education.

Ministry of Justice. (2006). Jamaica human rights: Panmedia. Retrieved from http://www.panmedia. com.jm/

Pogge, T. (2005). Severe poverty as a violation of negative duties. *Ethics and International Affairs*, 19(1), 55–84.

Stamford Interagency Workshop on a Human Rights-Based Approach in the Context of UN Reform. (2003). Statement on a common understanding of a human rights-based approach to development cooperation. Retrieved from http://www.undg.org/archive_docs/6959-The_Human_Rights_Based _Approach_to_Development_Cooperation_Towards_a_Common _Understanding_among_UN.pdf

Turner, R. (2008, July 21). Domestic violence statistics alarming. *Jamaica Gleaner*. Retrieved from http://jamaica-gleaner.com/gleaner/20080721/lead /lead6.html

United Nations (UN). (1948, December 10). *Universal declaration of human rights*. G.A. Res. 217 A (III). Retrieved from http://www.refworld.org /docid/3ae6b3712c.html

United Nations (UN). (1966a, December 16). *International covenant on civil and political rights*. G.A. Res. 2200A (XXI). Retrieved from http://www.ohchr.org /Documents/ProfessionalInterest/ccpr.pdf

United Nations (UN). (1966b, December 16). *International covenant on economic, social, and cultural rights*. G.A. Res. 2200A (XXI). Retrieved from http://www .ohchr.org/EN/ProfessionalInterest/Pages/CESCR.aspx

United Nations (UN). (1979, December 18). *Convention on the elimination of all forms of discrimination against women*. G.A. Res. 34/180. Retrieved from http://www.ohchr.org/Documents/ProfessionalInterest/cedaw.pdf

United Nations. (1989, November 20). *Convention on the rights of the child.* G.A. Res. 44/25. Retrieved from http://www.ohchr.org/Documents /ProfessionalInterest/crc.pdf

UNICEF Jamaica (2011). Caribbean Child Research Conference. Retrieved from http://www.unicef.org/jamaica/promoting_child_rights_20898.htm

UNICEF Jamaica. (2014a). 20th anniversary: Convention on the rights of the child. Retrieved from http://www.unicef.org/jamaica/promoting_child _rights_15284.htm

UNICEF Jamaica. (2014b). Caribbean Child Research Conference: Promoting child rights through research. Retrieved from http://www.unicef.org/jamaica /promoting_child_rights_13575.htm

University of Connecticut (UConn) School of Social Work. (2009). Our world, our people, our future: The University of Connecticut Academic Plan 2009– 2014. Retrieved from http://ssw.uconn.edu/wp-content/uploads/2010/05 /SSW_AcademicPlan_2009_2014.pdf

University of the West Indies (UWI). (2013). Vision and mission. Retrieved from http://myspot.mona.uwi.edu/socialwork/vision-and-mission

U.S. Department of Labor. (2008). The U.S. Department of Labor's 2008 findings on the worst forms of child labor. Retrieved from http://digitalcommons .ilr.cornell.edu/cgi/viewcontent.cgi?article=1653&context=key_workplace

U.S. Department of State. (2011). *2010 country reports on human rights practices: Jamaica.* Retrieved from http://www.unhcr.org/refworld/docid /4da56db97a.html

Why we should be outraged. (2010, April 4). Editorial. *Jamaica Gleaner.* Retrieved from http://mobile.jamaica-gleaner.com/gleaner/20100404/cleisure /cleisure1.php

Walker, H. S. (1995). Jamaica and the United Nations: 1962–1995. *Jamaica Journal, 25*(3), 2–9.

SECTION IV

Human Rights Education and Special Populations

The chapters in Section IV emphasize the integration of human rights education with regard to a number of special populations and topics. Although the principle of universality of human rights is embedded into the foundational treaties, numerous human rights declarations and conventions have been adopted to address the special concerns of vulnerable and exploited groups. These mesh well with social work's focus on vulnerable populations. This section contains chapters on the rights of children, migrants, and people of color. The final chapter addresses water as a human right, also highlighting the intersection of the right to water with women's and children's rights. The population-focused chapters expand the discussions in Section III of other vulnerable groups—women and persons affected by HIV/AIDS—as foci for study travel and exchange programs. One common thread that vulnerable groups share is their limited ability to advocate for themselves due to their social status, whether related to age, race, legal or citizenship status, or other factors. This often constrains their ability to claim their human rights.

Children are widely overlooked as rights holders and until recently were often treated as the property of parents. Robin Spath and Joyce Lee Taylor demonstrate how educators can connect the topic of human rights in special-ized courses focusing on children's issues, especially child protection and per-manency planning. They reference the Convention on the Rights of the Child and ways its principles can be used, even without treaty ratification. Their discussion includes suggestions and concrete exercises for reframing child pro-tection and permanency as human rights issues for social work students.

Immigrants, refugees, and other migrants often experience grave human rights violations. Once outside their countries of origin, they may lack pro-tection from exploitation and abuse; some even become stateless persons. To date, international law does not provide adequate protections for these groups, and governments are reluctant to expand legal and social protection to international migrants in their territory. The treaty protecting migrant rights, the International Convention on the Protection of the Rights of All Migrant Workers and Members of Their Families, has not been ratified by any of the major immigrant-receiving countries.

Two chapters in this section address teaching a rights-based approach to problems of immigrants and refugees. Uma Segal identifies the struggles of migrant workers and the violations they face as foreigners/guests within another country. She proposes that social work curricula must address the needs and concerns of migrant workers. Filomena Critelli illustrates the use of a 6-hour, two-session module to prepare students to develop a just and humane practice with immigrants. Her chapter provides not only an infor-mative overview of relevant human rights law related to immigrants, but also highlights for students the rights-based implications of working with undocu-mented and newly arrived immigrants.

In their chapter, "Deconstructing Mass Incarceration in the United States from a Human Rights Lens: Implications for Social Work Education and Practice," Kirk James and Julie Smyth paint a stark picture of the human rights implications of imprisonment of persons of color in the United States. Indeed, shadow reports submitted for the CERD Committee review of U.S. compliance with the Convention on the Elimination of All Forms of Racial Discrimination have emphasized the gross overrepresentation of African Americans in the criminal justice system. James and Smyth use a human rights framework to identify ways social work educators and practitioners can engage with this important domestic rights issue.

The final chapter focuses on a specific issue—the right to water—rather than a population. DeBrenna LaFa Agbenyiga and Sudha Sankar's contribution discusses water as a fundamental human right and underscores the effects water scarcity has on children. They make an argument that the lack of water supplies limits a child's ability to develop and thrive. In numerous developing countries the gendered responsibility of girls to obtain water for their families often forces young girls to miss school, compromising their futures. Health of the girls can be affected by long walks to and from water sources, bearing heavy loads. Furthermore, the water is often unsafe for drinking, putting family health in jeopardy. Indeed, the leading cause of child death in many countries is diarrhea related to unclean water and lack of sanitation. Climate change may make the right to water a more universal concern, as even countries with advanced economies suffer from drought and water shortages.

Social work educational programs already address vulnerable populations in their curricula. The chapters in this section will inspire educators to introduce or strengthen human rights content and rights-based practice considerations in their courses on race, gender, sexual minorities, special age groups, and other oppressed populations.

20 | Reframing Child Protection and Permanency Social Work as Human Rights Work

Robin Spath and Joyce Lee Taylor

Historically, the focus of the social work profession has been human rights based, including the involvement of social workers in the early years of the children's rights movement. In fact, many of the governmental regulations and programs that exist to protect children are due in large part to the effort of social workers over the last century (Healy, 2008). In the United States today, social workers focused on child protection are working under several basic philosophical tenets that are grounded in human rights. First, every child has the right to a safe and permanent home that is free of abuse and neglect. Additionally, in most cases children are best cared for in their own families. When parents are not able to care for their children, it is the responsibility of child protection to work in the best interests of the child to establish permanency as quickly as possible. Finally, children have the right to have their physical, mental, emotional, educational, and medical needs met (DePanfilis & Salus, 2003). These basic philosophical tenets align with rights outlined in the Convention on the Rights of the Child (United Nations, 1989) and the Convention on the Protection of Children and Co-Operation in Respect of Intercountry Adoption (Hague Adoption Convention; Hague Conference on Private International Law, 1993).

Therefore, it is critical that social workers look for ways to integrate a human rights perspective into curricula and trainings focused on child protection and permanency. This discussion includes an overview of the Convention on the Rights of the Child and the Hague Adoption Convention, as well as human-rights focused practice standards and competencies in child protection used in other countries. Current standards of practice in child protection in the United States also are examined to determine how well our work with this population aligns with these conventions. Finally, we provide suggestions for readings and exercises for social work educators to use to reframe child protection and permanency as human rights based social work.

Convention on the Rights of the Child

The Universal Declaration of Human Rights was adopted by the United Nations in 1948. However, more than two decades prior to the adoption of this treaty, Eglantyne Jebb, a British social reformer and founder of Save the Children, attended a meeting in Geneva of the International Union, where she drafted the Geneva Declaration, or the Declaration of the Rights of the Child (League of Nations, 1924). This charter drafted in 1923 focused on the responsibility of the international community to take into consideration the rights of children in their planning and was adopted a year later by the League of Nations. In 1959 an expanded version of the Declaration was adopted by the United Nations (Mulley, 2009). In the succeeding years world leaders felt that children needed their own convention recognizing that children's rights and that, as a more vulnerable population, children have their own set of unique needs and concerns.

In 1989 the Convention on the Rights of the Child (CRC) was developed and adopted by the United Nations to address this need. The CRC is a set of universally approved and legally binding standards for children. The CRC is guided by four key principles: nondiscrimination; right to life, survival, and development; a focus on the best interests of the child; and respect for the child perspective. Based on these principles, the CRC outlines children's rights and standards in health care; education; and legal, civil, and social services. These are delineated in 54 articles and two optional protocols. Although all the articles and protocols relate on some level to child protection and permanency, several relate directly to the key philosophical tenets of child protection and permanency social work:

- Best interests of the child (Article 3): Decisions affecting children should be made with the best interests of the child as the primary guiding concern.

- Protection from all forms of violence (Article 19): Children have the right to protection from neglect; physical, mental, or emotional abuse; and any other form of maltreatment by their parents or any other caregiver.

- Sexual exploitation (Article 34): Governments should protect children from all forms of sexual exploitation and abuse.

- Separation from parents (Article 9): Children have the right to live with their parent(s), unless it places them at risk. Children have the right to contact with both parents, even if they do not live together, unless the child is at risk.

- Children deprived of family environment (Article 20): Children who cannot be cared for by their own families have a right to an alternative permanent placement with people who respect their ethnic group, religion, culture, and language.

- Adoption (Article 21): Children who are adopted or who live in foster care have the right to the best care and protection. The primary concern in cases of adoption and foster care is what is in the best interest of the child. This applies to cases of in-country as well as intercountry adoption.

- Respect for the views of the child (Article 12): Children have the right to say what they think and have their opinions considered when adults are making decisions that affect them (UNICEF, n.d.).

In addition, Article 5 of the CRC explicitly recognizes parents and the significant role they play in raising children; it calls on governments to protect parents and provide any assistance needed to help them fulfill this essential role.

Two articles on the CRC would be especially helpful in educating students about this convention. Tang (2003) provides an overview of the process of implementation of the CRC in Canada and gives a helpful understanding of the implications of ratifying the CRC from a neighboring country. Bessant (2011) explores how the reporting mechanisms available through the CRC can be used to address children who continue to be at risk even after the state has intervened due to child abuse and/or neglect. This is particularly relevant considering the use of class action lawsuits in the United States to address issues with the child protection system and provides students an alternative approach to address systemic issues in the United States. These two articles provide content focusing on the CRC and human rights that can readily be infused into a course focusing on child protection and/or permanency.

In 2009, in honor of the 20th anniversary of the CRC, the United Nations General Assembly endorsed the Guidelines for Alternative Care of Children (United Nations, 2009). The aim of these guidelines is to provide further guidance to nation states implementing the CRC in terms of the protection and well-being of children not in parental care, as well as guidelines and goals for alternative care (Save the Children, 2012).

The Hague Adoption Convention

Another international agreement designed to safeguard the rights of children is the Hague Adoption Convention on the Protection of Children and Co-operation in Respect of Inter-Country Adoption (commonly known as the Hague Adoption Convention; Hague Conference on Private Law, 1993). The United States signed this convention in 1994, and it went into full force in the United States in 2008. The Hague Adoption Convention applies to adoptions from and to the United States with other nations that have joined the convention and provides additional protections for children, birth parents, and adoptive parents involved in intercountry adoption. One of the major goals of the Hague Adoption Convention is to prevent the abduction, sale, and trafficking of children. Additionally, the protocols and procedures established as a result of the Hague Adoption Convention are designed to ensure that adoption is in the best interests of each child. The convention requires nations to seek permanency options for a child in-country; intercountry adoption is seen as a last resort if all other possible options for permanency within a home country have been exhausted (U.S. Department of State, 2013). The U.S. Department of State is the central authority for intercountry adoption and provides accreditation for agencies interested in providing support to adoptive families under the Hague Adoption Convention process.

Since the adoption of the Hague Adoption Convention in the United States, several articles that are relevant to social work practice and education have been published examining this change in policy. Bailey and Delavega (2011) conducted a study that examined the public comment period prior to the implementation of the Hague Adoption Convention and the responsiveness of the Department of State to these public comments. Hollingsworth (2008) examines the protection of cultural identity in relationship to the convention and provides recommendations for social work practice and research. Bergquist (2009) discusses the convention and the emergency evacuation of children during a crisis or upheaval, using Chad as an example. Kim and Smith (2009) examine intercountry adoption in Korea, which implemented the convention in 2000. These readings focusing on intercountry adoption would provide a solid foundation of knowledge to students regarding the Hague Adoption Convention.

Building a Human Rights Perspective

The International Federation of Social Workers (IFSW) has developed a training manual for social work students, educators, and practitioners interested in implementing the ideals of the CRC. The IFSW (2002) outlines five building blocks that can be used as a starting point for working from a children's rights perspective:

1) Children are people rather than "people-in-the-making";
2) Childhood is not just a stage leading to adulthood, but a period that has significant value in the life of a person;
3) Children are "active agents of their own lives" and it is important that as professionals we never assume that our understanding and knowledge of a child's life is greater than that of the child;
4) Age discrimination is an issue that regularly impacts children and needs to be addressed; and
5) Children are especially vulnerable due to their size, strength, experience and intellectual and cognitive development; therefore they are more vulnerable to abuse and exploitation (p. 8).

These readings that focus on the CRC and Hague Convention, as well as those that outline key philosophical principles in child protection, provide a foundation for framing child protection and permanency as human rights issues.

Integrating a Human Rights Perspective in Social Work Education

As social work educators, it is critical that we look for ways to integrate a human rights perspective into curriculum and trainings focused on child protection and permanency. One approach that can be used to encourage critical thinking is assignments that compare and contrast child protection and permanency policies and practices in various countries. Students should be educated regarding how the United States compares with other countries in relation to child protection approaches and overall children's rights. In fact, most students are probably unaware that the United States is one of only three countries in the world (besides Somalia and South Sudan) that have not yet ratified the CRC (Child Rights International Network, 2013; United Nations, 2013). In the three countries that have not ratified the CRC, are children's rights the least protected? In comparing one country to another, instructors may assign small groups to choose among a list of countries and explore children's rights dilemmas in each country (see Appendix 4). For each country analyzed, students can assess whether a given set of problems exists, to what degree (severity and frequency), and political and societal responses to these problems. This student assignment, which asks students to consider multiple examples of human rights violations, is included in Appendix A. Students complete a worksheet for the United States and a comparative worksheet for another country of their choosing.

When such an analysis is conducted, it appears that children's rights in the United States are fairly well-protected, compared to other countries that have ratified the CRC. Therefore, it is important to examine with students the other essential components necessary to protect children's rights. The following list of seven essential components is derived from the literature focusing on leadership, policy, and evaluation in social work and child welfare:

- Commonly held societal values and public health standards
- Passage and adherence to national and international policies and legal protections
- Infrastructure and adequate systems to support children's rights
- Sustainable resources to operationalize prevention efforts and to respond to violations of children's rights
- Good practice behaviors at the frontlines, in addition to supervision, administration, and leadership that values and promotes children's rights
- Ongoing emphasis on best practices in the system (continuous quality improvement, education, training, data systems, and data-informed decision making)
- Attention to the actual lived experience of children and families

Social work programs typically cover human rights and children's rights during policy courses. However, the human rights perspective can be infused into child welfare practice courses. Instructors could deliver a historical overview of children's rights and guide a class discussion that analyzes which of these essential components (or lack thereof) influenced each milestone in the evolution of children's rights to the present day. Furthermore, these seven essential components can be applied to tragic cases that appear in the news headlines. Every child maltreatment fatality focuses attention on the actual details surrounding a child's death (using Component 7); therefore, students could be directed to view the child welfare system to identify strengths and areas needing improvement (using Components 1–6). An analysis of child fatalities becomes even more powerful as one views multiple instances within the same child protection jurisdiction. A report of 194 child deaths in New York City over a 2 year period not only identified the factors of each of those deaths individually, but also provided a lens to view weaknesses in New York City's child protection system (Freundlich, Gerstenzang, Diaz, & London, 2003).

Another productive topic to explore addresses the human rights dimensions of disproportionality of racial minorities within child protective services and the foster care system. Students can review documents that highlight racial disparities in the child welfare system from a human rights perspective and discuss how this framing might help impel more just practices at multiple levels. As a 2008 shadow report on New York City's record regarding racism and human rights to the Committee on the Elimination of Racial Discrimination noted, "the over-representation of children of color in the child welfare system is linked directly and indirectly to public and child welfare policies and practices, including: the targeting of impoverished neighborhoods; rash reactions to tragedies of family violence; insufficient social and economic support to poor families; and racial stereotypes that are ingrained in the minds of professionals that work with our nation's children" (Urban Justice Center, 2008, para. 8). The report highlights issues of intersectionality and the relationship between individual children's well-being and structural racism as human rights concerns.

Child Protection and Human Rights

In the United States, class action lawsuits have been filed against governmental child protection agencies in various states over the last 30 years when groups of children experienced similar circumstances in which their rights were not protected by the system. These lawsuits sought major improvements to the child welfare system in Connecticut (*Juan F. v. Malloy*), the District of Columbia (*LaShawn A. v. Gray*), Georgia (*Kenny A. v. Deal*), Massachusetts (*Connor B. v. Patrick*), Michigan (*Dwayne B. v. Snyder*), Mississippi (*Olivia Y. v. Barbour*), Missouri (*E. C. v. Sherman*), Missouri (*G. L. v. Sherman*), New Jersey (*Charlie and Nadine H. v. Christie*), New Mexico (*Joseph A. v. Bolson*), New York (*Marisol A. v. Giuliani*), Oklahoma (*D. G. v. Yarbrough*), Rhode Island (*Cassie M. v. Chafee*), Tennessee (*Brian A. v. Haslam*), Texas (*M. D. v. Perry*), and Wisconsin (*Jeanine B. v. Walker*) (as cited in Children's Rights, 2013). This list is not exhaustive and represents only a handful of the states involved in class action lawsuits. These lawsuits call attention to widespread failures to protect children's rights in the child welfare system. Students may be directed to any of these cases and instructed to start their analysis with Component 7 (stated previously), which pays attention to the actual lived experience of children as individuals.

As one considers the depth and breadth of flaws within the child protection system, the idea of systemic reform can feel overwhelming. It may be discouraging to consider all the time and work it would take to change policies, to build adequate infrastructure, to allocate the appropriate resources, and to create and maintain a workforce and leadership to implement effective interventions. By contrast, a different approach would be to view the child protection inadequacies as violations of children's rights. Rather than feeling overwhelmed, students may respond with strong feelings of urgency to join the advocacy efforts and to contribute to improved practices.

The following outlines an exercise that can be used with students to get them to see the effect of perspective and challenge them to view problems as a systems issue or as a children's rights issue, rather than as unique individual issues. After being organized into two workgroups, students analyze the child protection system using two perspectives. The first group would begin their analysis with any of the state jurisdictions involved in the class action lawsuits (see previous list). Students in the second group would start their analysis at the individual level by focusing on the plaintiffs in the cases. Each group would use the seven components discussed earlier as its framework for analysis. Class action lawsuits have been called regulation by litigation. As students will find in their analyses, the question of each component becomes one of sufficiency. Even if all the components were marginally met, we can take a second look to determine whether those components came together to sufficiently protect the actual lived experience of all children and families on a consistent and continuous basis. Another difference that may be observed between Group 1 and Group 2 may be the level of passion with which they speak of for the need for reform.

Students can also be assigned advocacy projects in child welfare courses that challenge them to advocate for changes in state and federal policy based on human rights issues. For example, students in a macro-level class focusing on programs and policies affecting women and children organized a group project focusing on state-level advocacy in support of a task force examining state-level compliance with the CRC. Students testified at the state legislature, developed and distributed flyers, and organized an e-mail list to engage people in contacting their legislators when the item came up for a vote. This assignment provided a real life experience in advocating for human rights within the context of social work education and practice.

Social work educators can also look for opportunities to develop interdisciplinary assignments with other students and professionals in related fields. For example, several law students working in a child dependency courtroom conducted a thorough legal review of existing laws related to children's rights and the protection of exceptional and special needs children. They discovered numerous states have child welfare protection rights to records, adoption search for birth families when children reach adulthood, and protection of children's rights to safety related to mandated reporting and the balance of parental rights (termination of parental rights or youth emancipation). Based on their work, this group of graduate students joined with social workers and community leaders in support of legislative aspirations for children's rights in Florida (Figarola & Cobb, 2014).

Additionally, video material can be used to engage students in a discussion on the ability of the United States to meet the mandates outlined in the CRC and the Hague Adoption Convention in cases involving child protection, permanency, and adoption. The film *The Taking of Logan Marr* tells the tragic story of a young girl who was killed while in state custody (PBS Video, 2003). The film *Aging Out* chronicles the stories of five youths as they reach legal age and leave the foster care system (Weisberg & Roth, 2005). Another film, *I Love You, Mommy,* shows the transformation of a girl, adopted from China at an older age, as she navigates her life and identity with a Jewish family living in Long Island, New York (Wang-Breal, 2009). These are just three interesting and thought-provoking films that provide case examples of children who have been adopted or ended up in the child welfare system and whose basic rights and needs have been overlooked. These videos provide a starting point for discussions focused on the human rights aspect of child welfare and challenge students to move from a child protection to a human rights perspective.

Enhancing Social Work Competencies to Support Children's Rights

Schools of social work sometimes seek partnerships and federal funding to deliver courses and field practica for aspiring public child welfare social workers (National Child Welfare Workforce Institute, 2012). Several universities from across the country worked collaboratively to design, deliver, and disseminate child welfare syllabi (child welfare practice courses; policy courses; diverse populations; and special topics such as supervision and leadership, systems of care, research, and trauma approaches). Reframing child protection and permanency social work as human rights social work would not require major alterations to the course content or assignments. The reframing might take the form of cross-referencing the content areas and assignments with the CRC, most particularly the articles mentioned earlier.

An instructor may choose to focus on particular issues in the United States, such as unmet basic needs and international comparisons or poverty and the gap between the haves and have-nots within the United States. Students may be asked to consider economic and social justice as issues of children's rights, and the ways in which children's rights often conflict with economic efficiencies (e.g., see Chapters 11 and 15). Shall we describe a family's economic struggles as child neglect? Nationally, the child protection system is shifting its approach in practice; for example, several states have implemented a differential response system (Gursky, Sullivan, & Welch, n.d.). The differential response system approach is a step toward acknowledging a human rights perspective and the idea of child neglect within an ecological perspective.

In addition, the Council on Social Work Education (2008) has developed Educational Policy and Accreditation Standards that outline competencies for social work education. This type of cross-referencing could be conducted for practice behaviors that are embedded in selected competencies (National Child Welfare Workforce Institute, 2012), which are required in social work education and relate to child welfare and specific articles of the CRC, such as the following:

- Best interests of the child (Article 3): Practice behaviors are applying good judgment in viewing a child's emotional and physical needs and his or her family's capacity to provide for those needs in developmentally appropriate ways; identifying the interventions that are most likely to be helpful; evaluating progress related to safety, permanency, and well-being in meaningful ways; and involving children and families in the planning, implementation, and evaluation of services.

- Protection from all forms of violence (Article 19): Practice behaviors are identifying physical violence; sexual abuse; emotional abuse; deprivation of food, water, or clothing; abandonment; predators; providing an adequate response to dangerous situations related to inadequate parental supervision, bullying, or serious emotional disturbances; delivering effective interventions to alleviate a child's suffering and assisting with strategies to reduce the effects of trauma.

- Sexual exploitation (Article 34): Practice behaviors are providing outreach to identify and involve victims in prevention; counseling/mentoring; building partnerships to coordinate a community-based multidisciplinary response that includes the police, prosecutors, lawyers, social workers, judges, schools, and community leaders to coordinate care and treat victims as victims rather than criminals.

- Separation from parents (Article 9): Practice behaviors are assessing risk and resiliency factors associated with maltreatment (various types, frequency, duration, severity); the child's development, behaviors, and functioning, and the caregiver's abilities and supports; making decisions to keep the family together unless risks cannot be ameliorated.

- Children deprived of family environment (Article 20): Practice behaviors are facilitating continued contact between parents and children if separating families is necessary; removing barriers that interfere with family preservation or reunification, understanding the dynamics of poverty and diversity, and identifying issues contributing to the racial disparities at multiple points during the life of a case (referral, substantiation, differential response, removals, types of placement settings, types of permanency decisions, and child outcomes).

- Adoption (Article 21): Promoting children's best interests when considering adoption or alternatives; providing support to families during transitions related to adoption or the adoption issues that arise throughout a child's development.

- Respect for the views of the child (Article 12): Teaching and supporting children's self-advocacy skills; creating opportunities for children to be asked for their views; using good interviewing skills to engage children and understanding communication abilities when interpreting their views; taking the children's views seriously (National Child Welfare Workforce Institute, 2012).

As shown, some of the practice behaviors are not mutually exclusive. They may overlap with multiple articles of the CRC. One article, however, was not addressed in the practice competencies outlined in the syllabi published by the National Child Welfare Workforce Institute: respect for the views of the child (Article 12). Perhaps this can be traced to the paternalistic origins from which the child welfare field originated. Another plausible explanation may be any combination of the harmful traditional attitudes that challenge our ability to honor children's right to be heard within child protection settings. The following harmful attitudes call into question a child's status, capacity, and influence:

- Children are dependent and therefore cannot qualify for human rights.
- Children are incomplete human beings.
- Family privacy is paramount.
- Parental authority should not be undermined.
- We must respect our elders.
- Traditional discipline works.
- Smacking, slapping, and spanking are not violence.
- Child protection is about ending child abuse (Willow, 2010).

As social work educators we need to challenge these harmful attitudes and assist students in reframing practice and, in particular, honoring the voices of children.

Conclusion

Social work practice in child protection and permanency in many ways is guided by the values and beliefs outlined in the CRC and the Hague Adoption Convention and are human-rights focused. However, many social work students do not view child welfare work through this lens. Educators can assist students to make concrete connections between human rights practice and social work practice in this area. This chapter cites and discusses numerous readings that provide a basic foundation for understanding child welfare and protection issues through the lens of human rights. For example, Link (2007) provides an excellent analysis of the CRC as it relates to child welfare practice in the United States. In particular, she provides the broader historical context in which the CRC was adopted and an interesting international example in Slovenia of the use of the CRC as a template for best practice with children and families. The use of films, followed by small and large group discussion exercises, also provides excellent opportunities for students to study concrete examples of child welfare practice and analyze them through a human rights lens. As noted earlier, *The Taking of Logan Marr* is an example of a very useful film for generating meaningful discussion regarding child protection, human rights, policy analysis, and advocacy. Numerous other films can provide rich examples and opportunities for critical discussion of child welfare practice through the lens of human rights.

It is also critical that social workers play a more active role in advocating for change, in particular from a human rights perspective. Social work educators have a unique opportunity to educate professionals and increase their skills in this area. The sample assignment outlined in Appendix A can be expanded to include either an individual or group oriented advocacy project. Students can use their findings in the final column to advocate for change. One potential project is to write and submit a letter to the editor of the local paper briefly outlining a particular human rights issue and advocating for social change, such as providing greater support to children aging out of the foster care system. Another potential project is organizing stakeholder groups to testify at meetings and hearings of elected officials to advocate for policy change—again framing child welfare challenges as human rights issues.

Finally, students can advocate for change through professional publications such as journals and other periodicals. For example, the newsletter of the New England Association of Child Welfare Commissioners and Directors, *Common Ground*, is an excellent venue for students' position papers that advocate for policy change. Ultimately, the goal for social work educators is to provide child welfare professionals a greater understanding of how human rights intersect with child protection and permanency work and to incorporate a human rights lens into policy and practice.

References

Bailey, J. D., & Delavega, M. E. (2011). Rules on the Hague and the intercountry adoption act: Public comments and the state's responsiveness. *Journal of Policy Practice, 10*(1), 35–50.

Bergquist, K. J. S. (2009). Operation baby lift or baby abduction? *International Social Work, 52*, 621–633.

Bessant, J. (2011). International law as remedy: When the state breaches child protection statutes. *Child & Youth Services, 32*(3), 254–275.

Child Rights International Network. (2013, October 4). *South Sudan: Children's rights in UN treaty body reports.* Retrieved from http://www.crin.org/resources/infodetail.asp?id=29213

Children's Rights. (n.d.). *Reforming child welfare.* Retrieved from http://www.childrensrights.org/reform-campaigns/phases-of-reform/

Council on Social Work Education. (2008). *Educational policy and accreditation standards.* Retrieved from http://www.cswe.org/File.aspx?id=13780

DePanfilis, D., & Salus, M. K. (2003). *Child protective services: A guide for caseworkers.* Washington, DC: National Clearinghouse on Child Abuse and Neglect.

Figarola, R., & Cobb, J. (2014, July 30). *Meeting of the Community-Based Care Subcommittee on Children's Rights.* [Unpublished research].

Freundlich, M., Gerstenzang, S., Diaz, P., & London, E. (2003). *Continuing danger: A report of child fatalities in New York City.* New York, NY: Children's Rights.

Gursky, T., Sullivan, L., & Welch, M. (n.d.). *Poverty and child neglect: Exploring solutions through differential response.* Medford, MA: Tufts University, Department of Urban and Environmental Policy. Retrieved from http://ase.tufts.edu/uep/degrees/field_project_reports/2007/Team3_CFS_Report.pdf

Hague Conference on Private International Law. (1993). *Convention on the protection of children and co-operation in respect of intercountry adoption.* Retrieved from http://www.hcch.net/upload/conventions/txt33en.pdf

Healy, L. (2008). Exploring the history of social work as a human rights profession. *International Social Work, 51*, 735–748.

Hollingsworth, L.D. (2008). Does the Hague convention on intercountry adoption address the protection of adoptees' cultural identity? And should it? *Social Work, 53*, 377–379.

International Federation of Social Workers (IFSW). (2002). *Social work and the rights of the child: A professional training manual on the UN convention.* Retrieved from http://cdn.ifsw.org/assets/ifsw_124952-4.pdf

Kim, S., & Smith, C. J. (2009). Analysis of intercountry adoption policy and regulations: The case of Korea. *Children and Youth Services Review, 31*, 911–918.

League of Nations. (1924). *Geneva declaration of the rights of the child of 1924,* adopted Sept. 26, 1924, League of Nations O.J. Spec. Supp. 21, at 43. Retrieved from http://www.un-documents.net/gdrc1924.htm

Link, R. J. (2007). Children's rights as a template for social work practice. In E. Reichert (Ed.), *Challenges in human rights: A social work perspective* (pp. 215–238). New York, NY: Columbia University Press.

Mulley, C. (2009). *The woman who saved the children: A biography of Eglantyne Jebb, founder of save the children.* London, UK: Oneworld Publications.

National Child Welfare Workforce Institute. (2012). *Collection of child welfare syllabi from the 12 NCWWI traineeship programs.* Albany, NY: National Child Welfare Workforce Institute.

PBS Video (Producer & Director). (2003). *Failing to protect: The taking of Logan Marr.* [Motion Picture]. Boston, MA: PBS Video.

Save the Children. (2012, November). *Guidelines for the alternative care of children: Policy brief.* Retrieved from http://www.crin.org/docs/International _Guidelines_on_Alternative_Care_of_Childen_Policy_Brief[1][1].pdf

Tang, K. (2003). Implementing the United Nations Convention of the Rights of the Child: The Canadian experience. *International Social Work, 46*, 277–288.

UNICEF. (n.d.). *Fact sheet: A summary of the rights under the convention on the rights of the child.* Retrieved from http://www.unicef.org/crc/files/Rights_ overview.pdf

United Nations. (1989). *Convention on the rights of the child.* G.A. Res. 44/25. Retrieved from: http://www.ohchr.org/Documents/ProfessionalInterest/crc.pdf

United Nations. (2009). *Guidelines for the alternative care of children.* G.A. Res.
  64/142. Retrieved from http://www.unicef.org/protection/alternative_care
  _Guidelines-English%282%29.pdf

United Nations. (2013). *Treaty collections: Status on the convention on the
  rights of the child.* Retrieved from http://treaties.un.org/Pages/ViewDetails.
  aspx?src=TREATY&mtdsg_no=IV-11&chapter=4&lang=en

U.S. Department of State. (2013). *The Hague convention.* Retrieved from
  http://travel.state.gov/content/adoptionsabroad/en/hague-convention.html

Urban Justice Center. (2008). *Local implementation New York, New York: Race
  realities in New York City, Response to the periodic report of the United States to
  the United Nations Committee to End Racial Discrimination.* Retrieved from
  http://www.ushrnetwork.org/sites/default/files/26_new_york.pdf

Wang-Breal, S. (Producer & Director). (2009). *Wo ai ni mommy (I love you,
  mommy).* [Motion Picture]. United States: New Day Films.

Weisberg, R., & Roth, V. (Producers & Directors). (2005). *Aging out.* [Motion
  Picture]. United States: PBS Video.

Willow, C. (2010). *Children's right to be heard and effective child protection. A guide
  for governments and children rights advocates on involving children and young
  people in ending all forms of violence.* Bangkok, Thailand: Save the Children
  Sweden.

21 Deconstructing Mass Incarceration in the United States Through a Human Rights Lens: Implications for Social Work Education and Practice

Kirk James and Julie Smyth

Few things in this world are considered as axiomatic and pervasive across all cultures as is the concept of human rights. Its very essence creates and demands unification among people, communities, and countries regardless of race, culture, or creed. The theory of human rights was fully operationalized on December 10, 1948, by the United Nations General Assembly. The formation of the United Nations in 1945, and the Universal Declaration of Human Rights (UDHR; United Nations, 1948) shortly thereafter, was largely galvanized by the unimaginable human atrocities committed during the Second World War. The UDHR states:

> Whereas recognition of the inherent dignity and of the equal and inalienable rights of all members of the human family is the foundation of freedom, justice and peace in the world, Whereas disregard and contempt for human rights have resulted in barbarous acts which have outraged the conscience of mankind, and the advent of a world in which human beings shall enjoy freedom of speech and belief and freedom from fear and want has been proclaimed as the highest aspiration of the common people (Preamble).

The United States was principal in the formation of United Nations and also instrumental in crafting the UDHR. The United States is often hailed as the epicenter of democracy and freedom for all people. Archetypical stories of immigrants arriving by the boatload at Ellis Island recall idealism after fleeing inhumane conditions or lack of liberties in their countries of origin. The

United States has undoubtedly created pathways toward democracy and has often upheld human rights and dignity in numerous countries throughout the world; however, the gross human rights violation of mass incarceration in this country has continued unabated for more than a century.

The first section of this chapter contends that mass incarceration in the United States is in violation of the UDHR and subsequent human rights treaties such as the International Covenant on Civil and Political Rights (ICCPR; United Nations, 1966) and the International Convention on the Elimination of All Forms of Racial Discrimination (ICERD; United Nations, 1965), both of which the United States is party to. To support this assertion, which may be audacious to many, the authors examine mass incarceration through a human rights lens, illuminating numerous historical and contemporary contexts of injustices carried out under the guise of criminal justice in America.

The second section of this chapter explores the implications of this human rights violation for social work education, a profession birthed to ameliorate human conditions perpetuating injustice. The International Federation of Social Workers (IFSW) has long asserted that the catalytic, driving force of the profession is the intrinsic belief in human rights and dignity for all people (IFSW, 1988). Yet Healy (2008) asserts "the [social work] profession is not widely regarded as a leader within the larger global human rights movement" (p. 735). The authors use key human rights documents related to criminal justice reform, namely the ICCPR (United Nations, 1966) and the ICERD (United Nations, 1965), and conclude by offering practical examples on the integration of a human rights analysis of mass incarceration throughout facets of social work education, including points of infusion for clinical practice, advocacy and through targeted field placements.

Neo-Slavery

This chapter makes no attempt at rehashing the history of slavery. Few would disagree that chattel slavery in the United States represents one of the darkest chapters in the history of humanity. Thus, this section will instead focus on the advent of a new peculiar institution that was birthed through the Thirteenth Amendment. The passage of the Thirteenth Amendment is hailed as a monumental achievement in ending legalized inequality and the subhuman treatment of Blacks in America. Although its passage theoretically ended slavery, it also served to create another peculiar institution—slavery—which was made unconstitutional "except as punishment for crime whereof the party shall have been duly convicted" (James & Smyth, forthcoming; U.S. Const. amend. 13).

The peculiar clause in the Thirteenth Amendment not only allowed the institution of slavery (albeit by another name) to persist, but it also violates the UDHR, signed by United States. Article 4 of the UDHR states, "No one shall be held in slavery or servitude; slavery and the slave trade shall be prohibited in all their forms" (1948). The Thirteenth Amendment has, in its own language, left the door open for the continuation of this practice, through the cloak of mass incarceration.

Historical Perspective of Mass Incarceration

Although many define the onset of mass incarceration as an era beginning in the 1970s through the present (Alexander, 2010; Mauer, 2006; Mauer & King, 2007), historical analysis reveals that mass incarceration in the United States commenced at the conclusion of slavery. The Black Codes were laws passed by Southern states in response to the emancipation of African Americans by the Thirteenth Amendment, the impetus of which was to legalize the control and criminalization of newly freed Blacks (James & Smyth, forthcoming). Laws were arbitrarily orchestrated to criminalize the social and economic conditions of the newly freed slaves in the South. Historians and critical thinkers of the era, such as W. E. B. Du Bois, felt that the codes were nothing more than neo-slavery (1910). The Black Codes criminalized a litany of arbitrary actions, such as unemployment among Blacks and Blacks looking Whites in the face. The Codes criminalized Blacks for walking on the same side of the street as Whites and often allowed for the legal beatings of Blacks by Whites to settle oppressive labor contracts with Whites (Alexander, 2010; Berry & Blassingame, 1982; Cohen, 1991; Muhammad, 2010).

Perhaps the most obtrusive manifestation of neo-slavery to validate Du Bois' contention would come in the form of the *convict leasing system.* The inhumane atrocities committed within the convict leasing system prompted a journalist writing an exposé of the era to open with a caveat: "please reader, do not read this chapter unless you can steal your heart against pain" (Tannenbaum, 1938, p. 74). The convict leasing system resembled and mirrored many facets of slavery, allowing Blacks to be arrested, convicted, and sentenced under the Black Codes to be leased out to plantations, often fulfilling roles similar to those they thought were eradicated with the passage of the Thirteenth Amendment. Furthermore, the dubious distinction of being a convict allowed and justified greater mistreatment of these men and women than during chattel slavery (DuBois, 1910; Tannenbaum, 1938).

Writing on the conditions of individuals incarcerated under convict leasing system, Freidman (1993) concluded that inmates were treated more like animals than human beings. Blacks in the convict leasing system had few resources and no influence, and as such were ruthlessly and mercilessly treated (Allen & Abril, 1997). The mortality rates of incarcerated Blacks were also exponentially higher than the nonincarcerated population (Freidman, 1993). The convict leasing system persisted in many Southern states well into the 1940s, whereas the Black Codes were at least publicly reprimanded as inhumane and undemocratic. Yet this attributed identity of Blacks as criminals slowly saturated an American consciousness, rationalizing the continued subhuman treatment of Blacks in America, which is a poignant reality for the profession of social work.

The social work profession values and functions under the premise that people do not exist in silos, but rather that a person's environment, including reciprocal relationships and the physical and social environment, is critical to understanding individuals (Barker, 2003; NASW, 2005). We argue that the environment social workers must take into account is inclusive of the historical context that brought forth the present circumstances. Therefore, social work educators can and are recommended to include examinations of the effects of the historical context on current social systems in their syllabi; doing so will permit students to gain the historical perspectives necessary to fully understand contemporary social issues. When social work educators fail to include the historical context of contemporary issues such as mass incarceration (Cnaan, Draine, Frazier, & Sinha, 2008; James, 2013) students enter the field with inadequate knowledge of the historically racial, social, psychological, and economic factors that have propelled mass incarceration in the United States. This lack of context funnels student learning, subsequent understanding, and eventual practice to be shaped by social stigmas, rather than rooted in a holistic multidimensional framework typically associated with the social work profession.

Contemporary Mass Incarceration

The ideology that has fueled this new wave of mass incarceration can best be understood by the seminal work of criminologist Robert Martinson, who blasted the concept of rehabilitation, proposing that severe punishment and heavy community surveillance were the best methods to combat crime (Cullen, Smith, Lowencamp, & Latessa, 2009; Martinson, 1974). Martinson (1974) espoused a "nothing works" ideology about criminal behavior, which the field of criminology then legitimized as their mantra. The nothing works mentality in the field of criminology propelled the onset of the "get tough on crime" movement, which is embodied by the War on Drugs.

War on Drugs is the term commonly used to describe a period beginning in the mid-1970s, when a substantial amount of political energy was focused on ending the illicit drug trade and even the use of drugs in America (Alexander, 2010; James & Smyth, forthcoming). In a matter of a few years, a slew of drug prohibition laws were introduced across the nation, starting in New York. The most draconian, the Rockefeller Drug Laws, were enacted in 1973. Individuals incarcerated for possessing 4 ounces of cocaine or selling 2 ounces of cocaine were often mandated to life sentences (Alexander, 2010; Department of Criminal Justice Services, 2014).

This concept of mandatory minimums was introduced during this period, establishing mandatory prison sentences, which removed judicial discretion and the consideration of mitigating factors in determining the length of a prison sentence (Alexander, 2010; James, 2013; Muhammad, 2010). Despite an array of policy changes throughout the early 21st century, the collateral consequences of the War on Drugs are still felt all across the country today, maintaining a profoundly negative effect on poor communities of color.

To highlight the colossal effect of the tough on crime movement, in 1972 the prison population stood at around 300,000, and today more than 2 million people are incarcerated in state and federal prisons in the United States. There are also many more than 5 million people on probation, parole, or other form of community supervision (Carson & Golinelli, 2013; Glaze & Herberman, 2013; Maruschak, 2012; United States Department of Justice, 2012). This means that one of every 104 people in the United States is currently incarcerated, and one of every 33 people is under correctional system control. One would naturally attribute this influx to higher crime rates, yet between 1960 and 1990, for example, "official crime rates in Finland, Germany and the United States were close to identical" (James, 2013, p. 40). Far more disturbing than the vast number of people incarcerated is the extremely disproportionate racial composition. In 2007 approximately 900,000 prisoners were African American (Mauer & King, 2007), with African American women being the fastest growing prison population (James & Glaze, 2006). In 2009 the Bureau of Justice Statistics reported that non-Hispanic Blacks accounted for nearly 40% of the total federal and state prison population; however, the 2010 census reported that Blacks comprised less than 14% of the U.S. population. In fact, more African American men are under some form of criminal justice supervision today than were enslaved in 1850 (Alexander, 2010; James & Smyth, forthcoming).

The Black Codes of the 19th century successfully germinated into present day processes such as "stop and frisk" policing strategies, mandatory minimum sentences, "three strikes"[1] and "truth in sentencing"[2] legislations. Each of these contemporary mechanisms has incarcerated millions of poor people of color in the United States. The Sentencing Project (Mauer, 2014) reports that 60% of those incarcerated are people of color or ethnic minorities and, more specifically, that two thirds of all those incarcerated for drug offenses are people of color.

The Vera Institute of Justice, in partnership with the Manhattan District Attorney's office, released a report in 2014 about the effects of race on prosecution and sentencing in the Borough of Manhattan (Kutateladze & Andiloro, 2014). The report found that "compared to similarly situated white defendants, black and Latino defendants were more likely to be detained at arraignment… receive a custodial sentence offer as a result of the plea bargaining, and to be incarcerated" (Kutateladze, Tymas, & Crowley, 2014, p. 3) and also that "Black defendants were 19% more likely… to receive a punitive sentence offer" (Kutateladze & Andiloro, 2014, p. 161) than their White counterparts. Most notably, the summary report concluded by stating that the causes of these racial disparities in sentencing "are complex, with historical underpinnings as deep as our nation's history is long…includ[ing] policies that are neutral on their faces, but produce unfair racial impacts" (Kutateladze, et al., 2014, p. 9) This report by the Vera Institute is a clear example that many laws, which on the surface appear to be race-neutral, continue to wreak havoc on communities of color.

Human Rights Framework for Criminal Justice Curriculum Infusion

A key human rights treaty directly related to criminal justice reform is the ICCPR, which was approved by the United Nations in 1966 and ratified by the United States in 1992 under the Clinton administration (Labelle, 2013). This treaty reiterates the basic human rights principles of the inherent dignity of all persons and places restrictions on harsh sentences and degrading treatment for children and adults in the criminal justice system. Despite the necessary and exhaustive principles presented within the ICCPR, the United States continues to incarcerate more of its citizens than any country in the world (Walmsley, 2013); the conditions of these jails and prisons are more than often egregious (Human Rights Watch, 2014; Weiser, 2014; Weiser, & Schwirtz, 2014; Winerip & Schwirtz, 2014).

Article 26 of ICCPR, taken in conjunction with the Vera Institute of Justice's report about racial discrimination in sentencing, highlights exactly why the human rights lens is critical to examining the criminal justice system. Article 26 of ICCPR states:

All persons are equal before the law and are entitled without any discrimination to the equal protection of the law. In this respect, the law shall prohibit any discrimination and guarantee to all persons equal and effective protection against discrimination on any ground such as race, colour, sex, language, religion, political or other opinion, national or social origin, property, birth or other status.

Furthermore, Article 10 of the ICCPR states, "All persons deprived of their liberty shall be treated with humanity and with respect for the *inherent dignity of the human person*" (emphasis added; United Nations, 1966).

Another important human rights treaty, which the United States ratified in 1994, is the ICERD (United Nations, 1965). Taken with the ICCPR, ICERD provides another human rights mechanism through which to draw attention to the mass incarceration of people of color in the United States. In 2008 the Committee on the Elimination of Racial Discrimination determined the United States was in violation of Article 5 of ICERD: a review of the U.S. record found that "young offenders belonging to racial, ethnic and national minorities, including children constitute a disproportionate number of those sentenced to life imprisonment without parole" (UN Committee on the Elimination of Racial Discrimination, 2008, para. 21). In August 2014 the Committee on the Elimination of Racial Discrimination reviewed an alternative or shadow report from Los Angeles-based Dignity and Power Now and UCLA's Law and Human Rights Project on incarceration and abuse of Black people with mental health conditions in Los Angeles, CA, jails (Dignity and Power Now, n.d.). This represents another instance in which U.S. organizations use international law and mechanisms to highlight human rights violations related to mass incarceration and racism.

This is the perspective with which social work education and advocacy should be practiced. This framework must be considered within the aforementioned historical context of contemporary mass incarceration and the effect of attributed identity of Blacks as criminal, and synthesized to inform practice and policy around issues of mass incarceration that are truly just.

Implications for Social Work Education

The marginalization of criminal justice coursework within the field of social work during an era of mass incarceration overlooks the role that social workers can play both within and adjunct to the criminal justice system. Even more concerning is that criminal justice content is not required for students to be placed in field settings in the realm of criminal justice (Epperson, Robert, Ivanoff, Tripodi, & Gilmer, 2013; James, 2013). Epperson et al. (2013) found that less than 5% of MSW programs offer a concentration in a justice-related field. As a result, students training to work with oppressed and marginalized populations learn very little about mass incarceration in the United States. As such, when contacted with individuals affected by the criminal justice system, the response tends to be myopic and espouses a paradigm that solely focuses on changing behavior, rather than adopting a broader social work perspective of understanding individuals in the context of their environment (Epperson et al., 2013; James, 2013). In light of this clear educational gap, the profession as a whole must question the competency among MSW students to engage and work directly (and in many cases indirectly) with people affected by the justice system.

This next section examines various micro/clinical and macro staples of social work education as indicated by the Council of Social Work Education, and their intersection with mass incarceration. The section concludes with strategies of infusion based on the experiential knowledge of the authors. Specifically, they examine the Goldring Reentry Initiative (GRI) at the University of Pennsylvania School of Social Policy and Practice, which they played key roles in developing.

Intersections With Clinical Social Work Practice
Mental Health & Trauma

Clinical social workers are among the foremost providers of mental health services in the United States. As a result, schools of social work identify mental health education as one of the primary expectations of incoming students. At midyear 2005, more than half of all prison and jail inmates had a mental health diagnosis, including 705,600 inmates in state prisons, 78,800 in federal prisons, and 479,900 in local jails. This represents approximately 56% of state prisoners, 45% of federal prisoners, and 64% of jail inmates (Bloom & Farragher, 2010; James & Glaze, 2006). These numbers show that approximately 1.2 million incarcerated people have diagnosed mental health conditions. Mental health problems are even more prominent among incarcerated women. Seventy-three percent of women incarcerated in state prisons and 75% of women in local jails have diagnosed mental health problems (James & Glaze, 2006).

A systematic review of 62 surveys from across the country reported inmates (N=23,000) had greater predispositions to both posttraumatic stress disorder and antisocial personality disorder than the general public (Fazel & Danesh, 2002). Many individuals with ties to the criminal justice system also possess what Kupers (2005) has described as double jeopardy for posttraumatic stress disorder. Kupers (2005) reported that prisoners are often the victims of interpersonal abuse and have witnessed untold violence during their own developmental trajectories, which are often exacerbated by the trauma of incarceration.

The critical syllabus revisions to social work curricula would include an examination of the justice response to people with mental health challenges. This would include an overview of the numbers of incarcerated individuals who suffer from mental illness, their treatment while incarcerated, and the effects of incarceration on preexisting mental health challenges. The effects of solitary confinement on these men and women both during their sentence and rippling into their reentry are also rich for clinical learning and subsequent practice and advocacy. In particular, much is written about the effect of solitary confinement on all persons and on individuals with preexisting mental health conditions (Smith, 2006). Also important to highlight is the fact that the United Nations has deemed solitary confinement, in the vast majority of cases, as a form of torture that persists at unprecedented levels throughout the United States (Méndez, 2011).

Children & Families

Children with incarcerated parents are referred to as the "hidden victims" of the criminal justice system (Miller, 2006; p. 473). As a result of increasing jail and prison populations, at least 2.4 million children in the United States have one or both parents incarcerated, one in nine Black children has a parent incarcerated on any given day (Boudin & Zeller-Berkman, 2010; Ehrensoft,

Khashu, Ross, & Wamsley, 2003). Since 1990 the number of incarcerated women in the United States has increased by more than 110%, and at least 75% of incarcerated women were the primary caretakers of at least one child before their incarceration (Margolies & Kraft-Stolar, 2006). The sudden removal of a caretaker from the home creates financial instability for children. Caretaker instability also increases children's risk of experiencing the traumatic effects of insecure attachment, sometimes leading to depression, anxiety, and other trauma-related stress (Smyth, 2012).

The Centers for Disease Control acknowledges parental/caregiver incarceration as an "adverse childhood event," reporting that these have been linked to a wide range of health outcomes in adulthood including substance abuse, cardiovascular disease, depression, and diabetes (Centers for Disease Control, 2011). Due to the significant number of children affected by mass incarceration, Sesame Street now has toolkits training professions and families about how to talk to children about parental incarceration (see http://www.sesame-street.org/cms_services/services?action=download&uid=784d4f44-425b-445a-842b-86b5088cbcc5).

Many MSW students aim to work clinically with children and families; therefore, we recommend that schools of social work require competency regarding the effects of parental incarceration on children, which includes infusing mass incarceration specific curricula items to all social worker courses about children, child development, and child welfare.

Homelessness

Social workers have long worked with homeless populations; yet there is a bidirectional relationship between homelessness and incarceration, meaning that incarceration often leads to homelessness, and homelessness often leads to incarceration (Fruedenburg, 2001). Metraux and Culhane (2006) found that "due to their marginal economic and social status and the public nature of their existence, homeless individuals are more prone to arrests and incarceration for misdemeanors and a range of minor crimes" (p. 3). The rate of recent homelessness among U.S. jail inmates was found to be very high (15.3%), approximately 7.5 to 11.3 times higher than that found in the general population (Greenberg

& Rosenheck, 2008). Homeless individuals with criminal records then have a greater challenge of obtaining housing due to the many systemic barriers experienced by formerly incarcerated people (Metraux & Culhane, 2006).

Social work curricula should be sure that when they address contemporary social issues such as homelessness, itself a key human rights concern, coursework takes a systems perspective toward this bidirectional relationship between homelessness and incarceration. In our minds it is impossible to discuss homelessness without discussing criminal justice, and therefore coursework and assignments should be established with this in mind.

Advocacy Infusion: Voter Disenfranchisement

Article 21 of the UDHR states, "everyone has the right to take part in the government of his country, directly or through freely chosen representatives." Universal suffrage is the foundation of the democratic process, and many Americans fought tirelessly for the rights of women and racial minorities in this regard (Uggen & Manza, 2002). President Lyndon B. Johnson said the following at the signing of the Voter Rights Act of 1965: "[T]he vote is the most powerful instrument ever devised by man for breaking down injustice and destroying the terrible walls which imprison men because they are different than other men" (American Civil Liberties Union, 2010).

The right to vote is clearly a cornerstone of democracy. Social workers, and especially social work education, have long championed this democratic process by involving themselves with voter registration or volunteering their spaces for polling during election periods; however, many do not realize that this universal human right is extinguished as a result of a felony conviction for many individuals. Since the surge in the prison population in the late 20th century, a significant number of citizens have lost the right to vote as a result of criminal convictions, some temporarily and others permanently. Although a number of countries deny voting rights to prison inmates, the United States is alone in restricting rights of nonincarcerated individuals who have prior felony convictions. Some activists call this denial of the right to vote "civil death." In fact, the United States is the solitary democratic country that can permanently disfranchise individuals with felony convictions.

Within the United States, Maine and Vermont are the only two states that allow individuals incarcerated on felony charges to submit absentee ballots from prison. Eleven states in the United States put people at risk of permanently losing voting rights. Twenty states reinstate the right to vote after all involvement in the criminal justice system is terminated, including probation and parole. Four states reinstate the right after the end of parole, and 13 states and the District of Columbia reinstate the right to vote after one's term of incarceration (American Civil Liberties Union, 2010).

Voter disfranchisement is an area ripe for social work student organizing and advocacy. In a social policy or advocacy course, voter disfranchisement can be presented as not only a social justice issue, but also as a human rights issue as outlined by the UDHR, the ICCPR, and ICERD. As an overarching assignment, students can be tasked to partner with existing advocacy organizations and creatively advocate on the issue. The outcome of the assignment could be organizing a community-based event that brings together advocates, elected officials, and affected communities to discuss the issue from a human rights perspective with the goal of continued co-creation of a policy and advocacy strategy to challenge the disfranchisement of millions of America's citizens.

Class and Field Placement Infusion Example: The GRI

Outside the classroom, field placements are considered the gold standard of social work education. Yet often very little consideration is given to the incongruities of values that could exist between field agencies and the profession of social work (James, 2013). The Council on Social Work Education reports that many students are placed in criminal justice settings (CSWE, 2010). This, is in spite of various reports indicating the absence of classroom education to guide their work (Epperson et al., 2013; James, 2013). Working in justice settings is essential for our profession, yet it is even more critical that our students have the prerequisite competency to work from a position that is informed not only by the values and ethics of social work education, but also by a thorough understanding of the human rights implications of mass incarceration presented in the first section of this chapter.

The GRI is a field and educational placement opportunity developed at the University of Pennsylvania's School of Social Policy and Practice. The GRI works in conjunction with the University of Pennsylvania, the Philadelphia Prison System, the Defender Association of Philadelphia, and other related community partners to provide a block field placement for MSW students. The mission of the GRI is to increase micro and macro competencies for MSW students regarding issues of mass incarceration and the criminal justice system (University of Pennsylvania, 2014).

The GRI was developed at the School of Social Policy and Practice in response to the high levels of recidivism faced by men and women returning to Philadelphia communities. Research indicates that almost 75% of people released will return to prison within 3 years; moreover, most of these men and women lack the necessary support to make a successful transition from prison (James, 2013). With this in mind, the GRI was designed not only to train MSW students through course work to better understand the historical and contemporary mechanisms of the justice system, but also to train them to work with men and women reentering society 3 months prerelease, and 3 months postrelease. The design was in part due to extensive research into various reentry programs across the country that demonstrated empirical success using a pre- and postrelease continuum of care model.

The GRI is unique, not only because it is probably the only program in a school of social work designed specifically to train social work students about issues of mass incarceration while they also work with men and women returning to society, but it also employs what is called a "block placement." Students entering the program take classes/orientations together to increase their knowledge of mass incarceration. Core courses were infused with information about mass incarceration to gain a more holistic understanding of the challenges facing people affected by the justice system.

For example, the first GRI cohort (12 second-year MSW students) was placed in the same advanced clinical practice class. The integration of facets of mass incarceration entailed that students examine clinical practice theories with a specific focus on how the theory could be appropriately used in juxtaposition to the systemic challenges faced by people affected by the justice system, as well as the inherent challenges for social work practitioners in justice set-tings. Motivational interviewing, for example, did not just examine the stages of change and strategies to empower people toward change in silos. Rather, it was taught with an understanding that although behavioral change is in many cases necessary, the social, economic, and racial barriers often experienced by incarcerated people must also be addressed for the desired results to occur. Connections between these structural barriers, racism, and human rights are explicitly discussed by students in the block placement, thus challenging the tendency in social work to pathologize or individualize social problems.

Conclusion

Mass incarceration is a human rights issue that is directly pertinent to social work practitioners and educators. It is imperative that social work education be infused with an informed historical understanding of the varying facets of mass incarceration. A human rights analysis galvanized by our organizing value of social justice must be a staple across all of social work education. In this chapter we highlighted numerous possibilities for infusion of criminal justice content across social work curricula, including points for clinical infusion; a relevant advocacy example; and an overview of the GRI, a functioning field and educational placement pertaining to mass incarceration and the related field of reentry.

Infusion of human rights-informed criminal justice content is the most efficient way to disseminate information across existing social work curricula. Historically, similar methods of infusion can be seen relating to cultural diver-sity (Doyle, 1997) and more recently with gerontology (Appleby & Botsford, 2006; Cummings, Cassie, Galambos & Wilson, 2006; Fredriksen-Goldsen, Hooyman, & Bonifas, 2006; Lee, Collins, Mahoney, McInnis-Dittrich & Boucher, 2006). It is imperative that we hold the social work profession accountable to its organizing values and principles of social justice and basic human rights.

Social work is a profession birthed to ameliorate the human plight. It may be argued that no greater social and human injustice exists in America today than mass incarceration's effect on individuals, families, and entire communities. The damage of incarcerating millions of people is incalculable. Informed responses at the micro, mezzo, and macro levels of social work education must happen now if we are to truly stand by our organizing value of social justice.

References

Alexander, M. (2010). *The new Jim Crow: Mass incarceration in the age of colorblindness.* New York, NY: New Press.

Allen, H. E., & Abril, J. C. (1997). The new chain gang: Corrections in the next century. *American Journal of Criminal Justice, 22*(1), 1–12.

American Civil Liberties Union. (2010). *ACLU history: Guaranteeing the right to vote.* Retrieved from https://www.aclu.org/voting-rights/aclu-history-guaranteeing-right-vote

Appleby, E., & Botsford, A. L. (2006). Research, macro practice and aging in the social work education curriculum. *Journal of Gerontological Social Work, 48,* 257–279.

Barker, R. L. (2003). *The social work dictionary* (4th ed.). Washington, DC: NASW Press.

Berry, M. F., & Blassingame, J. (1982). *Long memory: The Black experience in America.* New York, NY: Oxford University Press.

Bloom, S. L., & Farragher, B. (2010). *Destroying sanctuary: The crisis in human service delivery systems.* New York, NY: Oxford University Press.

Blomberg, T. G., & Lucken, K. (2010). *American penology.* New Brunswick, NJ: Transaction.

Boudin, K., & Zeller-Berkman, S. (2010). Children of promise. In J. A. Graham, Y. R. Harris, & G. J. Oliver Carpenter (Eds.), *Children of incarcerated parents: Theoretical, developmental, and clinical issues* (pp. 73–101). New York, NY: Springer.

Carson, A. E., & Golinelli, D. (2013). *Prisoners in 2012: Trends in admissions and releases, 1991–2012. Bureau of Justice Statistics.* Retrieved from http://www.bjs.gov/index.cfm?ty=pbdetail&iid=4842

Centers for Disease Control (CDC). (2011). *Adverse childhood experiences reported by adults.* Retrieved from http://www.cdc.gov/features/dsACEs/

Cnaan, R., Draine, J., Frazier, B., & Sinha, J. (2008). Ex-prisoner' re-entry: An emerging frontier and a social work challenge. *Journal of Policy Practice, 7*(2–3), 178–198.

Cohen, W. (1991). *At freedom's edge: Black mobility and the southern white quest for racial control.* Baton Rouge, LA: Louisiana State University Press.

Council on Social Work Education (CSWE). (2010). *Statistics on social work education in the United States.* Alexandria, VA: Author.

Cullen, F. T., Smith, P., Lowencamp, C. T., & Latessa, E. J. (2009). Nothing works revisited: Deconstructing Farabee's Rethinking Rehabilitaiton. *Victims and Offenders, 4,* 101–123.

Cummings, S. M., Cassie, K. M., Galambos, C., & Wilson, E. (2006). Impact of an infusion model on social work students' aging knowledge, attitudes, and interests. *Journal of Gerontological Social Work, 47,* 173–186.

Department of Criminal Justice Services. (2014). *2009 drug law changes: 2014 update.* (Report No. 5). New York, NY: Office of Justice and Research Performance.

Dignity and Power Now. (n.d.). *Advocates release United Nations report exposing incarceration and abuse of Black people with mental health conditions in LA jails as a violation of international law.* Retrieved from http://nationinside.org /campaign/dignity/posts/advocates-release-united-nations-reports-exposing -incarceration-and-abuse-o/

Doyle, C. (1997) Working with abused children. Basingstoke, UK: Macmillan/ BASW.

Du Bois, W. E. B. (1910). Reconstruction and its benefits. *American Historical Review, 15*(4), 784.

Epperson, M. W., Robert, L. E., Ivanoff, A., Tripodi, S. J., & Gilmer, C. N. (2013). To what extent is criminal justice content specifically addressed in MSW program? *Journal of Social Work Education, 49,* 96–107.

Fazel, S., & Danesh, J. (2002). Serious mental disorder in 23000 prisoners: a systematic review of 62 surveys. *Lancet, 359*(9306), 545–550.

Fredriksen-Goldsen, K. I., Hooyman, N. R., & Bonifas, R. P. (2006). Innovations in gerontological social work education multigenerational practice: An innovative infusion approach [Special section]. *Journal of Social Work Education, 42,* 25–36.

Friedman, L. M. (1993). *Crime and punishment in American history.* New York: Basic Books.

Freudenberg, N. (2001). Jails, prisons, and the health of urban populations: A review of the impact of the correctional system on community health. *Journal of Urban Health, 78*(2), 214-235.

Glaze, L. E., & Herberman, E. J. (2013). Correctional populations in the United States, 2012. *Bureau of Justice Statistics Bulletin.* Retrieved from http://www.bjs .gov/content/pub/pdf/cpus12.pdf

Greenberg, G. A. & Rosenheck, R. A. (2008) Jail incarceration, homelessness and mental health: A national study. *Psychiatric Services, 59*(2), 170–177.

Healy, L. M. (2008). Exploring the history of social work as a human rights profession. *International Social Work, 51,* 735–748.

Human Rights Watch. (2014). Prison and detention conditions. Retrieved from http://www.hrw.org/united-states/us-program/prison-and-detention-conditions

International Federation of Social Workers (IFSW). (1988). Human rights. In *International Policy Papers.* Geneva, Switzerland: Author.

James, D. J., & Glaze, L. E. (2006). Mental health problems of prison and jail inmates. *Bureau of Justice Statistics Special Report.* Retrieved from http://www .cmhda.org/go/portals/0/cmhda%20files/committees/forensics/handouts/ bureau_of_justice_statistics_mh_problems_of_prison_and_jail_inmates_(12 -18-08).pdf

James, K. (2013). *The invisible epidemic: Educating social work students toward holistic practice in a period of mass incarceration.* (Unpublished doctoral dissertation) University of Pennsylvania School of Social Policy and Practice, Philadelphia, PA. Retrieved from http://repository.upenn.edu/edissertations _sp2/34

James K., & Smyth. J. (In press). If George Zimmerman was found guilty, would the criminal justice system be considered just? A racial examination of American criminal justice in the aftermath of Trayvon Martin. In K. J. Fasching-Varner, A. Dixson, R. Reynolds, & K. Albert (Eds.), *Trayvon Martin, race and American justice: Writing wrong.* The Netherlands: Sense Publishers.

Kupers, T. A. (2005). Toxic masculinity as a barrier to mental health treatment in prison. *Journal of Clinical Psychology, 61*(6), 713–724.

Kutateladze, B. L., & Andiloro, N. R. (2014). Prosecution and racial justice in New York County—technical report. Vera Institute of Justice: Prosecution and Racial Justice Program. Retrieved from http://www.vera.org/sites/default/files /resources/downloads/race-and-prosecution-manhattan-technical.pdf

Kutateladze, B., Tymas, W., & Crowley, M. (2014). Race and prosecution in Manhattan: Research summary July 2014. Retrieved from http://www.vera. org/sites/default/files/resources/downloads/race-and-prosecution-manhattan -summary.pdf

Labelle, D. (2013). *Criminal justice & human rights in the United States.* Retrieved from http://www.ushrnetwork.org/site/ushrnetwork.org/files/criminal_justice _framing_paper_-_ushrn.pdf

Lee, E. K., Collins, P., Mahoney, K., McInnis-Dittrich, K., & Boucher, E. (2006). Enhancing social work practice with older adults: The role of infusing gerontology content into the master of social work foundation curriculum. *Educational Gerontology, 32,* 737–756.

Margolies, J. K., & Kraft-Stolar, T. (2006). *When "free" means losing your mother: The collision of child welfare and the incarceration of women in New York state: A report of the Women in Prison of Correctional Association of New York.* Retrieved from http://www.correctionalassociation.org/wpcontent/uploads/2012/05/When_Free_Rpt_Fe_2006.pdf

Martinson, R. (1974). What works? Questions and answers about prison reform. *The Public Interest, 35,* 22–54.

Maruschak, L. M. (2012). Probation and parole in the United States, 2011. Bureau of Justice Statistics. Retrieved from http://www.bjs.gov/content/pub/pdf/ppus11.pdf

Mauer, M. (2006). *Race to incarcerate.* New York, NY: The New Press.

Mauer, M. (2014). *The sentencing project: Racial disparity.* Retrieved from http://www.sentencingproject.org/template/page.cfm?id=122

Mauer, M., & King, R. S. (2007). *Uneven justice: State rates of incarceration by race and ethnicity.* Washington, DC: Sentencing Project.

Méndez, J. (2011). Solitary confinement should be banned in most cases, UN expert says. *UN News Centre.* Retrieved from http://www.un.org/apps/news/story.asp?NewsID=40097#.U_Z4-xzNX3M

Metraux, S., & Culhane, D. P. (2006). Recent incarceration history among a sheltered homeless population. *Crime & Delinquency, 52*(3), 504–517.

Miller, K. M. (2006). The impact of parental incarceration on children: An emerging need for effective interventions. *Child and Adolescent Social Work Journal, 23*(4), 472–486.

Muhammad, K. G. (2010). *The condemnation of Blackness.* Cambridge, MA: Harvard University Press.

National Association of Social Workers (NASW). (2005) *NASW standards for clinical social work in social work practice.* Washington, DC: NASW Press.

Sentencing Project. (2014). *Shadow report of the Sentencing Project to the committee on the elimination of racial discrimination: Regarding racial disparities in the United States criminal justice system.* Retrieved from http://sentencingproject.org/doc/publications/rd_CERD_Shadow_Report_2014.pdf

Smith, P. S. (2006). The effects of solitary confinement on prison inmates: A brief history and review of the literature. *Crime and Justice, 34*(1), 441–548.

Smyth, J. (2012). Dual punishment: Incarcerated mothers and their children. *Columbia University School of Social Work Review 3(1), 33–45.*

Tannenbaum, F. (1938). *Crime and the community.* Boston, MA: Ginn.

Uggen, C., & Manza, J. (2002). Democratic contraction? Political consequences of felon disenfranchisement in the United States. *American Sociological Review, 67*(9), 777–803.

United Nations. (1948). *Universal declaration of human rights.* G.A. Res. 217 A (III). Retrieved from http://www.refworld.org/docid/3ae6b3712c.html

United Nations. (1965*). International convention on the elimination of all forms of racial discrimination,* G. A. Res. 2106 (XX). Retrieved from http://www.ohchr.org /Documents/ProfessionalInterest/cerd.pdf

United Nations. (1966, December 16). *International covenant on civil and political rights.* G.A. Res. 2200A (XXI). Retrieved from http://www.ohchr.org /Documents/ProfessionalInterest/ccpr.pdf

United Nations Committee on the Elimination of Racial Discrimination. (2008, May 8). *Consideration of reports submitted by states parties under Article 9 of the Convention, concluding observations of the Committee on the Elimination of Racial Discrimination: United States of America.* CERD/C/USA/CO/6. Retrieved from http://www.refworld.org/docid/4885cfa70.html

United States Department of Justice. (2012). *Correctional populations in the United States, 2011.* (NCJ 239972). Bureau of Justice Statistics. Retrieved from http://www.bjs.gov/content/pub/pdf/cpus11.pdf

University of Pennsylvania. (2014). *Goldring reentry initiative (GRI).* Retrieved from http://www.sp2.upenn.edu/gri/

Wamsley, R. (2013). World prison population list (10th ed.). *International Centre for Prison Studies.* London, UK: University of Essex.

Weiser, B. (2014, July 21). New York City to pay $2.75 million to settle suit in death of Rikers Island inmate. *The New York Times.* Retrieved from http://www.nytimes.com/2014/07/21/nyregion/new-york-city-to-pay-2-75 -million-to-settle-suit-in-death-of-rikers-island-inmate.html?_r=0

Winerip, M., & Schwirtz, M. (2014, July 14). Rikers: Where mental illness meets brutality in jails. *The New York Times.* Retrieved from http://www.nytimes. com/2014/07/14/nyregion/rikers-study-finds-prisoners-injured-by-employees .html

Endnotes

1   Legislation allowed prosecutors to give life prison sentences to individuals convicted of a felony with two prior serious or violent convictions (Blomberg & Lucken, 2010).

2   A punitive policy enacted in 1987 to ensure that individuals convicted of a criminal offense would serve at least 85% of their sentence prior to being eligible for parole. Truth in sentencing did away with early release as a result of good behavior or completion of mandated programs (Alexander, 2010).

22 | Human Rights and Migration

Uma A. Segal

When human rights and human migration are coupled, thoughts immediately turn to human trafficking. Although this should certainly be an integral part of any discussion on human rights and the movement of peoples, it would be a grave error to overlook the breadth and depth of rights violations of both voluntary migrants (authorized and those without the requisite papers) and other types of involuntary migrants (refugees, asylum seekers, and stateless persons) as well as those who have been trafficked for sex or labor.

This chapter goes beyond attention to human rights violations perpetrated on trafficked adults and children, to raise awareness of the several ways in which international migrant groups are abused in transit and destination countries/regions. If migrants are without the requisite human capital to be in a position to negotiate equity or are in a country illegally, they are vulnerable to a number of forms of abuses, including a most common form that requires them to work long hours for low wages and in deplorable conditions.

With cross-national communication and possibilities for mobility increasing exponentially, migrant populations are present in all nations, and social work education must begin to include them in discussions of both diversity (population-focused courses) and human rights advocacy (issue-focused) courses. Although these discussions should be included in curricular offerings, social work in the United States and abroad has been slow to truly recognize immigrant and refugee issues as being important ingredients to integrate into courses, and concern about human rights is even further in the background.

Global Migration

Although people migrate for several reasons, underlying all is the search for opportunities for a better quality of life. To regulate migration, most nations have developed immigration policies that screen and limit entry, and a few also monitor and control exit. The desire for an improvement in opportunity, however, is not as easily regulated, and its search often puts individuals and groups at the mercy of those who can determine or influence their fate. Most countries differentiate between voluntary and involuntary migrants as well as between legal and unauthorized immigrants (in this chapter, *immigrant* is used to refer to all entrants, regardless of immigrant status) and the resources they may access are circumscribed by these categories (see Figure 1).

Figure 1   **Voluntary and involuntary immigrant groups**

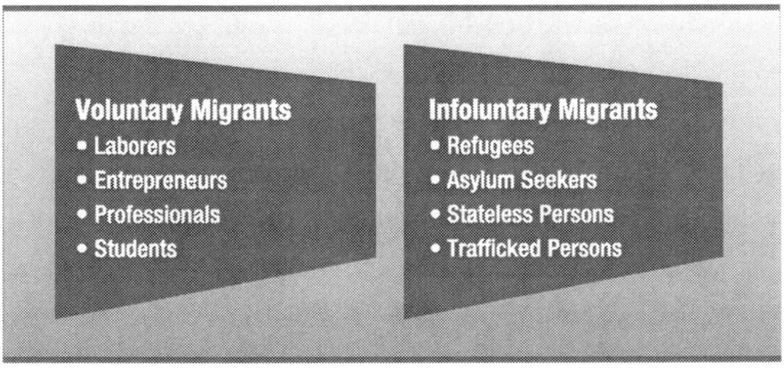

Voluntary Migrants
- Laborers
- Entrepreneurs
- Professionals
- Students

Infoluntary Migrants
- Refugees
- Asylum Seekers
- Stateless Persons
- Trafficked Persons

Voluntary Immigrants

Voluntary migrants leave their homelands and enter a country by choice (Global Commission on International Migration, 2005); some may be individuals with papers that permit them legal residence in a country, others may have entered the nation legally but overstayed the term of their visit, and some may have entered without authorization. Portes and Rumbaut (2006) identify three types of voluntary migrants: labor migrants, entrepreneurs, and professionals. *Labor migrants* usually are low skilled and work in low status, low paying jobs that, nevertheless, allow them a better lifestyle than would be available to them at home. *Entrepreneurs* usually have sufficient social and financial capital in their home countries and are able to identify and pursue business opportunities abroad. *Professionals* have traditionally been seen as the "brain drain" of their home countries and are highly educated with superior competencies in their disciplines. *Students*, though not mentioned as a specific category by Portes and Rumbaut (2006), compose a potential migrant pool because some change their temporary student status to permanency when they complete their education and decide not to return to their homelands.

Involuntary Migrants

Involuntary migrants are individuals who are forced to move out of their homelands despite a preference to remain. Among these are refugees, asylum seekers, stateless persons, and victims of human trafficking. *Refugees* are in a migrant category defined by the 1951 Convention (United Nations, 1951) and the 1967 Protocol of the United Nations High Commissioner for Refugees (United Nations, 1967) as a group that is outside its home country "owing to a well-founded fear of being persecuted for reasons of race, religion, nationality, membership of a particular social group or political opinion" (United Nations High Commissioner for Refugees [UNHCR], 2005, p. 11) and is unable or unwilling to return to the country for the same reasons. *Asylum seekers* may have entered a country legally or illegally; they are people who have requested international protection but whose cases are being investigated (UNHCR, 2012a). *Stateless people* are those without a nationality, perhaps because the borders have moved or because the nation state does not recognize them, and, hence they have no access to the country's resources or services (UNHCR, 2012b). They are marginalized in the land in which they reside and have limited or no opportunities to work or integrate into the country (UNHCR, 2012a). *Victims of human trafficking* are people who are trafficked and exploited for labor and/ or for sex (United Nations Office on Drugs and Crime, 2012).

Host Country Dilemma

Most countries of the developed world, barring the United States of America, are experiencing a declining workforce. As continuing population declines are evidenced because of dropping birthrates and aging workers, countries in the Global North are purposefully turning to immigrants from developing countries, where population numbers continue to grow (see http://www.census.gov/population/international/data/idb/informationGateway.php). Despite this logical solution to the labor shortage, there are numerous pitfalls and barriers, as Max Frisch's oft-quoted statement, "we wanted workers; we got people instead" rings forever true. Along with their workforce contributions, immigrants bring to a nation a diversity of cultures, experiences, and expectations, several of which either conflict with or question the norms of native populations. The dilemma for several countries is that although they need immigrants to fill their labor force and economic needs, they do not really want them (Ceobanu & Koropeckyj-Cox, 2012).

Issues Facing Immigrants and Refugees

As we begin, albeit slowly, to explore how social workers can become involved in working with immigrants and refugees, the profession has attempted to identify issues facing these populations. Interestingly, the focus has been on migration related concerns, even in the several publications (both recent and older) by this author (see Segal, 1991, 2004, 2012, 2013). However, to truly work with this population, as with any other, one must also take into account issues universal to all human beings. Migrant groups often are vulnerable or disfranchised, they are also subject to several human rights violations. Thus, Figure 2 portrays a holistic view of issues with which a large number of immigrants and refugees must contend.

Figure 2   **Issues facing immigrants and refugees**

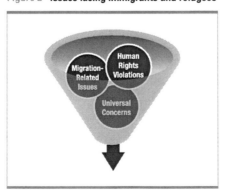

Universal Concerns

In its wonderful sensitivity to diversity and cultural competence, social work fails to recognize or pay heed to the reality that human beings are more similar than they are different. As the profession focuses on diverse issues, it becomes so enamored of differences that it seems to assume that issues of diverse populations can be addressed by focusing only on that diversity, and all issues are an outgrowth of that diversity. It is significantly more important to recognize that all peoples, regardless of origin or culture, experience certain universal issues in life and, although these can be exacerbated by migration experiences and/or human rights violations, they merit attention even in the absence of migration effects and rights abuses. For example, all individuals and families are concerned about their subsistence, their health, and their economic security. They seek opportunities to enhance their quality of life, and depending on the nation in which they live, this will include attempts to maximize use of opportunities such as education, work access, housing, and health care to promote general well-being.

Migration-Related Issues

Several migration-related issues do exist, and to suggest that they do not affect immigrants would be naïve. In addition, these are substantially different from those influencing the lives of native-born ethnic minorities. The ability of immigrants to manage migration-related concerns depends on the resources the migrant brings to the host country and the readiness of the host country to accommodate the migrant (Segal, 2002). These evidence themselves in the level of the immigrant's integration into the host country; his or her ability to adapt to the host country's norms, attitudes, and behaviors; and the willingness of the host country to address the needs of the immigrant. Immigrant and host must work in tandem to ease transitions and achieve stability in the country of immigration.

Migration-related issues can be numerous because immigrants leave all that is familiar, including their homes, families and friends, supports, culture, food, entertainment, climate, and perhaps language. They move to an alien land where people may look and sound different from themselves and where they may not understand the culture, the political system, the infrastructure, or many patterns and norms natives take for granted. Some may travel through difficult and dangerous circumstances, others may have made large financial investments at significant cost, and yet others may have had to leave behind spouses, children, parents, or other immediate family members. The vast majority of immigrants leave their homelands in their adult working years, when adaptation can be more difficult than it is when one is a child.

One expects migration-related issues usually in the first years following migration. However, concerns emerge and evolve throughout the migrant's lifetime, affecting even universal experiences such as (a) raising children, particularly when the second generation begins, once again, to challenge the norms of the immigrant group; (b) dealing with aging parents who refuse to leave the homeland; and (c) preparing for their own retirement and end-of-life decisions (Segal, 2013).

Human Rights Violations

An exploration of Amnesty International's website produces a wealth of recent news reports that underscores its statement that "immigrants' rights are human rights," and this includes information on human rights violations through human trafficking, isolation in immigrant detention, deplorable conditions in refugee camps, and expectations of the United States' 2013 immigration reform (http://www.amnestyusa.org/our-work/issues/refugee-and-migrant-rights/immigrants-rights-are-human-rights).

Social workers and many people around the world are now much more aware of several extreme violations and abuses because they have been brought to light by the news media in the last decade. It is significant that we are beginning to be cognizant of the human rights abuses experienced across the globe by myriad individuals and groups in a variety of ways. Although knowledge of abuses in immigrant detention and refugee camps and with trafficked victims is burgeoning, there is less focus on the insidious violations that other migrants experience and that are not labeled as human rights violations but should be so categorized. This chapter proposes *MOVED* (marginalization, oppression, violation, exploitation, and discrimination) as the acronym for human rights abuses among immigrants.

When immigrant communities or individuals are marginalized and not allowed access to a country's financial and social resources and are not permitted to integrate into the society, either overtly or otherwise, their human rights are violated. For example, several second and third generation Japanese Brazilians who were marginalized in Brazil returned to Japan only to find themselves further marginalized in their ancestral homeland (Tsuda, 2007). Although they are not physically harmed, lack of access to Japanese opportunities and absence of legal requirements for schooling for their children, for example, prevent them from maximizing their abilities (Teachers in the Brazilian School, Tsukuba, Japan, Personal communication, June 15, 2012).

If migrant workers, who may be authorized or not, are expected to work long hours and in deplorable conditions, with short breaks, poor housing, and inadequate health care, and have few alternatives, they are clearly oppressed and exploited. Such experiences are not uncommon for migrants across the globe. Nessel (2012) suggests that often migrant workers as seen as "disposable" and asks whether human rights concerns should be taken into account when these disposable workers become ill or are injured. If they are not provided with health care, and they know they do not have access to it if they should become ill, is the country not oppressing these migrants?

A recent publication suggests that "migration may be the single greatest behavioral risk factor for human rights abuse in the contemporary world" (Brysk, 2013, p. 10). Although human rights violations are recognized as being inflicted on several groups of immigrants and refugees who are considered vulnerable (e.g., trafficked or smuggled individuals, those in refugee camps), one may propose that many other immigrants are also exploited when they are hired at lower wages for jobs that natives occupy at higher income levels (Kee, 1995). Thus, wage discrimination that was prevalent when globalization was slower may now be even more rampant. Access to social capital seems to shrink wage differentials between immigrants and natives (Behtoui & Neergaard, 2010), but even immigrants with the requisite papers may not have the knowledge, the social capital, or the negotiating abilities to ensure that they receive wages that are commensurate with their capabilities and skills. Frequently, both low skill workers as well as professionals may receive salaries that are below those of their native born counterparts (Lofstrom, 2011). Therefore, not only are vulnerable immigrants' rights violated, but all immigrants are potentially vulnerable to this form of discrimination if they do not have both the human and social capital to negotiate equity.

Figure 3 categorizes some of the issues facing immigrants and refugees. The previous discussion provides an overview of the three general areas affecting immigrants and their lives in the host country, beginning with the universal and moving to the particular. Thus, (a) all human beings experience the universal concerns; (b) immigrants must deal with another layer of life experiences through which they must navigate successfully, adding a new lens through which universal concerns are viewed; and (c) several migrants experience a range of human rights violations that, in turn, exacerbate difficulties that emerge through or because of the migration process. Therefore, as portrayed in Figure 3, one must first understand the human rights violations a particular individual or group has experienced, explore the effect it has on the ability of the victim of the human rights abuse to adapt to the host country, and recognize implications for successfully negotiating life's many opportunities and obstacles. Woven through the figure is an intricate web that further describes the capability of individuals to manage their experiences and reflects a difference between specific people.

Figure 3   **Some issues of migrants and the direction of impact**

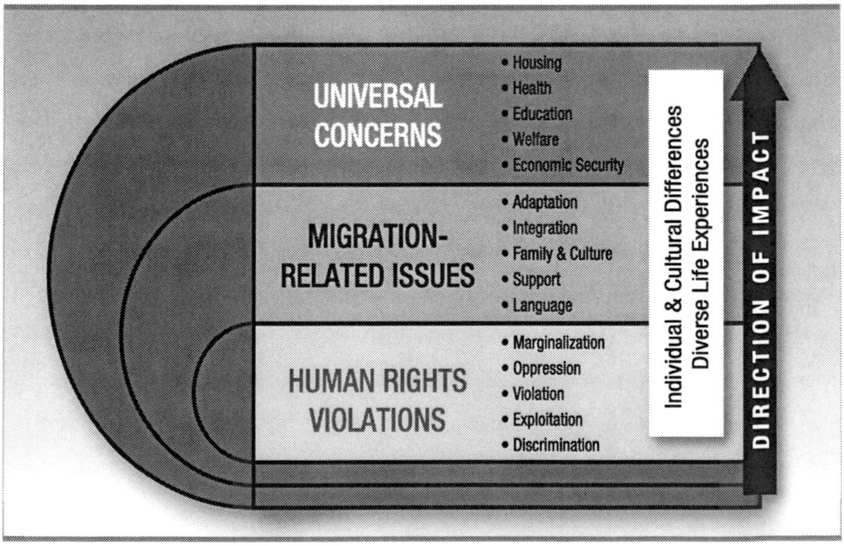

Differences Between People

Despite the universality of human need and emotion, and despite similarities across societies and in expectations, one cannot fail to recognize that there are cultural variations, unique experiences, and individual differences between people. These provide an overarching perspective on how individuals perceive and navigate the triage of universal concerns, migration-related issues, and human rights violations. The social, economic, personal, and psychological resources and supports of an individual can influence his or her ability to navigate migration related issues and to mitigate the effects of human rights violations.

Sufficient literature exists to indicate cultural variations in expectations and behavior and how societies may socialize their members to respond to particular occurrences (Church et al., 2013; Cross, Uskul, Gerçek-Swing, Alozkan, & Ataca, 2013; Gelfand et al., 2011). This can help individuals from particular cultures better manage or provide rationalization for the existence of untoward situations than those from other societies. Hofstede's (1980) cutting-edge work has generated much debate about the effects of culture, and although the final result is still pending, it is clear that culture does affect attitudes and behavior, although it is not the only influence and may not even be the most significant (Segal, Segal, & Niemczycki, 1993).

In addition to differences in culture, individuals evidence variations that reflect their unique personalities and life experiences, and these also influence their abilities to adapt to the continuing vagaries of their lives' trajectories. Although environmental influences affect one's development, and hence handling of particular experiences, personality characteristics, which may be genetically based, are also important determinants of behavior (Bouchard, Lykken, McGue, Segal, & Tellegen, 1990; Hatemi, McDermott, Eaves, Kendler, & Neale, 2013) that may differentiate individual responses to particular experiences and stresses. Furthermore, experience unrelated to a particular event may temper or determine behavior (Romero & Martínez-Román, 2012) and should be considered when assessing the effects of human rights violations and migration issues.

Human Rights Treaties and Migrants

The Universal Declaration of Human Rights (United Nations, 1948), with all nine current major conventions, embodies much that reflects universal humanity. The articles recognize human vulnerability to exploitation in a variety of ways and seek to offer the right to protection from harm. The United States has ratified some of the core human rights treaties, but it is distressing that it has yet to sign or ratify the Convention on the Protection of All Migrant Workers and Their Families (United Nations, 1990). Although signing a treaty does not necessarily indicate that protections will be forthcoming, the failure to sign does suggest, at the very least, that the country is undecided about migrants. Perhaps, with immigration reform, the nation will be ready to join other countries as a signatory to the Convention on the Protection of All Migrant Workers and their Families.

Wronka (2013) indicates that there are five critical notions that underlie the development of the treaties, and all areas of human rights are interdependent. These notions recognize the universality of the following: (1) human dignity; (2) nondiscrimination; (3) civil and political rights; (4) economic, social, and cultural rights; and (5) solidarity and unity among nations. Each of these is certainly relevant to all human beings, but each is also particularly pertinent to the migrant experience in which individuals and groups are in environments and among people who are not like them, who may not share their culture and values, and on whom they are dependent.

Undoubtedly, all human beings are vulnerable to human rights abuses, and immigrants and refugees are no exception. However, the manner in which migrants enter a country and the human and social capital they possess can have substantial implications for their level of protection from harm. The UNHCR reports that of the more than 200 million individuals living and working outside their countries of origin, some are found working in jobs that embody the three Ds—dirt, danger, and degradation—and many experience human rights violations, discrimination, and exploitation. UNHCR further states that human rights violations against migrants include denial of access to fundamental rights such as education and health, reflecting deep-seated prejudice that is embodied in law and implementation (UNHCR, n.d.a). Human

Rights Watch provides an ongoing and updated news report on human rights violations of migrants around the globe. The UNHCR proposes a human rights approach to migration that

> places the migrant at the centre of migration policies and management, and pays particular attention to the situation of marginalised and disadvantaged groups of migrants. Such an approach (ensures) that migrants are included in relevant national action plans and strategies, such as plans on the provision of public housing or national strategies to combat racism and xenophobia.
>
> Although countries have a sovereign right to determine conditions of entry and stay in their territories, they also have an obligation to respect, protect and fulfil the human rights of all individuals under their jurisdiction, regardless of their nationality or origin and regardless of their immigration status." (UNHCR, n.d.a)

The Convention specifies two general areas of the rights of migrant workers: those applicable to all migrant workers, including those who are unauthorized, and those applicable only to authorized migrants. The following rights apply to all migrants: (a) basic freedoms, (b) due process, (c) right to privacy, (d) equality with nationals, (e) transfer of earnings, and (f) right to information. Additional rights that apply only to regular or authorized migrants are the following: (a) right to be temporarily absent, (b) freedom of movement, (c) equality with nationals, and (d) protection from employment contract violations (United Nations Educational, Scientific, and Cultural Organization, n.d.).

Most nations that have ratified the convention are migrant sending countries. A large majority of host countries still have not taken this step. Because the United States, like several other nations, has not ratified this convention, it has not committed itself to protecting this group of its residents. Especially since the terror attacks in the United States on September 11, 2001, some of the basic freedoms and rights to due process and privacy for some immigrants have been jeopardized. Inequality in labor opportunities and benefits between nationals and immigrants can also be a reflection of human rights violations.

Furthermore, rights to family unity are violated when immigration policies prevent unauthorized parents from remaining in the United States with their children who are born in the country. Asylum seekers may also face real threats, particularly if they are from countries that send large numbers of unauthorized immigrants, because their rights to be heard and to due process may be violated and they may be treated as illegal immigrants. In addition to institutionalized rights violations, as reflected in laws and hiring policies, vulnerable migrants may experience more apparent rights violations at the hands of their employers and not understand they have the freedom to inform authorities. Human Rights Watch (2012) published a substantive report on the experience of farm workers subjected to sexual violence and harassment and discussed their fears of reprisal from employers if they shared this information with authorities. Thus, the failure of the United States to ratify the Convention on the Protection of All Migrant Workers and their Families, by process of omission, disallows immigrants' access to protections that should be the rights of all human beings.

In 1999 the Commission on Human Rights created the Special Rapporteur on the Human Rights of Migrants, whose jurisdiction includes all countries regardless of whether they have ratified the International Convention on the Protection of the Rights of All Migrant Workers and Members of Their Families. In addition to reporting to the General Assembly at its request, the main functions of the Special Rapporteur are to

a) examine ways and means to overcome the obstacles to the full and effective protection of human rights of migrants, recognizing the particular vulnerability of women, children, and those undocumented or in an irregular situation;

b) request and receive information from all relevant sources, including migrants themselves, on violations of the human rights of migrants and their families;

c) formulate appropriate recommendations to prevent and remedy violations of the human rights of migrants, wherever they may occur;

d) promote the effective application of relevant international norms and standards on the issue;

e) recommend actions and measures applicable at the national, regional, and international levels to eliminate violations of the human rights of migrants;

f) take into account a gender perspective when requesting and analysing information and give special attention to the occurrence of multiple instances of discrimination and violence against migrant women;

g) give particular emphasis to recommendations on practical solutions with regard to the implementation of the rights relevant to the mandate, including by identifying best practices and concrete areas and means for international cooperation; and

h) report regularly to the Human Rights Council, according to its annual programme of work, and to the General Assembly, at the request of the Council or the Assembly (UNHCR, n.d.b).

Although the Special Rapporteur can provide information and guidelines, the protection of human rights lies with nation states. Only with increasing awareness of the extent of the problem and the realization that the violation of the human rights of migrants does occur in all countries will each nation begin to take a look within its own borders.

Social Work Education

Social work and social work education in the United States have paid relatively little heed to their own country's human rights violations. Discussions of social justice are only just beginning to include a human rights focus, and the recognition that migrants may be victims of human rights abuses is still far from curriculum content. In other words, social work education has yet to emphasize both these areas: human rights and migration. Therefore, without proactive advocacy, attention to the human rights violations of migrants will remain an unaddressed topic in social work education.

Meetings such as the Working Seminar in Advancing Human Rights in Social Work Education, held at the University of Connecticut's School of

Social Work in May 2013, gives hope that discussions of migrant issues will also be included in studies of human rights. This seminar aided the realization that human rights abuses assume several faces, some more obvious than others. Thus, as human rights information becomes integrated into the social work curriculum, so will information on human migration.

Courses on human migration may be offered as electives in social work; however, at the very least, information on migration should be integrated into courses on human behavior, particularly in the United States, where increasingly there is acknowledgment that "we are a country of migrants." In addition, information on the migrant population can be included in courses on policy and practice. An assessment of migration policies, both in the United States and abroad, may provide insight into institutionalized discrimination. Program development and intervention skills may include an assessment of whether the rights of individual migrants or migrant groups have been violated, the effect on their functioning, and implications for intervention.

To bring awareness of human rights violations among migrant groups, the table in Figure 4 may be completed by students. Although obvious and well-recognized forms of violation will undoubtedly be included, this exercise will allow students to also identify areas that are often overlooked. This will permit them to critically assess policies, practices, programs, and behaviors that may reflect the variety of abuses perpetrated on migrants.

Figure 4 **Migrants and human rights violation**

	LEGAL MIGRANTS	**UNAUTHORIZED MIGRANTS**	**INVOLUNTARY MIGRANTS**
Human rights abuses	e.g., Lower pay for work done by citizens in similar occupations	e.g., Violation of right to family unity	e.g., Long working hours with limited benefits

Information from this completed table could help students understand the immigration experience from a human rights perspective. Discussions could center on how these open or hidden abuses could be mitigated and assess the possibilities for social work intervention at the individual, organization, community, program, and policy levels when human rights and social justice perspectives are used. At the very least, students should be made aware that the protection of basic rights of access to a safe environment and societal resources should be fundamental to all individuals, including migrants. This table may also be used by students as a self-assessment exercise regarding their own and prevalent societal values and attitudes.

A first step for social work education in taking a human rights approach to migration, however, is for social work academics to admit that migration and migration-related issues are areas of relevance to the discipline of social work. When 25% of the United States population is considered to be "new Americans," namely, immigrants and their offspring (Segal, 2013), ignoring their concerns is woefully short-sighted. Not all new Americans require social work intervention, but when they do, their issues may be more complex and may differ from those of citizens whose U.S. ancestry spans three or more generations (Figure 3).

Furthermore, social work educators should be alert to the wealth of information regarding migration and the effects of migration on immigrants, long-term residents of the country, and on the country itself. Focus on immigrants tends to address their adjustment; however, their presence has far-reaching effects (both positive and challenging) on all aspects of a nation's population and infrastructure. Only when the discipline includes this content in its curricula can human rights issues be found to be relevant. An exploration of human rights violations of individuals and families may be identifiable, such as the incarceration and physical abuse of asylees in detention; but institutionalized discrimination, such as the lack of access to certain public programs and services (as in the Welfare Reform Act; Congressional Research Service, 2003), even for legal residents, may be less evident.

A human rights perspective as related to migration may challenge students to address ethical dilemmas in a variety of circumstances. If human rights perspectives violate or conflict with state or federal laws, difficulties for students and for the social work profession increase. When a human rights approach directly requires the breaking of a law (e.g., providing services to an unauthorized migrant), citizen social workers find themselves at a crossroads that requires them to explore their own values and determine the personal risk they may be willing to take.

Concluding Comments

This chapter presents a cursory overview of some issues facing immigrants and refugees, regardless of country of origin or destination, and suggests that some groups within these populations are particularly at-risk for human rights violations. It also points a finger at social work as failing to educate itself about this sizable and diverse group of people and being remiss in integrating content on migration into social work curricula. When people choose to move, they are responsible to a large extent for their own adaptation and success; nevertheless, a nation that invites or accepts immigrants also has an obligation to ease and facilitate this process (Segal, 2013).

Some migrants and migrant groups have greater need for professional social work assistance than do others. Some groups may experience more human rights abuses than do others. Not all immigrants require social work assistance, but all social workers must be cognizant of potential issues, and when 25% of the United States is composed of new Americans, it behooves the profession to apprise itself of the benefits and challenges of migration effects on immigrants and the host country. With the ease of transnational travel, global migration will continue to increase. Recognizing that some immigrants experience human rights violations—which can be evidenced in the home, transit, or destination country—may help social workers purposefully include an exploration of this phenomenon in conducting client assessments and contributing to effective advocacy.

References

Behtoui, A., & Neergaard, A. (2010). Social capital and wage disadvantages among immigrant workers. *Work, Employment & Society, 24*(4), 761–779.

Bouchard, T. J., Lykken, D. T., McGue, M., Segal, N. L., & Tellegen, A. (1990). Sources of human psychological differences: The Minnesota Study of Twins Reared Apart. *Science, 250,* 223–228.

Brysk, A. (2013). *Human rights and private wrongs: Constructing global civil society.* London, UK: Routledge.

Ceobanu, A. M., & Koropeckyj-Cox, T. (2012). Should international migration be encouraged to offset population aging? A cross-country analysis of public attitudes in Europe. *Population Research and Policy Review.* doi: 10.1007/s11113-012-9260-7.

Church, A.T., Katigbak, M.S., Locke, K. D., Zhang, H., Shen, J., Vargas-Flores, J. de J., . . .Ching, C. M. (2013). Need satisfaction and well-being testing self-determination theory in eight cultures. *Journal of Cross-Cultural Psychology, 44*(4), 507–534.

Congressional Research Service. (2003). *The 1996 Welfare Reform Law.* Retrieved from http://royce.house.gov/uploadedfiles/the%201996%20welfare%20 reform%20law.pdf.

Cross, S. E., Uskul, A. K., Gerçek-Swing, B., Alozkan, C., & Ataca, B. (2013). Confrontation versus withdrawal: Cultural differences in responses to threats to honor. *Group Processes Intergroup Relations, 16*(3), 345–362.

Gelfand, M. J., Raver, J. L., Nishii, L., Leslie, L. M., Lun, J., Lim, B. C., … Yamaguchi, S. (2011). Differences between tight and loose cultures: A 33-nation study. *Science, 332,* 1100–1104.

Global Commission on International Migration. (2005). *Migration in an interconnected world: New directions of action.* Retrieved from http://www.iom .int/jahia/webdav/site/myjahiasite/shared/shared/mainsite/policy_and_research /gcim/GCIM_Report_Complete.pdf.

Hatemi, P. K., McDermott, R., Eaves, L. J., Kendler, K. S., & Neale, M. C. (2013). Fear as adisposition and an emotional state: A genetic and environmental approach to out-group political preferences. *American Journal of Political Science, 57*(2), 279–293.

Hofstede, G. (1980). *Culture's consequences: International differences in work-related values.* Thousand Oaks, CA: SAGE.

Human Rights Watch. (2012). *Cultivating fear: The vulnerability of immigrant farmworkers in the U.S. to sexual violence and sexual harassment.* Retrieved from http://www.hrw.org/sites/default/files/reports/us0512ForUpload_1.pdf.

Kee, P. (1995). Native-immigrant wage differentials in the Netherlands: Discrimination? *Oxford Economic Papers, 47,* 302–317.

Lofstrom, M. (2011). Low-skilled immigrant entrepreneurship. *Review of Economic Households, 9,* 25–44.

Nessel, L. A. (2012). Disposable workers: Applying a human rights framework to analyze duties owed to seriously injured or ill migrants. *Indiana Journal of Global Legal Studies, 19*(1), 61–103.

Portes, A., & Rumbaut, R. G. (2006). *Immigrant America: A portrait.* Berkeley, CA: University of California Press.

Romero, I., & Martínez-Román, J. A. (2012). Self-employment and innovation: Exploring the determinants of innovative behavior in small businesses. *Research Policy, 41*(1), 178–189.

Segal, U. A. (1991). Cultural variables in Asian Indian families. *Families in Society, 72*(4), 233–242.

Segal, U. A. (2002). *A framework for immigration: Asians in the United States.* New York, NY: Columbia University Press.

Segal, U. A. (2004). Practicing with immigrants and refugees. In D. Lum (Ed.), *Cultural competence, practice stages, and client systems* (pp. 230–286). Belmont, CA: Brooks/Cole.

Segal, U. A. (2012). Working with immigrants and refugees. In R. Link & L. Healy (Eds.), *Handbook of international social work* (pp. 73–80). New York, NY: Oxford University Press.

Segal, U. A. (2013). Immigration policy. In C. G. Franklin (Ed), *Encyclopaedia of social work* (21st ed., vol. 2). New York, NY: Oxford University Press.

Segal, M. N., Segal, U. A., & Niemczycki, M. A. P. (1993). Value network for cross-national marketing management: A framework for analysis and application. *Journal of Business, 27*(1), 65–83.

Tsuda, T. (2007). When minorities migrate: The racialization of the Japanese Brazilians in Brazil and Japan. In R. S. Parreñas & L. C. D. Siu (Eds.), *Asian diasporas: New formations, new conceptions* (pp. 225–251). Stanford, CA: Stanford University Press.

United Nations. (1948). *Universal declaration of human rights.* G.A. Res. 217 A (III). Retrieved from http://www.refworld.org/docid/3ae6b3712c.html

United Nations. (1951). *Convention relating to the status of refugees.* G. A. Res. 429 (V) of 14 December 1950. Retrieved from http://www.ohchr.org/EN /ProfessionalInterest/Pages/StatusOfRefugees.aspx

United Nations. (1967). *Protocol relating to the status of refugees.* G. A. Res. 2198 (XXI) of December 1966. Retrieved from http://www.ohchr.org/EN /ProfessionalInterest/Pages/ProtocolStatusOfRefugees.aspx

United Nations. (1990). *Convention on the protection of the rights of all migrant workers and members of their families.* G. A. Res. 45/158. Retrieved from http://www2.ohchr.org/english/bodies/cmw/cmw.htm

United Nations Educational, Scientific, and Cultural Organization. (n.d.). International migration convention. Retrieved from http://www.unesco.org /new/en/social-and-human-sciences/themes/international-migration /international-migration-convention/

United Nations High Commissioner for Human Rights (UNHCR). (n.d.a). *Migration and human rights.* Retrieved from http://www.ohchr.org/en/Issues /Migration/Pages/MigrationAndHumanRightsIndex.aspx.

United Nations High Commissioner for Human Rights (UNHCR). (n.d.b). *Special rapporteur on the human rights of migrants.* Retrieved from http://www .ohchr.org/EN/Issues/Migration/SRMigrants/Pages/SRMigrantsIndex.aspx

United Nations High Commissioner for Refugees (UNHCR). (2005). *Refugee status determination: Who is a refugee?* Retrieved from http://www.unhcr.org /cgi-bin/texis/vtx/home/opendocPDFViewer.html?docid=4d944d5b9&query =Who%20is%20a%20refugee?

United Nations High Commissioner for Refugees (UNHCR). (2012a). *A year in crisis: Global trends 2011.* Retrieved from http://www.unhcr.org/cgi-bin/texis /vtx/home/opendocPDFViewer.html?docid=4fd6f87f9&query=Global%20 trends%202010.

United Nations High Commissioner for Refugees (UNHCR). (2012b). *Guidelines on statelessness no. 1: The definition of "stateless person" in article 1(1) of the 1954 convention relating to the status of stateless persons.* Retrieved from http://www .unhcr.org/4ffa957b9.html.

United Nations Office on Drugs and Crime. (2012). *Global report on trafficking in persons.* Retrieved from http://www.unodc.org/documents/data-and-analysis /glotip/Trafficking_in_Persons_2012_web.pdf.

United States Senate. (2013). *Senate Bill S744, border security, economic opportunity, and immigration modernization act.* Retrieved from http://www .gpo.gov/fdsys/pkg/BILLS-113s744is/pdf/BILLS-113s744is.pdf.

Wronka, J. (2013). *An overview of human rights.* In T. Hokenstad, L. Healy, & U. A. Segal (Eds.), *Teaching human rights curriculum resources for social workers: A resource manual.* Alexandria, VA: CSWE Press.

23 Incorporating a Human Rights Framework to Advance Just Policy and Practice with Immigrants: A Teaching Module Within a Social Work/Human Rights Seminar

Filomena M. Critelli

Migration has become a truly global phenomenon, and multiethnic immigrant communities have been established in all of the advanced industrialized countries around the globe. Worldwide, one of 35 is an international migrant, with a total of 185 million worldwide, 3% of the world's population. In keeping with these trends, the United States has experienced the highest levels of immigration in recent years since the turn of the 20th century. By 2000 about 11% of the United States population was foreign-born. Many of these immigrants are parents of children who are either immigrants or, more commonly, U.S. citizens themselves. Currently, one in every five children in the United States lives in an immigrant family (Haskins, Greenberg, & Fremstad, 2004). A *refugee* is defined as a person legally admitted to the United States who cannot return to his or her country because of a "well-founded fear of persecution" (Martin & Hoeffer, 2009, p.1). Refugees comprise 7%—2.5 million—of the immigrant population of the United States (Capps & Passel, 2004). Immigration is no longer confined to traditional destination states such as California, New York, Florida, Texas, or New Jersey. Immigrants and refugees are increasingly dispersed throughout states in the Southeast, Midwest, and West of the United States (Fix & Capps, 2002). Additionally, international migrants include many who are undocumented or irregular migrants (Batalova & Terrazas, 2010).

These changing demographics underscore the fact that social workers in nearly every practice setting will interact with immigrants and also the value of a human rights framework as a critical tool for current policy discussions about immigration and social work practice with migrants. A host of bodies such as the International Federation of Social Workers and the United Nations Scientific and Cultural Organization (UNESCO) advocate for greater attention to immigrant rights, a growing but neglected area of human rights practice. Therefore, it is incumbent on social work educators to prepare students with competencies for just and humane policy and practice with immigrants with a deeper grounding in the rights-based perspective.

This chapter presents material from a 6-hour, two session module that was part of a course on social work and human rights titled Perspectives on Trauma and Human Rights: Contemporary Theory, Research, Policy, & Practice. This advanced year course offers students a survey of diverse ways of conceptualizing, researching, preventing, and redressing trauma and human rights violations with a range of vulnerable communities and populations, which includes immigrants. The learning objectives of the module are to (a) help students examine their attitudes and assumptions about immigrants and migration and challenge prevalent myths about migration; (b) provide an overview of the complexity of patterns of contemporary migration, the difficulties and dilemmas faced by many immigrants, and their vulnerability to trauma and human rights abuses; (c) examine the development of the various instruments within international and regional human rights law, international labor law, international criminal law, and refugee law that address the protection of migrants; (d) analyze current social, economic, and policy conditions that impede the basic liberties and rights of immigrants; and (e) discuss recommendations for policy and practice based on a human rights framework that protects and promotes the full range of civil, social, and economic rights of immigrants. Teaching methods include mini-lectures, film clips, dyadic and small group exercises, examination of texts of human rights instruments, and analyses of news items/case studies from a human rights perspective.

Since the 1948 adoption of the Universal Declaration of Human Rights (United Nations, 1948), an expanding body of international instruments, conventions, and treaties have codified a comprehensive range of rights that provide a framework for humane conditions for international migration. Underlying these is the fundamental principle of the universality of human rights as inherent to the dignity of every person. However, a tension is created because enforcement of these rights depends on states to observe and implement them, leaving a gap between the aspirations of universality of rights and the reality in the local practice of states regarding immigrants' rights. Globalization has facilitated the free movement of merchandise and information, but there are many barriers to the free movement of people, especially between the Global North and South. Although employers in countries such as the United States avail themselves of the physical labor of immigrants, laws restrict the number of legally issued visas and other avenues for legal migration. Furthermore, in response to economic downturns and the September 11, 2001, attacks, there has been an increasingly adversarial stance toward immigrants (Critelli, 2008; Gzesh, 2006). This renders many who live and work as noncitizens, especially those who are undocumented, susceptible to numerous political and social rights vulnerabilities.[1]

Confronting Myths and Biases and Sensitizing Students to the Complexities of Migration

The objectives of this portion of the module are to challenge some of the predominant misconceptions and stereotypes that lead to biased assumptions about immigrants. A beginning exercise, done in dyads, involves a series of statements that students discuss as true or false, with justifications for their responses. These address some of the common myths about migration, such as "The United States is a melting pot that has always welcomed immigrants from all over the world"; "It is easy for people to migrate to the United States"; "Immigrants are costly to the economy and a drain on the public welfare system"; or "Immigrants take jobs away from American citizens." After the students come back together from the discussion, the class unpacks these assumptions with corrective information and dialogue. Students are often surprised to learn of the difficulties and limited avenues for legal migration and how the lack of alternatives drives undocumented immigration.

The current policy framework stems from the Immigration Act of 1965, which placed a new emphasis on reuniting families and granting refugee status, while also favoring immigrants with desirable job skills. The act ended the longstanding preference for Western Europeans. This law established a quota of 20,000 immigrants per country from the eastern hemisphere, with a maximum of 120,000 immigrants from the western hemisphere. Admissions preference is based on employment skills or family reunification (immediate family exempted from quota). Administrative backlogs and the long waits for family reunification are serious challenges because the number of visas available by law each year is fewer than the number of prospective immigrants getting in line to wait for a visa. For example, as of the year 2011 there were more than 300,000 wives, husbands, and minor children of legal permanent residents waiting for immigrant visas, and there were more than 2.5 million siblings waiting for the 65,000 visas available each year (Jones, 2012). It has been widely recognized that the current immigration system is flawed and out of sync with current realities. Yet proposals for policy reform have been stalled by lack of political consensus, particularly regarding the path to citizenship for undocumented immigrants.

The exercise is followed by a mini-lecture that builds on the previous section. The lecture highlights the complexity of migration and explores theories regarding the multiple drivers of migration, with a focus on their relationship to human rights deprivations and violations. Migration is most commonly viewed as a process that involves "push" and "pull" factors (Potocky-Tripodi, 2002). Human rights are closely interrelated with the push and pull of the migration process. People migrate in response to push factors in the country of origin and/or pull factors in the country of destination. Push factors are generally considered to be undesirable because they often are related to human rights deprivations or violations by the countries of origin, such as political oppression, famine, war, or conflict. Some people are recognized as refugees whereas others become asylum-seekers. Violations of civil and political rights, including during civil conflict, that fall below the persecution threshold needed for a successful asylum claim also fuel much migration (Papademetriou, 2005).

Other factors that stimulate exit from a country of origin include poor economic conditions, extreme economic vulnerability in the home country, and unemployment or underemployment. Individuals may feel that they have no choice but to migrate for survival. These factors are all related to a search for economic and social rights. Pull factors are those that encourage a person to move and are considered to be more positive, such as better economic and educational opportunities, political freedom, and openness to immigrants (Potocky-Tripodi, 2002). Another strong motivator for migration is the opportunity for migrants to send money home (known as remittances), which enables their relatives to live better lives.

The mini-lecture also seeks to counter popular images of immigration as an invasion of impoverished individuals from abroad and the myth of immigration as simply random flows of people from poverty to wealth. In fact, international migration generally flows from regions and nations that are undergoing rapid change as a result of their incorporation into global trade, information, and production networks, rather than from regions with a lack of market development (Massey, 2004). Economic globalization disrupts existing social and economic arrangements and brings about the widespread displacement of people from customary livelihoods, creating a mobile population of people who actively search for new ways of achieving economic security and advancement. Furthermore, the lecture emphasizes that most industrialized countries have become economically dependent on migrants. Structural forces in developed nations have created a demand for migrants' services, so immigrant labor from less developed states becomes structurally embedded in the economies of industrialized states.

It is also important to highlight that the rewards to migrants, employers, and societies (both sending and receiving) are enormous (Castles & Davidson, 2000; Massey, 2004; Sassen, 1999). Receiving countries (such as the United States) benefit enormously from this pool of labor. The reluctance of native workers to perform specific jobs labeled as "3D jobs—dirty, demanding and dangerous" is well-documented (International Labour Organization [ILO], 2004). Industries including construction, domestic services, agriculture, food service, meatpacking, and landscaping rely heavily on undocumented labor (Workers Defense Project, 2013). Migrant sending countries are also interested in remittances, which play a key role in their economies (UNESCO, 2005). Therefore, there is an intricate web of global interdependence that links sending, receiving, and transit countries, creating self-feeding dynamics that encourage ever more migration, and these dynamics include both push and pull factors (Papademetriou, 2005). Discussion of this content promotes a more complex analysis of migration as part of broader global change and advances understanding of the multi-level structural forces that drive migration. It also counters some of the prevailing assumptions about migration as simply a matter of individual choice and the increasing tendency to view undocumented migration as a criminal act.

Film clips from New Americans Series (James & Tajima-Pena, 2003a, 2003b)[2] provide a visual illustration of the theories in action, including the physical, psychological, and human rights challenges throughout the migration process. A newer film, *La Americana* (Bruckman, 2008),[3] effectively illustrates how immigration policy affects families on both sides of the border. The film tells the story of a mother who makes the dangerous and illegal journey from Bolivia to the United States to work long hours to pay for her disabled daughter's medical care. The mother struggles unsuccessfully to legalize her immigration status, facing the prospect of never seeing her daughter again. The film depicts the risks, sacrifices, and agonizing choices that confront the undocumented. The goals are to foster empathy and deeper understanding of the struggles faced by members of this group who are so often a target of public demonization. The film also stimulates dialogue regarding the justness of immigration policies from a rights perspective and thoughts about elements for immigration reform.

Brief Overview of Immigration Statuses, Legal Framework, and Human Rights

Understanding immigration status is also a key element for social workers for determining immigrants' eligibility for various social benefits; the types of political, economic, and social rights and legal remedies they can claim; and an accurate assessment of their psychosocial needs. All of these factors are generally contingent on immigration status. In this section of the module, students are briefly introduced to key terminology and basic policy related to migration. An immigrant is defined as a person who enters and usually becomes established in a country where he or she is not a native. *Alien* is the technical term for a foreign-born resident who has not been naturalized and is still a subject or citizen of another country. Naturalization is the process by which U.S. citizenship is conferred on a foreign citizen. Lawful permanent resident ("green card") status grants foreign nationals the right to reside in the United States permanently and eventually (if the foreign national so chooses) apply to be naturalized (Potocky-Tripodi, 2002). Although this status is intended to be permanent, certain actions can lead to a legal permanent resident being placed in removal proceedings and being deported to his or her home country. These actions include convictions for certain crimes, remaining outside the United States for long periods of time, or committing immigration fraud (U.S. Dept. of Homeland Security, 2008). A refugee is defined as a person unable to return to his or her country of nationality because of a "well-founded fear of persecution on account of race, religion, nationality, membership in a particular social group, or political opinion" (Martin & Hoeffer, 2009, p.1). Based on 2012 figures, globally more than 10 million refugees who have fled violence and persecution are under the mandate of the UN High Commissioner for Refugee's mandate (UNHCR, 2013). Asylum and refugee statuses are closely related; however, they differ depending on where a person applies for the status.

The rights of an immigrant (often called *migrant* in the international literature) are largely defined by the migration category to which he or she belongs, and by the reasons underlying that migration. Some migrants, usually skilled workers who move to secure professional jobs in the formal sector, may have relatively fewer human rights problems. Voluntary migrants (who constitute most of the world's migrants) are protected under general principles of international human rights law. Among these, unskilled workers–who form the majority of migrants–are more vulnerable to rights violations, particularly when they work in the informal sector as domestic workers, and may have fewer protections. Migrants are especially vulnerable to human rights violations if they have been trafficked and exploited or smuggled. Women and girls are highly vulnerable to certain types of exploitation such as rape, sexual assault, and trafficking. Refugees and victims of trafficking, because of humanitarian concerns, have special rights protections in international law.

In the case of refugees, protections have become part of a separate and well-established protection regime covered by the 1951 Geneva Convention relating to the Status of Refugees (United Nations, 1951). The U.S. Refugee Act of 1980 provides the first permanent and systematic procedure for admission of persons fleeing persecution to the United States and establishes federal programs for resettlement. As a result, refugees are eligible for services and benefits that are not available to other types of lawful permanent residents, including assistance in locating appropriate housing, food, cultural orientation, school registration for children, health care, 8 months of cash assistance, and English as a second language (ESL) classes and employment services. As humanitarian entrants, refugees are entitled to apply for lawful permanent resident status 1 year after admittance and are eligible for benefits such as Temporary Assistance to Needy Families without a waiting period.

In 2000 the United Nations, after recognizing the need to address human trafficking more thoroughly, adopted the Palermo Protocols (United Nations, 2000). This requires states to criminalize acts of trafficking and smuggling and establish a framework for international cooperation. The United States further reinforced its commitment to protection of trafficking victims through the passage of the Victims of Trafficking and Violence Protection Act of 2000, which enables victims to come forward for assistance without facing the threat of deportation. One of its provisions is the T visa, which allows victims of severe forms of trafficking to become temporary residents of the United States. A recipient of a T visa may be eligible after 3 years for permanent residence status if he or she meets certain conditions. A primary condition is cooperating with the authorities in the investigation or prosecution of traffickers. A more in-depth discussion is beyond the scope of this chapter, but criticism of the law from a rights perspective focuses on the justness of the policy's emphasis on cooperation with law enforcement and testimony against the traffickers rather than the extensive needs of survivors (Goodey, 2004; Rieger, 2007).

Still, systematic governmental assistance is not available to other classifications of immigrants. In 2009 (the most recent date with reliable figures), an estimated 11.1 million undocumented immigrants lived in United States (Passel & Cohn, 2010) who experienced great disregard for their human rights. They were more likely to face discrimination and exclusion; violation of labor rights, exploitation, and abuse; and to become targets of hate crimes. Undocumented immigrants are often prevented officially from being able to access adequate health care or renting decent accommodation, or from exercising their right to freedom of association, labor rights, and other basic rights.

The Human Rights Framework:
Examining Key Human Rights Treaties

This section of the module examines the core instruments within international and regional human rights law, international labor law, international criminal law, and refugee law that address the protection of migrants. In conjunction with a presentation on human rights and the core treaties that address migration, students receive handouts that include summaries of the Universal Declaration of Human Rights, International Covenant on Civil and Political Rights (ICCPR; United Nations, 1966a), Convention on the Elimination of Racial Discrimination (CERD; United Nations, 1965), and International Convention on the Protection of the Rights of All Migrant Workers and Members of Their Families (CMW; United Nations, 1990) (the last treaty has yet to be ratified by the United States).

Understanding the principles of human rights is fundamental to social work. A rights-based approach is predicated on the concept of the inherent dignity and worth of every individual, promoting the belief that immigrants should be viewed as human beings first. A basic principle of a human rights framework that must be clarified is that entering a country in violation of immigration laws does not deprive a person of the most fundamental human rights, nor does it negate the obligation of the host state to protect these individuals. Several articles from the Universal Declaration of Human Rights are reviewed, such as Article 1, which guarantees "all human beings are born free and equal in dignity and rights." Article 2 provides that these rights should be granted to all persons "without distinction of any kind, such as race, color, sex, language, religion, political or other opinion, national or social origin, property, birth or other status." Article 7 prohibits discrimination based on citizenship or immigration status, because "all are equal before the law and are entitled without any discrimination to equal protection of the law." Massive global flows of people and the effects of migration on countries have fostered recognition that more specific laws and policies on state and international levels are warranted to provide political and social rights protections and legal remedies to migrants (Office of the United Nations High Commissioner for Human Rights, 2005).

Key international legal instruments that address the rights of migrant workers are introduced with some background history: the CMW, which was built on the foundation of the International Labor Organization's Migration of Employment Convention and the Migrant Workers (Supplementary Provisions) Convention.[2] The CMW was adopted by the General Assembly and opened for signature by all member states of the United Nations in December 1990. This convention was the culmination of several decades of rising concern among international bodies on the subject of migrants' rights.[3] The CMW entered into force on July 1, 2003. It includes 93 articles and extends fundamental human rights to all migrant workers. A migrant worker is defined in Article 2 as "a person who is to be engaged, is engaged or has been engaged in a remunerated activity in a State of which he or she is not a national" (Office of the United Nations High Commissioner for Human Rights, 2005). CMW recognizes that legal migrants have the legitimacy to claim more rights than undocumented migrants, but stresses that undocumented migrants must also see their fundamental human rights respected.

All migrants, including regular and irregular migrants (documented or undocumented), are guaranteed general human rights that include the right to life (Article 9); prohibition of torture or cruel, inhuman, and degrading treatment (Article 10); freedom from forced labor (Article 11); and the right to liberty and security of their person (Article 16). Part III of the Convention (Articles 8 to 35) relates to human rights of all migrants, granting a fairly broad series of rights to all migrant workers and members of their families, irrespective of their migratory status. Many of these articles specify the application of rights to migrant workers articulated in the International Covenant on Civil and Political Rights and on Economic, Social and Cultural Rights and the other core human rights treaties.

Notably, all migrant workers and members of their families are entitled to specific human rights. These include equality before the law regardless of a migrant's legal status; protection from the confiscation or destruction of identity documents; prohibition of collective expulsion; the right to equal treatment with regard to remuneration, other conditions and terms of employment, and social security; the right to join and participate in meetings and activities of trade unions; the right to receive urgent medical care; and basic rights of access to education on the basis of equality of treatment with nationals (Office of the United Nations High Commissioner for Human Rights, 2005).

Together with the more general human rights treaties, these instruments set out a very comprehensive set of civil, political, economic, social, and cultural rights for migrants, including the right to equal protections under labor laws, antidiscrimination laws, and family laws. The CMW in particular has become a cornerstone of the rights-based approach to migration advocated by many international organizations and nongovernmental organizations concerned with the protection of migrant workers (Ruhs, 2012). As of June 2012, 97 countries have ratified, acceded to, or signed at least one of the three international conventions on migrant workers. The Committee on the Rights of Migrant Workers has identified the low level of ratifications to the CMW as a key challenge (Ruhs, 2012). The majority of countries that have ratified the CMW are predominantly countries of net emigration rather than net immigration, signaling resistance on the part of many of the countries that receive immigrants to commit to better protection for migrants. For example, the CMW has one quarter of the ratifications of the Convention on the Rights of the Child (United Nations, 1989), passed a year before the CMW, and has received fewer ratifications than the Convention on the Rights of Persons with Disabilities (United Nations, 2006), although that convention was passed 16 years after the CMW.

Although the United States has yet to ratify the CMW, many immigrants' rights are protected in core human rights treaties that the United States has ratified, such as the International Convention on the Elimination of all Forms of Racial Discrimination and the International Covenant on Civil and

Political Rights. The failure of the United States to address human rights violations facing migrant workers has drawn sharp criticism from the UN Special Rapporteur on the Rights of Migrants, the UN Human Rights Committee, and the UN Committee on the Elimination of Racial Discrimination (Ruhs, 2012).

The International Covenant on Civil and Political Rights gives everyone freedom from abuse, such as arbitrary killing, torture, and inhuman treatment; slavery; forced labor; child labor; arbitrary arrest; unfair trial; and invasion of privacy. All persons also have the right to marry, to be protected as minors, to peaceful association and assembly, to equality, and to freedom of religion and belief. These rights apply to everyone irrespective of his or her nationality and must be guaranteed without discrimination between citizens and aliens (United Nations, 1966a).

The CERD, ratified by the United States in 1994, requires that laws against racial discrimination must apply to noncitizens regardless of their immigration status. It also has great relevance to immigrants' rights. It is designed to protect individuals and groups from discrimination based on race, whether or not the discrimination is intentional or the result of seemingly neutral policies. When states ratify the CERD, they accept a three tier set of obligations: to "engage in no act or practice of racial discrimination," to "ensure" conformity by public authorities, and to "prohibit" discrimination by private groups (Grant, 2005b).

Examining Human Rights Violations in the United States: Case Study Analysis

The final section of the module examines and analyzes some of the prominent areas of rights violations based on case examples drawn from the news or advocacy reports. Students work in small groups to read the case examples to identify rights violations. Additionally, students contrast the experiences explored in the vignettes with the rights extended in key human rights treaties that were reviewed. Finally, students have a discussion and create recommendations for rights-based policy and practice. The issues related to the violation of human rights are vast and can be focused on any number of topics that may be of particular interest to the class (e.g., hate crimes, trafficking victims, and labor rights violations; access to economic and social rights such as health care or social services). Unfortunately, human rights obligations in the United States have been overshadowed by intensification of xenophobia, restrictive and exclusionary social policies, and aggressive mechanisms of immigration enforcement and deportations. In the post-9/11 era, immigrants may be the first to be suspected or scapegoated as security risks. The linking of antiterrorism measures and immigration control in the context of the "war on terror" has also encouraged discrimination and hate crimes against migrants and refugees (Critelli, 2008). Case studies used in this chapter focus on two prominent issues: the effects of aggressive mechanisms of immigration enforcement and security measures resulting in deportation and family separation and labor exploitation in the form of "wage theft."

Aggressive Mechanisms of Immigration Enforcement and Security Measures

A case example, "Silverio's Story" is examined with a flowchart that outlines the deportation process and illustrates the effects on families and children of escalated detentions and deportations (Applied Research Center, 2011). In the last decade the United States has relied heavily on enforcement-only approaches to address migration, using deterrence-based border security strategies to control its borders. The U.S. government has expanded the powers of federal authorities and has increasingly criminalized unauthorized migration by expanding criminal prosecution of individuals who violate federal immigration laws rather than relying on the extensive federal civil enforcement system (American Civil Liberties Union [ACLU], 2012).

Since the passage of the Illegal Immigration Reform and Immigrant Reform Act of 1996 there has been enhanced funding for Border Patrol. This has fostered the detention of aliens, has increased penalties for unlawful entry, and has swelled the numbers of deportations. U.S. immigration laws criminalize immigrants and migration itself by allowing the arrest, detention, and deportation of people based on their immigration status. The tightening of immigration and deportation laws and the stepped-up enforcement policies of the United States have led to the removal of hundreds of thousands of individuals each year with strong family ties in the United States, including tens of thousands of lawful permanent residents. Two 1996 laws, the Antiterrorism and Effective Death Penalty Act and the Illegal Immigration and Immigrant Responsibility Act greatly increased the grounds for deportation from the United States by expanding the sorts of criminal convictions that result in mandatory deportation (Center for Human Rights and International Justice, 2013). Two additional federal policies exacerbate the violations of civil and political rights of immigrants, Section 287(g) Agreements and Secure Communities programs, which are operated by the Department of Homeland Security. Section 287(g) of the federal immigration law allows state and local law enforcement agencies to enter into an agreement with Immigration and Customs Enforcement (ICE) to enforce immigration law within their jurisdictions. It effectively turns state and local law enforcement officers into immigration agents (although with minimal training and virtually no oversight or accountability). Secure Communities is a program under which those who are arrested and booked into a local jail have their fingerprints checked against ICE's immigration database, regardless of the state's or locality's assent to the practice (ACLU, 2012; Kohli, Markowitz, & Chavez , 2011).

As a result, ICE detained 363,000 people in a network of 350 detention centers, and the federal government deported close to 400,000 people in 2010. Annual deportations have increased more than 400% since 2010 and more than a million people have been removed from this country since the beginning of the Obama administration. In the first 6 months of 2011 the federal government removed more than 46,000 mothers and fathers of children with U.S. citizenship. Deportations break up families and have traumatized the children left behind. It is estimated that 5,100 children have been placed in foster care as a result (Applied Research Center, 2011).

In addition to the previously mentioned federal policies, discriminatory antiimmigrant measures have been adopted at the state level. Following the 2010 passage of Arizona's notorious antiimmigrant law SB 1070 (Support Our Law Enforcement and Safe Neighborhoods Act, 2010), several other states have passed similar legislation targeting immigrants and people of color for harassment, intimidation, and punitive sanctions. Similar bills have passed in Alabama, Georgia, Indiana, South Carolina, and Utah (ACLU, 2012). The laws all focus on the investigation and detention of persons who are suspected of lacking the required authorization to live or work in the United States. Another problematic aspect of these bills is that they have no standards to guide law enforcement personnel in assessing whether there is a reasonable suspicion that a person is an undocumented immigrant. Because all of these bills rely on state and local police to make a preliminary assessment of whether an individual may be unauthorized, it is asserted that they encourage profiling based on perceived race, nationality, and language proficiency (ACLU, 2012; *New York Times*, 2012).

Federal courts have at least partially blocked implementation of the laws in all six states; however, the Supreme Court has reinstated the core provisions of SB 1070 that require ordinary state and local police to demand immigration status documentation if they have "reasonable suspicion" about a person's authorization to be in the United States (ACLU, 2012, p. 6). Although the U.S. Department of Justice has also filed lawsuits challenging Arizona's SB 1070 and similar measures in other states, federal policy contributes to exacerbate the violations of civil and political rights permitted by state legislation (Section 287(g) and Secure Communities).

The ACLU, along with other groups, also filed lawsuits in all six of the states that have passed such laws, charging that these laws violate the United States Constitution. They argue that the laws discriminate on the basis of perceived race or nationality, requiring unreasonable searches and seizures, arrests, and illegal detentions, and interfering with federal authority over immigration. They also cite violations of the International Covenant on Civil and Political Rights including Article 2 (right of nondiscrimination), Article 9 (right of protection from arbitrary arrest or detention), and Article 26 (right of equal protection).

Advocates and human rights organizations argue that this overly wide dragnet deports many undocumented immigrants with no criminal histories who were arrested for minor offenses, scooping up noncriminals, lawful immigrants, and even victims of crime, and that it encourages racial profiling and erodes trust in law enforcement among immigrants (Media Matters, 2011).

Tightened border controls have not stopped irregular migration, but rather have been linked to increased risk for immigrants. Measures to strengthen and fortify borders have been accompanied by reports of the use of excessive force on the part of border guards (ACLU, 2012; National Foundation for American Policy, 2013).

Labor Exploitation

A second case example for discussion is drawn from the news regarding a case of a worker who is deported after alleging wage theft (Jamieson, 2013). About 22 million immigrants currently work in the United States, including more than 6 million undocumented and 240,000 temporary guest workers in low-wage industries (National Employment Law Project, 2013). Immigrants are significantly more likely to be employed in riskier, lower–paying occupations than U.S.-born workers or victims of wage-theft. Many are paid low wages and work in unsafe workplaces, and those without documents are more likely to work in sectors where labor standards are not applied and are vulnerable to abuse and exploitation by employers (ILO, 2004; Meissner, Kerwin, Chishti, & Bergeron, 2013). Some employers exploit the fear of deportation to discourage unauthorized immigrants from reporting violations of law and protesting substandard conditions. Further, immigrant workers often have fewer options for recourse when violations occur, and in some cases they are not granted equal protections before the law (Workers Defense Project, 2013).[4] Women in an irregular status are doubly vulnerable because of their legal status and the high risk of sexual exploitation (Grant, 2005a). Migrant women domestic workers are among the world's most vulnerable workers.[5] Working conditions vary enormously, and although some may be treated as members of the employer's family, others are subjected to conditions that may amount to virtual slavery and forced labor (Grant, 2005a).

Conclusions

Although greater awareness of migrants' rights has evolved in recent decades with new laws and protection tools such as the Convention on Migrant

Workers, much needs to be done to translate these rights into practice. The United States supported the effort to internationalize human rights standards after the Second World War through passage of the Universal Declaration of Human Rights and frequently holds itself up as an example for the rest of the world, yet it increasingly ignores its own violations of human rights of immigrants. Concurrently, the social work profession in the United States has been slower than in other parts of the world to embrace human rights as an essential foundation for practice, although this has been changing in recent years.

Immigration has become a polarizing, hot-button issue within the United States, where a heightened climate of hostility and xenophobia often obscures the humanity of those involved. Consequently, integrating a human rights-based approach to migration into social work education is an important vehicle to promote a human rights framework for humane and just policy and practice with immigrants. A human rights framework is an especially effective tool for assisting social work students to frame the current political debates about immigration policies and proposals for immigration reform. Teaching from this perspective normalizes a human rights discourse and offers guiding principles for the development of best practices with immigrants. From a pedagogical standpoint, the use of film and case studies to examine human needs at the core of migration, as well as various right violations of immigrants, are effective tools to build greater awareness and empathy by putting a human face on the issues. They also pose a counter-narrative to the pervasive demonization of immigrants and the current policy emphasis on criminalization and exclusion. Therefore, when students are engaged in framing the issue in terms of human rights rather than immigrants' rights, their thinking can be transformed. It has been observed that reframing one's work in human rights terms enables people to understand the primacy of equality and dignity no matter what the circumstance. When basic human rights principles are asserted, perceptions of the problem change, and new avenues for advocacy and policy considerations open up (Ford Foundation, 2004).

References

American Civil Liberties Union. (2012). *United States compliance with the International Covenant on Civil and Political Rights.* Retrieved from http://www2.ohchr.org/english/bodies/hrc/docs/ngos/HRI_1_USA107.pdf

Applied Research Center. (2011). *Shattered families: The perilous intersection of immigration enforcement and the child welfare system.* Retrieved from http://www.sph.sc.edu/cli/word_pdf/ARC_Report_Nov2011.pdf

Batalova, J., & Terrazas, A. (2010). Frequently requested statistics on immigrants and immigration to the United States. Migration Policy Institute. Retrieved from http://www.migrationpolicy.org/article/frequently-requested-statistics-immigrants-and-immigration-united-states-1

Bruckman, N. (Director). (2008). *La Americana.* United States: Cinema Guild.

Capps, R., & Passel, J. (2004). *Describing immigrant communities.* Retrieved from the Urban Institute website http://www.urban.org/UploadedPDF/DescribeImmigrants.pdf

Castles, S., & Davidson, A. (2000). *Citizenship and migration.* Basingstoke, UK: MacmillanPress.

Center for Human Rights and International Justice. (2013). Brief of the post-deportation human rights project in support of the Request for Public Thematic Hearing Concerning U.S. Deportation Policy and the Rights of Migrants before the Inter-American Commission on Human Rights 149th Period of Sessions. Retrieved from http://www.bc.edu/content/dam/files/centers/humanrights/doc/PDHRP%20IACHR%20brief%208%2021%202013%20FINAL.pdf

Critelli, F. M. (2008). The impact of September 11th on immigrants in the United States. *Journal of Immigrant and Refugee Studies, 6*(2), 141–167.

Fix, M., & Capps, R. (2002). *U.S. immigration: Trends and implications for schools,* Washington, DC: Urban Institute.

Ford Foundation. (2004). *Close to home: Case studies of human right work in the United States.* Retrieved from http://www.wcl.american.edu/endsilence/documents/ClosetoHome.pdf

Goodey, J. (2004). Sex trafficking in women from Central and East European countries: Promoting a "victim centered" and "woman centered" approach to criminal justice intervention. *Feminist Review, 76,* 26–45.

Grant, S. (2005a). *Migrants' human rights: From the margins to the mainstream.* Washington, DC: Migration Policy Institute. Retrieved from http://www.migrationinformation.org/feature/display.cfm?id=291

Grant, S. (2005b). International migration and human rights. Paper prepared for the Policy Analysis and Research Programme of the Global Commission on International Migration. Retrieved from https://www.iom.int/jahia/webdav /site/myjahiasite/shared/shared/mainsite/policy_and_research/gcim/tp/TP7.pdf

Gzesh, S. (2006). *America's human rights challenge: International human rights implications of U.S. immigration enforcement actions post–September 11.* Washington, DC: Migration Policy Institute.

Haskins, R.; Greenberg, M.; & Fremstad, S. (2004). Federal policy for immigrant children: Room for common ground? *The Future of Children, 14*(2), 2.

International Labour Organisation (ILO). (2004). *Towards a fair deal for workers in the global economy.* Retrieved from http://www.ilo.org/public/portugue /region/eurpro/lisbon/pdf/rep-vi.pdf

James, S. (Director) & Tajima-Pena, R. (Director). (2003a). *The Ogoni refugees.* United States: Kartequim Films.

James, S. (Director) & Tajima-Pena, R. (Director). (2003b). *Mexican story.* United States: Kartequim Films.

Jamieson, D. (2013). Undocumented worker alleges wage theft, ends up in deportation proceedings. *Huffington Post.* Retrieved from http://www.huffingtonpost.com /2013/07/09/undocumented-worker-wage-theft_n_3567024.html

Jones, T. (2012). *Practical solutions for immigrants and for America.* Retrieved from http://immigrationforum.org/images/uploads/FamilyBacklogBackgrounder.pdf

Kohli, A., Markowitz, P., & Chavez, L. (2011). *Secure communities by the numbers: An analysis of demographics and due process.* Retrieved from http://www.law .berkeley.edu/files/Secure_Communities_by_the_Numbers.pdf

Martin, D., & Hoeffer, M. (2009). *Annual flow report, refugees and asylees: 2008.* Retrieved from http://www.dhs.gov/immigrationstatistics

Massey, D. (2004). *Patterns and processes of international migration in the 21st century.* Paper presented at the Conference on African Migration in Comparative Perspective, Johannesburg, South Africa.

Media Matters. (2011). *Fox obfuscates the fact that a majority detained By ICE program are nonviolent immigrants.* Retrieved from http://mediamatters.org /research/2011/06/03/fox-obfuscates-the-fact-that-a-majority-detaine/180277

Meissner, D., Kerwin, D. M., Chishti, M., & Bergeron, C. (2013*). Immigration enforcement in the United States: The rise of a formidable machinery.* Washington, DC: Migration Policy.

National Employment Law Project. (2013). *Immigrants and work.* Retrieved from http://www.nelp.org/site/issues/category/immigrants_and_work/

National Foundation for American Policy. (2013). *How many more deaths? The moral case for a temporary worker program.* Retrieved from http://www.nfap .com/pdf/NFAP%20Policy%20Brief%20Moral%20Case%20For%20a %20Temporary%20Worker%20Program%20March%202013.pdf

New York Times. (2012, July 20). A challenge to a brutal anti-Latino law. [Editorial] Retrieved from http://www.nytimes.com/2012/07/21/opinion/a -challenge-to-arizonas-brutal-anti-latino-law.html?_r=0

Office of the United Nations High Commissioner for Human Rights. (2005). *The international convention on migrant workers and its committee* (Fact sheet No. 24). Retrieved from http://www.ohchr.org/Documents/Publications /FactSheet24rev.1en.pdf

Papademetriou, D. (2005). *The global struggle with illegal immigration: No end in sight.*Retrieved from http://www.migrationinformation.org/feature/display. cfm?ID=336

Passel, J. S., & Cohn, D. (2010). *U.S. unauthorized immigration flows are down sharply since mid-decade.* Retrieved from http://pewhispanic.org/files/reports /126.pdf

Potocky-Tripodi, M. (2002). *Best practices for social work with refugees and immigrants.* New York, NY: Columbia University Press.

Rieger, A. (2007). Missing the mark: Why the Trafficking Victims Protection Act fails to protect sex trafficking victims in the United States. *Harvard Journal of Law & Gender, 30,* 231–257.

Ruhs, M. (2012). The human rights of migrant workers: Why do so few countries care? *American Behavioral Scientist, 56,* 1277–1293.

Sassen, S. (1999). *Guests and aliens.* New York, NY: New Press.

Support Our Law Enforcement and Safe Neighborhoods Act. (2010). 49th Arizona Legislature, 2nd Session. Retrieved from http://www.azleg.gov/ legtext/491eg/2r/bills/sb1070s.pdf

United Nations. (1948). *Universal declaration of human rights.* G.A. Res. 217 A (III). Retrieved from http://www.refworld.org/docid/3ae6b3712c.html

United Nations. (1951). *Convention relating to the status of refugees.* G. A. Res. 429 (V) of 14 December 1950. Retrieved from http://www.ohchr.org/EN /ProfessionalInterest/Pages/StatusOfRefugees.aspx

United Nations. (1965). *International convention on the elimination of all forms of racial discrimination,* G. A. Res. 2106 (XX). Retrieved from http://www.ohchr .org/Documents/ProfessionalInterest/cerd.pdf

United Nations. (1966a, December 16). *International covenant on civil and political rights*. G.A. Res. 2200A (XXI). Retrieved from http://www.ohchr.org /Documents/ProfessionalInterest/ccpr.pdf

United Nations. (1989, November 20). *Convention on the rights of the child*. G.A. Res. 44/25. Retrieved from http://www.ohchr.org/Documents /ProfessionalInterest/crc.pdf

United Nations. (1990, December 18). *International convention on the protection of the rights of all migrant workers and members of their families*. G. A. Res. 45/158. Retrieved from http://www2.ohchr.org/english/bodies/cmw/cmw.htm

United Nations (2000). *Protocol to prevent, suppress and punish trafficking in persons, especially women and children, supplementing the United Nations convention against transnational organized crime*. Retrieved from http://www .unhcr.org/refworld/docid/4720706c0.html

United Nations. (2006). *Convention on the rights of persons with disabilities*. G.A. Res. A/RES/61/106. Retrieved from http://www.ohchr.org/EN/HRBodies /CRPD/Pages/ConventionRightsPersonsWithDisabilities.aspx

United Nations Educational Scientific and Cultural Organisation (UNESCO). (2005). *Information kit: United Nations Convention on the Rights of Migrants*. Retrieved from http://unesdoc.unesco.org/images/0014/001435/143557e.pdf

United Nations High Commissioner for Refugees (UNHCR). (2013). *UNHCR statistical yearbook 2012*. Retrieved from http://www.unhcr.org/52a722c49.html

U.S. Department of Homeland Security. (2008). *Annual report: Immigrant enforcement actions: 2006*. Retrieved from https://www.dhs.gov/xlibrary/assets /statistics/publications/enforcement_ar_06.pdf

U.S. Refugee Act of 1980, Pub. L. 96-212, tit. I, 101(b), 94 Stat. 102 (1980).

Victims of Trafficking and Violence Protection Act of 2000. (2000). 114 Stat. 1464.

Workers Defense Project. (2012). *Build a better nation: A case for comprehensive immigration reform*. Retrieved from *workersdefense.org/IMMIGRATION %20wdp%20color%20FINAL.pdf*

Endnotes

1   Human rights organizations (including civil rights organizations in the United States) recommend using the term *undocumented* for immigrants with irregular status and consider the term *illegal alien* to be derogatory and legally inaccurate. Moreover, the word *illegal* carries a series of negative connotations. It is often assumed that "illegal" people have no civil or workplace rights, when in fact all people have rights regardless of immi-

gration status. Additionally, some people falsely think that entering the country without a visa is a felony crime, when in fact it is a civil violation. *Undocumented* is viewed as a more accurate term because it simply means immigration authorities have not documented an immigrant's status (Workers Defense Project, 2013).

2   ILO Convention 97, adopted in 1949, deals with international migration for employment, providing foundations for equal treatment between nationals and regular migrants in recruitment procedures; living and working conditions; and access to justice, tax, and social security. It sets out details for contract conditions, participation of migrants in job training or promotion, provisions for family reunification, and appeals against unjustified termination of employment or expulsion. The protections of ILO Convention 97 apply only to migrant workers who are legally residing and working in the host country. The ILO Migrant Workers Convention No. 143 was adopted in 1957 and provides specific guidance regarding treatment of irregular migration and facilitating integration of migrants in host societies. Article 1 establishes the obligation of ratifying states to "respect the basic human rights of all migrant workers," independent of their legal situation in the host state. Its Part II details standards for integration of long-term migrant workers (Ruhs, 2012).

3   It evolved from initial United Nations concerns in 1972 about the illegal transportation of labor to European countries, the exploitation of workers from African countries in conditions similar to slavery and forced labor, and discriminatory treatment of foreign workers. In 1973 recommendations were made by the Economic and Social Council for the establishment of a United Nations convention on the rights of migrant workers, which was echoed by the World Conference to Combat Racism and Racial Discrimination in Geneva in 1978. The UN General Assembly began to propose measures to improve the situation and protect the human rights of migrant workers (Office of the United Nations High Commissioner for Human Rights, 2005).

4   Other examples of violations such as wage theft and retaliation for asserting labor rights are available in the National Employment Law Project's 2013 *Testimony Regarding Retaliation Against Immigrant Workers in California*. Retrieved from http://nelp.3cdn. net/43a4ff6fea3fd41526_q8m6b1zi0.pdf.

5   Additional information and relevant case vignettes are available in *Home Economics: The Invisible and Unregulated World of Domestic Work* released by an advocacy group, the National Domestic Workers Alliance (2012; see http://www.domesticworkers.org/ pdfs/HomeEconomicsEnglish.pdf . It is the first large-scale national survey of domestic workers in United States.

24 | Addressing the Human Right to Water in Global Social Work Education

DeBrenna LaFa Agbényiga and Sudha Sankar

The World Health Organization defines *safe water* as water that does not contain any physical, biological, or chemical contaminants detrimental to health, is free of objectionable odors and tastes, and is available in adequate amounts for the sustainability of a hygienic lifestyle (World Health Organization, 2009). As of 2012, 783 million people around the world had lower than minimum access to safe water for drinking and sanitation (United Nations International Children's Emergency Fund [UNICEF], 2012). Deprivation of water is a matter of serious concern because it is more detrimental and dangerous for human beings than the deprivation of food. Water accounts for more than 60% of the average body weight (Bulto, 2011) and affects human health, agriculture, and livelihood. Although more than 70% of the earth's surface is covered in water, only 3% of this water is freshwater suitable for human consumption (Chen & Altschuller, 2010; Stockholm International Water Institute, 2013a). Approximately three quarters of this consumable water (and up to 90% in some of the fastest growing economies) is consumed by agriculture and industrial use (Stockholm International Water Institute, 2013b) with less than 2% available for household use (Bulto, 2011; Chen & Altschuller, 2010).

Although water deprivation and human beings' right to access clean water is undeniably a topic of ever increasing global importance, an examination of social work journals for water related research returns very few results. As a field, social work seems to be disconnected from research and discourse on the issue of human access to and use of water in various related fields including economics, politics and governance, and international and environmental development. Although several local and international organizations such as the International Water Management Institute, World Watch Institute, and the Stockholm International Water Institute conduct extensive research on the topic of water availability, access, use, governance, and management, the social work perspective is absent from this important work. Major subtopics of water availability and access include assessment and management of the quality/quantity of water, effects of climate change and pollution, and sustainability of technological solutions. However, research in this area is often assumed to fall under the realm of the physical and statistical sciences. This is reflected in the professional identities of individuals generating knowledge on water resource issues. Much work in this area is carried out by economists and engineers finding solutions to problems of access to water safe for drinking and sanitation. However, the matter of battling water scarcity and distribution is more complex than just finding engineering solutions such as irrigation and wetland restoration (although these are of key importance). In fact, this issue requires a multidisciplinary approach, as outlined in the focus case in Sidebar 1.

Sidebar 1

CASE IN FOCUS: In West Bengal (India), where groundwater is abundant, a social scientist from the International Water Management Institute, Aditi Mukherji, was tasked with assessing and addressing drops in agricultural productivity. She discovered that "an outdated permit system" required for "electrification of small groundwater wells" was "mired in red tape and corruption" and "preventing farmers from accessing water," thereby "causing a production bottleneck." Aditi convinced the state government of West Bengal to scrap "the permit system and also to give Farmers some one-time financial assistance for electrification of their wells thereby boosting agricultural productivity (International Water Management Institute, 2013).

The following exploration of challenges and trends in the field of water security is intended to help social workers better understand and envision their contributions to problems in this area of research and practice. It clearly illustrates how the practice skills we use as social workers in a community setting could be useful in identifying, addressing, and supporting change efforts as they relate to global water concerns.

Commodification and Privatization: Water in the Open Market

A key challenge in the fight for universal access to water is the push toward privatization and commodification of water. *Commodification* refers to the process by which a resource is converted into a tradable entity (like gold, silver, and land) by creating policies and laws that permit one or more private parties to claim ownership or distribution rights (privatization) to that resource. Large private corporations, with the support of organizations such as the World Bank are moving to take over ownership and distribution of water. The claim is that this is the only way to ensure that water is managed well and distributed to those who need it. However, those who oppose this stance recognize that turning water into a tradable good will ultimately increase access for those who can pay for it while further exacerbating poverty and inequalities across the world. Worldwide, countries have been caught between this struggle of commodification and privatization. Ultimately, the cost of this struggle lies within impoverished communities as illustrated in the case in Sidebar 2.

Sidebar 2

CASE IN FOCUS: In the 1990s, backed by World Bank, Bolivia sold water management rights for its poorest regions to private corporations. At the outset, access to water increased; but soon, rising costs led to many of the country's poorest communities losing access to water as a result of inability to pay. The people eventually engaged in riots and forced the company out of the country (Shultz, 2005).

Developing countries desperately searching for solutions to their water distribution and management problems are particularly vulnerable to being persuaded to hand over the management of public water services to large multinational corporations, which stand to profit from developing countries' plights. This vulnerability arises from the fact that governments are susceptible to influence through undue pressure exerted by powerful funding agencies.

The problem is compounded by the fact that people in the poorest communities of the world have very little voice and little or no power. Therefore, social workers need to recognize their role in both preventive advocacy and intervention work with communities. The act of supporting and guiding communities in organized community advocacy and action can prove powerful in combating movements toward privatization, as in the case of India demonstrated in the focus case in Sidebar 3.

The Multidimensional Effects of Water Scarcity

Access to water is intricately linked to health, education, quality of life, agricultural development, and opportunity for economic growth (Kumar, Sivamohan, & Bassi, 2013) at the individual and community level. There are strong intersections between poverty and all measures of human well-being including access to clean water. In the 2010 Human Development Report, the United Nations Development Programme presented the complex relationships between various indices of well-being and poverty as the Multi-Dimensional Poverty Index (Human Development Report, 2010; see Figure 1). The report consolidates three large international surveys, namely the Demographic and Health Survey, the Multiple Indicators Cluster Survey, and the World Health Survey. It presents the multiple deprivations in health, education, and living standards with which individuals in poor households must contend as a part of their daily survival. The Multi-Dimensional Poverty Index not only reflects the prevalence but also the intensity of poverty by counting the number of deprivations each individual experiences. In this way, differential experiences of oppression and deprivation by gender, age, geographic location, ethnic group, and social class are examined. According to the 2013 Human Development Report (UNDP, 2013), about 1.6 billion people (30%) of the 5.4 billion people in the 104 countries covered (76% of the world total) "lived in multidimensional poverty between 2002 and 2011" (p. 13).

Figure 1   **Components of the Multidimensional Poverty Index. This figure illustrates the three dimensions and 10 indicators of multidimensional poverty first published in the Human Development Report, 2010.**

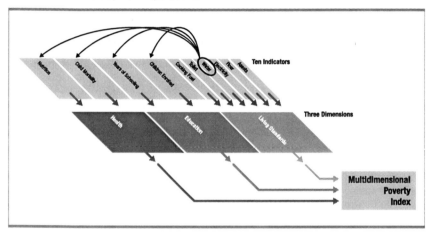

The concept of multidimensional poverty is a complexity-based approach or framework (discussed later in this chapter) that proves very useful in understanding the multidimensional effects of water deprivation at the microsystemic level. We have marginally modified and expanded the model to illustrate the fact that water is not just an independent indicator of living standards but also a predictor of other indicators including enrollment in school, years of education, nutrition, and child mortality. All of these aspects violate individuals' human rights and access to opportunities that lead to an improved way of life that is directed away from various levels of poverty.

The Right to Water: A Fundamental Human Right

Since the inception of the United Nations Millennium Development Goals (MDGs) in 2000, research in the field of social work has shown increased attention to important development indices including poverty, inequality, and sustainable living. The discourse on access to water has also gained some momentum across disciplines in the past decade or so. Yet there are significant barriers, including concern that water has remained secondary to other development issues within the field. In social work this is due, in part, to the role ambiguity of social workers previously discussed in this chapter. Another key challenge, however, is the simple fact that national and international human rights charters and legal regimes do not always recognize the right to water as a fundamental human right but rather as a subset of other seemingly larger rights (Bulto, 2011; Chen & Altschuller, 2010). For example, the African Charter on Human and Peoples' Rights lacks an explicit legal mention of the right to water (Bulto, 2011). The right to this important resource is thus left to the creative and ethical interpretation of the charter (as a derivative of the right to health and dignity) by the African Commission on Human and Peoples' Rights, thereby never guaranteeing the right to water. Similarly, although the issue of access to safe water for consumption and sanitation (United Nations, 2009) is at the heart of the MDGs (including environmental sustainability, eradicating poverty, hunger, and diseases), the recognition of water comes largely in an indirect manner. For example, the fourth MDG specifies the commitment to reduce child mortality. Knowing that child mortality rates are linked to diarrheal disease and hygiene related illnesses, it becomes clear that access to clean water for drinking and sanitation are key processes in the reduction of child mortality rates (World Health Organization, 2009). Unfortunately, water is still invisible as a basic right and as an important indicator of development.

Recognizing water as a fundamental human right is important for several reasons as we seek to alleviate poverty and fully embrace the challenge of achieving the MDGs. First, ignoring the impact of access to water places water at a much greater risk of large scale privatization and commodification, particularly in developing nations. Currently, there seems to be an unspoken recognition that those counted among the most vulnerable deserve access to water only to the extent that it contributes to survival. However, without an explicit legal recognition of water as a natural resource to which every individual is entitled—a human right—there is no legal ground on which to protect water from privatization and consequently from being subject to commodification and market forces. Thus, a risk exists for this resource to be monopolized by private entities standing to benefit from its sale. Moreover, access to water necessary for daily survival could be threatened, which in turn could significantly affect and further marginalize communities. This perspective is clearly illustrated in the case outlined in Sidebar 4.

Sidebar 4

CASE IN FOCUS: In 2012 India's Ministry of Water Resources released a draft of a national water policy that proposed the nationwide privatization of water delivery and sanitation. The government entity claimed that the intent of the proposed policy change was to maximize value, recover administrative costs of water management and distribution, reduce waste, and promote efficient use of water. The move is believed to have come following international pressures from the U.S. government and policies proposed by water lending organizations such as the World Bank and International Monetary Fund. Several private and political groups as well as Supreme Court judges spoke out vehemently against this, emphasizing that several past Supreme Court rulings have clearly stated that air, water, and forests are natural resources that cannot be privately owned, thereby preventing this proposal from passing. However, although privatization on a national scale has thus far been prevented, several cities have subcontracted water management to private companies. Results of such moves have been discouraging, to say the least (Prakash & Kumara, 2012; Ramachandran, 2013).

Second, the issue of water needs to be examined through the lens of human rights. In the Human Development Report published in the year 2000, the United Nations Development Programme defined *human rights* as "the rights possessed by all persons, by virtue of their common humanity, to live a life of freedom and dignity" (p. 15). According to the UNDP (2010) report, human rights "give all people moral claims on the behavior of individuals and on the design of social arrangements—and are universal, inalienable and indivisible."

Central to this definition is the concept of equality as a human being and hence equal rights to all resources on earth. The common discourse within both academic and non-cademic organizations centers on water to the extent necessary for survival. For example, the MDGs lay out some core human development priorities and goals that are based on minimum necessary levels of access and not equalities, barriers, intersections, and process freedoms (United Nations Development Programme, 2010). This essentially becomes a vehicle of exploitation wherein those more privileged deny individuals and communities their basic rights by refusing to recognize this lack of access as a problem. Furthermore, individuals living in these conditions are less likely to complete school and obtain economic stability and are further disempowered.

Finally, this refusal to acknowledge the right to water as a fundamental human right implies that the primary value of water is restricted to economic, agricultural, and survival potential. The social and qualitative elements of water that add to human well-being (Alston & Mason, 2008) are not counted as important values of water, thereby privileging these aspects of water solely to those who have the economic wherewithal to benefit from the social uses of water. As with the risks of commodification, here too, there is an embedded hierarchy wherein the possibility of equal access is eliminated and those in more privileged positions are guaranteed much more than their equal share of access to water.

More recently, the discourse on the right to access to water has been moving toward acknowledging water as a fundamental right. In a general comment in 2002 the United Nations Committee on Economic, Social and Cultural rights declared the right to water as autonomous. Similarly, the African Charter on the Rights and Welfare of the Child requires states to ensure the provision of adequate safe drinking water for children (African Commission on Human and Peoples' Rights, 1990). From this stance, one would infer that we are globally and collectively headed in the right direction. However, as a field social work has not been actively engaged in this process, even though the individuals, families, groups, and communities we work with are often severely affected by the lack of access to water. Therefore, social workers need to take a proactive stance in this debate for water rights. By not contributing to the global dialogue on water rights, we perpetuate the message that we accept water as a secondary and derivative right. The case of water rights presented here also presents the opportunity for social work educators to engage students to think critically about what this refusal to acknowledge the right to water as a fundamental right implies for people, for human rights, and for society as a whole.

Water Scarcity and Political Conflict

Around the globe, water scarcity has resulted in political tensions and transnational conflicts that threaten to result in war over this important resource. Governments and international organizations alike work toward developing policy that allows the safe resolution of such disputes. For example, the case in Sidebar 5 illustrates an issue with access to water that cuts across three African nations.

Sidebar 5

CASE IN FOCUS: In Southern Africa the Okavango River, which is shared by Angola, Namibia, and Botswana, proves to be an ongoing source of conflict, particularly during times of drought or water scarcity. In the late 1990s severe droughts in Namibia threatened livelihoods and prompted Namibia to propose the construction of a 250 km pipeline to divert water from the Okavango River into their dams. To resolve such conflicts, the three countries signed an agreement to establish a common commission, the Permanent Okavango River Basin Water Commission, which has thus far managed to keep major conflict and unfair use of the river water at bay (Green, Cosens, & Garmestani, 2013; Mbaiwa, 2004).

Unfortunately, the outcomes of such conflicts are not always amicable and are often (such as in the case illustrated in Sidebar 6) strongly influenced by political motives rather than the best interests of the people. Advocating for policy that benefits those most affected by water scarcity should be a key role adopted by social workers. To date, areas of Namibia continue to struggle with access to water. This struggle has moved from remote rural areas into the city because individuals have migrated in search of water.

Sidebar 6

CASE IN FOCUS: The Krishna River in India is primarily shared by three states: Maharashtra, Karnataka, and Andra Pradesh. In the 1960s the Krishna Water Dispute Tribunal was established to resolve conflicts and ensure fair use and distribution of Krishna River waters. However, in the recent past there has been a stark rise in internal conflict between northern and southern parts of Andra Pradesh over the distribution of the river water. Communities in the northern part of the state claimed loss of development and agriculture due to heavy diversion of water by southern Andra Pradesh. In September 2013 the conflict was addressed by granting a division of Andra Pradesh into two separate states (Telangana and Seemandra) with the central government proposing the creation of the Krishna Control Board to oversee and establish new guidelines for fair use of the river water between the two new states. As of October 2013 the state of Seemandra is experiencing riots and protests against the divide. A curfew was set and police were given orders to shoot at sight to contain the conflict. Power plant employees across the state are protesting the divide by unanimously abandoning their jobs, leaving much of the state in darkness and costing the state millions.

The outcomes in the case above illustrate not just the importance of policy and governance, but also the need for a complexity view that places greater emphasis on incorporating historical, cultural, political, and public policy considerations in social work practice, teaching, and research. This is important if we hope to truly contribute to the advancement of water access in developing nations. For example, in the case discussed in Sidebar 6, this state divide is suspected of giving several politicians an advantage in upcoming elections. On the other hand, people in at least one of the new states are expected to suffer job loss, slowed economic growth, and loss of other important resources. Interestingly, although driven largely by water-based conflict, the division is also closely tied to linguistic differences between the two parts of the state. In addition, the current geographic line of division closely mirrors that which existed between the boundaries of the British Empire and local kingdoms during British colonization of the region. Thus, social work educators have the responsibility to establish practical and theoretical training that is grounded in a commitment to understand and voice the people's opinions and needs to the governing systems, while carefully considering the macrosystemic factors including historical, cultural, and political motives contributing to the state of water access in local regions. Examining international models of policy and community structures that have proven to work in favor of communities in need also proves useful in establishing multisystemic solutions to problems of water access (see Sidebar 7).

Sidebar 7

CASE IN FOCUS: In the case discussed in Sidebar 3 (village of Plachimada in Kerala, India, versus the Coca Cola company), one of the key strengths of the people of the village was the political hierarchy and organization in the region. To run the plant, Coca Cola was required not only to obtain state and central government consent but also to obtain a valid operating license issued by the Perumatty Grama Panchayat, the local village council, a community level democratic system acting on behalf of village residents. This license was first issued by the council in 1999. However, following complaints from village residents, the local council refused to renew the license in 2003 on the grounds of acute scarcity of safe groundwater caused by abuse of the resource by the manufacturing plant. A legal battle lasting many years ensued, with the state of Kerala eventually challenging Coca Cola on behalf of the village council. The plant was eventually closed, and fights for compensation are ongoing (India Resource Center, 2006, 2010; Rights to Water and Sanitation, 2010; Singh, 2011).

Water and Women

Although a look at world averages might mislead one to believe that we are making significant progress toward increasing access to clean water, a closer look shows that there are striking inequalities across countries and regions with respect to access to clean water and proper sanitation. Not only does this access and its effects on individuals vary by geographical locations, but it also varies by socioeconomic status, rural living, age, and gender (World Health Organization, 2009), with the most vulnerable and resource-deprived populations facing the most severe consequences.

It is commonly seen that in many cultures, particularly in the poorest segments of societies, traditional gender roles assign women to the task of obtaining access to and managing use of water for domestic activities including drinking, cooking, and sanitation (see Figure 2). This automatically places women in a disadvantaged position, particularly with respect to access to education, contribution to the workforce, self-sufficiency, and ultimately power and safety.

Figure 2   **Who collects water for households?**

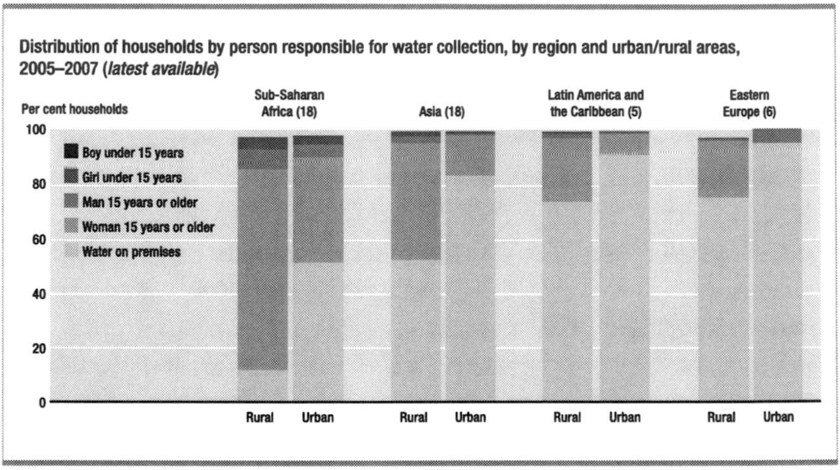

Distribution of households by person responsible for water collection, by region and urban/rural areas, 2005–2007 (*latest available*)

Source: United Nations Department of Social and Economic Affairs, 2010

Gender adds additional dimensions of deprivation for women, with the challenges and costs of water scarcity extending far beyond the matter of time and distances traveled to obtain water. Many young girls and women drop out of or fail to attend school because they may have to walk many miles every day to obtain and carry water (which may not be clean) to their families. For women, lack of access to clean water and toilets for sanitation means a lack of dignity and privacy. In many cultures it is not permissible for women to relieve themselves during the day because they risk being exposed or seen. Without adequate sanitation they are forced to wait many hours to relieve themselves after nightfall. This also poses a threat to their health and heightens the risk of assault and rape because they may have to travel to uninhabited areas after dark for cleansing and sanitation. When young girls reach puberty, lack of access to clean water and private cleansing facilities similarly poses difficulties in sanitation in the school environment, causing them to drop out of school. Women are primary caregivers in most communities and families, and lack of access to safe water diverts their valuable time and energy to caring for family members who contract waterborne diseases. Access to safe water also plays a key role in women's health, with more than 40 million pregnant women contracting waterborne illnesses (UNICEF, 2003) every year, thereby endangering both themselves and their unborn children.

While acknowledging the increased challenges posed to women as a result of water scarcity, it is equally important to acknowledge that women are uniquely placed to change and revolutionize how water is used and the policies that govern it. In many societies women are the first to recognize water pollution and scarcity and raise voices in protest. They control the use and distribution of this resource within their communities and families even when they do not have exclusively recognized power in the system. This is shown in the case example in Sidebar 8, which demonstrates the strength and determination of women in community environments struggling to have access to water that is clean and safe.

Sidebar 8

CASE IN FOCUS: In the case discussed in Sidebar 3 (village of Plachimada in Kerala, India, versus the Coca Cola company), the women of the village were the first to congregate and raise their voices in protest against the drying of their groundwater wells and the contamination of water used for household purposes. They stated that what little water was left proved toxic to their skin, thereby forcing them to walk up to 5 km a day to fetch water. It was on the grounds of this protest that the community and the village council moved to take action against the continued operation of the Coca Cola plant (India Resource Center, 2006, 2010; Rights to Water and Sanitation, 2010; Singh, 2011).

One important role of social workers lies in their efforts to empower women in economically challenged communities to initiate work and engage themselves in enhancing access to water for their communities. Some of the identified barriers to achieving these goals include the absence of participation of the targeted individual or community in implementing solutions; competing agendas between various parties including government, local communities, external actors, and funding sources; and gaps between suggested solutions and policy mandates that prevent solutions from being implemented. Social workers may thus have to advocate for women when needed, open communication channels between various stakeholders, and offer collaboration and energy to help maintain progress and ensure the sustainability of change. For social work educators, it has become increasingly important to introduce trainees to the concepts of capacity development, including an understanding of operating spaces (see Baser, Morgan et al., 2008, for a detailed description of operating spaces for change) that can endure and sustain changes through participant and stakeholder engagement. The field of capacity development has much to offer in the way of solving social problems that includes access to water across global communities.

Conceptualizing Water Scarcity in Social Work: A Complexity Framework

In the human service and development fields, experts and practitioners have been moving away from privileging predictability and toward acknowledging complexity and uncertainty (Bolland & Atherton, 1999; European Centre for Development Policy Management, 2008; Pearson, 2011). Unlike traditional theory, complexity approaches do not encompass a set of interrelated propositions but rather, a framework for how to think about complex human problems (Bolland & Atherton, 1999). The field of social work, like other social sciences, claimed to take a subjective and contextual view of human experience for a long time. The emphasis on linear cause and effect mechanisms thought to be privileged by the pure sciences and strongly attested to by the social sciences tells a different story. For example, in social work theory a complexity view of systems seems to be limited primarily to the interconnectedness of systems within which any individual is embedded versus the examination of multiple complex relationships between indicators of well-being and specific resources within the context of ecological systems. To truly adopt a complex understanding of the human experience—teaching, learning, research, and service in social work—we need to move away from simplistic, linear, cause-and-effect explanations. Instead, explanations can be embedded in multidimensional, multidirectional, and hierarchically nested theoretical models such as the one presented in Figure 3.

Figure 3 Complexity based framework for multidimensional effects of water availability and access

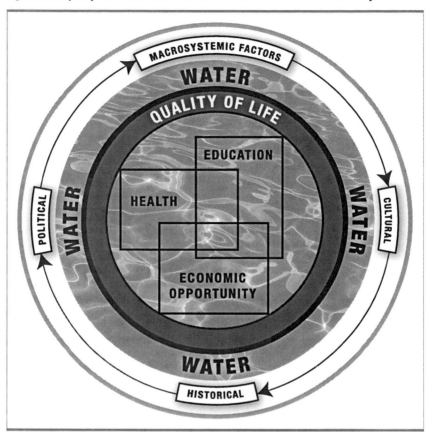

To understand the effects of access to and availability of water, we need to consider the multidirectional effects that individual, micro-, mezzo-, exo-, and macrosystems have on each other and the effects of water access on various development indices, particularly education, health, growth, and opportunity, and consequently quality of life across these systemic levels. Therefore, the profession needs to bring advocacy informed by complex systemic analysis and considerations to bear on practice issues.

Role of Social Work

As a profession, social work has the potential to play a significant role in creating a heightened level of understanding and awareness of global water issues.

As change agents consistently engaged in communities across various regions of the world, we are well-positioned to help establish and manage sustainable changes at all systemic levels. To be truly responsive to global needs, social work has to attend to four major callings:

- To recognize its responsibility to the most vulnerable populations it serves and to identify and create a place for itself in the interdisciplinary efforts to improve access to water among poor communities in developing nations.
- To examine and comprehend the complex factors influencing access to and availability of water and its consequences for individuals, communities, and the world, and to incorporate this lens into social work practice.
- To take an active role in the global discourse on the human right to water and to actively influence water use and distribution policies.
- To advocate for, engage, and collaborate with vulnerable individuals and communities in finding multisystemic solutions to problems of water scarcity, availability, and access.

As social work educators, we need to immerse ourselves in this important calling. We need to actively incorporate not just research from within social work academia, but also the complex and ever changing landscape of knowledge from organizations and individuals directly engaged in human capacity development around the world such as the Stockholm International Water Institute, International Water Management Institute, the United Nations commissions, and others who serve the most vulnerable and oppressed populations globally. We also need to model the need for a shift toward incorporating complexity approaches (including a multidisciplinary, multidimensional conceptualization) not only to systems of thinking, but also to models of engagement including those that guide our research, teaching, and service. Social work educators carry an immense responsibility to not just pass information on to students but also to help them become aware of complex and often invisible implications. In social work education the emphasis on the significance of small shifts in thinking (such as this) for social change can be instructive and enlightening. The importance of these shifts in thinking are enhanced in the context of human rights issues where the focus is on setting up structural safeguards. Of particular importance is a more vocal and pervasive attention to access to water as an autonomous human right, to the resolution of the inequalities and barriers to accessing this basic right, and to capacity development as a complex tool that can be used to engage communities in finding solutions to their water problems. Ultimately, we must commit to inspiring social workers in training to serve as the voice of those unable to speak for themselves and join hands with those who stand to lose the most in this battle over water—our most precious resource.

Conclusion

As a profession that works within the context of the person and his or her environment, social work has a duty to become an active participant in all global human rights initiatives like water availability and access. We must break disciplinary boundaries and advocate for change on the global stage. Water scarcity affects the livelihood of the most vulnerable populations we serve, thereby necessitating a professional immersion in the topic. Our training frameworks must also be scrutinized and restructured to accommodate a focus on water availability and access and its impact on livelihoods.

References

African Commission on Human and Peoples' Rights. (2010). African charter on the rights and welfare of the child. (OAU Doc. CAB/LEG/24.9/49) Retrieved from http://www.achpr.org/instruments/child/

Alston, M., & Mason, R. (2008). Who turns the taps off? Introducing social flow to the Australian water debate. Rural Society, 18(2), 131–139.

Baser, H., Morgan, J., Bolger, J., Brinkerhoff, D., Land, A., Taschereau, S., ... Zinke, J. (2008). Capacity change and performance study report. European Centre for Development Policy Management. Retrieved from http://www.ecdpm.org/Web_ECDPM/Web/Content/Download.nsf/0 /5321BD4DC0C1DB09C1257535004D1982/$FILE/PMB21-e _capacitystudy.pdf

Bolland, K. A., & Atherton, C. R. (1999). Chaos theory: An alternative approach to social work practice and research. Families in Society, 80 (4), 367.

Bulto, T. S. (2011). The human right to water in the corpus and jurisprudence of the African human rights system. African Human Rights Law Journal, 11(2), 341–367.

Chen, E., & Altschuller, S. A. (2010). Corporate accountability and human rights in the age of global water scarcity. Natural Resources & Environment, 24(3), 9–14.

European Centre for Development Policy Management. (2008). Capacity change and performance: Insights and implications for development cooperation. (Policy Management Brief No. 21). Maastricht, The Netherlands: Author.

Green, O. O., Cosens, B. A., & Garmestani, A. S. (2013). Resilience in transboundary water governance: The Okavango River Basin. Ecology and Society 18(2), 23.

India Resource Center. (2006, June 19). Kerala government assures proactive action against Coca-Cola. Retrieved from http://www.indiaresource.org/news/2006/1069.html

India Resource Center. (2010, March 22). Coca-Cola liable for $48 million for damages in Plachimada, Kerala. Retrieved from http://www.countercurrents.org/irc220310.htm

International Water Management Institute (IWMI). (2013). IWMI annual report 2012. Retrieved from http://www.iwmi.cgiar.org/About_IWMI/Strategic_Documents/Annual_Reports/2012/IWMI_Annual_Report_2012.pdf

Kumar, M. D., Sivamohan, M. V. K., & Bassi, N. (2013). Food security and sustainable agriculture in developing economies. In M. D. Kumar, M. V. K. Sivamohan, & N. Bassi (Eds.), Water management, food security and sustainable agriculture in developing economies (pp. 1–14). New York, NY: Routledge.

Mbaiwa, J. E. (2004). Causes and possible solutions to water resource conflicts in the Okavango river basin: The case of Angola, Namibia and Botswana. Physics and Chemistry of the Earth, Parts A/B/C, 29(15–18), 1319–1326. doi:10.1016/j.pce.2004.09.015Pearson, J. (2011). Training and beyond: Seeking better practices for capacity development, OECD development co-operation working papers (No. 1). Retrieved from http://dx.doi.org/10.1787/5kgf1nsnj8tf-en

Prakash, A., & Kumara, K. (2012, March 30). India's government orients towards privatizing water. Retrieved from http://www.wsws.org/en/articles/2012/03/indi-m30.html

Ramachandran, S. K. (2013, March 20). Water privatization is not for India. *The Hindu*. Retrieved from http://www.thehindu.com/news/cities/Delhi/water-privatisation-is-not-for-india/article4528871.ece

Rights to Water and Sanitation. (2010). *Case against Coca-Cola Kerala State: India.* Retrieved from http://www.righttowater.info/ways-to-influence/legal-approaches/case-against-coca-cola-kerala-state-india/

Shultz, J. (2005, January 28). The politics of water in Bolivia. *The Nation*. Retrieved from http://www.thenation.com/article/politics-water-bolivia

Singh, J. (2011, February 24). India Coca-Cola compensation law is passed in Kerala. *BBC NEWS South Asia*. Retrieved from http://www.bbc.co.uk/news/world-south-asia-12567542

Stockholm International Water Institute. (2013a). Facts and Statistics: Water resources and Scarcity. Retrieved from http://www.siwi.org/media/facts-and-statistics/1-water-resources-and-scarcity/

Stockholm International Water Institute. (2013b). Facts and statistics: Food, agriculture and bioenergy. Retrieved from http://www.siwi.org/media/facts-and-statistics/6-food-agriculture-and-bioenergy/

United Nations. (2009). *UN millennium development goals report, 2009*. Retrieved from http://www.un.org/millenniumgoals/pdf/MDG_Report_2009_ENG.pdf

United Nations Department of Social and Economic Affairs. (2010). The world's women 2010: Trends and statistics. Retrieved from http://unstats.un.org/unsd/demographic/products/Worldswomen/WW_full%20report_color.pdf

United Nations Development Programme. (2000). *Human development report 2000: Human rights and human development*. New York, NY: Oxford University Press. Retrieved from http://hdr.undp.org/en/content/human-development-report-2000

United Nations Development Programme. (2010). *Human development report 2010: The real wealth of nations: Pathways to human development*. New York, NY: Oxford University Press. Retrieved from http://hdr.undp.org/en/media/HDR_2010_EN_Complete_reprint.pdf

United Nations Development Programme. (2013). *Human development report 2013: The rise of the south: Human progress in a diverse world*. New York, NY: Oxford University Press. Retrieved from http://www.undp.org/content/undp/en/home/librarypage/hdr/human-development-report-2013/

United Nations International Children's Emergency Fund (UNICEF). (2003). WASH and women. Retrieved from http://www.unicef.org/wash/index _womenandgirls.html

United Nations International Children's Emergency Fund (UNICEF). (2012). Progress on drinking water and sanitation: 2012 update. Retrieved from http://www.unicef.org/media/files/JMPreport2012.pdf

World Health Organization. (2009). Integrating poverty and gender into health programmes: A sourcebook for health professionals. Manila, Philippines: Author.

EPILOGUE | **Future Directions in Human Rights and Social Work Education**

S. Megan Berthold, Rebecca L. Thomas, Lynne M. Healy, and Kathryn R. Libal

This volume provides conceptual frameworks and practical guides for integrating human rights into social work pedagogy. It addresses curriculum development, teaching methodologies, and strategies that can be used in foundation and advanced courses, travel study and exchange models to promote human rights education, and in electives with special populations and problems. It promotes a rights-based approach to policy practice and social work research and explores the relationship between human rights and social justice. As such, the volume supports the ongoing efforts of social work educators and educational institutions to infuse human rights into the curriculum and profession.

It is vital to further this work to more fully realize social work as a human rights profession. Educational standards are an excellent place to begin. Many of the chapters refer to the 2008 Educational Policy and Accreditation Standards (EPAS) and the efforts made to implement the standard on human rights (Council on Social Work Education [CSWE], 2008). This underscores the importance of curriculum standards in encouraging development of new curriculum areas. As this volume is being published, the 2008 version of EPAS is about to be replaced. It is critical that the new standards retain and optimally strengthen the emphasis on human rights. This will reinforce the progress made to date and underpin further work on the areas identified in following paragraphs.

Among other areas needing additional development in scholarship and pedagogy are incorporating discussion of human rights philosophy and values into the foundation level social work curriculum, field education, the education of current and future social work educators, interprofessional practice, and program evaluation and research. Even as social work educators integrate human rights concepts into the classroom, embedding human rights practice in the profession also requires developing field educators' capacities to recognize and engage human rights principles (Dominelli, 2007; see also Chapters 5 and 21 in this volume) and reshaping doctoral training of future social work educators. The latter is crucial for the development of innovative approaches to teaching about human-rights based practice in all domains of social work and to foster a deeper understanding of the interconnectedness of human rights and social work in our educational institutions. Chapters in this volume provide examples of projects that have advanced student learning of human rights through interprofessional practice (Chapter 18) and research (Chapter 12). Another addresses the education of social work faculty (Chapter 5). Further contributions to the literature are needed in these areas to advance the integration of human rights into all domains of social work practice.

Foundation Level Human Rights Education

As Wronka (2008) has consistently asserted in his scholarship, human rights education cannot be relegated to an elective course or a single unit or two in a course that all students are required to take to complete their degree. Creative ways to incorporate human rights concepts, values, and ideas about rights-based practice will be most effective when incorporated throughout the curriculum, thereby underscoring its fundamental importance to the foundation of all social work education. The University of Buffalo, Monmouth University, and Fordham University each provide examples of this integrative approach.

Steen (2012) has pointed out that human rights philosophy is a good companion to the person-in-environment perspective and is especially relevant to human behavior curriculum. She notes that a key challenge is that most human rights content developed for social work texts in the past has tended to focus on the macro level, and attending to the mezzo and micro practice dimensions of human rights is critical to social work too. Steen (2012) notes, "When the concept of human rights is introduced as inherently connected with human development, students can more easily transition into understanding how development is impacted by oppression, which is essentially the violation of human rights" (p. 860). Moreover, Steen (like Androff & McPherson, Chapter 3 this volume), regards incorporating human rights philosophy into human behavior courses as promoting vertical integration of macro, mezzo, and micro domains of human life and social work practice.

Field Education

Field education has long been recognized as the signature pedagogy in social work (Wayne, Raskin, & Bogo, 2010) and as a medium for promoting the development of competent social work practitioners (Bogo, 2010). The social work literature includes attention to addressing topics such as sexual orientation (Newman, Bogo, & Daley, 2009), racism, and gender oppression in field education. Human rights are highly relevant to competent social work practice and the life experiences of these and many other historically marginalized and oppressed populations served by social workers. Despite this reality and the recent emphasis in the EPAS and by international social work organizations on human rights, there is a relative dearth of literature on human rights and field education. On the international level, the Global Standards for the Education and Training of the Social Work Profession, adopted by the International Federation of Social Workers (IFSW) and the International Association for Schools of Social Work (IASSW; 2004) mention human rights but do not specifically address the link to field education. Perhaps one of the most useful guides setting standards for rights-based approaches to field education and practice is one developed by the United Nations in collaboration with IFSW and IASSW (United Nations Centre for Human Rights, 1994). Although this document is now two decades old, it is still highly relevant. The IFSW Europe Division (IFSW European Region e.V., 2010) has established guidelines for integrating human rights into social work practice that provide substantive recommendations that merit consideration in the United States. Although not a widely known document in the United States, it addresses important dimensions of practice such as the need for appropriate caseloads and the use and misuse of information. Given that the EPAS guidelines provide little concrete direction for how to train social workers to consciously integrate human rights into their practice, we suggest thorough review and professional dialogue about the IFSW European Standards document. The document addresses several themes relevant to the U.S. context, including the effects of neoliberal policies on social welfare systems broadly and the influence of such processes on everyday micropractices of social workers because of increased case loads, reduced social benefits for individuals and families, and rising numbers of individuals and families seeking public assistance.

Field instructors and social work interns alike often struggle to identify opportunities in field for students to apply human rights to their assignments and develop practice behaviors to promote the advancement of human rights and social and economic justice in keeping with the EPAS standards. Without clear guidance and instructions, social work students miss valuable opportunities to identify and address human rights issues in their internships, such as ensuring that their clients' rights to food, housing, health care, and self-determination are realized.

Field education is a formative and pivotal experience that significantly shapes the orientation and practice behaviors of beginning social workers. One could argue that, given the resource constraints and heavy caseloads emblematic in our field, it may be challenging to integrate in-depth human rights education at a later stage of professional development. Further scholarship related to human rights and field education is urgently needed, along with the development of practical materials that can provide guidance in the field setting. Some field instructors may also benefit from continuing professional education to build their understanding of human rights and the application to social work.

Education of Current and Future Social Work Educators

Another important area for development is in fostering new learning in existing and emerging generations of social work educators to prepare them to build competencies in human rights in the next generation of professionals. One venue for capacity-building for the integration of robust human rights knowledge and practice is in social work doctoral programs.

The current EPAS standards do not apply to doctoral education; thus, it is left up to individual institutions to decide whether (and how) human rights belong in doctoral education. This is a critical issue because doctoral students are the future social work educators. Exposing them in a robust way to human rights theory and practice will shape their teaching and scholarship. This might be accomplished, for example, by a required course in the first year covering human rights theory and pedagogical approaches to teaching social work from a rights-base, followed by substantial attention to human rights in the rest of the doctoral curriculum. This is only one of a number of possible ways of accomplishing this goal.

If human rights are not core to the areas of expertise and approach of existing senior faculty, they are not likely to encourage doctoral students to integrate a rights-based approach in their work. Ideally, a multipronged educational strategy is needed to build a cadre of social work educators to ensure that social work truly is the embodiment of a human rights profession. The authors' university has a well-attended human rights and social work faculty and doctoral student reading group that has served to build increased knowledge and enthusiasm for faculty integrating human rights into their curriculum. Human rights education can be offered in bachelor's, master's, and doctoral programs and in continuing education programs, workshops, and colloquiums. Mentoring and ongoing supervision by seasoned human rights practitioners also can make a valuable contribution. A special interest group, Human Rights & Social Work, has been formed for researchers, educators, and students interested in advancing the role of human rights within social work. The group meets regularly at national conferences, including the Society for Social Work and Research (SSWR) and the CSWE annual conferences. A manual published in 2013 with human rights curriculum and classroom teaching modules also makes a significant contribution to moving the field forward (Hokenstad, Healy, & Segal, 2013).

Interprofessional Efforts

Interprofessional collaboration is frequently an integral part of human rights efforts around the world because campaigns often call on the expertise and mobilization of members of many disciplines and sectors of society. Academic human rights institutes such as that at the editors' home institution, bring together scholars and practitioners from diverse disciplines. Social workers have long been engaged in interprofessional practice across multiple practice settings and methods (Crawford, 2012; Quinney & Hafford-Letchfield, 2013). Medical social workers, for example, are part of interdisciplinary treatment teams and play prominent roles in such areas as assessing the needs of patients, safeguarding their access to health care and supports they are entitled to, and ensuring that patient and family members' rights are respected in difficult treatment and end of life decisions. Social workers active in child welfare arenas may routinely collaborate with law enforcement, policy makers, educators, and health care providers to safeguard the rights and safety of children and advance their overall best interests. Community organizers working to combat the dumping of toxic waste in poor neighborhoods may join forces with a diverse array of actors such as community members, school and church leaders, attorneys, health care providers, local legislators, researchers, and policy analysts. Social work policy practitioners may collaborate with economists, legislators, and public interest lawyers to advance equitable access and the right to affordable food, housing, and health care.

Social workers, even those with traditional roles, can practice in a human rights framework. Numerous opportunities exist for social workers to transcend disciplinary boundaries and work in alliance with other professionals doing rights-based practice. Working across disciplines can strengthen efforts to address complex and multifaceted problems and human rights issues that require expertise from diverse professions. Studies have found, for example, that this approach enhances competence, effectiveness, and cultural sensitivity in the delivery of health care (Pecukonis, Doyle, & Bliss, 2008).

At the same time, interprofessional efforts may also bring challenges. Disparately trained professionals do not always speak the same language, share the same goals or code of ethics, or define the problem and solution in compatible ways. They may not have a clear understanding of the skill set and scope of practice of their colleagues. There may be professional turf wars for some. When the various professionals engaged in the care of a person or community do not coordinate their efforts, there is great risk of unintended negative consequences and suboptimal care in violation of the rights of those they serve.

Expanded curricular efforts have recently been made to prepare social work students to work as part of interprofessional health care teams (Bonifas & Gray, 2013; Pecukonis et al., 2013). Some universities have developed interprofessional graduate programs to train students across a number of disciplines to be able to collaborate with colleagues from other professions. These include the University of Maryland's summer interprofessional research project in Malawi (see Chapter 18), the Toronto Rehabilitation Institute's interprofessional education clinical placement (Lumague et al., 2006), and the Urban Service Track Program at the University of Connecticut (Clark-Dufner, Gould, Dang, Goldblatt, & Johnson, 2010). These programs prepare students across medicine, social work, and allied health disciplines to research and address issues of health disparities and serve urban poor, underserved, and otherwise marginalized communities. What is often lacking, however, is an explicit human rights frame in this work. Some models of interprofessional teams exist that directly use a rights-based approach. Social workers have long worked closely with attorneys serving asylum seekers, for example, safeguarding and advocating for their clients' rights in therapeutic and legal contexts, providing expert witness testimony documenting rights violations, and collaborating to fight against the impunity of perpetrators. Further efforts using this cross-disciplinary model are needed, along with a more robust infusion of human rights principles and approaches in social work curricula.

Program Evaluation and Research

Social work textbooks and course curriculum regarding program evaluation and research largely lack inclusion of human rights (see Chapter 12). These materials typically place heavy emphasis on the technical aspects of methodology and statistical analysis with little or no explicit attention to human rights concerns, although some of the material could be reframed with a human rights lens. For example, some texts attend to issues of human subjects protection, but generally in the context of institutional review board concerns and applications, without always connecting this discussion to broader human rights issues.

A community-based participatory research (CBPR) approach is increasingly gaining momentum as a tool for conducting research and evaluation in collaboration with communities (Campus-Community Partnerships for Health, 2013; University of Kansas, 2013). A CBPR approach aims to create an equal partnership between researchers/evaluators and community members and involves an ongoing collaborative process of assessing the research/evaluation needs of a community, implementing research/evaluation projects, analyzing community data, and carrying out action plans. This approach promotes growth in the capacities of community organizations and communities to conduct research and evaluation and seems to inherently be embedded in a human rights orientation and framework. Pittaway, Bartolomei, and Hugman (2010) address the ethics of participatory action research grounded in human rights to advocacy-focused research with vulnerable populations. Fisher (2012) addresses various ethical dimensions of qualitative research and stresses that the human rights of vulnerable individuals are advanced by ensuring their ability to participate in these studies. The social work literature and curriculum would greatly benefit from further in-depth and explicit exploration of rights-based approaches to research and program evaluation.

Engaging a Robust Array of Human Rights Documents and Practices

International social work educators participating in the working seminar on Advancing Human Rights in Social Work Education that led to this volume noted that the Universal Declaration of Human Rights (United Nations, 1948) has often been the key (and at times only) point of departure for linking social work to human rights practice in the United States. Still latent in the U.S. context is robust engagement with the myriad human rights treaties and related documents available to analyze and use in a range of practice settings (Pollack & Rosman, 2012), such as precedents set by committees monitoring treaties through their quasi-judicial review of individual complaints and petitions (see Chapter 8). General comments or recommendations by specific treaty committees offer rich insights for rights-based practice in a number of social work realms, whether at macro, mezzo, or micro levels. United Nations special rapporteurs or experts in a given area of human rights concern often produce country reports and provide substantive guidance for interpreting the content and implementation approaches that are most promising (see the Office of the High Commissioner for Human Rights at www.ohchr.org).

Although the Universal Declaration of Human Rights provides the foundation for expression of the moral bases of human rights mobilization and practice (Chapter 2), the growing corpus of treaty law ("hard law") and related documentation ("soft law") enables social work educators and practitioners to frame more nuanced and particular claims for the realization of human rights (Chapter 8). Thus, for example, even though the United States is one of few countries that does not recognize the right to adequate food as a human right, social workers can still use the well-elaborated definition and content of this right established at the international level when thinking about their own community practice or advocacy campaigns (see, e.g., International Human Rights Clinic, 2013). Developing the ability to navigate the documentation available at the United Nations website, as well as resources available at various regional human rights bodies, will deepen social work engagement with human rights at local, national, and international levels. Through such efforts, social workers in the United States may play more central roles in the burgeoning human rights movement that is taking place across professional lines and within communities (Libal & Healy, 2015). They may also raise questions concerning human rights implications of practice in settings where such framing has yet to take hold, thus helping to challenge U.S. exceptionalism and build a society in which human rights is perceived as both a domestic and an international concern (Berthold, 2015).

Conclusion

Social workers come into contact with a wide range of populations whose members experience human rights violations. Although not exhaustive in its coverage of all population groups (e.g., indigenous communities, people with disabilities, LGBTQ individuals, the elderly), the contributions to this volume demonstrate the application of a human rights framework in educating social work students and practitioners that could be adapted and applied to other issues and populations. Notwithstanding the areas for further development discussed here, this contributory volume provides valuable resources for social work educators seeking to infuse a rights-based approach into their curriculum. It is hoped that this book will further fruitful dialogue and collaborations in our field and contribute to the multipronged efforts to realize social work as a human rights profession. It is only by educating and supporting the new generation of social workers to adopt a rights-base to their practice that this will be possible.

The pedagogy advanced here is new for many social work educators and programs in the United States. Those who have been engaged in implementing such curricular innovations, such as the authors in this volume, have formed an informal learning collaborative. Ongoing faculty and institutional support and the sharing of ideas and lessons learned will be invaluable if we are to further realize the integration of human rights into social work pedagogy. In addition, insights gained from further research on the effects of rights-based education on social work graduates, including their efforts and experiences of applying human-rights approaches in practice, will enhance our understanding of how best to teach human rights to further the establishment of a human rights culture in the social work profession.

References

Berthold, S. M. (2015). *Human-rights based approaches to clinical social work*. New York, NY: Springer.

Bogo, M. (2010). *Achieving competence in social work through field education*. Toronto, ON, Canada: University of Toronto Press.

Bonifas, R. P., & Gray, A. K. (2013). Preparing social work students for interprofessionalpractice in geriatric health care: Insights from two approaches. *Educational Gerontology, 39,* 476–490. doi:10.1080/03601277.2012.701137.

Campus-Community Partnerships for Health. (2013). *Community-based participatory research*. Seattle, Washington: University of Washington, 2013. Retrieved from http://depts.washington.edu/ccph/commbas.html

Clark-Dufner, P., Gould, B., Dang, D. K., Goldblatt, R. S., & Johnson, J. (2010). The University of Connecticut Urban Service Track: An effective academic-community partnership. *Connecticut Medicine, 74*(1), 33–36.

Council on Social Work Education (CSWE). (2008). *Educational policy and accreditation standards.* Alexandria, VA: Author.

Crawford, K. (2012). *Interprofessional collaboration in social work practice.* Thousand Oaks, CA: SAGE Publications.

Dominelli, L. (2007). Human rights in social work practice: An invisible part of the social work curriculum? In E. Reichert (Ed.), *Challenges in human rights: A social work perspective* (pp. 16–43). New York, NY: Columbia University Press.

Fisher, P. (2012). Ethics in qualitative research: "Vulnerability," citizenship and human rights. *Ethics and Social Welfare, 6*(1), 2–17.

Hokenstad, M. C., Healy, L. M., & Segal, U. A. (Eds.). (2013). Teaching human rights: *Curriculum resources for social work educators.* Alexandria, VA: CSWE Press.

International Federation of Social Workers (IFSW) & International Association of Schools of Social Work IASSW). (2004). *Global standards for the education and training of the social work profession.* Retrieved from www.iassw-aiets.org

International Human Rights Clinic. (2013). *Nourishing change: Fulfilling the right to food in the United States.* New York: NYU School of Law.

International Federation of Social Workers European Region e.V. (2010). *Standards in social work practice meeting human rights.* Retrieved from http://cdn.ifsw. org/assets/ifsw_45904-8.pdf

Libal, K. R., & Harding, S. (2015). *Human-rights based approaches to community practice in the United States.* New York, NY: Springer.

Lumague, M., Morgan, A., Mak, D., Hanna, M., Kwong, J., Cameron, C., … Sinclair, L. (2006). Interprofessional education: The student perspective. *Journal of Interprofessional Care, 20*(3), 246–253.

Newman, P. A., Bogo, M., & Daley, A. (2009). Breaking the silence: Sexual orientation in social work field education. *Journal of Social Work Education, 45,* 7–27. doi: 10.5175/JSWE.2009.200600093

Pecukonis, E., Doyle, O., & Bliss, D. L. (2008). Reducing barriers to interprofessional training: Promoting interprofessional cultural competence. *Journal of Interprofessional Care, 22,* 417–428.

Pittaway, E., Bartolomei, L., & Hugman, R. (2010). Stop stealing our stories: The ethics of research with vulnerable groups. *Journal of Human Rights Practice, 2*(2), 229–251.

Pollack, D., & Rosman, E. (2012). An introduction to treaties for international social workers. *International Social Work, 55,* 417–427.

Quinney, A., & Hafford-Letchfield, T. (2013). *Interprofessional social work: Effective collaborative approaches* (2nd ed.). Thousand Oaks, CA: SAGE Publications.

Steen, J. A. (2012). The human rights philosophy as a values framework for the human behavior course: Integration of human rights concepts in the person-in-environment perspective. *Journal of Human Behavior in the Social Environment, 22,* 853–862.

United Nations. (1948). *Universal declaration of human rights.* Retrieved from http://www.un.org/en/documents/udhr/

United Nations Centre for Human Rights. (1994). *Human rights and social work: A manual for schools of social work and the social work profession* (Professional Training Series No. 1). Retrieved from http://www.ohchr.org/Documents/Publications/traininglen.pdf

University of Kansas. (2013). *Community tool box.* Retrieved from http://ctb.ku.edu

Wayne, J., Raskin, M., & Bogo, M. (2010). Field education as the signature pedagogy of social work education. *Journal of Social Work Education, 46,* 327–339. doi: 10.5175/JSWE.2010.200900043

Wronka, J. (2008). *Human rights and social justice: Social action and service for the helping and health professions.* Thousand Oaks, CA: SAGE.

ABOUT THE AUTHORS

DeBrenna LaFa Agbényiga, PhD, MBA, MSW, is associate dean for graduate studies and inclusion in the College of Social Science and associate professor in the Department of Human Development and Family Studies and the School of Social Work at Michigan State University. She has led study abroad courses in Ghana and Jamaica and is a core faculty member of the African Studies Center, the Center for Advanced Study of International Development, the Center for Gender in Global Context, the African American and African Studies Program, and the Research Consortium on Gender-Based Violence. She has worked as a consultant to numerous international ministries and nongovernmental organizations. Her research interests focus on organizational culture, international social and economic development, community development and sustainability, women's rights, children's rights, gender-based violence, cross-cultural learning, and diversity. She has published extensively and presented her work broadly in the domestic and international arena.

David Androff, PhD, MSW, is assistant professor in the School of Social Work at Arizona State University. He earned his MSW and PhD in social welfare from the University of California at Berkeley. His work examines the intersection of human rights and social work and has focused on immigration policy, human trafficking, restorative justice, and Truth and Reconciliation Commissions. His research has been recognized with the 2011 Frank Turner Prize for best article in *International Social Work* and the 2011 Emerging Scholar Award from the Association of Community Organization and Social Administration.

Androff currently serves on the Council on External Relations for the Council on Social Work Education, and chairs the Publicity and Public Promotion working group of the Special Commission to Advance Macro Practice. He has organized international conferences in Indonesia and Singapore and teaches in the areas of international social work, community practice, and social policy.

Rosemary A. Barbera, PhD, MSS, has been working in human rights since the 1980s in the United States and Latin America. Her areas of practice include human rights, surviving torture, community rebuilding after human rights violations, participatory action research, and social work in Latin America. Current research examines the role memory plays in postdictatorship society, community resilience after disaster, and building human rights social movements. She also participates in Juntos/Casa de los Soles, the Agrupación de Familiares de Detenidos Desaparecidos, and the Junta de Vecinos Concierto y Cultura. For the past 20 years she has brought students to the población La Pincoya in Santiago, Chile, where they learn about past and present human rights issues and participate in human rights activities. She is associate professor and field coordinator in the Department of Social Work at La Salle University.

S. Megan Berthold, PhD, LCSW, is assistant professor at the University of Connecticut's School of Social Work. She has worked with diverse refugee and asylum seeking survivors of torture, war traumas, human trafficking, female genital mutilation, and other traumas since the mid-1980s. She was a clinician and educator in refugee camps in Nepal, the Philippines, and on the Thai-Cambodian border and worked with the Program for Torture Victims in Los Angeles, CA, before joining the faculty of the University of Connecticut. Megan conducts National Institute of Mental Health-funded research examining the prevalence of mental and physical health consequences postgenocide and other traumas among Cambodian refugees. Her community based participatory research in Cambodian communities across the United States has contributed to building community capacity to conduct research to address their health disparities. She frequently testifies as an expert witness in U.S. Immigration Court. Megan was selected as the 2009 National Social Worker of the Year by the NASW.

Sandra Chadwick-Parkes, PhD, is a lecturer in the Social Work Unit of the Department of Sociology, Psychology, and Social Work at the University of the West Indies, Mona Campus, Jamaica. Her research interests span the many dimensions of community development, specifically, building community resilience and sustainability and reducing poverty through local and community economic development, partnerships, and interventions targeting the informal economy. She has been involved in research on successful youth gang exit programs, community-based disaster risk reduction and management, and urban squatting. Chadwick-Parkes received her doctoral degree in rural studies from the University of Guelph in Ontario, Canada. She specialized in local economic development and community economic development. She also holds an MSc in development studies and a BSc in public administration, both from the University of the West Indies.

Anusha Chatterjee, MA, is a doctoral student at the University of Maryland, Baltimore. Her dissertation interest is in the area of global philanthropy and funding mechanisms. Her research interests include international social work, gender-based violence, and health. Before moving to the United States to obtain her PhD, Chatterjee worked in the area of corporate social responsibility in Delhi, India, where she worked in partnership with nonprofits and community based organizations to develop social projects nationally and locally. She was also involved in project monitoring and evaluation and documentation. Chatterjee received her MA in social work from the Tata Institute in Mumbai, India, and her BA in sociology from University of Calcutta. She also received the Maria Mies Award for Student Scoring the "Highest Marks in a MA Dissertation on Issues of Gender and Justice" for her MA dissertation on the issue of violence against women with disabilities.

Christina M. Chiarelli-Helminiak, PhD, MSW, is assistant professor of social work at West Chester University. She received her doctorate from the University of Connecticut, where she was recognized as an Outstanding Woman Scholar. Her dissertation focused on organizational factors affecting job satisfaction and burnout among forensic interviewers. Chiarelli-Helminiak also researches the integration of human rights in social work curriculum. Her extensive practice experience includes working with survivors of domestic violence, sexual assault, and child abuse. Her greatest professional achievement is leading the development of a children's advocacy center providing community-based services in rural north Georgia. Chiarelli-Helminiak received her BA in social work from Shippensburg University and an MSW from Marywood University, where she was the first social work student awarded the Sister M. Eva Connors Peace Medal.

Elaine P. Congress, DSW, ACSW, LCSW, is professor and associate dean at Fordham University Graduate School of Social Service. She is on the International Federation of Social Workers (IFSW) United Nations team and is a member of the executive committees of the NGO Committee on Migration and the NGO Committee on the United Nations International Decade of the World's Indigenous Peoples. In addition she serves on the IFSW International Committee on Ethical Issues. Currently, Congress is the chair of the Council on Social Work Education Council on Publications and on the Governing Council of APHA. Congress has many publications on cultural diversity and ethics in social work. Her books include *Social Work with Immigrants and Refuges: Legal Issues, Clinical Skills, and Advocacy; Multicultural Perspectives in Working With Families, Social Work Values and Ethics;* and *Teaching Social Work Values and Ethics: A Curriculum Resource Guide.*

Filomena M. Critelli, PhD, LCSW, is associate professor in the School of Social Work at the University at Buffalo, where she teaches courses in social welfare policy, community social work, and international social welfare. She is co-director of the Institute for Sustainable Global Engagement. Prior to entering academia she directed a number of programs in immigrant communities in New York City. Her research is focused on women's activism and gender based violence in domestic and international contexts. Another area of research is devoted to human rights of immigrants and refugees and global migration. As a recipient of a 2014 research grant from the International Association of Schools of Social Work, she is currently conducting a study to examine the effects of separation on transnational families with scholars from the Ukraine, Moldova and Azerbaijan.

Brunilda Ferraj, MSW, is a senior public policy specialist at the Connecticut Community Providers Association. She graduated from the University of Connecticut School of Social Work MSW program with a concentration in policy practice. While completing her MSW, Ferraj was a research assistant for a program evaluation, monitoring one public organization's program aimed at increasing civic engagement among immigrants and facilitating community integration. She also researches remittances, focusing on the untold experiences of immigrants who send money home.

Shirley Gatenio Gabel, PhD, MSW, is associate professor at Fordham University's Graduate School of Social Service. Her research increasingly focuses on how public policies improve the well-being of children from a child rights perspective. She has served as a consultant over the last 7 years to UNICEF and UNESCO on child poverty and advocacy strategies, social protection in developing countries, and social inclusive policies and programs in developing countries. She was a senior Fulbright scholar in Bulgaria in 2005–2006 and a Fulbright specialist in Argentina in 2014. She is a member of the Board of Directors of the Council on Social Work Education (CSWE), chairs CSWE's Commission on Global Education, and is a member of the Katherine A. Kendall Institute for International Social Work Education and the International Network on Leave Policies and Research. She co-edited (with Lynne Healy) a special issue of the *Journal of Social Work Education* on the globalization of social work education and is the editor of a book series on rights-based approaches to social work practice.

Lynne M. Healy, PhD, MSW, is Board of Trustees Distinguished Professor at the University of Connecticut School of Social Work and founding director of the Center for International Social Work Studies. Her areas of publication include human rights, internationalizing social work curriculum, international social work, human service administration, and ethics. She has written several articles on human rights and social work, co-edited (with Rosemary Link) the recently published *Handbook of International Social Work: Human Rights, Development and the Global Profession* (Oxford, 2012), and co-edited a 2012 special issue of the *Journal of Social Work Education* on globalization and social work education (with Shirley Gatenio Gabel). Healy chairs the International Association of Schools of Social Work (IASSW) Human Rights Committee, represents the IASSW on the United Nations NGO Committee for Social Development, and is a member of the Council on Social Work Education Katherine A. Kendall Institute Advisory Committee.

Kirk A. James, DSW, MSW, completed his doctoral degree at the University of Pennsylvania School of Social Policy and Practice in 2013. His dissertation, "The Invisible Epidemic: Educating Social Work Students Towards Holistic Practice in a Period of Mass Incarceration," provides critical insight into the need for social work education and practice that addresses racism and mass incarceration in the United States. James developed and directed The Goldring Reentry Initiative (GRI) at the University of Pennsylvania. The GRI prepares social work students to complete a year of their field placement working with men and women transitioning from Philadelphia prisons pre- and postrelease to reduce the likelihood of recidivism. James is currently based in New York City and is the newly appointed senior director of policy at the David Rothenberg Center for Public Policy at the Fortune Society, one of the nation's preeminent reentry service organizations.

Hugo A. Kamya, PhD, MSW, MDiv, is professor at the Simmons College School of Social Work, where he teaches clinical practice, trauma, and narrative therapies. Originally from Uganda, Kamya came to the United States more than 20 years ago. He studied at Harvard University, Boston College, and Boston University and began a career in interrelated practices and trainings in social work, psychology, and theology. Kamya's work has focused on immigrant populations and international efforts to assess social service needs of people affected by HIV/AIDS. Over the last few years Kamya has facilitated bilateral cultural and educational exchanges between Uganda and the United States. In

2003 he received an award from the American Family Therapy Academy for Distinguished Contribution to Social and Economic Justice. Kamya's work internationally has focused on human rights and developing effective international partnerships. In 2014 Kamya was accepted into the Fulbright Specialist Roster Program.

Kathryn Libal, PhD, MA, is associate professor of social work and associate director of the Human Rights Institute at the University of Connecticut. She earned her doctorate in anthropology at the University of Washington. She specializes in human rights, social welfare, and the state and has published on women's and children's rights movements in Turkey and on advocacy efforts of international nongovernmental organizations on behalf of Iraqi refugees. Her current scholarship focuses on the localization of human rights norms and practices in the United States, including a co-edited volume with Dr. Shareen Hertel, *Human Rights in the United States: Beyond Exceptionalism*, and a new project on U.S. politics of food security and food policy as a human rights concern. She has also co-authored, with Dr. Scott Harding, a short text, *Human Rights-Based Approaches to Community Practice in the United States*.

Barris P. Malcolm, PhD, MSW, STM, is associate professor of social work administration at the University of Connecticut. Malcolm earned his PhD from Columbia University, the MSW from the University of Connecticut, and holds degrees from Yale University Divinity School and the University of the West Indies. Malcolm teaches financial management, substance abuse, analysis of social welfare policy, and HBSE-macro theories. He has worked in administration at the Cornell Scott Hill Health Center and Columbus House in New Haven. His special interests include international social work, human rights, substance abuse, health disparities, and homelessness, and he has publications on some of these areas Malcolm is an officer on the board of Connecticut Multicultural Health Partnership and Cross Roads Inc.

Susan Mapp, PhD, MSSW, is professor and chair of the Department of Social Work at Elizabethtown College, PA. She has authored *Human Rights and*

Social Justice in a Global Perspective: An Introduction to International Social Work and Global Child Welfare and Well-Being and numerous journal articles, and she is currently completing a book on domestic minor sex trafficking. Her areas of specialty include human trafficking, international social work, violations of children's rights, and program evaluation. She serves on the board of directors for the Association of Baccalaureate Social Work Program Directors and the board of the International Consortium for Social Development. Mapp is on the editorial boards of several leading journals dealing with social work education and international social work.

Jane McPherson, MSW, MPH, LCSW, is a doctoral candidate at Florida State University. Her work is located at the intersection of human rights and social work. Recent projects include designing a framework for human rights practice in social work, developing scales to measure human rights exposure and engagement in social workers, incorporating human rights activism into the social work classroom, and examining models of rights-based social work intervention in Brazil. McPherson is a clinical social worker with more than 20 years of experience in the field. Motherhood, trauma, torture, and the special treatment needs of women have been her areas of clinical specialization. Her work has been global and local in scope, extending from rural Florida to New York City, Egypt, and Brazil.

Vimla Nadkarni, PhD, is professor emerita and founding dean at the School of Social Work, Tata Institute of Social Sciences, Mumbai, India. She is currently president of the International Association of Schools of Social Work. She is an internationally recognized leader, scholar, and educator in the field of international social work, social work education, and practice. She specializes in health ethics and human rights, community health, health management, HIV/AIDS policy and intervention, reproductive health, and ecology and health. Her publications include *NGOs, Urban Health and the Poor* and articles on the right to health, poverty and human need, HIV/AIDS, and human rights perspectives in social work. Nadkarni is a founding member of the International Social Work Network in Health Inequalities. She has presented at numerous national, regional, and international conferences and has received Kellogg and Fulbright fellowships. She gave the International Hokenstad lecture at the 2008 Council on Social Work Education Annual Program Meeting.

Jody K. Olsen, PhD, MSW, is a visiting professor at the University of Maryland School of Social Work and director of the university Center for Global Education Initiatives (CGEI). CGEI has sponsored student teams from dentistry, law, medicine, nursing, pharmacy, and social work to Malawi for interprofessional research projects and smaller interprofessional university grant-funded teams to nine countries in 2014. She teaches international social work courses and online graduate interprofessional global health courses. Olsen was deputy director and acting director of Peace Corps (2001–2009). She was a Peace Corps volunteer in Tunisia and in other Peace Corps positions has designed, facilitated, and evaluated numerous volunteer and staff programs. She also directed the Fulbright Senior Scholar Program. She has spoken frequently throughout the world on international training, education, and development. Her MSW and PhD in human development are from the University of Maryland.

Nivedita Prasad, PhD, studied social pedagogy at the Free University in Berlin and earned her PhD at the Carl von Ossietzky University in Oldenburg. The topic of her PhD thesis was "Utilizing the Issue of Violence against Migrant Women in Order to Restrict Migration; Responsibility of Social Work as a Human Rights Profession." In 2012 she was awarded the first Anne Klein Prize for her ongoing dedication to the human rights of migrant women. From 1997 to 2012 she was the project coordinator and researcher at Ban Ying, an antitrafficking nongovernmental organization. Since 1993 she has taught at various universities in Berlin, Maastricht, and Vorarlberg and given trainings for social workers, police, judges, prosecutors, and lawyers. Since 2010 she has been the director of the master study program "Social Work as a Human Rights Profession." In April 2013 she became a professor at the Alice Solomon University of Applied Sciences.

Michael Reisch, PhD, MSW, MA, is the Daniel Thursz Distinguished Professor of Social Justice at the University of Maryland School of Social Work. He has held faculty and administrative positions at five major U.S. universities and visiting appointments at the University of California, the New Bulgarian University (Sofia), the Chinese University of Hong Kong, and the University of Queensland (Australia). He is the author or editor of nearly 30 books and monographs and more than 400 other publications and papers on contemporary social policy and social welfare history, philosophy, and practice. His work has been translated into nine languages, and he has lectured widely in other nations. Reisch has held leadership positions in major advocacy, professional, and social change organizations; directed and consulted on political campaigns in four states; and received numerous honors from local and state legislatures, nonprofit organizations, universities, and professional associations, including the CSWE Significant Lifetime Achievement Award in October 2014.

Dennis Ritchie, PhD, MSW, serves as the Elisabeth Shirley Enochs Endowed Chair in Child Welfare, professor of social work, and MSW program director at George Mason University, Virginia. He directs the Enochs Technical Assistance Program, the mission of which is to promote and maintain a regular exchange of experts in the field of child and family welfare between Latin America and the United States. His practice experience includes providing consultation, education, and direct services in school settings, and over the past 22 years he has been actively involved in international social work with a special interest in participatory action research and the connection between social work and human rights. Ritchie has held a number of professional leadership positions related to international social work and human rights and has been a visiting professor at the University of Costa Rica, Vytautas Magnus University in Lithuania, and the National Autonomous University of Honduras as a Fulbright scholar.

Sudha Sankar, MS, is a third-year doctoral student in the Department of Human Development and Family studies at Michigan State University, specializing in couple and family therapy. She received her bachelor of science in psychology in India and her master of science in psychology at Pittsburg State University. Her research and practice focus is development and ongoing transformation of the concept of self, constructed identity, and sense of belonging as modes of resilience in the context of dislocations and traumas and human rights issues in developing countries. She is a strong advocate for women's and children's rights. Sankar was originally from India but spent most of her early years in Africa and has migrated to several countries.

Uma A. Segal, PhD, MSSW, is professor at the University of Missouri–St. Louis and fellow in its International Studies and Programs. Her current research focuses on immigrant integration and the Dekasegi movement between Brazil and Japan and on older immigrant health in the United States. Segal is author/co-editor of a number of books on human migration, has several peer-reviewed and invited publications, and has presented her research on all continents. From 2004–2012, she was editor-in-chief of the *Journal of Immigrant & Refugee Studies*, a journal she moved into the international and interdisciplinary realm. Segal serves on the Advisory Board of the Council on Social Work Education's (CSWE's) Katherine A. Kendall Institute and on CSWE's Board of Directors. In 2013 she received CSWE's Partners in Advancing International Education award. A 2013–2014 Fulbright fellowship took her to Bangalore, India, to establish a new school of social work with a dual international and rural focus.

Louise Simmons, PhD, is professor of social work at the University of Connecticut. She received her PhD in urban and regional studies from the Massachusetts Institute of Technology. Her research interests include urban social and political movements, community organizing, community–labor coalitions, welfare reform, and urban policy issues. She is author of *Organizing in Hard Times: Labor and Neighborhoods in Hartford* (Temple University Press, 1994), editor of *Welfare, the Working Poor and Labor*, (M. E. Sharpe, 2004) and co-editor with Scott Harding of *Economic Justice, Labor and Community Practice* (Routledge, 2010). She is a former co-editor of the *Journal* *of Community Practice* and on editorial boards of several journals. Simmons is past a chairperson of the governing board of the Urban Affairs Association. She was elected as a councilperson on the Hartford City Council from 1991–1993. She has been active in civil rights, labor, and community struggles in Hartford since the 1970s.

Julie Smyth, LMSW, received her master of science in social work from Columbia University in 2012. Following her graduate studies she was a mitigation specialist and sentencing advocate at the Defender Association of Philadelphia, PA, the city's public defender's office. Her writing focuses on various issues related to mass incarceration, specifically pertaining to the effects of incarceration on families and communities. She is published on the topics of incarcerated mothers and on systemic racism relating to policing and the prison system. In 2013 Smyth presented at the Council for Social Work Education's Annual Program Meeting in Dallas, TX, on the topic of integrating mass incarceration coursework into social work core curricula. She is currently a criminal defense practice social worker at the Bronx Defenders in New York City.

Robin Spath, PhD, MSW, is associate professor and chair of the Women and Children in Families Substantive Area at the University of Connecticut, School of Social Work. Her direct practice experience is in the areas of child welfare, family violence, and program administration. Her research and scholarly interests include women's issues, child welfare and permanency for children, program evaluation, human services administration, and organizational change/culture. Spath has published journal articles and book chapters and conducted presentations nationally and internationally in these areas. Most recently, she presented a paper at the International Conference on the Challenges of Living in Poverty and Experiencing Maltreatment on Children's Future in Padova, Italy.

Laura Guzmán Stein, PhD, received her *licenciatura* in social work from the University of Costa Rica and doctoral degree in social work from Arizona State University. She is an international consultant in human rights and professor emeritus in the Department of Social Work of the University of Costa

Rica in San Jose. During her career she also has coordinated the Programa de Derechos Humanos (Women and Human Rights Program) at the Instituto Interamericano de Derechos Humanos (Interamerican Institute of Human Rights). Guzmán has extensive background in research and teaching on the intersection of social work and human rights. She has published on such topics as women and feminism in Costa Rica; gender, globalization, and religion; women's labor rights in Costa Rica; and feminist theoretical analysis of women's organizations. She also has served as a consultant for social work curriculum development in Panama, Ecuador, and Guatemala.

Joyce Lee Taylor, PhD, has 24 years of experience in the child welfare field. Her career began at the Connecticut Department of Children and Families (DCF) juvenile justice facility, and she was a child protection services worker in investigations, treatment, foster care, and adoption. After serving in a wide range of supervisory and management roles, Taylor was appointed to a key leadership position as the DCF deputy commissioner. In 2006 she moved to Massachusetts, where she led 22 programs in a large nonprofit agency. Then she coordinated Community Services Reviews for the Rosie D Court Monitor, evaluating children's mental health reform throughout Massachusetts. Currently, Taylor teaches full-time at Springfield College, School of School of Social Work, and is a consultant for the Yale Program on Supervision. In 2014 she advocated for children's rights while serving as the interim CEO at Our Kids, Miami-Dade, Monroe.

Viviene Taylor is head of the Department of Social Development at the University of Cape Town. She teaches social policy, development planning, and social development. Her career consists of national and international development experience spanning more than 30 years. Her publications include articles, chapters, and books such as *Social Mobilisation: Lessons from the Mass Democratic Movement* (1997), *Gender Mainstreaming in Development Planning: A Reference Manual for Governments and other Stakeholders* (1999), and *Marketisation of Governance: Critical Feminist Perspectives from the South* (2000). Her research in South Africa and Africa focuses on addressing poverty and social inequalities. She undertook a 50 country study for the African Union on Social Protection called Social Protection in Africa: An Overview of the Challenges. Taylor currently serves as a commissioner on South Africa's National Planning Commission and is also the chair of the Ministerial Committee on the review of South Africa's White Paper on social welfare.

Rebecca L. Thomas, PhD, MSW, is associate professor at the University of Connecticut, School of Social Work, and the director of the Center for International Social Work Studies. She is appointed to the City of Hartford Commission on Refugee and Immigrant Affairs. She was the principal investigator for a 3-year process and outcome evaluation, "Building Relations and Bridging Social Capital: An Inclusive Approach to Immigrant Civic Engagement Within Libraries." Her areas of research include micro credit, disasters, remittances, and building social capital. She serves on the Global Affairs Advisory Board of the University of Connecticut, charged with the task of developing a strategic plan and proposing concrete strategies for deepening global education at the university. Recently, she was a Fellow in the Costa Rica Professional Women's Empowerment Program sponsored by the Global Training and Development Institute of the University of Connecticut and funded by the U.S. Department of State.

Joseph Wronka, PhD, is professor of social work at Springfield College, Massachusetts, where he teaches social policy, international social work, human rights, and qualitative research. He serves as main representative to the United Nations in Geneva for the International Association of Schools of Social Work and is Fulbright senior specialist in social work with major specialties in social justice and poverty and minor ones in phenomenology, human rights, and psychology. He is also the author of numerous scholarly and popular articles and four books, such as, *Human Rights and Social Policy in the 21st Century: A History of the Idea of Human Rights* and *A Comparison of the U.S. Federal and State Constitutions With the Universal Declaration of Human Rights* (UPA, 1992), *The Dr. Ambedkar Lectures on the Theme Creating* *a Human Rights Culture* (NISWASS, 2002, [India]), and *Human Rights and Social Justice: Social Action and Service for the Helping and Health Professions* (SAGE, 2008).

INDEX